THE MPLS PRIMER

An Introduction to Multiprotocol Label Switching

SEAN HARNEDY

ISBN 0-13-032980-0

9 780130 329806

90000

Prentice Hall PTR
Upper Saddle River, NJ 07458
www.phptr.com

Library of Congress Cataloging-in-Publication Data

CIP data available

Production Supervisor: Wil Mara
Acquisitions Editor: Victoria Jones
Editorial Assistant: Michelle Vincenti
Marketing Manager: Debby van Dijk
Buyer: Maura Zaldivar
Cover Designer: Anthony Gemmellaro
Composition: Gail Cocker-Bogusz

© 2002 Prentice Hall PTR
Prentice-Hall, Inc.
Upper Saddle River, NJ 07458

The publisher offers discounts on this book when ordered in bulk quantities. For more information contact: Corporate Sales Department, Prentice Hall PTR, One Lake Street, Upper Saddle River, NJ 07458. Phone: 800-382-3419; FAX: 201-236-7141; E-mail: corpsales@prenhall.com.

Printed in the United States of America

10 9 8 7 6 5 4 3 2 1

ISBN 0-13-032980-0

Pearson Education LTD.
Pearson Education Australia PTY, Limited
Pearson Education Singapore, Pte. Ltd
Pearson Education North Asia Ltd
Pearson Education Canada, Ltd.
Pearson Educación de Mexico, S.A. de C.V.
Pearson Education—Japan
Pearson Education Malaysia, Pte. Ltd
Pearson Education, Upper Saddle River, New Jersey

*This book is dedicated to
my wife Andrea and our three sons,
Ryan, Sean and Drew*

Contents

CHAPTER   2

MPLS Background   *45*

CHAPTER   3

MPLS Documentation and Resources   *87*

CHAPTER   8

Current MPLS Developments and Directions   *261*

CHAPTER   9

Current MPLS Implementations   *269*

CHAPTER   10

Future MPLS Developments and Directions   *281*

List of Figures

List of Tables

Preface

Today's providers of networks and network services are faced with many daunting challenges. Figure P–1 on the next page depicts the key demands of network customers. These include an appetite for new types of value-added network services, especially services based on the Internet Protocol (IP), the need to utilize an upgraded networking infrastructure, and the sheer increased demand for more bandwidth.

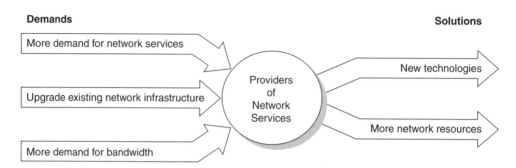

Figure P-1 The challenges of today's network service providers.

The personnel that provide networking within the various tiers of a network, Internet service providers (ISPs), and other organizations that deal with existing telecommunications and data communications networks must wear many hats. Network administrators, operators, planners, and architects may assume, at times, functional roles similar to those of fire fighters, police officers, teachers, mathematicians, programmers, and many others. The administration of today's networks is indeed a challenge. To cope with all of this change, a person dealing with this generation and the next generation of networks must even take on the role of philosopher!

The ancient Greeks are generally credited with inventing philosophy. It is interesting to note that without precedence in most matters, many important Greek philosophers created theories that, at first glance, seem irreconcilably opposed.

Heraclitus felt that the only constant in the world was change; he is famous for his comment that one never steps into the same river twice. His contemporary, Democritus, had the completely opposite view. He was one of the first proponents of atomic theory and the notion that in spite of all outward appearances, everything is essentially made up of the same thing—atoms. For Democritus, change was somewhat of an illusion, merely a rearrangement of atoms.

An important point to take from this duality of vision is that change is a matter of perspective. Understanding what change is and managing its consequences is an important task, one that is fundamental in successfully moving forward and progressing. Nowhere is change more apparent and more dramatic than in networking technology and the Internet. A prime example of this is that estimates on the doubling of the bandwidth demand for Internet traffic range from three months to one year! This is change that needs to be understood and managed.

Our Heraclitus-like selves can be easily panicked and overwhelmed by all the latest technological changes that are thrust upon us every-day—from MPLambdaS and dense wave division multiplexing (DWDM) to quality of service (QoS) and service level agreements (SLAs) for voice, data, and video traffic. It is becoming difficult enough to understand the basic concepts, let alone make intelligent decisions on what is to be done about them and how they relate to any strategic network planning.

Our Democritus-like selves then come to the rescue. We understand basic networking concepts. Most of us know that the Open Systems Interconnection (OSI) model has seven layers, and while technology is rapidly evolving, it can be understood within the framework of enhancements and new development of established products and network architectures.

The fundamental routing that occurs in the Internet has changed little since its beginnings. IP version 6 (IPv6) has only recently made inroads into the original IP version 4 (IPv4), which has been with us for almost 20 years, little changed since Request for Comments (RFC) 791. Routing protocols such as Open Shortest Path First (OSPF) and the Border Gateway Protocol (BGP) have been around for several years and are evolving to match newly emerging routing and signaling demands. IP technologies coexist with other prevalent networking frameworks such as Frame Relay (FR) and Asynchronous Transfer Mode (ATM).

Providers of networks and network services need to offer solutions for these many daunting challenges. As shown in Figure P–1, there are two primary solutions being explored: new technologies and more network resources. If we ponder for a moment, we can see how these two approaches are complementary, how they marry the view of Heraclitus and Democritus to provide a way of mastering change for today's networks. We must adapt networks by developing and using new technology as these approaches become integrated into the network infrastructure that is already in place.

So how does Multiprotocol Label Switching (MPLS) fit in? MPLS is a new development that builds on technologies that have already proven themselves successful in the networking arena. MPLS is a fresh approach that synthesizes the best of the connection-oriented model with the existing packet-based Internet and IP. By looking closely at MPLS and all of the many associated topics and developments, one can begin to assess whether MPLS is a new and positive change to the Internet and network technology. Is MPLS an evolutionary step for the Internet architecture, or is it an attempt at something different that may or may not succeed? Either way, one has to be ready...

This book is titled as a primer on MPLS in the hopes of providing a comprehensive introduction to the topic, as well as documenting all of the associated subjects and developments that are occurring in "Internet-time" in this area.

I will use the convention of calling out parenthetical topics by giving more information that the reader may find interesting as follows:

Because this is a **primer** ...

A **primer** is a small, beginning book that introduces the reader to a subject, often for the first time. The word is derived from the Latin word primarius, meaning primary, or first. Its original use, dating back to the fourteenth century, is as the reference to a small book for teaching children how to read.

MPLS is an exciting new technology. It is not being developed in a vacuum, but rather under the auspices of the Internet Engineering Task Force (IETF) whose motto of "running code, rough consensus" will make this technology a prominent Internet standard. Implementations of MPLS are being fielded and tested as you read these words. Implementation experience and further development in new areas—particularly in the emerging optical area—will determine MPLS's success. Stay tuned.

This is the preface. It contains a general introduction to the book. It describes the goals of the book, the book's audience, how the book is organized, and the conventions used. It also includes the "Acknowledgments" section. It is my sincerest wish that this book broadens the reader's knowledge base of MPLS and its related technologies, and serves as a valuable guide and reference on these topics.

GOALS ....

This book is written to introduce the reader to MPLS. There are several specific goals:

- Introduce key definitions and terminology.
- Explain the technologies that have come together to create MPLS. This includes explaining the Internet-based technologies, routing and switching, earlier efforts in cell and tag switching, and the other important technologies that are key to understanding MPLS's evolution.
- Provide pointers to more information on standards, frameworks, and implementations. This includes the IETF documentation and frequently referenced Web sites.
- Explain the MPLS core technologies and protocols, including how label switching is used and the various signaling and label distribution protocols that are needed.
- Introduce first-generation MPLS applications and services.
- Indicate the current and future directions for MPLS and its role in the Internet and networking technology.

AUDIENCE ....

This book is intended for network administrators, planners, architects, and operators who are dealing with, or will soon be confronted with, the adaptation of new Internet technologies such as MPLS. Many more people will find this book interesting and worthwhile also, including people interested in routing and switching and the delivery of IP services. People interested in emerging network applications such as traffic engineering (TE), delivering QoS, and virtual private networks (VPNs) will find this book worthwhile as well. Network and systems management people interested in management standards and the Simple Network Management Protocol (SNMP) as it relates to MPLS will gain knowledge of work being done in these areas. People interested in the use of MPLS with the latest optical technologies such as Generalized MPLS (GMPLS) will also find this book informative.

HOW THIS BOOK IS ORGANIZED ....

This book includes a complete discussion of MPLS and all of the issues dealing with it.

The book is organized into ten chapters with six appendices. There is also a bibliography with important Web sites, a glossary and acronyms section, and an index.

Chapter 1, "Introducing Multiprotocol Label Switching," provides an introduction and overview to MPLS by asking the "five W's and H": who, what, why, when, where, and how. Key MPLS terms are defined. This chapter also contains a review of internetworking technology basics. It concludes with a discussion of what MPLS is promising in regard to advancing current Internet-based networking technology.

Chapter 2, "MPLS Background," looks at all of the many topics and trends that must be understood; MPLS cannot be looked at in isolation. This chapter includes an introduction to the TCP/IP protocol suite, the concepts underlying switching and routing, a brief history of MPLS, and several other related issues.

Chapter 3, "MPLS Documentation and Resources," describes the key documents relating to MPLS. These include the latest RFCs, MPLS Working Group (WG) Internet drafts (IDs), and other related IDs. It also describes other key resources, such as associated standardization efforts, industry forums, and MPLS books.

Chapter 4, "MPLS Core Technologies and Protocols," introduces the core MPLS technologies and protocols in detail. It explains the central MPLS control plane and data forwarding plane concepts. It also documents key MPLS acronyms and details general MPLS design and implementation issues.

Chapter 5, "MPLS Signaling and Label Distribution," introduces signaling and how labels are distributed among MPLS-enabled routers. It explains the hop-by-hop signaling of the Label Distribution Protocol (LDP) and the traffic-engineered signaling done by Resource Reservation Protocol with Traffic Engineering Extensions (RSVP-TE) and Constraint-based Routing Label Distribution Protocol (CR-LDP). Other label distribution techniques are introduced and several associated issues are discussed.

Chapter 6, "MPLS Operation and Uses," introduces current major uses of the technology. The key MPLS applications such as TE, VPNs, QoS, path restoral services, and others are described.

Chapter 7, "The Management of MPLS," describes MPLS-related management issues. These include SNMP-based management and the current MPLS management information bases (MIBs). Associated management issues are also discussed.

Chapter 8, "Current MPLS Developments and Directions," describes current topics and MPLS technology developments. Protocol improvements are also discussed.

Chapter 9, "Current MPLS Implementations," introduces the companies and enterprises that are using and developing MPLS implementations. These include equipment vendors, stack providers, service providers, and other organizations involved with MPLS.

Chapter 10, "Future MPLS Developments and Directions," describes topics that are just emerging and promise to be important in the future as MPLS develops and matures. These include MPLambdaS and GMPLS. Two current MPLS optical forums—the Optical Internetworking Forum (OIF) and Optical Domain Service Interconnect (ODSI) Forum—are introduced.

Appendix A, "An MPLS Chronology," presents a timeline of MPLS's short history.

Appendix B, "MPLS-Related RFC Index," contains a list of RFCs for MPLS and related topics.

Appendix C, "RFC 3031: Multiprotocol Label Switching Architecture," specifies the MPLS architecture.

Appendix D, "RFC 3032: MPLS Label Stack Encoding," contains the specification for MPLS label stacks and other associated issues such as label encoding with various protocols.

Appendix E, "A Detailed Introduction to SNMP," describes the Simple Network Management Protocol, or SNMP. This appendix includes the SNMP reference model and a discussion of the protocol, Structure of Management Information (SMI) #data definition language, and related MIBs. The three major versions of SNMP are also explained.

Appendix F, "RFC 2570: Introduction to SNMPv3," provides an overview for the third and current version of SNMP.

The bibliography contains the list of references used. This includes books, periodicals, and related Web sites. Finally, there is a section that contains a glossary of terms and their associated acronyms.

CONVENTIONS USED IN THIS BOOK ....

Listed below are the conventions for the various fonts used in this text:

`Constant Width`	Used for source code examples, and for quotations from source code within the text, including variable and function names. This font is also used for output printed by a computer and for the contents of files.
Constant Bold	Used for commands typed word for word by the user.
Italic	Used for command names, directory names, and filenames. It is also used for words that are being defined.
Bold	Used for command options. In addition, **bold** is used for vectors in the mathematical sense.

ACKNOWLEDGMENTS ....

Once again, I have to thank my family for their love and support. Without the help of my wife, Andrea, and our three boys, Ryan, Sean, and Drew, this book would not have been possible. I would also like to thank Charlotte Harnedy and Andrew and Gloria Laspino.

I would like to thank my partners at Enjelis Networks, Inc.: Lawrence Bressler, Ed Kuczynski, and Nick Lekkas. Special thanks to the MPLS development team at my former company, Iron Bridge Networks, especially David Aha, John Renwick, Jim Cervantes, Chris Knight, Joseph Muollo, Lingesh Rao, and Ev Tate. I would also like to thank several other people that I worked with at Iron Bridge Networks, including Todd Thompson, Scott Koumjian, and Sean McCormick. Thanks also to Joan Cucchiara for answering my LDP MIB questions.

I would like to doubly thank David Aha who also reviewed the manuscript and offered suggestions for improving it.

I would like to thank all the people I met on the Internet and through the MPLS Working Group for all of their thought-provoking e-mail exchanges and all of the additional pointers and information they provided concerning MPLS and networking technologies.

Additionally, I would like to thank Wil Mara, Victoria Jones, and everyone else at Prentice Hall PTR who helped see this project through to completion. Finally, I would like to especially thank Mike Meehan for keeping this project going.

Sean J. Harnedy
August 2001
Westborough, Massachusetts

REFERENCES FOR PREFACE ....

1. Barlett, John (Emily Beck, general ed.). *Bartlett's Familiar Quotations, 15th ed.* Boston: Little,

2. Brown and Company, 1980, p. 70.

3. Barlett, John (Emily Beck, general ed.). *Bartlett's Familiar Quotations, 15th ed.* Boston: Little, Brown and Company, 1980, p. 79.

4. *Reader's Digest Treasury of Modern Quotations.* New York: Reader's Digest Press, 1975, p. 283.

Introducing Multiprotocol Label Switching

> Do not go where the path may lead,
> go instead where there is no path and leave a trail. [1]
>
> — *Ralph Waldo Emerson*

"It's the bandwidth, stupid."

This flip response from your favorite service provider after all of your keyboard pounding, all that excessive mouse clicking, and all of your "What's taking so long?" whining hit close to the mark in the past. The lack of bandwidth—that is, the carrying capacity of the communications channel—was the primary culprit for long delays, low throughput, and even poor reliability problems. The constantly increasing demands on the Internet and its services require planning and technological innovation for its undeniable success to continue and grow. Indeed, there is an increasing requirement for networking technology in general to accommodate and expand to satisfy the seemingly insatiable appetite for bandwidth resulting from more users and the deployment of new bandwidth-intensive applications.

1

The Internet is flourishing. Traffic is increasing at a dramatic rate as the Internet becomes a vital part of the communications infrastructure used today. The Internet has become the cornerstone of the Information Age, and Internet technologies are used extensively for many types of new, large-scale enterprise and private networks.

The types of traffic that flow on these networks now include dizzying arrays of voice, data, and video applications, each having their own particular set of services and resource demands. There is significant momentum in the convergence of the Internet and Public Switched Telephone Network (PSTN) that is introducing many new design, deployment, and management challenges. The number of users and devices that support and access the Internet is exploding. Also, many new and important networking technologies are being introduced and integrated throughout the Internet, from the core backbones all the way down to the edges and home access devices in "the last mile." Fiber optics and optical-based communications are also being introduced to work with packet-based networks with unprecedented urgency and resolve. The core of the Internet is being upgraded with high-speed glass fiber links that connect optical cross-connects (OXCs), wave division multiplexers (WDMs), and soon, photonic switches (PXCs).

A hallmark of the Internet has always been that packet traffic has been delivered on a "best-effort" basis using the TCP/IP protocol suite. Service level requirements are usually met by over-provisioning more and faster links and connecting more numerous and sophisticated routers and switches while assuring that network utilization does not get too high. Conventional routing protocols such as BGP, OSPF, and Intermediate System-Intermediate System (IS-IS) orchestrate routes for the routers placed throughout the network to facilitate the delivery of data packets from source to destination. The routers use these various routing protocol algorithms and signaling techniques to efficiently direct the traffic flow within the Internet.

The new and increased demands for more and different services with varying requirements are quickly forcing network and Internet service providers (NSPs and ISPs, respectively), and other specialized internetworking service providers, to realize that new technologies, in addition to more and faster equipment, are what is needed to keep pace.

Perhaps in the not-too-distant future, when a frustrated network user is pounding the keyboard and asking why the response time is so slow, a network administrator can update the standard reply with a snappier retort such as: "It's your quality of service, stupid."

MPLS is a new network technology that promises to offer QoS and many other new and timely applications to current best-effort, IP-based internetworking. MPLS is designed to operate with the current set of Internet routers and switching equipment, as well as become an important enabling technology for the next generation of Internet devices such as IP terabit (and soon, petabit!) routers and OCX switches. MPLS is also a vital solution that will allow current Layer 2 transport technologies such as ATM, FR, and Ethernet to seamlessly interoperate and coexist with IP-based networks. By allowing new disruptive technologies and current soon-to-be legacy implementations to coexist, MPLS provides network planners flexibility in migration and replacement tactics for their desired networking strategies. MPLS is often spoken of as the "glue" for next-generation networks because of this fact.

MPLS is a hybrid of a traditional network's Layer 3 routing protocols and Layer 2 switching technologies. The concepts are not new, but the way they are combined in MPLS may offer a fresh spin on evolving the Internet routing architecture. MPLS separates the control functions from the data forwarding functions in a manner that allows for new, flexible, and operational efficiencies. MPLS introduces a single forwarding model that is based on label swapping. It offers a richer model for routing packets based on additional and configurable input parameters. It also allows a stack of labels within a packet that can be used in a hierarchical fashion for several innovative, new applications. MPLS can coexist with many existing Layer 2 and Layer 3 protocols and provide scalability for how these protocols are used in today's networks.

MPLS allows for the rapid deployment of multiservice applications, which will allow service providers and network users to realize revenues in new ways. MPLS may be the enabling technology for the next information "gold rush."

MPLS is being developed within a working group of the IETF as an open and standardized way of doing label switching. The MPLS Working Group (WG) is also responsible for defining how to implement label-switched paths over various link level technologies. MPLS includes procedures and protocols for the distribution of labels between the network devices that do label manipulation and swapping.

MPLS was derived mainly from several proprietary efforts that were being done in the early and mid-1990s to marry switching and routing. This allowed MPLS's direction to be expanded into several new areas. Some view MPLS as an attempt to take the best features of the ATM technology and add them to IP. These include the connection-oriented nature of setting up paths and the ability to offer various levels of QoS to packet traffic. MPLS will also allow the interoperability of IP with ATM and FR in an integrated fashion to create a single manageable network infrastructure. Finally, the MPLS label framework is being expanded as a more general model for routing in optical switching networks and additional physical layer technologies, such as time division multiplexing (TDM) and the spatial switching of incoming fiber to outgoing fiber.

To better introduce MPLS, the "five W's and H"—a long-standing journalistic device that asks: who, what when, where, why, and how—is effective in presenting and summarizing the basics. Because MPLS is integrated as an Internet technology, it is also important to understand the basics of the Internet, its key models, and other closely related topics.

What Is MPLS? ....

MPLS is an exciting new hybrid technology that integrates the best of the current approaches for delivering packets from their source to their destination across an internetwork[1]. A formal definition is presented in Figure 1–1[2]:

> Multiprotocol Label Switching is a set of open, standards-based Internet technologies that combines Layer 3 routing with Layer 2 switching to forward packets by utilizing short, fixed-length labels.

Figure 1–1 A formal definition of MPLS.

By using existing and newly enhanced Internet routing and control protocols, MPLS provides virtual connection-oriented switching across Internet routes by supporting labels and the label swapping paradigm. MPLS includes the implementation of label-switched paths (LSPs) over the most popular link level technologies. MPLS also provides the neces-

---

1. Throughout the book, the words *"internet"* and *"internetwork"* are used interchangeably to mean a network of networks. The Internet is, of course, the global internetwork.

2. It is interesting to note that in the main MPLS specification (RFC 3031, *"Multiprotocol Label Switching Architecture"*), MPLS is simply defined as "an IETF working group and the effort associated with the working group."

sary procedures and protocols for the distribution of labels between MPLS-enabled routers and switches.

MPLS work is being done under the auspices of the MPLS WG within the IETF.[3] MPLS is still a very new development; it just entered the Internet standards track in the RFC format at the beginning of 2001. (An RFC is the specification format that is used to place a protocol on the standards track and allow it to progress from proposed to draft to full Internet standard.) Current MPLS RFCs are described in Chapter 3, "MPLS Documentation and Resources." For a full discussion of Internet standards, see Appendix B, "MPLS-Related RFC Index."

Because they are being actively worked on, many MPLS specifications are still largely in Internet draft (ID) format. As such, the exact specifics of the protocol and other ancillary issues are being regularly discussed, revised, and improved. IDs can advance to RFCs. Note that all IDs carry with them the caveat that they are "draft documents valid for a maximum of six months and may be updated, replaced, or obsoleted by other documents at any time. It is inappropriate to use Internet-Drafts as reference material or cite them other than as "works in progress"." The current MPLS IDs as of this writing are also described in Chapter 3, "MPLS Documentation and Resources."

The MPLS WG arose from a consensus at the Tag Switching Birds of a Feather (BOF)[4] meeting held at the 37th IETF meeting in December 1996 in San Jose, California.[5] The first official meeting of the MPLS WG was held the following April at the 38th IETF meeting in Memphis, Tennessee, where the acronym MPLS first came into common use. The MPLS WG has been working ever since in continuing its efforts to advance the MPLS specifications on the standards track.

The original MPLS WG charter statement is shown in Figure 1–2. Now that the MPLS architecture and signaling protocols are on the standardization track, the MPLS WG has undertaken additional tasks. These include investigating multicast issues, specifying extensions for authentication, defining and completing SNMP MIB definitions, specifying fault

---

3. For the main URL of the MPLS WG, view:
www.ietf.org/html.charters/mpls-charter.html

4. A Birds of Feather (BOF) is a gathering of parties at an IETF meeting interested in a new and related topic. Typically, if the BOF meets two or more times, a working group is formed.

5. The BOF minutes are very interesting to read. They are available on the Web at:
http://www.ietf.org/ietf/96dec/tagsw-minutes-96dec.txt

tolerance and recovery mechanisms, and documenting additional encapsulation methods for the latest lower layer technologies.

Currently, none of the solutions that employ label-swapping based forwarding ("label switching") in conjunction with network layer routing are based on standard technology. In order to achieve the benefits of this new technology, a standard solution is necessary.

The working group is responsible for standardizing a base technology for using label swapping forwarding paradigm (label switching) in conjunction with network layer routing and for the implementation of that technology over various link level technologies, which may include Packet-over-Sonet, Frame Relay, ATM, Ethernet (all forms, such as Gigabit Ethernet, etc.), Token Ring, [and others.]

This includes procedures and protocols for the distribution of labels between routers, encapsulations, multicast considerations, use of labels to support higher layer resource reservation and QoS mechanisms, and definition of host behaviors.

Figure 1–2   The original MPLS WG charter. [2]

Using MPLS for switching TDM slots, optical lambdas (wavelengths), and spatial switching (between incoming and outgoing fibers) are some of the latest developments. These efforts are collectively called Generalized MPLS, or GMPLS. GMPLS is discussed in Chapter 10, "Future MPLS Developments and Directions."

The MPLS WG also originally created a list of eight high-level requirements of "should's" and "must's" to further define the "what" of MPLS:

1. MPLS should work with most data link technologies.
2. MPLS should be compatible with most network layer routing protocols and other associated Internet technologies.
3. MPLS must operate independently from any routing protocols.
4. MPLS should support a wide range of forwarding granularities for any given label.
5. MPLS should support operation, administration, and maintenance (OAM).
6. MPLS must contain loop prevention or detection.
7. MPLS must operate in a hierarchical network.
8. MPLS should be very scalable.

These eight requirements are the cornerstones for the major development efforts that have ensued since they were defined. The requirements can be traced through the architecture and the additional supporting specifications.

In conjunction with these requirements, the MPLS WG also set forth a set of eight key objectives. These important MPLS aims are:

1. The specification of standard protocols to maintain and distribute label binding information to support unicast destination-based routing, where the forwarding is done by swapping labels. (Unicast routing specifies exactly one interface; destination-based routing refers to routing based on the final destination of the packet.)

2. The specification of standard protocols to maintain and distribute label binding information to support multicast destination-based routing, where the forwarding is done by swapping labels. (Multicast routing specifies more than one interface. The work of integrating multicast techniques and MPLS is still in the discussion phase.)

3. The specification of standard protocols to maintain and distribute label binding information to support a hierarchy of routing knowledge, where the forwarding is done by swapping labels. (A routing hierarchy refers to knowing the topology within an autonomous system (AS), and also between ASs.)

4. The specification of standard protocols to maintain and distribute label binding information for supporting explicit paths based on label swapping. These paths may be different from the ones calculated by conventional IP routing, which are based on destination-based forwarding. (Explicit paths are the key to the TE applications that are part of MPLS's prime advantage over conventional routing.)

5. The specification of standardized procedures for carrying label information over different Layer 2 link level technologies. (MPLS link layer encapsulation makes the technology flexible and scalable.)

6. The specification of a standard way to interoperate with ATM at the user and control planes (an excellent way to have ATM and IP interoperate, and also a migration path to TCP/IP-only networks).

7. The specification of support for QoS technologies (such as the Resource Reservation Protocol, or RSVP). (QoS is also one of the most important MPLS applications. MPLS QoS will be a important enabler for the derivation of revenues from next-generation networks.)

8. The specification of standard protocols to allow hosts to utilize MPLS. (Much like ATM, this objective was never met, as MPLS was implemented from the core outward. Host-based MPLS appears not to be feasible due to scalability and performance issues.)

As can be seen, most of these MPLS objectives serve as the basis for creating and designing the major MPLS technologies and protocols discussed in Chapter 4, "Core MPLS Technologies and Protocols," and Chapter 5, "MPLS Signaling and Label Distribution."

WHY IS MPLS NEEDED? ....

After the initial BOF meeting in December 1996, the MPLS WG convened in early 1997 and addressed four original problems:

1. Layer 3 network layer routing scalability
2. Forwarding performance increases
3. Cell switched-based technologies integration
4. Increased routing services delivery flexibility

These four problems are central to the current challenges facing internetworking today. These include integrating the various technologies that must coexist, evolving and scaling to include increased traffic and new equipment, and providing new functionality, including new Internet services and applications.

MPLS was originally envisioned as a technology that could improve the scaling of Layer 3 IP routing by avoiding the large number of "fully connected" routers that were required for the Internet core. It has since been shown that there are other ways to extend IP routing over such meshes.

Also, the argument that forwarding performance could be greatly improved because the table lookup for short, fixed-length labels is much quicker than the longest destination address match that is required for conventional IP routing has been mitigated by hardware solutions done in application-specific integrated circuits (ASICs) and field-programmable gate arrays (FPGAs). The IP header analysis that is required is no longer the computational bottleneck for router performance, and is now done at "wire speed."

Because many service providers employ an ATM-based backbone and offer FR access services, MPLS has an important new way of offering value-added IP services over these existing transports. The cell switching-based technologies of ATM and frame-based FR are being integrated, migrated, and in some cases, supplanted by standards-based IP solutions such as MPLS.

A great deal of interest has been generated for new applications such as QoS, TE, VPNs, and fast path restoral. There is also interest in integrating new technologies under the MPLS umbrella, including MPLS use in optical networking and switching, voice over MPLS, placing certain types of Layer 2 traffic over MPLS, and many others.

While MPLS is being developed to address these original concerns, the major driving force for promoting the technology is to offer a method of providing alternate routing to the best-effort, shortest path first (SPF) routing that is utilized by the conventional IP routing done today. New types of applications and services will have new requirements that demand updated techniques to offer proper QoS to users.

How Is MPLS Done?...

MPLS can be thought of as a set of technologies that works together to deliver packets from source to destination in a controlled, efficient, and predictable manner. It uses label-switched paths (LSPs) for Layer 2 forwarding that have been set up with Layer 3 routing and signaling protocols.

Because the concepts of forwarding, switching, and routing are central to understanding how MPLS works, it is important to state and understand their definitions.

> **Because this is a primer...**
>
> Three important concepts that set the groundwork for understanding MPLS are forwarding, switching, and routing.
> **Forwarding**—The process of receiving a packet on an input port and sending it out an output port.
> **Switching**—The knowledge of directing the forwarding process to choose the correct output port. A switch is a device that operates on Layer 2 header information to direct the forwarding process.
> **Routing**—The process of setting up routes to understand the next hop a packet should take toward its destination between networks. A router is the device that sets up the tables that understand the network to accomplish this. The router operates on the Layer 3 packet header to analyze the best forwarding path a packet should take to go from network to network.

A router network device forwards a packet from source to destination by receiving, switching, and then forwarding it from device to device until it reaches its destination. Figure 1–3 shows this general model. The control plane maintains the set of possible routes that a packet may use to get to its next hop. In the general model, a packet enters a network device through an input interface or port. The packet is processed by a receive logic that passes the necessary information about the packet to the decision logic. The decision logic, which has information continually

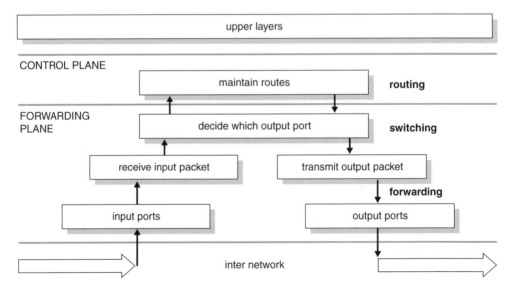

Figure 1–3   Routing, switching, and forwarding.

supplied to it from the control plane process that maintains the routes, gives the updated packet information to the transmit logic, which forwards the packet via the proper output port to its next destination device.

This is a greatly simplified model that varies between networking technologies, but it is a good starting point for discussing how MPLS is done. MPLS technologies offer a new model for how routing, switching, and forwarding play together to move packets within the Internet.

Another often-encountered model for how packets should flow between network devices such as routers is shown in Figure 1–4. The traffic that flows in the network can be thought of as essentially two types: control traffic, which includes routing and management information, and data traffic, which is, well, everything else.

The data traffic follows the "fast path" and is processed by the network devices in an efficient and timely manner. In most modern network devices, the fast path is realized in hardware. Any time the network device encounters a packet that is not data (and it can tell this by examining the packet header), the information about the packet is sent "up" to the control path for processing. Control packets include the information that is required for routing packets destined for that particular network device, any other packets that contain management information, data packets with options, exceptions, and so on. These packets are processed more slowly because they need to be examined by software. Because of this, this processing path is often called the "slow path."

This model is also important for introducing how MPLS works because it depicts the separation of the control path and the forwarding path. The ability of MPLS to decouple these important functions is what makes it a serious new contender for changing how data packets will be sent over the Internet.

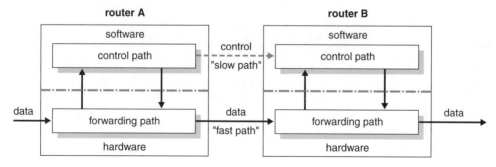

Figure 1–4   The "fast path" and the "slow path."

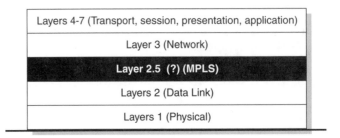

Figure 1–5   The MPLS "shim layer."

MPLS has been specified to work with many different Layer 2 and Layer 3 protocols, and also to function in many different types of network devices.

"Layer 2.5 technology" is another phrase that is often used to describe what MPLS is. Figure 1–5 shows that MPLS is often depicted as a new "shim layer" that has interposed itself between the network and data link layers.

While this initially appears to be a gross violation of the OSI communication model used to explain network protocols and interfaces, as well as the partitioning of functionality and services within a layer, it will be shown that MPLS is not an explicit new layer, but rather a binding of the control plane at the "bottom" of the network layer with the data forwarding plane at the "top" of the data link layer. MPLS is not a new network layer protocol because it does not have its own routing capabilities or an addressing scheme, which are required for a Layer 3 protocol. MPLS uses IP addressing and IP routing protocols (with the necessary modifications and extensions). MPLS is also not a new data link layer protocol because it has been designed to work over many of the popular data link technologies that provide the requisite Layer 2 addressing and functionality.

WHEN AND WHERE IS MPLS USED?..............................

One general model of the Internet is to view the entire set of communicating computers and networks as a set of concentric circles. The inside core routes lots of traffic at very high speeds. Moving outward, various types of traffic that need to flow together somehow move at many different speeds.

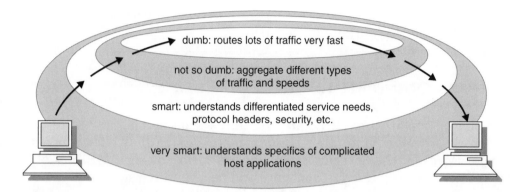

Figure 1–6   Internet traffic and devices.

It is often said that the Internet is a "dumb" network.[6] As shown in Figure 1–6, the intelligence of the Internet is dispersed to the edges, where very "smart" applications use networking technologies to perform all those amazing things computers are capable of doing. When using the Internet, packet flow begins at one host, travels through the various strata of communication technologies that comprise the Internet, and ends at the destination host.

This model relates directly to when and where MPLS is used. MPLS is being deployed first from the core outward as a transport technology. In a sense, it is an attempt to add a new type of internetworking intelligence by introducing more control over how traffic flows and what services can be delivered. The first deployments of MPLS have primarily been by large, top-tier service providers that need more control in how traffic flows through their networks. Naturally, because the communication technologies must all interoperate, there is an ongoing interest by second- and third-tier service providers, metropolitan equipment vendors, and large enterprises to enable MPLS within their networks. As the technology matures, it will gain more use in a variety of important areas, such as TE, VPNs, QoS, packet-based voice services, and various optical-based technologies. MPLS is being viewed as a strong, enabling mechanism for generating revenues for service providers. It is also interesting to note that MPLS in its current form will not migrate to the hosts. It is

---

6. It is interesting to note that this is often viewed as the opposite model of the deployed public phone system: millions of relatively dumb phones all interconnected in a global voice network via very intelligent switches.

an Internet technology that is transparent to the end-user and will reside within the internetworking infrastructure.

WHO IS DOING MPLS?...

The initial deployers of MPLS are large ISPs, some second- and third-tier network providers, and other similar organizations that offer products and services for the core and regional areas of the Internet. MPLS is also currently in use by carrier backbones and large-enterprise wide area networks (WANs). It is beginning to be rapidly introduced into metropolitan area networks (MANs), also.

Many different types of organizations are interested in MPLS, including MPLS equipment vendors, major service providers, MPLS software stack vendors, testing equipment manufacturers, testing organizations, universities, research centers, and others. See Chapter 9, "Current MPLS Implementations," for a sample of the many companies and organizations that are actively involved in MPLS implementation and deployment.

After reading the "five Ws and H," a quick introduction to the label switching paradigm and then MPLS will expose the reader to a sound overview of the main facets of the technology.

THE LABEL SWITCHING PARADIGM.................................

The label switching paradigm is the central mechanism that is employed in the data forwarding plane for advancing packets from source to destination while in the MPLS network. Primarily based on the ATM and FR model and earlier proprietary tag-based techniques, labels are assigned to packets as they enter the network, get swapped as the packets traverse the network, and are then removed as the packets exit the MPLS portion of the network.

Figure 1–7 on the next page shows the basic label swapping model. In a network, there is an entry point called the ingress node, intermediate nodes called transit nodes, and an exit point named the egress node for a particular path. The set of nodes that participate in the label swapping is called the label swapping domain.

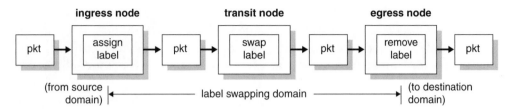

Figure 1–7   The label switching paradigm.

It should be noted that the values of the labels can be assigned and distributed before any label swapping of the data occurs, or the labels can be generated as packets belonging to a specified flow or class enter the network. These two types of label assignment are called control-driven and traffic-driven, respectively. After the label switching domain has been configured for handling the packet traffic that is to be forwarded by label swapping, packets are all processed in the same simple and straightforward manner.

A label is a short, fixed-length value that is carried in the packet header. The label identifies which forwarding path a packet will traverse based on a configurable set of input parameters (destination address, prefix, QoS, etc.). A process running at the ingress node determines any incoming packet's label value based on the information of how the packet maps to its forwarding path set. The ingress node assigns an initial label value to each packet and sends it into the network. Labels have only local significance, and the actual value of a label is only understood between any two communicating nodes. After a label is added by the ingress node, it is swapped at the transit nodes based on its configured label map until the packet reaches its destination at the egress node. Remember, the label maps that direct the packet through its LSP have been set up before the packet has begun its journey. Labeled paths are, therefore, roughly equivalent to a virtual circuit (VC). Also, a labeled path is always unidirectional. If you want packet traffic to flow in the opposite direction on the same route, you must set up two labeled paths.

Label swapping has several advantages over the hop-by-hop routing employed by conventional IP routers. It is simple and efficient. Packet analysis is done only once—at the ingress node. Label swapping within the label swapping domain is quick because the operation simply recognizes the label and swaps it for the packet's next label value. The egress node recognizes that the packet is at the edge of the domain and then removes the label and forwards the packet based on other information, such as the packet's network layer header, into the destination domain.

While label swapping is the heart of MPLS, a quick introduction reveals several more concepts that are necessary to begin to understand the technology more completely and to know why MPLS is more than just label swapping.

A QUICK INTRODUCTION TO MPLS ....

The MPLS technologies are a set of procedures for combining the Layer 2 label swapping paradigm with Layer 3 routing functionality. The basic premise of MPLS is that by assigning short, fixed-length labels to packets and then using only these pre-assigned labels for forwarding, certain efficiencies and additional, desirable network behaviors can be achieved.

There are three major steps in setting up and using an MPLS-enabled network:

* Enabling network devices for MPLS
* Setting up forwarding equivalence classes (FECs) and configuring LSPs
* Passing MPLS traffic, and monitoring and controlling the network

The initial step is adding the MPLS technology to the network and appropriate devices. This includes adding the appropriate hardware and software to the network devices, configuring the signaling software to assign and distribute the labels, performing any additional configuration duties such as setting up the interfaces, working with other routing and control software, interfacing to the data forwarding logic, and so on. MPLS-enabled routers are called label-switched routers (LSRs). ATM switches that have the MPLS capability added to them are often called ATM-LSRs. For an ATM-LSR, the TCP/IP stack is required for the MPLS control plane signaling and data forwarding logic to process the MPLS labels that become part of the ATM cells.

Figure 1–8 on the next page shows the MPLS domain. Again, the MPLS domain is defined as a set of nodes that is capable of supporting MPLS functionality. The packet traffic flow is always unidirectional, thereby enabling the definition of an entrance to the domain, intermediate hops, and an exit back to conventional Layer 3 routing. The roles of

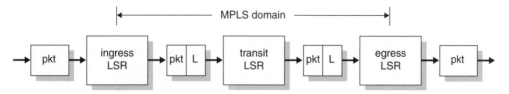

Figure 1–8   The MPLS domain.

the MPLS-enabled routers within the MPLS domain are called the ingress LSR, the transit LSR, and the egress LSR, respectively. Because the ingress and egress LSRs are at the edge of the domain, they are often called label edge routers (LERs). In other words, an LER is an MPLS node that is connected to a neighboring node that is outside the MPLS domain, and therefore not running MPLS.

The second step in setting up an MPLS network is configuring the forwarding equivalence classes (FECs) and LSPs.

An FEC is a group of IP packets that will be forwarded in the same manner, that is, over the same path, with the same forwarding treatment. The input FEC classification decision is shown in Figure 1–9. Because MPLS generally uses control-driven label assignment, which label is applied to which incoming network layer packet is predetermined by setting up these FECs ahead of time. There should be an FEC to assign any unlabeled incoming packet into a group that will become MPLS-labeled packets. A table within the MPLS-enabled router then assigns the MPLS label, the outgoing interface for forwarding, and other MPLS-related information based on which FEC the incoming packet is a member of.

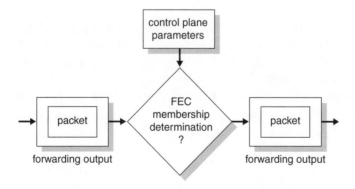

Figure 1–9   The forwarding equivalence class decision.

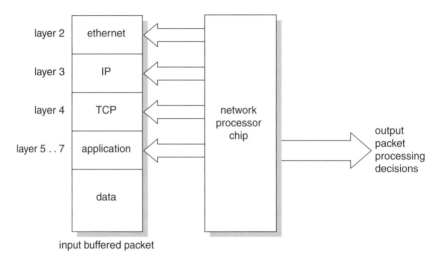

Figure 1–10   Packet header analysis.

An important point to remember is that FEC membership determination is done only once—at the ingress LSR. In conventional IP routing, a lookup must be done at every router to determine the next hop for a packet and a full packet header analysis must be done at every hop. In MPLS, because the path has been set up ahead of time, there is no further analysis of the network layer packet header required at the intermediate nodes, only the swapping of labels in the data forwarding mechanism. Determining which route (LSP) an incoming packet will use is one of the important improvements over conventional IP routing in terms of routing flexibility.

Packet header analysis can be used to give an even finer grained FEC determination classification. Much work, particularly in network processor hardware design, is being done in this area. Whereas conventional IP routing is based on the destination address found in the network layer header only, newly developed techniques are offering finer resolution in analyzing fields in packet headers in other layers. This deeper analysis will enable a next generation of IP-based services and applications such as TE and QoS by analyzing the traffic more closely.

Figure 1–10 shows a network processor chip that can interrogate (ideally, at wire speed) preprogrammed fields in the header of an input buffer queued packet. At Layer 2 (Ethernet, in this example), various prioritization fields in the header can be recognized. For instance, in Ethernet, the 802.1p standard specifies three bits that can be used for Layer 2

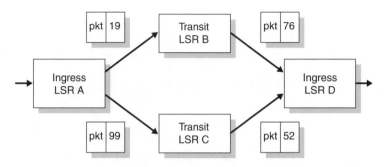

Figure 1–11 Passing traffic in the MPLS domain.

packet prioritization. At Layer 3, there are many additional header fields that can be analyzed to help define packet treatment. By looking at source and destination IP addresses, various flow prioritization schemes can be implemented. Port values for transport services are often investigated at Layer 4, and applications can be classified by using logic to categorize each recognizable application flow type.

Before the FEC classification has determined the label value and outgoing interface for any particular packet's LSP, the MPLS signaling and label distribution protocols must have distributed the proper labels within the domain to create those LSPs. The MPLS architecture does not mandate a specific label signaling and distribution protocol; therefore, today there are several protocols that are in use to create various types of LSPs. The main MPLS label protocols include the Label Distribution Protocol (LDP), RSVP-TE, and CR-LDP. A complete discussion of these protocols is included in Chapter 5, "MPLS Signaling and Label Distribution."

Network management plays a major role in configuring MPLS LSRs and LSPs. Via SNMP and Command Line Interfaces (CLI), network administrators set the proper values to enable MPLS on their networks.

Finally, the network is ready to pass traffic down its MPLS LSPs. Figure 1–11 shows a sample network configured to pass traffic. When the ingress LSR A recognizes that an incoming Layer 3 packet is to be sent down an LSP based on which FEC the packet is a member of, the ingress LSR encodes the MPLS label onto the packet. In this example, one FEC would place label 19 for LSP A-B-D, and another FEC would place an MPLS header with label value 99 on the packet for LSP A-C-D. At the transit LSR, the incoming label becomes an index into a table that assigns a new label and other associated information. Transit LSR B swaps label 76 for incoming packets that contain 19 as their top label value. The transit LSR then uses the corresponding outgoing interface to send the packet to egress LSR D. The transit LSR performs a similar operation for packets arriving at its incoming interface with label 99. At egress LSR D, the label is removed and the packet is forwarded as necessary using conventional network layer routing. The packet has left the MPLS domain.

Network management also plays a vital role in monitoring and controlling an MPLS network once has been configured. LSP usage and how the label distribution protocols are operating are only two of the tasks that are necessary for managing a properly running MPLS network.

The future of MPLS is in refining and extending network services and adding new applications based on tested and implemented MPLS deployments.

EVOLUTION OF INTERNET NETWORK MODELS ....

The need for MPLS can be traced through the recent evolution of the Internet by looking at several network models that were developed to handle the routing of data.

There are four models that are of interest:

- The IP over ATM overlay model
- The multilayer switching model
- The "pure IP" model
- The MPLS-only model

Overlay Networks

In the early-to-mid 1990s, ATM became a popular solution for providing transport services within service provider networks. The ATM speeds of up to 622 Mbps were greater than the TDM T-1 and T-3 speeds that were currently in use in the Internet. Since higher level applications were always primarily IP-based—there were very few "native" ATM applications ever developed—the IP over ATM overlay model was created as a reliable and cost-effective way to multiplex IP data over an ATM core. The model is presented in Figure 1–12.

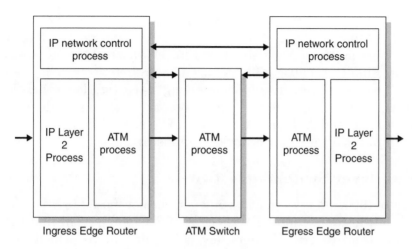

Figure 1–12   The IP over ATM overlay model.

The main feature of an overlay network is that the model presents two independent networks: a Layer 2 network that is running ATM in the core, and a Layer 3 network that is IP-based and running at the edges of the networks. Thus, at the IP layer, the IP devices are only logically connected from edge to edge. The IP and ATM protocols work concurrently, but in a totally independent fashion; the phrase "ships in the night" is often used to refer to this configuration.

There are several advantages of the overlay model. When VCs are set up in ATM, TE and QoS parameters can be specified because of the connection-oriented nature of the protocol. Protection and failover are often provided by an underlying SONET physical network in these types of networks, also. The ATM switches are arranged in a full-mesh configuration to guarantee the any-to-any connectivity that is required from the routed edge traffic's point of view. At the time, this arrangement provided state-of-the-art transport for service providers. It is still in use today with a large installed base.

There are also several disadvantages of the model. The full-mesh topology of the ATM switch core does not scale well when new switches or edge routers need to be added (this is called the "n-squared" problem). The full-mesh configuration can also cause a routing convergence problem for Internal Gateway Protocols (IGPs) during a link failure because of the number of updates that need to be sent. Because the Layer 2 and Layer 3 networks are independent, they must be managed and administered by two completely separate management platforms. This is a complex and costly situation. Also, ATM has a problem scaling past the OC-48 speed because it is not cost-effective to create the required segmentation and reassembly (SAR) chips to do the cell assembly and reassembly functions. Finally, because ATM is based on 53-byte fixed cells, there is a "cell tax" when transporting variable-length-packet IP traffic. Some of the data payloads are empty. There is work going on in developing a longer, frame-based ATM, but it has yet to be seen if this effort will have a place in the current internetworking landscape.

Multilayer Switching Networks

In the mid-1990s, many innovative ideas were proposed to bring the best features of the connection-based, VC, label swapping ATM and FR technologies to the Internet. Vendors developed innovative—albeit not standard, and therefore non-interoperable—solutions for the market. Such concepts as IP switching, the cell-based router, and products from Cisco, IBM, Ascend (Lucent), and others were attempts to integrate the overlay model of ATM and IP by combining the Layer 3 IP control plane with the Layer 2 ATM label swapping forwarding capabilities. This multilayer switching model is shown in Figure 1–13.

With multilayer IP switching, the IP routing control process is used with ATM label handling for data forwarding of the ATM cells carrying the packet traffic in the data payload. The ATM control plane protocols are not used. In this model, there are no longer "ships in the night," but rather "one boat." There is only one management and administration of the network, making it simpler and cheaper than the overlay model. Another big advantage is that it uses standard IP addressing. IP services and applications run natively on the network.

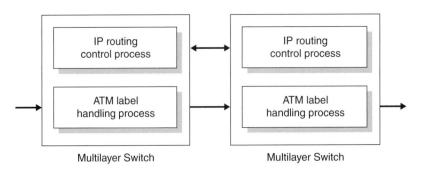

Figure 1–13   Multilayer switching model.

The big gotcha, however, is that these solutions were never standardized; therefore, the devices could not work with each other. Several important desirable ATM and FR features were also lost, including QoS and the ability to do TE and management.

"Pure IP" Networks

IP has become the predominant network layer protocol in use today, and the evolution to a "pure IP" network seems a natural direction, especially with the development of IP-based routing at very high speeds. This type of model is shown in Figure 1–14. Both the control and data forwarding planes are based solely on IP technologies.

This is the current direction in the Internet core as IP-based terabit routers now begin to outperform ATM switches. New optical technologies are allowing for the creation of OC-192 and OC-768 speeds in these devices. These devices add an even greater dimension of simplicity and ease of management. The introduction of new standardized technologies such as MPLS will also add the missing features from the ATM protocol. Required applications such as QoS and TE, plus the ability to have deterministic performance when required by using connection-like paths and the label swapping data forwarding plane, will be added to the network.

MPLS-Only Networks?

If the ideas of a universal control plane and label swapping data forwarding plane are advanced even further, a case may be made for MPLS-only networks as the next natural evolutionary step for certain classes of net-

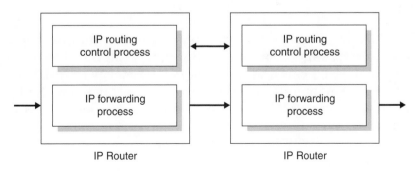

Figure 1–14   "Pure IP" model.

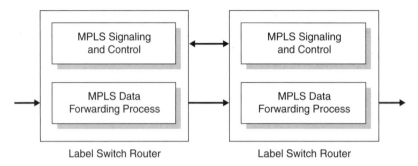

Figure 1–15   The MPLS-only model.

work devices within the Internet. Figure 1–15 shows two communicating LSRs that exclusively use the MPLS control and forwarding planes:

This scenario is currently not feasible because MPLS is tightly coupled with other TCP/IP protocols. The MPLS domain sits "inside" a larger IP domain to provide the necessary end-to-end connectivity that is required for host-to-host communications with the Internet. If deployment of MPLS becomes ubiquitous, MPLS-only networks may evolve for specific purposes, such as "fat" tunnels for moving large amounts of special data, many new evolving optical applications, and other uses that have not been developed—or imagined—yet. An MPLS-only device is a current development topic, and such development may produce devices that fill a specific niche in some networking situations.

To come full circle after looking at the future of the Internet, it is beneficial to look at the basics of the Internet to see how we got here in the first place.

BASICS OF THE INTERNET ....

MPLS cannot be understood outside the context of the Internet and its associated networking technologies. Since the Internet began over 30 years ago, it has become the most important global infrastructure for exchanging information. It is important to understand how the Internet evolved by presenting a quick history and taking a look at its current direction.

A Short History of the Internet

In 1969, the Internet began as the experimental data network called the Advanced Research Projects Agency Network (ARPANET). The Department of Defense (DOD) used the network as a testing ground for research and emerging network technologies, primarily for military purposes. The original network connected four universities: UCLA, the Stanford Research Institute, the University of California at Santa Barbara, and the University of Utah. It was viewed as a success and was expanded by adding computers and connectivity throughout the U.S. In the following year, the ARPANET host computers began using the first host-to-host protocol: Network Control Protocol (NCP). Also in 1970, AT&T installed the first transcontinental connection. It was a 56-Kbps line between UCLA and Bolt, Beranek, and Newman (BBN).

In the early 1970s, computer scientists started developing network applications and protocols to enhance the use of this internetwork. In 1972, scientists at the National Center for Supercomputing Applications (NCSA) developed the Telnet application. Telnet allowed a user to log in to remote computers. The following year, the File Transfer Protocol (FTP) was released. This application standardized the transfer of files between computers on the internetwork. In the late 1970s, e-mail and Usenet user groups were standardized and came into frequent use.

In the 1980s, the TCP/IP protocol suite became the only set of protocols used on the ARPANET. This was an important decision because it set the stage for the Internet as a set of networks that could successfully communicate and interoperate. The early 1980s also saw the dramatic rise in the deployment of the personal computer (PC) and host applications. The Berkeley version of the UNIX operating system (OS) included TCP/IP-based network software. UNIX PCs and minicomputers could FTP and Telnet to share and distribute files and applications over the Internet. In 1982, the Exterior Gateway Protocol (EGP) routing specification (RFC 827) was released. EGP was the first routing protocol used for gateways between networks. The Internet Activities Board (IAB) was established in 1983. This group was later renamed to the Internet Architecture Board; it is now the guiding organization for development activities within the Internet.

A major step in expanding the Internet occurred in the mid-1980s, when the National Science Foundation (NSF) connected the six primary supercomputing centers. This internetwork was called the NSFNET "backbone." The backbone was expanded by the NSF by creating regional networks that allowed universities and other institutions connectivity and access to the Internet. In 1987, the NSF granted Merit Network, Inc. the right to operate and manage the future development of the NSFNET backbone. Merit Network worked with International Business Machines (IBM) and MCI Telecommunications Corporation to research and develop newer, faster networking technologies. By 1987, there were over 10,000 hosts connected to the Internet. By 1989, the number of hosts had exploded to over 100,000!

Also in 1989, the NSFNET backbone was upgraded to "T1" trunks. This allowed backbone traffic to run at 1.544 megabits per second. Less than four years later, the backbone was upgraded to "T3" trunks (45 megabits per second). The NSFNET backbone was replaced in the mid-1990s by an even newer network architecture called the Very High-Speed Backbone Network System (vBNS). This system has a hierarchical layout that uses NSPs, regional networks, and network access points (NAPs). As this book was being written, there was discussion beginning on the design and deployment of Internet 2 (the sequel!).

An important Internet service called Gopher was developed at the University of Minnesota in 1991. It made accessing information in the format of files much easier by providing a set of file lists. These lists were accessible via hierarchically arranged menus. In the Gopher client/server model, the client could use a text viewer interface to read individual files.

Two years later in 1993, the European Laboratory for Particle Physics (CERN), located in Switzerland, released the World Wide Web (WWW). The WWW was developed by Tim Berners-Lee and others the previous year as a way of exchanging research and other information over the Internet. The Web introduced other essential Web technologies, including the Hypertext Transfer Protocol (HTTP), Hypertext Markup Language (HTML), hypertext and hypermedia links, and the Universal Resource Locator (URL) addressing scheme. With the development and release of the Mosaic graphical browser in the same year from the NCSA, the Internet got exposure to a much wider audience.

As of this writing, the Internet has millions of computers allowing tens (or perhaps hundreds) of millions of users to exchange information throughout the world.

Latest Internet Directions

In the new millennium, the Internet continues to grow, the user population doubling every few months. By January 2001, the number of hosts passed 100,000,000! Change will not only be in the number of users, but in the number and types of devices plugging into this matrix. The use of personal digital assistants (PDAs) and wireless telephones that can access the Internet is growing at an unprecedented pace. Technology is rapidly being upgraded to meet these new scaling and performance requirements. There is a definite place for new technologies such as MPLS. The rise of the optical core and use of associated frameworks such as GMPLS may figure prominently in the new Internet.

INTERNETWORKING TECHNOLOGY BASICS......................

"Open" and "standards-based" are two related attributes that are highly desirable for the multivendor, heterogeneous device environment that is required for today's networks. These two factors are often cited as the prime reasons for the tremendous growth of the Internet and the evolution of its technologies, including MPLS.

Open Standards-Based Frameworks

The open and standards-based attributes are highly desirable for any communication framework. Open systems can be analyzed and expanded in ways that are not possible with closed, proprietary systems. Open systems allow for the interoperability of multivendor, multiversion devices. Standards-based means that the appropriate enterprise framework must be based on well-established and agreed-upon rules.[7] Being open and standards-based allows an enterprise to field hardware and software from many vendors, creating a "best-in-breed" solution. The first efforts in the 1980s for device standardization were defined using the OSI seven-layer reference model (OSI-RM). The OSI-RM is universally used as the lowest common denominator for the basis of explaining how open systems based on standards communicate on a network and how networks can support communications with each other over an internetwork such as the Internet.

---

7. There are two common categories of standards: *de facto* and *de jure*. *De facto* standards are created for a special purpose and then come into standard use though general consensus. *De jure* standards are created by an authorized standards body by design.

The OSI Reference Model

For any communication system to be effective, it must be able to interoperate with the largest number of networks, devices, applications, services, and whatever else it communicates with. Also, for the underlying network to support communications on an internetwork, it must support common and interoperable protocols that allow for this communication.

The OSI-RM is used to explain how open systems are architected. The model was standardized by the International Organization for Standardization (ISO) in 1978 and was approved as a standard in 1983 (OSI guideline IS #7498). It defines the communication between two end-systems in terms of seven layers. Each layer communicates with its corresponding peer-level layer via its protocol. A layer provides a well-defined set of services. Each layer (*n*) communicates and uses the services of the layer below it (*n* minus 1) through its well-defined interface. This layering allows the functionality to be modularized and understood in manageable, logical units. Figure 1–16 shows the layers of the model using two computers connected over an internetwork.

The OSI-RM is often shown with intermediate devices that support just the lower three layers. These devices exist for aiding network traffic flow and do not support the higher-level user services. Examples of intermediate devices include routers, bridges, hubs, and other similar equipment. An MPLS LSR is also an example of an intermediate device.

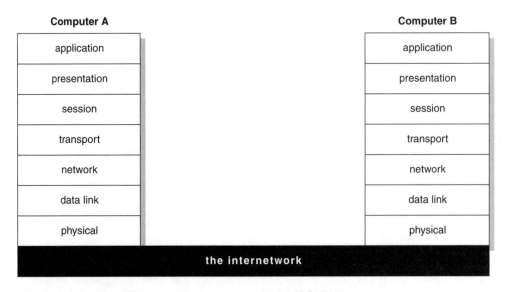

Figure 1–16   The OSI seven-layer reference model (OSI-RM).

The seven OSI layers are:

1. **Physical layer**—This is the lowest level in the model. This layer handles the interface to the physical medium and deals with the various physical characteristics of the medium such as voltages, data rates, and so on. Physical layers now include optical and wireless technologies.

2. **Data Link layer**—This layer provides error-free transmission for the network layer above. It handles flow control, error detection, and data delivery for the link between two connected points.

3. **Network layer**—Layer 3 establishes, maintains, and terminates the connections between two communicating end-devices. It handles routing, congestion, and other internetworking issues.

4. **Transport layer**—This layer ties together the process-to-process communication of the upper three user levels. It guarantees error-free, end-to-end data transfer between communicating devices.

5. **Session layer**—Layer 5 establishes and maintains the connection between different processes that are running on different machines. It handles connection establishment and data transfer between the sessions.

6. **Presentation layer**—This layer handles any data representation, translation, and presentation duties for communicating applications.

7. **Application layer**—The highest layer in the model provides user application access to the communication facilities provided by the lower six layers for exchanging data between applications that can be running on different machines.

Before we go deeper into the details of communication technology, it is important to fully understand the key concepts of this reference model. These include layers, services, protocols, and data encapsulation.

Layers The layers of the model were created to handle complexity by abstracting how the various required services would be arranged. Each layer performs a well-defined set of functionality by providing services to the layer above and using the services of the layer directly below. With this in mind, Figure 1–17 on the next page is another look at the OSI reference model with the levels named by their responsibilities.

This view of the model shows that the application layer at one computer knows what it wants to do, that is, what application it wishes to run. In a client/server model, the user at computer A would be the host client, initiating an application that may use a program running at the host server on computer B.

Each layer, in turn, presents the data to each successive layer below it to perform the duties that are required to deliver the information from one application to the application running at the remote computer. The data is successively transformed into the proper format, prepared for the right session, packed for the correct transport end location, routed to the appropriate network, framed to the link format, and then (finally!) transformed into the physical bits that are moved across the communication medium.

At the receiving computer, the process is reversed and the message eventually reaches the corresponding application. It becomes quite evident that this process involves a large number of related and cooperating processes. Each process is modeled as a service or set of services.

With MPLS and conventional routing, the seven OSI-RM layers can be condensed into a simplified model as shown in Figure 1–18 on the next page. Often, when dealing with layered communications models, it is important to understand that a layer represents a "bundle," or collection of functionality. Because communications models were developed at dif-

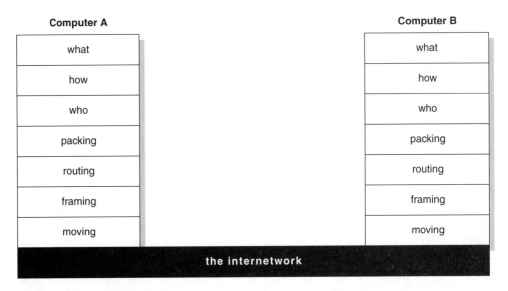

Figure 1–17 The OSI-RM functions.

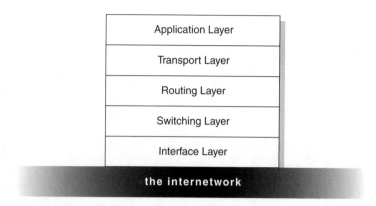

Figure 1–18   Simplified communication layer model.

ferent times for different purposes (protocols, services, etc.), the number of layers varies, but the idea of what a layer represents remains the same. The best example is that the OSI-RM is seven layers, while the TCP/IP reference model only contains four layers, yet both are used in successful network implementations.

With MPLS, the routing and switching layers contain the key functionality: the control plane where the paths are set up and maintained, and the data forwarding plane where the label manipulation occurs.

Services   Services are the set of well-defined functions (also called "primitives," "operations," or "methods") provided and used by the layers in the model. A layer provides services to the service user in the layer above. The service communicates in an established way through an unambiguously defined network service access point (NSAP).

Figure 1–19 on the next page shows the general OSI service model. The line between the layer N service provider and its corresponding service user at layer $N + 1$ is called the "interface." Interfaces separate the layers. Figure 1–20 further refines the service model by showing the intra-layer relationships.

Both the OSI and TCP/IP models include the concepts of layers, services, and protocols. Before these two models and their protocols can be compared, the seven layers of the OSI model need to be further divided into three major parts: the end-to-end services (Layers 1, 2, 3), transport layer (Layer 4), and application services (Layers 5, 6, and 7).

In this view, the lowest layer, end-to-end services, focuses on the data transmission among end-systems across the internetwork communi-

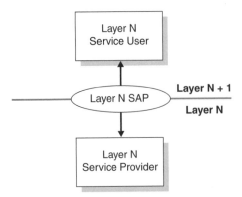

Figure 1–19   General OSI service model.

cations facility. The upper layer, application services, focuses on the user requirements and applications. The transport layer and its interfaces separate these two types of services. The transport layer's main purpose is to shield the application services from the internetwork details of the end-to-end services below. The relationships between services within the OSI model are shown in Figure 1–21 on the next page.

Protocols   Protocols are the sets of rules that control the information flow between two cooperating peer layers. Within each protocol, there is a definition of the data that is passed during communication. The exact definition of the protocol data unit (PDU) is dependent on the protocol. The PDUs include header information and the data portion. Each

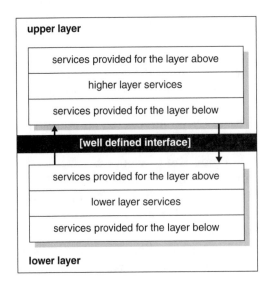

Figure 1–20   Layer services.

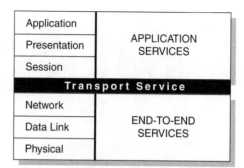

Figure 1–21   Network services model.

layer encapsulates the layer above's PDU with its own header. This header provides the information that is required for the communication services at that level. The PDU of the layer above becomes the data portion for the layer below.

Data Encapsulation   Closely related to the topics of layers, services, and protocols is data encapsulation. Figure 1–22 shows the basic model of data encapsulation when used with layered communications protocols. Encapsulation places the header and data into the data "capsule" of the protocol in the layer below it. There are four protocols in this example. Typically, the only minor exception to pure encapsulation in actual implementations is at Layer 2, where a data link trailer field is maintained for a checksumming feature.

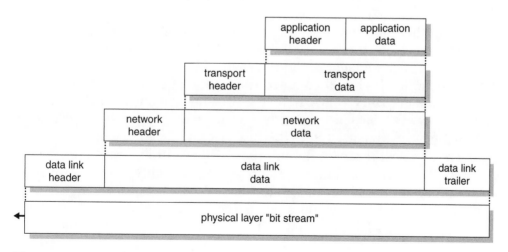

Figure 1–22   Data encapsulation.

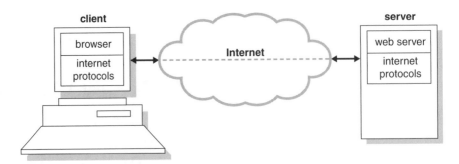

Figure 1–23 A top-level model of the Internet.

Models

Models can be used to reduce the complexity of a system by decomposing that system into simpler, more understandable representations. Models can be created to group the many components of a system into larger, more abstract building blocks that can be more easily understood by the designers, architects, and analysts who will flesh out these models into designs, and eventually into products. Models can be used to simulate the behavior of systems and their subsystems. In an abstract fashion, models can also represent other functional requirements of a system, such as how data will be defined and stored, how the design will accommodate security, which protocols will be used, and others.

The main idea behind modeling is to make things easier to understand, but there is a danger in complex systems—such as communication protocols and technologies—to oversimplify. We are kept honest by Albert Einstein's famous adage: "Everything should be simple as possible, but not simpler." [3] It should be noted that many of the topics presented in this primer are very complex and have filled volumes by themselves. Models, however, have consistently shown themselves to be an excellent starting point when discussing the Internet and its technologies.

The simplest model of the Internet is shown in Figure 1–23.

The route that communications packets actually traverse involves going through several distinct collections of network devices. In the general model, the hosts are located in the "outer" shell called the local domain, or often, "the last mile." The local domain is connected to an access layer that contains, among other things, the devices to which the home and enterprise computers attach to access the Internet.

The access layer includes customer premise equipment (CPE), routers, digital subscriber line access multiplexers (DSLAMs), Data Over Cable Service (DOCS) terminations, and other technologies that offer these connections. The access layer often uses local area networks (LANs) because the devices are usually in close proximity.

Access networks are often connected to metropolitan area networks (MANs). MANs typically span distances of up to several hundred kilometers and serve large, concentrated urban areas. MANs bridge the service requirements between the wide area, long-haul, regional network carriers and the access networks. MANs are responsible for interconnecting a wide variety of enterprise host traffic in the form of all the protocols that are running in the Internet today such as TCP/IP. Transport technology within the metropolitan area is evolving from T1/T3 TDM to high-speed routers and optical switches for the next generation of multiservice information needs that is currently including the use of MPLS. There is also a new type of MAN called a metropolitan optical network (MON) that uses optical technologies. New directions in the metropolitan area also include the use of gigabit Ethernet and the integration of new optical technologies.

Metropolitan traffic is often sent to regional areas that consist of long-haul carriers and equipment that carries the packet traffic over longer distances. All regional areas connect to the Internet core.

Finally, the heart of the Internet is the core. Here, large devices shunt vast amounts of data as quickly as possible. The backbone of the Internet comprises companies and organizations known as ISPs, which are often ranked in "tiers" depending on their size; a tier one ISP would be the largest. The largest ISPs actually have overlapping areas where their equipment is deployed and must be connected at junctures called network access points (NAPs). Each ISP comprises a set of devices called points of presence (POPs). These POPs are where access layer routers can connect to the ISP. Within each POP, there are actually several types of routers that are used for various purposes. These include access routers, border routers, hosting routers, and core routers. Access routers are used for connecting to remote customers, border routers connect various ISPs, hosting routers connect to various Web servers, and core routers provide inter-POP connections.

The diagram that best sums up these relationships is often called the "onion-skin" model. This view of the Internet is shown in Figure 1–24 on the next page. The Internet "cloud" can be viewed as a set of concentric circles, with each circle containing a vast array of different host and net-

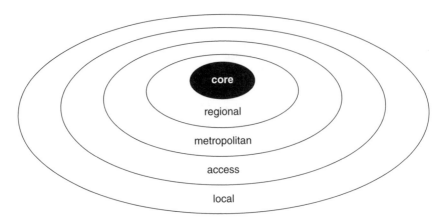

Figure 1–24   The "onion-skin" model of the Internet.

work devices. This model includes a global communications infrastructure that offers nearly universal access to the services and applications available on the Internet.

This top-level model can be further divided into logical models and physical models to delve deeper into the complexities of the devices, protocols, and technologies—such as MPLS—that are used.

A sample logical model that includes three hosts and seven routers is shown in Figure 1–25. This model contains two types of network nodes: hosts and network devices. The hosts initiate and terminate applications that use the internetworking communications infrastructure to exchange

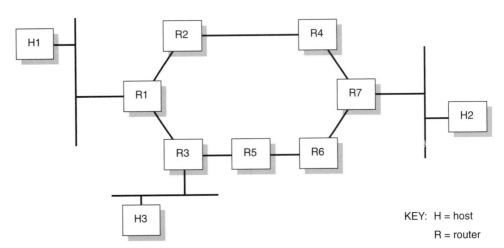

Figure 1–25   A logical model of the Internet.

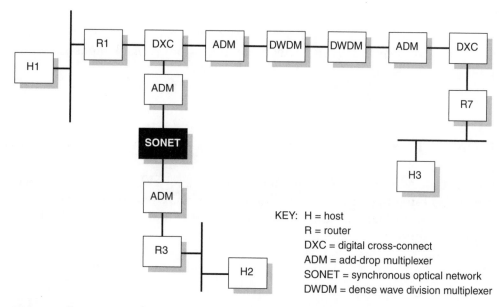

Figure 1–26   A physical model of the Internet.

information with any other hosts that they know the addresses for. The network devices, that is, the routers, connect the various networks that comprise this internetwork example. The routers know how to send packets between other routers to deliver the information from source to destination for any hosts that wish to communicate with each other.

This logical model can be used to introduce MPLS and how it is beginning to be deployed in the Internet as a new transport method. The routers can become LSRs, and various LSPs can be set up to deliver packet traffic between the three hosts if the network administrators wish to take advantage of the new benefits that MPLS offers. These benefits include the major MPLS applications of TE, QoS, VPNs, and path restoral.

The logical model can be refined to depict a physical model that is closer to an actual internetwork. The physical model based on the logical model of Figure 1–25 is shown in Figure 1–26.

This physical model contains several new network devices that are included in an MPLS data flow path, but are not MPLS-enabled devices. As the new Internet integrates optical technologies, devices such as DXCs, ADMs, SONET rings, and DWDMs will deliver more packet traffic over longer distances in much less time. In this physical model, for example, MPLS would only be operating in the three routers. These would be LSRs.

To more fully understand the various types of network models, it is important to study some additional basic background information. Two such basic topics are graph theory and a standardized modeling language.

MORE BASICS: GRAPH THEORY AND MODELING LANGUAGE ....

Graph theory and the Unified Modeling Language (UML) standardized modeling language are two ancillary topics that one often encounters when first approaching new communications technologies such as MPLS. Although these two areas are not essential to the MPLS domain knowledge, understanding the basics can enhance one's knowledge in the area.

Graph Theory

Graph theory is a branch of mathematics that uses diagrams called graphs as mathematical models to help simplify complex problems. Pictorially, a graph can be drawn as a finite number of small circles linked together by lines. Each small circle is called a vertex, and the collection of all the dots in the graph is called a set of vertices. The links—the lines that connect the circles—are called the edges. Each edge connects two vertices. Graph theory is a common technique frequently used for describing communication networks. There is also additional terminology that one can learn if one wishes to delve deeper into this discipline. For example, the valence of any vertex in a graph model is the number of edges that meet at a point. Additionally, a graph is a connected graph if for each pair of its vertices there is at least one path of edges connecting the two vertices.

Figure 1–27 on the next page is a common graph model used in explaining MPLS; it is called the "fish" network. Obviously, it is called this because of its shape. This connected graph has several properties that make it applicable for discussing basic routing concepts.

Figure 1–28 shows a (slightly unbalanced) fish model that demonstrates how routes can be set up in a network. This model can be used to simulate and model traffic flows for setting up applications such as TE. Conventional IP routing would most likely set up a route from C to D to G for traffic that is being sent from host H1 to host H2. The routing protocols running on these nodes would create forwarding information bases

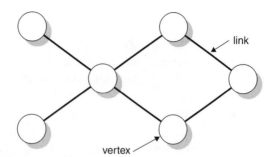

Figure 1–27 The "fish" network model.

that would direct the packets along this route using the SPF, longest destination address match algorithm. MPLS can use a TE application and constraint-based signaling and label distribution (such as RSVP-TE or CR-LDP) to set up an LSP tunnel from C to E to F to G as an alternative route. The overall network resources are now more evenly utilized as alternate paths that would be under-utilized in the IP routing only case begin carrying the MPLS traffic.

To further specify, document, and design networks, modeling languages are often used. The standardized modeling language, UML, has come to the forefront as the most commonly used tool for this purpose. Before MPLS applications such as TE can be designed, modeling languages must be typically employed to do the top-level network engineering that is required. The first step in modeling a network is to understand the traffic, what resources are required, and where the bandwidth needs to be placed. After the network engineering has been modeled, the use of Internet technologies such as MPLS can be successfully configured and deployed.

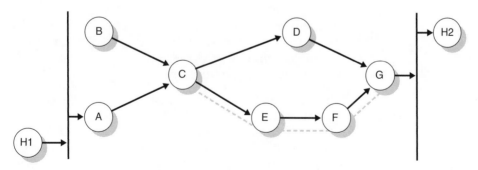

Figure 1–28 IGP and MPLS route model.

Unified Modeling Language (UML)

Understanding the role of MPLS in a network is a complex enough activity that there is a need for standardized modeling. UML has become the premier industry-standard language for network modeling. The Object Management Group (www.omg.org) adopted UML as a standard in November 1997, and it has been in popular use since then.

UML comprises a number of graphical elements that are combined to form various types of diagrams. UML can be used for a variety of modeling needs. These include models for the initial process, class and object modeling, modeling of system components, and even distribution and further development modeling. The most important UML diagrams are the class diagram (CD), the object diagram, the use case diagram, the state diagram, the sequence diagram, the collaboration diagram, the component diagram, and the deployment diagram.

When one delves deeper into MPLS design and implementation, these various types of UML diagrams are often encountered.

THE PROMISE OF MPLS ....

The promise of MPLS is the benefits it will bring to the current and future Internet architecture. The top ten MPLS benefits are summarized in Table 1–1.

Table 1–1   The Promise of MPLS Top Ten List

Benefit	Description
1. Scalability	With the ever-increasing demand for more bandwidth for Internet usage from users and the increased access requirements from "last time" technologies such as DSL and cable modems, wireless, and so on, MPLS may prove a scalable technology to keep abreast of bandwidth requirements for the Internet.
2. New applications	With the ever-increasing demand for new IP-based applications such as QoS, TE, path restoral, and VPNs, MPLS will leverage the Internet services of data, voice, and video to deliver robust and cost-effective solutions. MPLS is also flexible enough to provide support for new applications as they arise.

Table 1–1   The Promise of MPLS Top Ten List (continued)

Benefit	Description
3. Standards-based	MPLS is a standards-based IETF specification developed by the MPLS WG. MPLS interoperates as part of the TCP/IP protocol suite with various signaling and label distribution protocols, SNMP management, and other standard IETF protocols.
4. Complements installed routing base	MPLS complements existing routing and builds on what is already there—no "forklift" replacement of existing router infrastructure is required. MPLS uses a number of label distribution and signaling techniques and protocols. MPLS gives "new life" to the Resource Reservation Protocol (RSVP), uses LDP developed from scratch, and works with conventional routing algorithms such as the Border Gateway Protocol (BGP).
5. Complements installed switching base	MPLS works with ATM and IP/ATM overlay networks, FR, Ethernet, PPP, SONET, and others.
6. Elegant, efficient, and extensible design	MPLS separates the control and forwarding functions. It offers an elegant evolutionary path to include new innovations and technology directions: voice over MPLS, multicast, label swapping in silicon (ASICs and FPGAs), etc. MPLS is an extensible solution that includes GMPLS to offer label swapping to new optical technologies.
7. New Internet services	MPLS is the enabling technology that will accommodate new advances in Internet services such as data, voice, and video.
8. Pivotal role in optical networking	MPLS may be the "glue" for the new optical world: GMPLS. MPLS progresses beyond ATM's limitations, but includes ATM's best features. MPLS fits well with next-generation terabit routers, core backbone switches, and other new devices. MPLS will end the need for overlay networks as optical networks are deployed.

Table 1–1   The Promise of MPLS Top Ten List (continued)

Benefit	Description
9. Reliability	MPLS offers fast restoral for telecommunications-like robustness akin to the Automatic Protection Switching (APS) feature found in SONET. MPLS is designed to handle many failure scenarios for both node and link failure types.
10. Top vendor and NSP/ISP support	MPLS is backed and being implemented by the top vendors in the network industry. It is enjoying initial success from ISP and service provider deployment at many levels.

THE PROMISE OF THE PROMISE OF MPLS ....

MPLS is enjoying great initial success as it begins to be deployed in several service provider networks as a new Internet transport technology. While MPLS will never be a host-to-host solution, it offers an enabling technology for delivering new Internet applications that would not be possible with just current IP routing or other networking technologies such as ATM. MPLS is not faster than IP prefix lookup due to advances in hardware technology such as ASICs and FPGAs; therefore, its promise as purely a performance enhancement to conventional routing has not proven true. However, in its current incarnation, MPLS is closely wedded to current IP technology and all of the major Layer 2 protocols. The flexibility, simplicity, and control that MPLS offers make it so appealing that it just may find a place in the set of technologies that operate the Internet, especially at the core. Current investigation also involves the feasibility of future MPLS-only network devices.

This introduction to MPLS serves as a starting point to the many associated topics that are included in this area. The remainder of this book will cover Internet technology background, specifications and supporting documentation, MPLS core technologies and protocols, label signaling and distribution, MPLS applications, network management, current and future MPLS developments, and a sample of implementers using MPLS and developing products for it.

SUMMARY...

This chapter introduced MPLS by presenting the "five W's and H" of MPLS.

- **What is MPLS?** MPLS is a set of open, standards-based Internet technologies that combines Layer 3 routing with Layer 2 switching to forward packets by utilizing short, fixed-length labels. A more narrow definition of MPLS is that it is an IETF working group and its associated efforts.
- **Why is MPLS needed?** MPLS is not so much a performance gain to conventional routing, but rather it provides an innovative approach by offering a virtual connection-type label switching technology that will enable a new set of Internet applications for providing TE, QoS, path restoral, and VPNs.
- **How is MPLS done?** MPLS complements IP technology by using a label swapping, data forwarding paradigm and introducing a new set of MPLS control procedures that are partially based on existing IP routing protocols with extensions.
- **When is MPLS used?** MPLS is used when Internet applications such as TE, QoS, path restoral, and VPNs need to be deployed. Service providers have begun deploying MPLS to more fully utilize their networks.
- **Where is MPLS used?** Initial MPLS deployments have moved from test labs and university test sites into the core of several large service providers. MPLS is also beginning to be deployed in metropolitan areas for a variety of application scenarios. The opportunity to derive revenue from providing provider-based VPNs is a current driver for deploying MPLS.
- **Who is doing MPLS?** In addition to service providers, initial MPLS developers, users, and investigators include many large network equipment vendors, test equipment makers, larger service providers, and communication stack providers.

Since MPLS is an Internet technology, this chapter also introduced the Internet and several of its main models. Background topics such as graph theory and the UML modeling language were also exposed. Finally, the promise of MPLS was introduced for consideration throughout the book on how the flexibility and simplification offered by MPLS will be realized.

REFERENCES FOR CHAPTER 1 ....

1. from `www.quoteland.com`.

2. from the original MPLS Working Group Web site:
   `www.ietf.org/html.charters/mpls-charter.html`.

3. Esar, Evan. *20,000 Quips and Quotes*. Garden City, New York: Doubleday and Company, Inc., 1968, p. 736.

MPLS
Background

2

In historical events great men—so called—are but the labels that serve to give a name to an event, and like labels, they have the least possible connection with the event itself. Every action of theirs, that seems to them an act of their own free will, is in an historical sense not free at all, but in bondage to the whole course of previous history, and predestined from all eternity. [1]

— *Leo Nikolaevich Tolstoi,* **War and Peace**

To understand the wider context in which MPLS is being developed, several important background topics need to be introduced. Figure 2–1 on the next page shows six interrelated areas that are key topics that need to be understood for a fuller comprehension of MPLS.

Since MPLS is an Internet-based technology and in the process of being standardized by the IETF, it is mandatory to understand the TCP/IP protocol suite. At the minimum, every MPLS LSR must run the TCP/IP stack to operate the required control plane protocols. Closely related to the TCP/IP protocols are the topics of routing and switching within the network nodes. It is requisite knowledge to understand the basics of these types of network nodes, which will be used to run MPLS. These

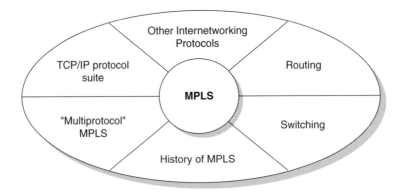

Figure 2–1   MPLS and key related topics.

basics include the routing and switching processes, the forwarding mechanism, the input and output interfaces, and the links that connect these devices together. Figure 2–2 displays this important general router/switch model.

In addition, since TCP/IP is not the only protocol suite used in internetworking today, there are several other important networking protocols that people come in contact with on a regular basis. This MPLS background needs to explain the roles of the ATM, FR, and OSI protocols, and several other networking technologies. Two other important background MPLS topics include its brief history with proprietary vendor implementations and other pre-MPLS standards efforts and the flexible and elegant "multiprotocol" design of the MPLS architecture.

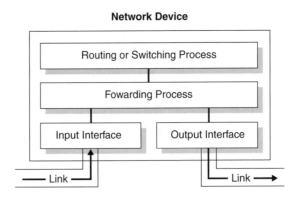

Figure 2–2   General router/switch model.

THE TCP/IP PROTOCOL SUITE...

Even a brief introduction shows that the full seven layers of the OSI model are exceedingly complex. Except for their implementation in the OSI protocol suite, which today is primarily used only in a limited role in telecommunications, most communication protocol suites use only a well-defined or slightly redefined subset of the model.

A case in point is the TCP/IP protocol suite. The TCP/IP protocol family is primarily the set of protocols used on the Internet. Nearly all of the new applications being introduced are based on TCP/IP. The TCP/IP model, while loosely based on OSI concepts, uses a redefined and simplified four-layer model.

The TCP/IP protocol suite is the primary set of protocols used for internetworking communications today. It is used both in the network infrastructure and for the applications that run on top. The original TCP/IP protocol efforts actually predate the OSI–RM and were originally developed from the ARPANET research and development efforts in the late 1960s and early 1970s. By the early 1980s, however, all the computing systems wishing to communicate on the ARPANET internetwork were required to speak the TCP/IP in use today. Its use and development are still on the rise, and TCP/IP is a protocol that is allowing more and more devices to communicate with each other on the Internet. The basic TCP/IP protocol suite and newly emerging compatible protocols, such as MPLS, offer the communication fabric for Internet evolution.

Although any networking architecture must include services for communications, the TCP/IP suite has been designed expressly from the start with reliable internetworking communications in mind. Four reasons for this fact are:

- Network technology independence
- Universal interconnection
- End-to-end acknowledgments
- Application protocol standards

TCP/IP is based on the premise of sending information as a set of packets. These packets are also called "datagrams." This common format helped to make the protocol independent of the many proprietary, single-vendor hardware or software platforms that were evolving at the time. TCP/IP allows any end-user or end-device to communicate to any other known end-user or end-device in a reliable manner because they all understand the common format. Acknowledgments can be optionally configured to verify that all messages have been properly received. The fourth reason listed above, application protocol standards, is the most important for MPLS applications and the SNMP enterprise management standard. SNMP has become the management protocol that allows end-user and network entities to manage and be managed, and is an important component in the monitoring and controlling of MPLS.

The TCP/IP model provides the core functionality of the OSI seven-layer model, but is represented in a more condensed fashion by its four-layer model. Figure 2–3 compares the TCP/IP model with the OSI-RM. The specific protocols of the TCP/IP family that run within each layer are discussed later in the chapter.

The four TCP/IP layers are:

1. **Network Access layer**—The lowest layer provides reliable host-to-network data exchange.

2. **Internet layer**—This layer handles device-to-device internetworking data exchange.

3. **Host-to-Host layer**—This layer provides reliable end-to-end internetworking exchange.

4. **Process layer**—This layer provides application services for the end-user.

The network access layer is the layer closest to the physical network. It includes both the physical and data link layers of the OSI-RM. This layer accepts and delivers packets between the Internet layer above it

OSI	TCP/IP
Application	Process
Presentation	Process
Session	Process
Transport	Host-to-Host
Network	Internet
Data Link	Network Access
Physical	Network Access

Figure 2–3   OSI-RM and TCP/IP model comparison.

and the physical internetwork media—that is, the bit stream—below. This layer has been developed for nearly every available network type, including most LANs and wide area networks (WANs) such as Ethernet, token ring, optical, and wireless.

The next layer, the Internet layer, contains the famous Internet Protocol (IP). This layer is equivalent to the network layer in the OSI-RM. By utilizing a 32-bit standardized global addressing scheme, the Internet layer provides a delivery service that is independent of the network access layer below it. IP is a connectionless, datagram internetworking protocol that does not guarantee end-to-end delivery. Its features include the ability to specify type of service, Internet layer addressing, fragmentation and reassembly, checksumming, and rudimentary security. The source reference for the current version of IP in common use—IPv4 (version 4)—is RFC 791, "Internet Protocol." Another important protocol included in the Internet layer is the Internetwork Control Message Protocol (ICMP) for error and congestion reporting. The source reference for ICMP is RFC 792, "Internet Control Message Protocol." There is a later version of IP—IP version 6 (IPv6)—that offers 128 bits of address space, but it has not yet become widely deployed.

The host-to-host layer offers the transport service necessary for allowing one host to communicate with another regardless of where it is on the internetwork. It offers similar functionality to the transport layer in the OSI model. This suite offers two transport protocols: the Transport Control Protocol (TCP) and the User Datagram Protocol (UDP). The source reference for TCP is RFC 793, "Transmission Control Protocol." For UDP, the relevant RFC is RFC 768, "User Datagram Protocol." TCP is a reliable, connection-oriented service that provides end-to-end reliability, resequencing, error checking, and flow control. UDP is an unreliable (i.e., not guaranteed), connectionless datagram service. UDP is used as a transport service for application protocols such as Domain Name Service (DNS), Network Time Protocol (NTP), and SNMP, where acknowledgements for individual messages are not required.

The top TCP/IP layer, the process layer, is the application layer that provides services to the end-user. This layer contains the services provided by the session, presentation, and application layers in the OSI model. The process layer includes the application protocols and a variety of common system functions. Popular TCP/IP applications include the Telnet terminal program, the FTP file transfer program, the Simple Mail Transfer Protocol (SMTP) electronic mail program, HTTP, and many others.

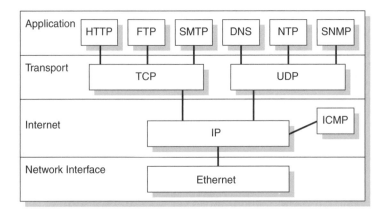

Figure 2–4 TCP/IP protocol suite layer protocols

Each of the four layers is implemented with many cooperating proto-cols (that is what makes it a suite!). The full complement of the TCP/IP protocol suite now comprises many dozens of protocols. A sample of the major TCP/IP protocols from the suite is shown in Figure 2–4. Note that the four TCP/IP layers are often called application, transport, Internet, and network interface instead of their "official" model layer names.

Network Access Layer Protocols

The network access layer is the lowest layer of the protocol stack. It is closest to the hardware. This layer's chief function is to provide reliable host-to-network data exchange. While there are a wide variety of possible network access protocols, each one corresponding to the many types of different networks that can be connected on the internetwork, Ethernet is the network access layer protocol now used most commonly.

Internet Layer Protocols

The Internet layer is responsible for carrying data from a source host to a destination host. The Internet layer's prime component is the IP. IP is a connectionless datagram protocol that does not guarantee end-to-end delivery. IP's features include the ability to specify the type of service, Internet layer addressing, fragmentation and reassembly, checksum-ming, and rudimentary security. Another important protocol included in the Internet layer is the ICMP, which is used for error and congestion reporting. There are several other protocols that talk directly to IP via the "raw IP" interface. The RSVP-TE MPLS signaling protocol is one such example.

Internet Protocol (IP)   The primary Internet layer protocol is the IP. IP is without a doubt the key protocol in the TCP/IP protocol suite, and it is well on its way to becoming the *lingua franca* for the Internet. Today, most new applications being written to run on the Internet are coded to run over IP.

IP provides a connectionless network layer service. This means it is the responsibility of the higher layers to assure accurate data transfer. The messages that are transferred between the transport layer and the IP are called datagrams; they are limited to 64K bytes. These datagrams are exchanged with the network interface layer to be sent and received over the Internet. If intermediate devices cannot handle large datagrams, these datagrams are broken up into fragments for reassembly at their final destination.

An IP datagram comprises two major parts: the IP header and the IP data area. The header comprises a 20-byte fixed portion and an optional header portion. Note that the length of the header is stored in the fixed portion. The IP packet header layout is shown in Figure 2–5.

The header comprises 14 fields of various bit lengths. Table 2–1 on the next page gives a brief description of each of these fields.

One requirement for the successful operation of IP is that every network device must have a unique IP address. A discussion of the IP header format must include the five formats that the IP source and destination addresses can assume from this 32-bit field. For the 32 bits of the address, there are a total of over four billion possible addresses. Figure 2–6 shows

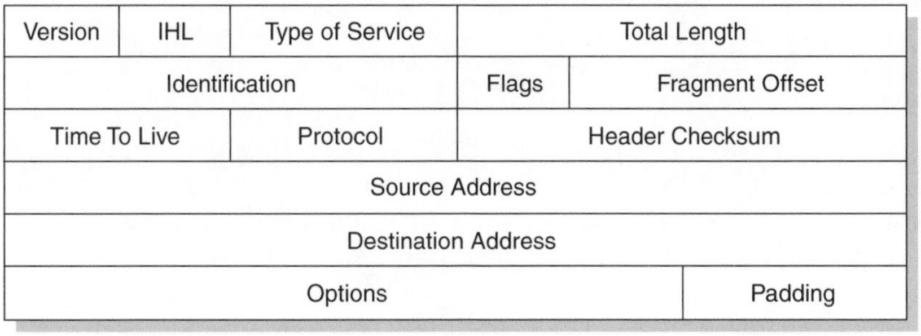

Version	IHL	Type of Service	Total Length	
Identification			Flags	Fragment Offset
Time To Live		Protocol	Header Checksum	
Source Address				
Destination Address				
Options				Padding

Figure 2–5   The IPv4 packet header format.

Table 2–1   IPv4 Packet Header Fields

Field	Size (in bits)	Description
Version	4	Identifies the IP version.
IP Header Length (IHL)	4	Header length in 32-bit words. Minimum value is 5, i.e., 20 octets.
Type of Service (TOS)	8	Used to specify: reliability, precedence, delay, and throughput.
Total Length	16	Total length of datagram, including the header, in octets.
Identification	16	Datagram originator ID used with addresses and protocol number to uniquely identify each datagram.
Fragment Flags	3	Bit flags used for fragmentation operation.
Fragment Offset	13	Indicates fragment's position in the datagram for reassembly; measured in 64-bit units.
Time To Live (TTL)	8	Lifetime counter measured in one-second increments. When it reaches 0, datagram is discarded.
Protocol	8	Transport protocol number.
Header Checksum	16	Checksum calculated when IP is sent and then recalculated when received with the same algorithm; if the checksums are not equal, the datagram is discarded.
Source Address	32	Sender's IP address.
Destination Address	32	Destination IP address.
Options	(variable)	Various IP options can be specified here.
Padding	(variable)	Added to make IP header end on a 32-byte boundary. Zeros are used.

the bit positions for the five possible formats of Internet addresses. Note that the bits are in network order with the left-most bit as bit 0 and the right-most bit as bit 31.

The five formats comprise three major portions. The leading significant bits determine the class of the address. There is a field for the network identification, the "netid," and also a field for the ID of the host, the "hostid." The IP address is usually written as four decimal numbers separated by decimal points. This is called "dotted decimal notation." Each decimal number represents eight bits of the address.

The Class A format is used when there are a large number of host computers and a small number of networks. Class A addresses use seven bits for the netid and 24 bits for the hostid. This allows for 16,777,214 host network devices and only 128 networks. The dotted decimal notation range is from 000.*nnn.nnn.nnn* to 127.*nnn.nnn.nnn*.

The Class B format strikes a compromise between the number of hosts and the number of networks by allocating 14 bits for the netid and 16 bits for the hostid. This allows for 16,384 network addresses and 65534 host device addresses. The dotted decimal notation range for Class B is from 128.000.*nnn.nnn* to 191.255.*nnn.nnn*.

When there is a need for a large number of networks with fewer network devices attached, the Class C addressing format is used. It uses 21 bits for the netid and 8 bits for the hostid. This allows for 2,097,152 networks, each with a maximum 254 attached host devices. The dotted decimal notation range is from 192.000.000.*nnn* to 223.255.255.*nnn*.

Class D addresses are reserved for multicasting, a limited broadcasting facility where traffic can be sent to a group of hosts arranged in a multicast group. This allows hosts to operate on more than one physical network for sending certain types of traffic. The possible dotted decimal notation range is from 224.000.000.000 to 239.255.255.254, although the

Class A	0		Netid (7 bits)			Hosted (24 bits)		
Class B	1	0		Netid (14 bits)			Hostid (16 bits)	
Class C	1	1	0		Netid (21 bits)			Hostid (8 bits)
Class D	1	1	1	0		Multicast Address		
Class E	1	1	1	1	0	(Reserved for future use)		

Figure 2–6   The IP address formats.

Internet does not allow 244.000.000.000 to be used, and reserves 244.000.000.001 for the special "all hosts" designation.

For completeness, we will include Class E, although this format is for experimental purposes and should never be used for general internetwork IP communications. The possible dotted decimal notation for this group is from 244.000.000.000 to 255.255.255.254.

There is another important concept that is closely aligned with IP address formats: subnetting. Subnetting is a way of dividing networks into logical subnetworks by assigning a special subnet addressing scheme. A 32-bit address called the subnet mask can make the netid/hostid pair into a netid/siteid/hostid triple by stealing some of the bits. Which bits are used is a function of the IP class format used.

As the use of (uniquely) IP-addressable devices exploded, it soon became apparent that without modifications to the IP subnetting scheme, the available addresses would become completely depleted. A solution that introduced variable-length subnet masks provided temporary relief that would be used until IPv6 came into popular use. (IPv6 defines 128-bit addressing, allowing for many millions of unique addresses. This solution is called classless inter-domain routing (CIDR, often pronounced "cider").

With CIDR notation, the subnet is specified as the number of bits that are applied as a mask. For example, a CIDR mask of 15 applied to an IP route would create a binary mask of 11111111.11111110.00000000.00000000. It is really an elegant extension of address class notation. The CIDR notation for Class A addresses would be /8, for Class B, /16, and for Class C, the /24 mask.

Today, the actual IP address blocks are usually controlled by ISPs. As the size of the Internet routing table soars past 100,000 entries, the ISPs get large portions of address space and then distribute smaller, controlled networks from this pool. RFC 1519, "An Address Assignment and Aggregation Strategy," contains all the details about CIDR.

The use of servers to match numeric IP addresses to a more friendly format of human-recognizable names is done by the Domain Name Service (DNS). There can be a hierarchy of name servers throughout the internetwork that maintain varying views of a database that correlate IP addresses to IP names. IP names are also represented in a dotted fashion, reflecting their place in an internetwork hierarchy.

There are also two important protocols from the TCP/IP protocol suite that handle name resolution between the physical network access address and the IP address: the Address Resolution Protocol (ARP) and the Reverse Address Resolution Protocol (RARP). These two protocols are

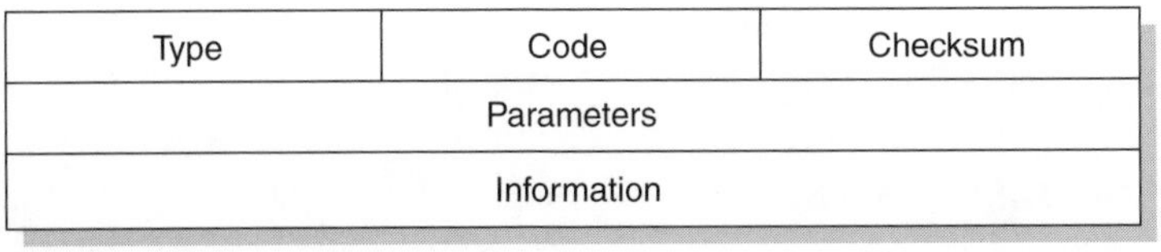

Type	Code	Checksum
Parameters		
Information		

Figure 2–7   The ICMP message format.

necessary for resolving the different addressing schemes and formats used in each of these two layers. The lowest level address is typically assigned by the manufacturer, and the IP address is derived from one of the Internet IP address classes and then administratively assigned.

ARP allows a network device to find the network access address, also called the media access address (MAC), of another device by only knowing the target device's IP address. This is done through a low-level broadcasting scheme. RARP allows a network device to find its IP address from a network server that maintains a table that correlates physical MAC and IP addresses. RARP is especially important for diskless workstations that do not know their IP addresses at power-up time.

Internetwork Control Message Protocol (ICMP)   The ICMP is a required protocol that must be implemented with IP in the Internet layer. The RFC for ICMP is RFC 792. It uses IP services to send various error and status messages. Figure 2–7 presents the key fields of an ICMP message:

Table 2–2 lists the size and a brief description of each ICMP message field:

Table 2–2   The ICMP Header Fields

Field	Size (in bits)	Description
Type	8	Specifies the ICMP message type.
Code	8	Used when message parameters can be encoded in a few bits.
Checksum	26	Checksum of entire ICMP message.
Parameters	32	Used for longer parameter values.
Information	(variable)	Contains any additional information that goes with the message.

There are 13 ICMP messages, each with a unique type value. Table 2–3 lists the various ICMP messages and their associated type values:

Table 2–3   ICMP Message Types

Message	Type Value
Echo Reply	0
Destination Unreachable	3
Source Quench	4
Redirect	5
Echo Request	8
Time Exceeded	11
Parameter Unintelligible	12
Timestamp Request	13
Timestamp Reply	14
Information Request	15
Information Reply	16
Address Mask Request	17
Address Mask Reply	18

The ICMP is most famous for its use in the Packet Internet Groper (PING) program. PING sends an ICMP message of type Echo Request and waits for an Echo Reply to signify that there is an IP connection between two end-points.

Transport Layer Protocols

The transport layer provides for the end-to-end transfer of data between processes, either reliably by using TCP or unreliably by using UDP.

Transmission Control Protocol (TCP)   Because the underlying IP is an unreliable service, the transport level can provide the required

Source Port							Destination Port
Sequence Number							
Acknowledgement Number							
Length (rsvd)	U R G	A C K	P S S H	R S T	S Y N	F I N	Window
Checksum							Urgent Pointer
Options (variable)							Padding (variable)

Figure 2–8   The TCP header format.

reliability features for network applications by using TCP. TCP offers this measure of reliability by providing various time-out, sequencing, and checksum features. Its source RFC is RFC 793.

As with IP, the maximum message in the TCP layer is 64K bytes. TCP messages are also called datagrams. TCP handles fragmentation and message sequencing so that if datagrams and/or fragments arrive out of order at the destination, TCP will reassemble the fragments and present the datagrams in the correct order to the application. TCP sequences each data byte by providing private sequence numbers. Because 32 bits are available for a sequence number, the probability that sequence numbers will be repeated because of wrapping is nearly zero. Duplicate retransmissions are also handled with the use of a three-way handshake.

A TCP datagram also comprises two major parts: the TCP header and TCP data portion. Just as with IP, the minimum TCP header comprises a 20-byte fixed portion and an optional header portion. The length of the header is stored in the fixed portion. Figure 2–8 shows the layout of the TCP header.

The header, shown in Table 2–4, consists of 17 fields of various bit lengths.

TCP's service interface provides functions for setting up and shutting down connections, transmitting and receiving data, and inquiring about the status of a connection.

Table 2–4   TCP Header Fields

Field	Size (in bits)	Description
Source Port	16	Identifies sender's source port.
Destination Port	16	Identifies destination port.
Sequence Number	32	Assigned sequence number for each datagram used for reassembly of larger message.
Acknowledgement Num.	32	Acknowledgement number for received datagrams.
TCP Header Length	4	Header length in 32-bit words.
(Reserved)	6	Reserved for future use.
URG	1	Urgent pointer flag.
ACK	1	Acknowledgement flag.
PSH	1	Push function flag.
RST	1	Connection reset flag.
SYN	1	Sequence number synchronization flag.
FIN	1	End of data flag.
Window	16	Flow control parameter. Octet number count that sender is able to accept.
Checksum	16	Checksum calculated when datagram is sent, and then recalculated when received with the same algorithm; if the checksums are not equal, the datagram is discarded.
Urgent Pointer	16	Points to data following urgent data, thereby indicating length of urgent data.
Options	(variable)	Options, such as maximum acceptable segment size.
Padding	(variable)	Added to make IP header end on a 32-byte boundary. Zeros are used.

Source Port	Destination Port
Datagram Length	Datagram Checksum

Figure 2–9   The UDP header format.

User Datagram Protocol (UDP)   The UDP is a simple transport service that allows applications to use IP network services. Its source RFC is RFC 768. It is a datagram-oriented protocol. The service that it provides is connectionless; therefore, it is unreliable in the sense that the higher level application protocol is responsible for making sure that the messages are delivered properly. It does not provide transport-level acknowledgement or the ability to detect and retransmit lost datagrams. An application must use mechanisms such as time-outs to determine whether retransmissions are necessary. UDP is also incomplete in its lack of flow control, congestion control, and datagram sequencing.

UDP has two transport services:

- The capability of distinguishing between multiple destinations, called ports, from multiple sources
- The support for an additional and optional checksum facility

The UDP header has four components: the source port, the destination port, the length of the datagram's data, and the transport-level checksum. Figure 2–9 depicts this layout. Note that each of these four components is two octets in length.

Table 2–5 lists the size and meaning of each header field.

Table 2–5   UDP Header Fields

Field	Size (in bits)	Description
Source Port	16	Indicates the port number of sending process. Optional; if not used, should be 0.
Destination Port	16	Indicates the port number the receiving process is waiting on.
Datagram Length	16	Contains datagram length in octets. This length includes the length of the header; therefore, the minimum value is 8.

Table 2–5   UDP Header Fields (continued)

Field	Size (in bits)	Description
Datagram Checksum	16	16-bit one's complement of the one's complement of the pseudo-header from the IP header. The data is padded with zero octets at the end, if necessary, to make a multiple of two octets.

Application Layer Protocols

The upper layer of the TCP/IP protocol stack is the process or application layer. This layer provides services directly to the end-user, such as Telnet, FTP, or SMTP, or it can provide common system functions that are used indirectly by routing protocols, SNMP, and user applications.

Routing Protocols

Routing is one of the key concepts behind MPLS. Routing is the process of getting packets from their source to their destination in a controlled fashion. The protocols that control routing come in a variety of flavors, depending on their functions, algorithms, and usage. Routing protocols understand the topology of the network in which they are operating and can be grouped as either Interior Gateway Protocols (IGPs) or Exterior Gateway Protocols (EGPs). IGPs distribute routing information inside an autonomous system (AS), and EGPs are used for routing among ASs. (An AS is a collection of routers usually controlled by a central administration; it is the set of routers in a single domain.)

Because this is a primer …

There are two basic types of routing protocols: distance vector and link state. A distance vector protocol uses the Bellman/Ford algorithm to calculate hop counts between routers. This algorithm also sends routing table updates at periodic intervals. This type of routing protocol is not computationally intensive, but is generally slow to converge for large networks. A link state protocol uses the Dijkstra algorithm to calculate routes for each router. The protocol only sends the information about its routes to the routers it is connected to. This protocol is computationally intensive, but allows for much quicker convergence for the routers in the network.

The most popular routing protocols in use today include:

- Open Shortest Path First (OSPF) Protocol
- Intermediate System-Intermediate System (IS-IS)
- Routing Information Protocol (RIP)
- Border Gateway Protocol (BGP)

Open Shortest Path First (OSPF) Protocol   OSPF is one of the most popular IGPs used in the Internet today. It is a link-state protocol. It is defined in RFC 1247.

OSPF was developed to overcome the limitations of the RIP routing protocol. RIP was the first widely deployed IGP. OSPF is a link state protocol that sends messages called link state advertisements (LSAs) to all of the other OSPF-aware routers in its area. These LSAs include information on the router interfaces and their metrics.

As routers running OSPF gather information about the network topology, they run the shortest path first (SPF) algorithm to calculate routes to each other node the router has in its database. An important concept in OSPF is the OSPF area. This area is a logical subdivision of an AS that is running OSPF as its IGP. OSPF areas allow another level of hierarchy that is not the same as that provided from the IP network information. Areas aggregate OSPF routing information and help hide the explicit details of the network. This and other features make OSPF a very scalable routing protocol for very large networks.

Intermediate System-Intermediate System (IS-IS)   A key OSI protocol is the IS-IS routing protocol. IS-IS is a link–state, intra-domain routing protocol. It is defined in ISO/IEC 10589, and its use in the Internet for IP-based routing is described in RFC 1142. It is similar to OSPF in functionality, but differs in the details of how it operates.

Routing Information Protocol (RIP)   RIP is an IGP that preceded OSPF. It is described in RFC 1388. RIP is a distance vector IGP that works best in small, homogeneous networks. RIP has several limitations that prevented it from scaling to larger networks. These limitations include a maximum hop count of 15, a lack of support for the CIDR variable-length subnet masks (although this was added in RIP-2), a generally inefficient use of bandwidth, and slow convergence between routers.

Border Gateway Protocol (BGP)   BGP is the prevalent EGP used in the Internet today. As such, it is used to let different transit ASs exchange routing information for the purpose of forwarding packets between them. This is often called "inter-domain routing." The current version of BGP is 4.

BGP is based on distance vector (DV) algorithms and uses TCP as its transport protocol. BGP is specified as a session between two nodes, although a network will have many BGP sessions running concurrently, and a single router may be involved in multiple BGP sessions.

In a BGP session, BGP peers exchange BGP messages over a TCP connection. The types of messages include opening the BGP session, informing the peer that new routes are active and old routes are not, reminding the peer that the connection is up, and receiving any unusual or error conditions.

BGP is a hard-state protocol, and routing information successfully exchanged between peers does not need to be refreshed. It is considered valid until one peer notifies the other that it is not or the BGP session between them ends.

A key principle behind BGP is that when one peer informs its partner that an IP address is reachable via an advertised path, the partner can be sure that its peer is successfully using the path for its own traffic already. This implies that the paths advertised to a peer are always usable when they get advertised. In combination with the usability of a path, a set of attributes is associated with the IP prefix.

Attributes are a strong design feature of BGP in that they allow the protocol to be extended for new uses. The most important BGP attributes include:

• Next hops
• Route preference metrics
• AS paths a routing announcement has traveled
• The way an IP prefix was added to the routing table
  at the source AS

Several new attributes are being defined for BGP to provide MPLS TE extensions, distribute MPLS labels, and add the multiprotocol capability required for BGP/MPLS VPNs. For more information on BGP, see BGP4: Inter-Domain Routing in the Internet. [2]

Other Routing Protocols   Other routing protocols include the standards-based Hello protocol and other proprietary routing protocols such as the Interior Gateway Routing Protocol (IGRP) and Exterior Gateway Routing Protocol (EGRP) from Cisco. IGRP is a DV interior gateway routing protocol developed by Cisco Systems. IGRP uses a combination of metrics such as internetwork delay, bandwidth, reliability, and load to create the forwarding table. Also from Cisco, the Enhanced Interior Gateway Routing Protocol (EIGRP) is an enhanced version of IGRP that combines the advantages of link state protocols with DV protocols. EIGRP includes features such as fast convergence, variable-length subnet masks, partially bounded updates, and support for multiple network layers.

Resource Reservation Protocol (RSVP)

RSVP is an Internet protocol that was developed for IP resource signaling to routers in a path for an application flow. RSVP is an important protocol in the Integrated Services (IS) model that is used for providing IP-based QoS. It allows host devices and routers in the application path to negotiate specific QoS attributes. The applications that require specific QoS characteristics signal an RSVP request to reserve the required resources from the source to the destination along their routes. The RSVP-enabled routers verify that a route is possible and then handle the scheduling and prioritization duties. RSVP is a dynamic protocol, and while RSVP is running, reservations for bandwidth and other required network resources are permitted or denied based on current network conditions. RSVP can also consider policies that refer to these reservations. RFC 2205 contains the current RSVP standard.

RSVP has been enhanced with TE extensions to perform MPLS signaling and label distribution.

Simple Network Management Protocol (SNMP)

SNMP is the recommended management framework for monitoring and controlling devices connected to the Internet. It contains five key elements:

- The overall architecture
- A mechanism for describing and naming managed objects and events called the Structure of Management Information (SMI)

- The management protocol for transferring management information between a managed entity and a managing entity
- Protocol operations for accessing management information
- A set of management "applications"

SNMP is discussed in detail in Appendix E, "A Detailed Introduction to SNMP."

Other Important TCP/IP-Related Protocols

As was introduced earlier, the TCP/IP protocol suite comprises many dozens of cooperating protocols. Table 2–6 lists several additional TCP/IP protocols that are often encountered when dealing with communications, networking devices, and MPLS:

Table 2–6   Other Important TCP/IP Protocols

Protocol Name	Description
Real-Time Transport Protocol (RTP)	RTP provides end-to-end network transport functions for real-time data applications such as audio or video.
Network-Time Protocol (NTP)	NTP provides a common clock for a consistent time for all of the devices on a network.
Simple Mail Transfer Protocol (SMTP)	SMTP is used to send and receive electronic mail. It is specified in RFC 821.
BOOTP	BOOTP is used to distribute the boot-up images for powered-up devices on the network.
Dynamic Host Control Protocol (DHCP)	DHCP is used to configure the computers that use TCP/IP by automatically assigning IP addresses, delivering TCP/IP stack configuration parameters such as the subnet mask and default router, and providing other configuration information such as the addresses for printer, time, and news servers.

Table 2–6   Other Important TCP/IP Protocols (continued)

Protocol Name	Description
Point-to-Point Protocol (PPP)	PPP is used for transmitting IP packets over serial lines and other physical media (such as SONET). It is an encapsulation that supports several types of link layer encapsulation formats.
Point-to-Point Tunneling Protocol (PPTP)	PPTP is the protocol that allows PPP to be tunneled through IP networks.
Telnet	Telnet is used as a remote terminal program protocol.
File Transfer Protocol (FTP)	FTP is used for transferring ASCII and binary format files.
Hypertext Transfer Protocol (HTTP)	HTTP is the TCP-based protocol used for transferring Web pages.

OTHER IMPORTANT INTERNETWORKING PROTOCOLS.....................................

In addition to the IETF developments for the TCP/IP protocol suite, there are several other standards bodies that have developed significant networking and communications technologies. These include ATM from the ATM Forum, FR from the Frame Relay Forum, the OSI protocol suite from the International Organization for Standardization (ISO), Ethernet from the IEEE, and additional protocols from ANSI, and the ITU-T Author: What technologies apply to these organizations? These technologies figure prominently as lower layers for transporting MPLS packets over different types of networks.

Asynchronous Transfer Mode (ATM)

ATM is the set of network standards originally derived from the earlier Broadband ISDN (B-ISDN) standards that were developed by the CCITT (now the ITU) in the mid-1980s. The intent of ATM is to provide a way of creating a multiplexing hierarchy of fixed bandwidth channels. ATM is a multilayered, connection-oriented technology. When used with MPLS, ATM is viewed as a Layer 2 technology.

The main specification for ATM principles is defined in CCITT Recommendation I.150. The four most important principles are:

- ATM is on 53-byte, fixed-length cells: 5 bytes for the header and 48 bytes for the data payload. The header specifies the virtual channel and aids in routing a cell. Each cell's header contains an identifier for the virtual connection of which the cell is a member. The connection identifier in every cell header explicitly associates a cell with a given virtual channel on a physical link. The connection identifier contains two subfields: the Virtual Channel Identifier (VCI) and the Virtual Path Identifier (VPI). As a pair, the VCI/VPI are used in multiplexing, demultiplexing, and switching a cell through the network. They are not addresses, per se, but rather explicitly assigned values assigned at each link between ATM switches. Using the VCI/VPI identifier pair, an ATM layer can asynchronously interleave cells from many connections at the same time.

- ATM is connection-oriented. Header values get assigned to each section of a connection for the complete duration of the connection. Also, in ATM, the signaling and user information are carried on separate virtual channels.

- The information field of ATM cells is carried "transparently" through the network, that is, no error control processing is performed on this field as it goes through the network.

- All ATM-based services such as voice, video, and data can be transported through the ATM network. To accommodate the special needs of a particular service, various adaptation functions in the ATM adaptation layers are provided to insert the necessary information into the ATM cells at the starting point of the connection. This is required to provide any of the service-specific functions such as clock recovery, cell loss recovery, and other necessary procedures.

There are four ATM adaptation layers (AALs) currently defined:

1. AAL1—This layer supports connection-oriented services that require constant bit rates and have specific timing and delay

requirements. These services include constant bit rate services like DS1 and DS3.

2. AAL2—This adaptation is a method for carrying voice over ATM. It consists of variable-size packets up to a maximum of 64 bytes that get encapsulated within the ATM payload.

3. AAL3/4—This layer is the merging of AAL3 and AAL4. It provides variable bit rate services for both connectionless and connection-oriented flows.

4. AAL5—This service layer supports connection-oriented variable bit rate data services. It is a pared down version of AAL3/4 with error recovery and built-in retransmission removed. This compromise offers less bandwidth overhead, simplified processing requirements, and reduced implementation complexity.

The ATM reference model can be compared to the OSI-RM, as shown in Figure 2–10. In terms of how ATM relates to MPLS, only the bottom two layers are considered. The MPLS layer is on top of the "ATM" layer.

The key point of ATM, as it differs from IP, is that it is connection-based. As such, it enjoys the benefits of using connections. These include the ability to time the flow of cells and support predictable traffic flows. ATM is designed to support the major services—voice, data, and video—effectively. ATM also has several other desirable attributes such as built-in QoS, loop prevention, automatic load balancing, and automatic failover.

ATM is a firmly established networking technology, but it has several drawbacks that are allowing newer technologies such as MPLS to gain a foothold.

Application, Presentation, and Session	Services and Applications
Transport	
Network	ATM Adaptation
Data Link	ATM
Physical	Physical
OSI Layers	ATM Layers

Figure 2–10 OSI and ATM layers.

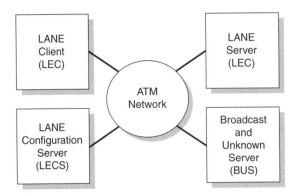

Figure 2–11   LAN emulation model.

Like TCP/IP, ATM also comprises a protocol suite. There are several associated ATM protocols in this suite that are relevant for running IP over ATM. These include:

- LAN Emulation (LANE)
- Classical Model of IP over ATM
- Multiprotocol over ATM (MPOA)
- Next-Hop Resolution Protocol (NHRP)
- ATM Address Resolution Protocol (AARP)

LAN Emulation (LANE)   LANE is an ATM protocol that was developed to transport legacy protocols and IP over ATM circuits in a LAN environment. It does not deal with internetworking, and essentially divides an ATM network into several emulated LANs that communicate with each other using routers or bridges. The LANE model is shown in Figure 2–11.

The LECS determines which hosts (that is, LECs) belong in which emulated LAN. The BUS network node supervises the broadcast and multicast traffic, and the LES handles the address resolution done by the LANE Address Resolution Protocol (LE_ARP). LE_ARP allows LECs to configure VCs for normal unicast packet traffic.

Classical Model of IP over ATM   Another technique for running IP over ATM is called the "classical model." It has this name because it uses the conventional IP subnetting architecture. It is a much more IP-centric approach than LANE and makes the ATM adapters IP interfaces to the IP protocol stack. The ATM network is subdivided into a number of logical IP subnets (LIS). Within an LIS, each interface shares a common IP network ID, subnet number, and network mask. Because each interface is directly connected via the lower layer ATM network, a full mesh of VCs is created. Any interface on an LIS can talk to any other interface. This model is described in RFC 1577.

Multiprotocol over ATM (MPOA)   MPOA is an extension to LANE to allow the setup of "shortcuts" across emulated LAN segments. It is a set of standards for transporting non-IP routing protocols over LANE and NHRP. It is a joint development by the ATM Forum and IETF. Its design is an attempt to bring existing ATM equipment and other non-ATM devices into a common communications infrastructure. The goals of MPOA include the ability to provide end-to-end connectivity across ATM networks for network layer traffic such as IP. MPOA allows devices that are either directly connected to the ATM network or devices indirectly connected through routers on non-ATM IP subnets to communicate. MPOA is a very complex framework, especially in the area of internetworking. MPLS may offer a simplification for how devices operate in such heterogeneous environments and eliminate much of the MPOA complexity.

Next-Hop Resolution Protocol (NHRP)   NHRP is a helper protocol that was developed by the IETF. It is used by communication protocol frameworks such as MPOA. NHRP resolves addresses between different subnets. NHRP uses a special server called the next-hop server (NHS) instead of traditional routing tables to determine the best next hop for a route. This was an alternative protocol to improve routing that may be supplanted by MPLS in several areas.

ATM Address Resolution Protocol (AARP)   AARP allows a client machine to receive a destination IP address and a corresponding ATM address so a VC can be made to the destination. The ARP process is responsible for maintaining a table for this resolution. The AARP server performs a broadcast of an AARP translation request to all connected ATM devices. Hosts on the network must register their ATM addresses with the server to avoid the lookup.

Frame Relay (FR)

FR is also a connection-oriented protocol. It allows both switched and permanent VCs to be configured to send variable-length frames. It is used in LAN and WAN environments, and many ISPs use FR to carry IP application traffic.

FR was developed in the late 1980s, but came into widespread use in the 1990s. FR evolved from the older X.25 protocol. The FR VCs that are on one physical port can cooperatively share all the available bandwidth so that applications that require extra bandwidth can temporarily borrow from the unused total idle bandwidth for those short durations to accommodate bursts of traffic. FR uses the bottom two layers in the OSI model and improves end-to-end efficiency by only doing error detection at the intermediate nodes and making the end-hosts responsible for retransmission. By dropping bad frames, greater throughput is realized and there is less overhead in sending the information. FR has built-in congestion management, which allows QoS for bandwidth requirements for the various traffic flows on the network. Because of this, FR is used to provide data, voice, and video Internet services.

ISO Protocols

The ISO has developed its own suite of communication protocols for the seven layers of the OSI reference model. Several of the ISO protocols are being used, particularly in telecommunications environments. These protocols include the File Transfer Acesss and Management (FTAM) protocol for file transfers and the Virtual Terminal Access and Management (VTAM) for virtual terminal access. These two protocols are similar in functionality to FTP and Telnet, respectively, in the TCP/IP world.

Other Important Related Protocols

There are other important related internetworking protocols that have been deployed in various network environments. These include Integrated Services Digital Network (ISDN), System Network Architecture (SNA) from IBM, Internet Packet Exchange (IPX) from Novell, and the ANSI Fiber Distributed Data Interface (FDDI) standard used in MAN environments. It is not clear that any of these other related protocols will have any interworkings with MPLS.

ROUTING...

It is very important to understand routing because MPLS complements it and intervenes between the network and data link layers. Routing in the conventional sense without MPLS is the process of setting up routes to understand the next hop a packet should take toward its destination between networks. This is accomplished by analyzing the Layer 3 network header. The routing process in each router uses various routing algorithms to discover the routes and create the forwarding table that is sent down to the data forwarding plane. With MPLS, different inputs are used to create MPLS routes (called LSPs) to route traffic in different ways. It is important to understand what a router is and how routing works with MPLS to create an LSR from a router.

A router is the device that is responsible for getting packets from one network to another by processing the Layer 3 network header. The router sets up the tables that understand the network topology to accomplish its routing duties. The different types of routing algorithms that may be running on the router—BGP, OSPF, IS-IS, RIP, and others—differ in the exact mechanisms they use, but their overall objectives are in line with understanding the router's role within its AS. The addition of MPLS to a router makes it an LSR.

SWITCHING ....

It is also critical to understand switching in the context of MPLS. Switching is the knowledge of directing the forwarding process to choose the correct output port. A switch is a device that operates on Layer 2 header information to direct the forwarding process. Switching is the process that operates in the data plane by using indexes that are set up as virtual connections so that forwarding can occur. The switching process accepts packets at the input ports, uses its internal switching tables that have been populated by the control information, and then forwards the packets to the proper output ports.

A switch does Layer 2 switching by processing the data link layer header. Switches are generally faster than routers, but have less functionality. The addition of MPLS to a switch makes it an LSR.

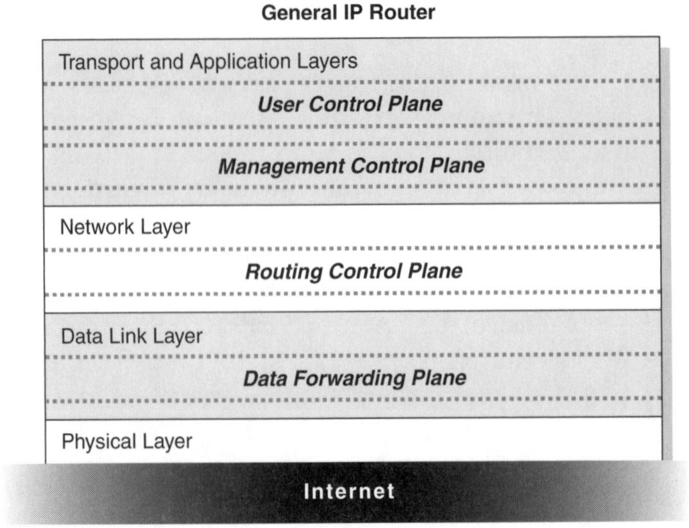

General IP Router

Transport and Application Layers
User Control Plane
Management Control Plane
Network Layer
Routing Control Plane
Data Link Layer
Data Forwarding Plane
Physical Layer

Internet

Figure 2–12   User, management, control, and forwarding planes.

THE CONTROL PLANE AND FORWARDING PLANE

The model of the various processes that run in a general IP router can be viewed as a stack of layers. These layers can be further refined by viewing a particular set of related functions within a layer as a slice, or "plane." In every router, there are four key planes of interest when dealing with networking: the user control plane, the management control plane, the routing control plane, and the data forwarding plane.

In the top layers, the user control plane provides the user interface for a particular device. The management control plane provides the monitoring and control functionality that is realized through SNMP, CLI, and other technologies. Within the network layer, it is the routing control plane that deals with routing details, including creating and downloading the forwarding table for the data link layer. The data link layer contains the data forwarding plane for receiving information from and sending information to the physical layer interfaces. These planes are shown in Figure 2–12.

IP Router Control and Forwarding Planes

The routing control and data forwarding planes shown in Figure 2–13 are responsible for accepting input traffic and deciding where to send it next.

Figure 2–14 on the next page shows the routing control plane. Inside the routing control plane, several key activities are done to set up routes, keep the routes current, and perform other route management activities. A key data structure in any IP router is the Route Information Base (RIB), which contains all of the possible routes that are known by a device. The router must cull the best routes for its next hops and create a Forwarding Information Base (FIB) to download to the data forwarding plane. The FIB only contains active routes. The various routing protocols, OSPF, IS-IS, BGP, and others, keep the route information up-to-date for each router.

The data forwarding plane is shown in Figure 2–15 on the next page. This plane is in charge of receiving input packets and having the knowledge of placing them in the proper output port. It uses the FIB it receives from the control plane to make these decisions. The data forwarding

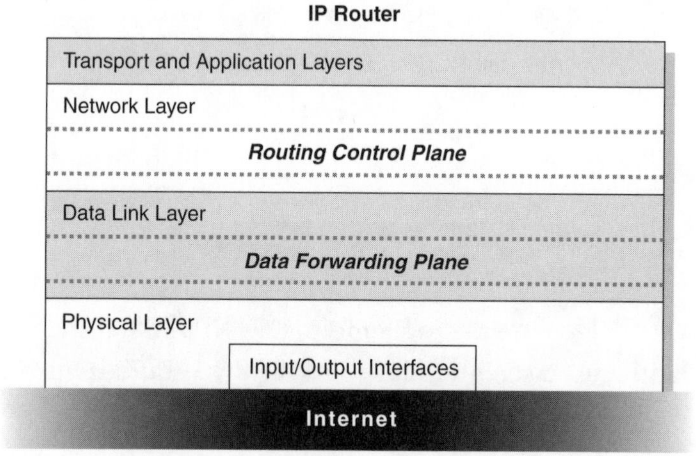

IP Router

| Transport and Application Layers |
| Network Layer |
| *Routing Control Plane* |
| Data Link Layer |
| *Data Forwarding Plane* |
| Physical Layer |
| Input/Output Interfaces |

Internet

Figure 2–13 Control plane and forwarding plane model.

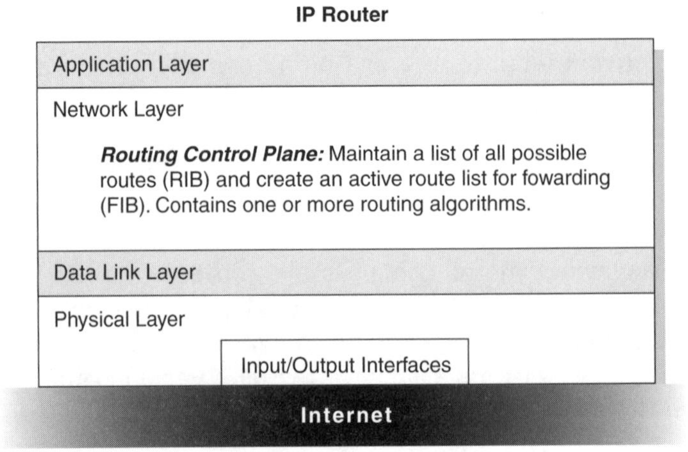

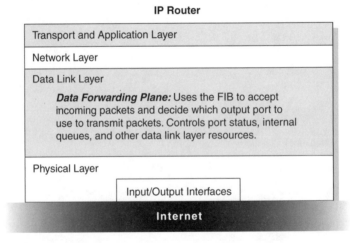

Figure 2–14 The network layer routing control plane.

Figure 2–15 The data link layer data forwarding plane.

plane also manages associated data link layer resources such as queues, ports, and so on.

MPLS-Enabled
IP Router Control and Forwarding Planes

Since planes aren't true layers, they can be visualized as sublayers. If the routing control plane and data forwarding plane "float" together, their functionality becomes closely coupled. The mating of the routing control

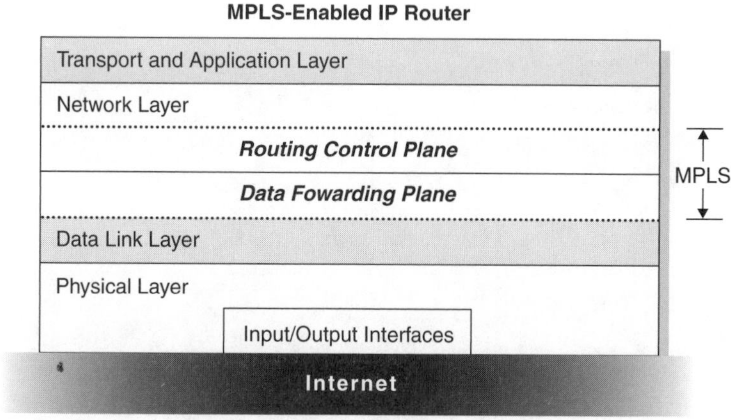

MPLS-Enabled IP Router

| Transport and Application Layer |
| Network Layer |
| *Routing Control Plane* |
| *Data Fowarding Plane* |
| Data Link Layer |
| Physical Layer |
| Input/Output Interfaces |
| **Internet** |

MPLS

Figure 2–16   The MPLS control and forwarding planes.

plane and data forwarding plane at the network layer and data link layer interface becomes the representation for "Layer 2.5" MPLS. This is shown in Figure 2–16. One of the strengths of the MPLS technology is the flexibility of this organization. MPLS can operate with a varied set of routing control plane techniques, but they all operate seamlessly with a data forwarding plane based on the label switching paradigm.

Figure 2–17 shows the routing control plane for an MPLS-enabled device. In a high-level sense, the control plane functionality is similar to a conventional IP router in that it sets up routes and creates the forwarding information that is necessary to send packets to their next hop. It dif-

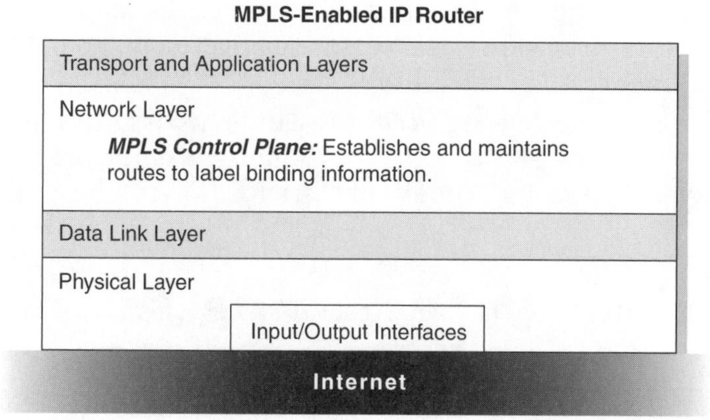

MPLS-Enabled IP Router

| Transport and Application Layers |
| Network Layer |
| *MPLS Control Plane:* Establishes and maintains routes to label binding information. |
| Data Link Layer |
| Physical Layer |
| Input/Output Interfaces |
| **Internet** |

Figure 2–17   The MPLS-enabled routing control plane.

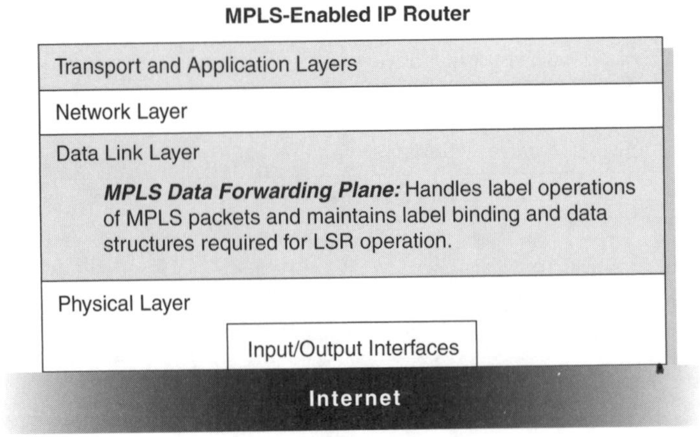

MPLS-Enabled IP Router

Transport and Application Layers

Network Layer

Data Link Layer

> **MPLS Data Forwarding Plane:** Handles label operations
> of MPLS packets and maintains label binding and data
> structures required for LSR operation.

Physical Layer

Input/Output Interfaces

Internet

Figure 2–18   The MPLS-enabled data forwarding plane.

fers in several key points, however, such as how the LSPs are set up and
actually used after the FECs have been created.

Figure 2–18 shows the data forwarding plane for an MPLS-enabled
device. This is the plane where label swapping is done. Key MPLS data
structures accept incoming labeled packets, swap the labels at the transit
locations, and then remove the labels as the packets exit the MPLS
domain.

By making the forwarding plane protocol-independent, multiple protocols can be used over the same forwarding path. There are no longer
"ships in the night," but an integrated network that can be managed as
one logical network. A key aim of MPLS is to create a modularity and
flexibility by separating the control plane from the data forwarding
plane, and an anticipated side-effect of this separation is the potential for
increased performance and scalability.

Another vital MPLS feature is that it can be used with many protocols at both the network and link layers. To date, it is important to note
that at the network layer, its primary use is with IPv4.

THE "MULTIPROTOCOL" PART OF MPLS.......................

MPLS is a standards-based technology that unites data link layer protocols with network layer protocols by providing connection-oriented, label-
based switching and forwarding, plus a loosely coupled control plane and

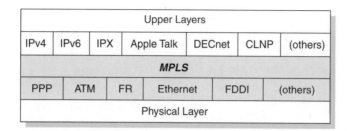

Figure 2–19 Multiprotocol MPLS model.

data forwarding plane. This allows for its use with a wide variety of network and data link protocols. MPLS can be considered a kind of mediator. It is an interposer layer that by design can permit a wide variety of network layer protocols to operate over a wide assortment of link layer protocols at the same time. The MPLS framework has proposed the common sets of network layer protocols and data link layer protocols used in the Internet today, as shown in Figure 2–19.

This figure represents the breadth of the MPLS WG. Its implementations are currently centered on sending IPv4 network traffic over PPP, ATM, FR, and Ethernet. Work is progressing in several other protocols as special cases.

Figure 2–20 shows that MPLS encapsulation has been specified for use with all of the major Layer 2 technologies. The top label can use the existing Layer 2 format, as is the case with ATM and FR, or it can be placed as the MPLS shim header when Ethernet or PPP is used. In all

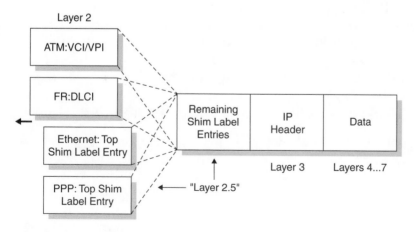

Figure 2–20 MPLS label stack encapsulation model.

cases, any optional label stack entries (i.e., any additional labels) are found between the top label stack entry and the Layer 3 IP header.

MPLS and Network Layer Protocol Use

While the MPLS framework has been specified to work with a number of network layer protocols—and in theory, because of its use of the MPLS shim header, any network protocol—its initial acceptance has been with the current version of IP: IPv4. Work on IPv6 is continuing and deployments of this protocol have been slowly rolled out.

MPLS and IPv4   Nearly all current MPLS deployments involve the use of IPv4 as the network protocol. Most of the major service providers use IPv4 exclusively. The MPLS shim header is placed in front of the IPv4 network header, and then in the proper place, depending on the Layer 2 protocol used below.

MPLS and IPv6   Just as with IPv4, IPv6 places the MPLS header in front of the network layer header, and depending on the Layer 2 protocol, in the proper place as a shim header or within the Layer 2 header. Also like IPv4, IPv6 runs on all popular Layer 2 technologies. The use of MPLS and IPv6 is a current topic of investigation by several vendors and universities, however, and is not yet in wide deployment.

MPLS and Other Network Layer Protocols   In theory, MPLS can be used with any network layer protocol. The initial MPLS designers included IPX, AppleTalk, DECnet, and CLNP, although there is little current interest in this development. Much of the new work in MPLS is centered in the lower layer technologies and the use of optical techniques to transfer IP network packets. It seems safe to say that IP will be the predominant network layer protocol used with MPLS.

MPLS Data Link Layer Protocol Encapsulations

A key part of the MPLS design is the data link layer protocol encapsulation. The specific data link layer encapsulation is dependent on the Layer 2 protocol, and is realized in several different formats depending on which Layer 2 protocol is used. The top label uses the specific format of the link layer protocol and any additional labels will use the "shim" label format and get inserted between the data link and network layer headers. The specific formats of how the MPLS label stack is placed into the lower layer message are presented in Chapter 4, "MPLS Core Technologies and Protocols."

MPLS and PPP MPLS can be used with PPP. PPP is actually a family of related IETF protocols that is used for sending multiprotocol datagrams over point-to-point links. PPP specifies a method for encapsulating the network layer datagrams from a variety of network layer protocols, a Link Control Protocol (LCP) for setting up, configuring, and maintaining the link connection, and a set of Network Control Protocols (NCPs) for controlling the various network layer protocols that the standard supports.

An NCP for MPLS that controls the sending of MPLS packets over a PPP link has been defined. It is known as MPLSCP. The PPP protocol field is assigned a special value that indicates that this PPP packet contains an MPLSCP control packet (hexadecimal 8281). When MPLS data packets are sent over the PPP link, the PPP protocol field is encoded with hexadecimal 0281 for MPLS unicast and hexadecimal 0283 for MPLS multicast.

MPLS and ATM The use of MPLS over ATM is in current use today, especially for transporting IP traffic over ATM networks. The ATM switches that are MPLS-enabled run the TCP/IP routing protocols and use ATM data forwarding based on 53-byte, fixed-size ATM cells. Within these ATM-LSRs, the top MPLS label entry is placed in the VCI/VPI fields of the ATM header and the MPLS label stack entries are placed in the data portion of the ATM cells.

MPLS and FR MPLS in FR networks has been deployed by several major service providers and is still in general use. Like ATM, MPLS-enabled FR switches use TCP/IP routing protocols to set up the control plane for the FR-controlled data forwarding. With FR, the current label is placed in the Data Link Connection Identifiers (DLCI) field of the FR header. Any additional MPLS label stack entries are carried after the FR header, but before the Layer 3 header contained in the FR data portion of the frame. The MPLS standard allows either the two- or four-octet Q.922 address that is used by FR.

MPLS and Ethernet Using MPLS over Ethernet, especially in metropolitan areas, is a growing opportunity for MPLS. The Ethernet standard itself is being extended to increase the speed and distance that

Ethernet packets can travel. Current Ethernet speeds are beginning to be deployed with 1–gigabit and soon 10-gigabit interfaces.

When MPLS is used with Ethernet, one labeled packet is placed in each frame. The MPLS label stack entries are placed between the network layer header and data link layer header (for example, the 802.1Q header may be there). In the Ethernet header, the Ethertype value 8847 hexadecimal is used to indicate that a frame is carrying an MPLS unicast packet; 8848 hexadecimal indicates that this Ethernet frame is carrying an MPLS multicast packet. The Ethertype values can be used with either of the popular Ethernet formats used today: the standard Ethernet encapsulation or the 802.3 LLC/SNAP encapsulation.

MPLS and Other Data Link Layer Protocols   Since MPLS can be made to operate over just about any data link technology, the original MPLS architects included several other popular link layer protocols like FDDI, token ring, and others.

THE HISTORY OF MPLS ....

In the mid-1990s several noteworthy proprietary attempts at marrying label switching and routing were realized. Two key areas for pre-MPLS efforts included vendor proposals and two standards developments. For a complete discussion of pre-MPLS developments, see Switching in IP Networks: IP Switching, Tag Switching, and Related Technologies and IP Switching: Protocols and Architectures. [3] [4]

Pre-MPLS Vendor Evolution

While the specifics of the frameworks varied greatly, all the pre-MPLS vendor solutions shared the common trait that the solutions were based on the label switching paradigm. The aim of these efforts was to increase the data forwarding performance of the devices and to gain cost and ease of management advantages. The five major efforts that are of most interest are:

- IP switching, designed at Ipsilon
- Cell switching router (CSR), done by Toshiba
- Cisco's tag switching architecture
- IBM's aggregate route-based IP switching (ARIS)

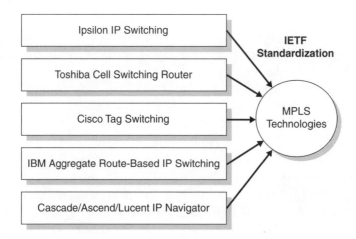

Figure 2–21 Pre-MPLS vendor evolution.

• IP Navigator, from Cascade/Ascend/Lucent

Pre-MPLS vendor implementations as they aided in MPLS evolution are shown in Figure 2–21.

Many of the pre-MPLS vendors have switched to MPLS development and products to promote the interoperability that is derived from offering standards-based products.

Toshiba: Cell Switching Router (CSR)   The CSR is generally given credit as being the first proposal to look at IP switching. At the IETF IP over ATM meeting in early 1994, the CSR concept was presented. The following year, the CSR was again presented at an IETF BOF meeting. Although it was recognized as a novel approach, interest did not pick up until Ipsilon formalized the concept of IP switching and introduced its proposal in 1996. The CSR enjoyed little commercial success.

The CSR was originally developed at the Tokyo Institute of Technology. It was then made into a product by Toshiba Corporation. The original purpose of the CSR was to connect the ATM LISs from LANE and RFC 1577 (classical model of IP over ATM) specifications with each other. The CSR uses UNI 3.1 Q.2931 signaling, which is specified as the Flow Attribute Notification Protocol (FANP). The CSR also uses ATM ARP for address resolution. The CSR can perform both cell switching and IP forwarding.

Ipsilon (Nokia): IP Switching   Ipsilon (now part of Nokia) is generally credited with getting the IP-based label switching MPLS-like model rolling, by introducing IP switching in 1996. The specific product developed by Ipsilon was called the IP switch. The IP switch comprised an ATM switch and an IP switch controller for the control plane functions. The IP switch controller was actually a separate device that contained the routing and forwarding functions linked to an ATM switch through one of its OC3c ATM ports. In this design, the ATM switch was only used as a switching fabric for forwarding cells. None of the native ATM signaling and control plane protocols were used.

Label switching was actually based on flow classification and could be configured based on parameters such as source IP address and port number, destination IP address and port number, and protocol type. Flows were classified as persistent (such as FTP transfers, HTTP, and Telnet traffic) or short-lived (such as DNS lookups, SNMP messages, and NTP).

The IP switching framework also specified several support protocols to help in setting up the data forwarding paths. The Ipsilon Flow Management Protocol (IFMP) classified the traffic and helped set up the VC that was required to forward a particular class. The Generic Switch Management Protocol (GSMP) was used to configure the ATM switch fabric.

IP switching was important in presenting a viable implementation of the label swapping paradigm and also in introducing a method for classifying IP traffic. After much debate, it was generally agreed that any approach based on flow switching, however, would not scale.

Cisco: Tag Switching   Slightly after the Ipsilon effort, Cisco developed a technology that used the label switching paradigm called tag switching. Tag switching is much closer to how MPLS has been designed, and indeed, MPLS is largely derived from the Cisco tag switching effort. A tag is very similar to a label. This approach was designed to be used with a number of lower layer protocols and included a label distribution protocol called Tag Distribution Protocol (TDP). Like MPLS, tag switching provided for a stack of tags. All of the Cisco routers that implemented tag switching have been updated to run MPLS.

IBM: Aggregate Route-Based IP Switching (ARIS)   IBM developed an IP switching technology called aggregate route-based IP switching, or ARIS. ARIS was intended to be used with ATM and FR switches, as well as LAN Layer 2 switches. The device that implemented ARIS was called an ARIS integrated switch router (ISR). The main difference between ARIS and tag switching is that it is route-based as opposed to flow-based. The routes in an ARIS-based domain are egress-centric. The egress nodes are configured and routes are propagated backwards toward possibly multiple ingress nodes. The egress can be specified by a number of identifiers: IPv4 destination prefix, egress router IP address, OSPF router ID, or multicast pair identifier. The establishment of the paths is done independently of the traffic flows. Essentially, routes are established from egress to ingress, and then data flows in the opposite direction, from ingress to egress. ARIS supports both source routing and point-to-multipoint multicast. The route signaling protocol is soft–state, and messages are periodically exchanged to maintain route status as needed.

Cascade/Ascend/Lucent: IP Navigator   The IP Navigator is a technology that was originally offered by Cascade. Cascade was subsequently acquired by Ascend, which in turn became part of Lucent. IP Navigator was originally based on many of the IP switching concepts developed earlier by Ipsilon, Cisco, and IBM.

Pre-MPLS Standards Evolution

In addition to the vendor developments, there were several important pre-MPLS standards efforts that engendered much debate.

Two notable pre-MPLS efforts were:

- The Unified Approach to Inter-Domain Routing
- The Nimrod Routing Architecture

The pre-MPLS evolution from standardization efforts is shown in Figure 2–22.

The Unified Approach   The Unified Approach was presented as an Informational RFC in May 1992. RFC 1322, "A Unified Approach to Inter-Domain Routing," was written by Estrin, Rekhter, and Hotz. This proposal outlined an approach for global inter-domain routing. It was an expansive and far-reaching look at scaling the Internet. The proposal included creating and supporting an environment for services and route selection criteria. Many of the ideas were adopted and have shaped how the Internet has evolved in the ensuing decade.

The Nimrod Routing Architecture The Nimrod Routing Architecture was another pre-MPLS architecture that had several new ideas
on progressing the architecture of the Internet. It was presented as an
Informational RFC in August 1996. RFC 1992, "The Nimrod Routing
Architecture," was written by Castineyra, Chiappa, and Steenstrup. The
focus of the Nimrod project was to examine the Internet architecture and
how to scale the routing for a global scope. Nimrod introduced two basic
mechanisms: the idea of "maps" over routing tables and the host selection
of routes as opposed to router-selected routes. The latter mechanism is a
twist on the source routing procedure. The project actually proposed the
use of client proxies, or agents, that selected routes for applications over
which they had control. The Nimrod architecture was very innovative
and several of its ideas have been subsequently incorporated into Internet technologies and products.

SUMMARY ....

Chapter 2 provided the essential background information on MPLS that
is required for a full understanding of what the technology is and how it
came to be. This background was divided into six areas: the TCP/IP protocol suite, other internetworking protocols, routing, switching, the "multiprotocol" aspect of MPLS, and the history of the events leading up to the
creation of MPLS.

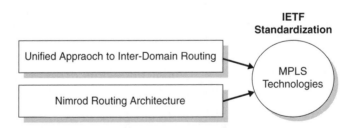

Figure 2–22 Pre-MPLS standardization efforts.

REFERENCES FOR CHAPTER 2..

1. Barlett, John (Justin Kaplan, general ed.). *Bartlett's Familiar Quotations, 16th ed.* Boston: Little, Brown and Company, 1992, p. 510.

2. Stewart, John W., III. BGP-4: *Inter-Domain Routing in the Internet.* Reading MA: Addison-Wesley, 1999.

3. Davie, Bruce S., Paul Doolan, and Yakov Rekhter. *Switching in IP Networks: IP Switching, Tag Switching, and Related Technologies.* San Diego: Academic Press, 1998.

4. Metz, Christopher Y. IP *Switching: Protocols and Architecture.* New York: McGraw-Hill, 1999.

MPLS Documentation and Resources

3

> Knowledge is of two kinds. We know a subject ourselves,
> or we know where we can find information upon it. [1]
>
> — *Samuel Johnson*

Around MPLS's rich set of technologies is an ever-expanding set of documentation that describes, explains, and specifies the architecture, protocols, and all of the associated applications and services. Because MPLS is a current and rapidly evolving standard based on a number of concurrent specifications being developed within the MPLS WG, it is paramount to keep abreast of the RFCs and latest IDs and their revisions.

The sheer amount of MPLS documentation is staggering. At this writing, there are over 110 MPLS IDs, translating into thousands of pages of text! With the core set of the WG's RFCs published as proposed standards in early 2001, MPLS is striving to do a great deal of "standardization" as quickly as possible. Remember, vendors are reluctant to continue too far down a path specified only by IDs. Standards-track specifications published as RFCs serve as a much more solid foundation from which to build open, standards-based products.

In addition to RFCs, IDs, and other IETF-related documentation, it is important to know about and refer to other available MPLS resources. These include MPLS conferences and tutorials, relevant books and periodicals, industry forums, vendor product announcements and white papers, other standardization activities, and URLs for the many interesting Web sites that pertain to MPLS topics.

The MPLS documents produced by the MPLS WG and other IETF-related activities can be grouped into several major categories:

- The MPLS standards-track RFCs
- Additional MPLS-related RFCs
- IDs being developed within the MPLS WG
- Additional MPLS-related IDs (individual submissions)

There are also several key supplemental MPLS resources that aid in the understanding of this technology. These include:

- MPLS-related industry forums
- Key Web sites containing MPLS information
- Books on MPLS

Finally, in addition to documentation and resources, terminology is very important when endeavoring to learn a new technology such as MPLS. To understand all of the new terms that you will encounter, please refer to the glossary at the end of the book for any words or acronyms that are unclear.

MPLS STANDARDS-TRACK RFCS ....

RFCs are the primary documents for progressing a technology through the IETF standardization path. While all RFCs are not standards-track specifications, the RFCs that are destined to become part of the standardized technology of the Internet begin as numbered RFCs with a proposed level of standardization.

Because this is a **primer** …	
There are three levels of standardization for a standards-track RFC: **proposed**, **draft**, and **full**. Non-standards-track RFCs can be **informational**, **experimental**, or **historical**.	

All the RFCs that deal with MPLS are listed in the "RFC Pages" Web page of the IETF at `www.ietf.org/rfc.html`. The RFCs can be accessed individually, or the entire RFC index can be viewed by clicking on the appropriate link. The entire list of all the RFCs related to MPLS and more information about the RFC process can be found in Appendix B, *"MPLS-Related RFC Index."*

There are currently 10 MPLS RFCs[1] as shown in Table 3–1.

Table 3–1   MPLS WG RFCs

Title	RFC Number	Date
Requirements for Traffic Engineering Over MPLS	RFC 2702	September 1999
Multiprotocol Label Switching Architecture	RFC 3031	January 2001
MPLS Label Stack Encoding	RFC 3032	January 2001
The Assignment of the Information Field and Protocol Identifier in the Q.2941 Generic Identifier and Q.2957 User-to-User Signaling for the Internet Protocol	RFC 3033	January 2001
Use of Label Switching on Frame Relay Networks Specification	RFC 3034	January 2001
MPLS Using LDP and ATM VC Switching	RFC 3035	January 2001
LDP Specification	RFC 3036	January 2001
LDP Applicability	RFC 3037	January 2001
VCID Notification Over ATM Link for LDP	RFC 3038	January 2001
MPLS Loop Prevention Mechanism	RFC 3063	February 2001

---

1. As this book was being completed, an eleventh RFC was published: RFC 3107, "Carrying Label Information in BGP-4."

Requirements for
Traffic Engineering Over MPLS

RFC 2702, "Requirements for Traffic Engineering Over MPLS," presents a set of requirements for TE in an MPLS environment. The specification identifies the functional capabilities needed to implement policies that make reliable operations more efficient in an MPLS network. TE is used to more fully utilize network resources and improve performance over conventional routing methods.

This RFC was written by Daniel Awduche, Joe Malcolm, Johnsom Agogbua, Mike O'Dell, and Jim McManus in September 1999. Its current status is "informational."

The MPLS Architecture

The MPLS architecture document, RFC 3031, "Multiprotocol Label Switching Architecture," is the main document that specifies the architecture. It is a proposed level standard that was released in January 2001.

The MPLS architecture document includes a description of the network layer control plane and link layer data forwarding plane. It introduces the label switching paradigm and all of the important core MPLS issues. The document introduces the terminology, all of the key MPLS basic features, some MPLS applications, and it also contains an overview of hop-by-hop label distribution procedures.

"Multiprotocol Label Switching Architecture" was written by Eric Rosen, Arun Viswanathan, and Ross Callon. The complete text for the current MPLS architecture specification is listed in Appendix C, "Multiprotocol Label Switching Architecture."

The original working group created an MPLS framework specification after the 38th IETF meeting held in April 1997. This document provided the first overview of MPLS and presented the issues and several possible approaches. This framework document evolved to include the requirements, terminology, and a discussion of the core MPLS components and technologies. The document "A Framework for Multiprotocol Label Switching" was refined and reissued several times before expiring in March 2000. The framework document was written by Ross Callon, Paul Doolan, Nancy Feldman, Andre Fredette, George Swallow, and Arun Viswanathan. The information presented by the framework document was incorporated into the architecture specification and other documents, and it was felt by the working group that the framework document was no longer needed as a separate specification (i.e., as an informational RFC).

MPLS Label Stack Encoding

The MPLS label stack encoding specification is an important specification that complements the architecture document. This document is RFC 3032. It is a proposed standard that was released in January 2001.

This document gives detailed information about MPLS labels and how they are used with various network technologies. This document defines the central MPLS concept of the "label stack." The label stack is seen as a key MPLS innovation. The ability to specify more than one label entry in a stack will allow the creation of label hierarchies, which may open the door to many new MPLS applications. When a label stack is added to a network layer packet, it becomes an "MPLS labeled packet." This is the basic unit that gets routed in an MPLS-enabled networking environment as shown in Figure 3–1.

The main focus of this RFC is to specify the encoding to be used by an LSR when transmitting labeled packets on PPP, Ethernet LAN, or other types of Layer 2 data links. The specification notes that on some types of data links, the label at the top of the stack may have to be encoded in a different manner because of the header format. The techniques described in the document must be used to encode the remainder of the label stack. The draft also specifies the rules and procedures that need to be used for processing the various fields of the label stack encoding.

The draft includes germane discussions on MPLS header processing. These include generating ICMP messages for error conditions, time to live (TTL) processing, maximum transmit unit (MTU) size, and message

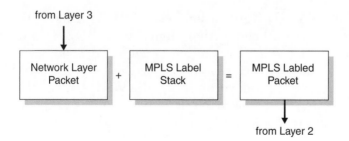

Figure 3–1   An MPLS labeled packet.

fragmentation. Other discussions include the specifics of running MPLS over PPP, MPLS over LAN media (especially Ethernet), and security issues dealing with this type of encapsulation.

"MPLS Label Stack Encoding" was written by Eric Rosen, Yakov Rekhter, Daniel Tappen, Dino Farinacci, Guy Fedorkow, Tony Li, and Alex Conta.

MPLS Frame Relay and ATM RFCs

There are four current proposed level RFCs that deal mainly with FR and ATM issues in an MPLS network:

RFC 3033, "The Assignment of the Information Field and Protocol Identifier in the Q.2941 Generic Identifier and Q.2957 User-to-user Signaling for the Internet Protocol," provides the framework for the implementation of long-lived sessions and QoS-sensitive session transfers over ATM. This RFC appeared in January 2001, and was written by M. Suzuki.

RFC 3034, "Use of Label Switching on Frame Relay Networks Specification," defines the model for using MPLS on FR networks. This enables FR switches to be MPLS-enabled and used as LSRs. This RFC was written in January 2001 by A. Conta, P. Doolan, and A. Malis.

RFC 3035, "MPLS using LDP and ATM VC Switching," specifies additional information about using LDP signaling with MPLS-enabled ATM switches. When an ATM switch runs IP-based network layer control routing protocols (such as OSPF or IS-IS), and their forwarding decisions are based on the results of these algorithms, they are called ATM-LSRs. The MPLS labels that are inserted into the ATM cell headers signify FECs for the paths that are determined on a hop-by-hop basis by IGP routing protocols. This RFC was written by B. Davie, J. Lawrence, K. McCloghrie, E. Rosen, G. Swallow, Y. Rekhter, and P. Doolan in January 2001.

RFC 3038, "VCID Notification over ATM Link for LDP," introduces the concept of a virtual connection identifier (VCID). Because the MPLS label is used in the VCI/VPI position of the ATM header when MPLS is used, the VCID needs to be created to keep the same value at both ends of the VC. The proposed notification sends the VCID between the connected ATM LSRs. This RFC was written in January 2001 by K. Nagami, Y. Katsube, N. Demizu, H. Esaki, and P. Doolan.

MPLS LDP RFCs

Two RFCs dealing with the Label Distribution Protocol (LDP) have recently been published. The LDP specification was placed on the standards track at the proposed level. The document detailing LDP applicability is at the informational level.

RFC 3036 is the main RFC that specifies LDP. "LDP Specification" was written by L. Anderson, P. Doolan, N. Feldman, A. Fredette, and B. Thomas in January 2001. LDP is a set of procedures that is used by LSRs to distribute labels for MPLS forwarding along the hop-by-hop routes that are set up by this type of signaling protocol. This specification also includes the main LDP controller state machine that handles LSP session initialization, address mapping message management, and routing interfaces.

RFC 3037, "LDP Applicability," by B. Thomas and E. Gray, refers to the LDP procedures used by LSRs for distributing MPLS labels. This document also includes a suggested requirement level for LDP. This requirement proposes that the implementation of LDP is recommended for devices that use hop-by-hop routes for forwarding MPLS packets. Scalability and security issues are also considered.

MPLS Loop Prevention Mechanism RFC

There is also an experimental RFC that discusses loop prevention: RFC 3063, "MPLS Loop Prevention Mechanism." It was written in February 2001 by Y. Ohba, Y. Katsube, E. Rosen, and P. Doolan. This RFC explains why packet looping is a very undesirable activity in a network. A prevention scheme for MPLS is presented in this document. This scheme is based on threads that prevent LSPs with loops from being set up.

ADDITIONAL MPLS-RELATED RFCS...........................

There are other MPLS RFCs that were developed outside of the WG that are of interest. Two RFCs have been published that deal with VPNs. This is a very important MPLS application from which ISPs are hoping to derive revenues. VPNs are discussed in detail in Chapter 6, "MPLS Operation and Uses."

- "BGP/MPLS VPNs" (RFC 2547)—This informational status RFC deals with the use of BGP-4 and MPLS in setting up standardized VPNs. This RFC was written by Eric Rosen and Yakov Rekhter.
- "A Core MPLS IP VPN Architecture" (RFC 2917)—This informational status RFC by Karthik Muthukrishnan and Andrew Malis introduces the concept of a virtual router service as a technology to provide VPNs using MPLS. It differs from RFC 2547 in that this document does not specify a particular IGP protocol, such as BGP-4, as a way to carry the routes for the VPN.

The reader can poll the RFC index to inquire when additional RFCs dealing with MPLS are being published. The URL for the RFC index is: `http://www.ietf.org/rfc.html`.

MPLS WORKING GROUP
INTERNET DRAFTS ....

As all of the MPLS specifications are being developed, draft versions for additional topics are being distributed via the IETF Web site in the "Internet-Drafts" directory (see `www.ietf.org/ID.html`). The MPLS WG members discuss, modify, and refine these drafts on the mailing list and also at the IETF meetings held three times a year. A draft is reviewed and revised periodically until it either becomes an RFC or it expires and work on it is discontinued. The maximum expiration date on every ID is six months. Note that when searching the MPLS WG IDs, use the following format: `draft-ietf-mpls-[topic]-[nn].txt`, where [*topic*] is the subject of the draft and [*nn*] is the revision number. Revision numbers start at zero (`[00]`). For example, at this writing, the current Internet draft for MPLS support of differentiated services (Diff-Serv) is `draft-ietf-mpls-diff-ext-08.txt`.

Table 3–2 is a snapshot from the MPLS WG page.[2] It shows the IDs the WG is reviewing (dated April 25, 2001). The columns include the ID title, the current filename for the revision of the specification, and the expiration date.

IDs are fluid; therefore, they should not be referenced directly by a specific version of a draft. It is irresponsible for a vendor to claim compli-

---

2. See the bottom of the MPLS WG home page: `http://www.ietf.org/html.charters/mpls-charter.html`

ance with any ID. It is, however, according to RFC 2026, acceptable to reference a standards-track specification that may reasonably be expected to be published as an RFC using the phrase "work in progress" without directly referencing the associated ID. This is currently the case with most MPLS documents. Because MPLS is still mainly in the Internet proposed standard stage of its evolution, it is very important to continually visit the IETF MPLS WG Web site and poll for the status of the constituent specifications. If you are serious about MPLS, please bookmark `http://www.ietf.org/html.charters/mpls-charter.html.`

Table 3-2   MPLS WG ID "Snapshot"

Title	Filename	Exp. Date
Carrying Label Information in BGP-4[1]	`draft-ietf-mpls-bgp4-mpls-05.txt`	July 2001
Definitions of Managed Objects for the Multiprotocol Label Switching, Label Distribution Protocol (LDP)	`draft-ietf-mpls-ldp-mib-07.txt`	February 2001
LDP State Machine	`draft-ietf-mpls-ldp-state-04.txt`	September 2001
RSVP-TE: Extensions to RSVP for LSP Tunnels	`draft-ietf-mpls-rsvp-lsp-tunnel-08.txt`	August 2001
Constraint-Based LSP Setup Using LDP	`draft-ietf-mpls-cr-ldp-05.txt`	August 2001
MPLS Traffic Engineering Management Information Base Using SMIv2	`draft-ietf-mpls-te-mib-06.txt`	September 2001

Table 3–2   MPLS WG ID "Snapshot" (continued)

Title	Filename	Exp. Date
MPLS Support for Differentiated Services	`draft-ietf-mpls-diff-ext-08.txt`	August 2001
Framework for IP Multicast in MPLS	`draft-ietf-mpls-multicast-05.txt`	July 2001
MPLS Label Switch Router Management Information Base Using SMIv2	`draft-ietf-mpls-lsr-mib-07.txt`	July 2001
ICMP Extensions for Multiprotocol Label Switching	`draft-ietf-mpls-icmp-02.txt`	February 2001
Applicability Statement for CR-LDP	`draft-ietf-mpls-crldp-applic-01.txt`	January 2001
Applicability Statement for Extensions to RSVP for LSP-Tunnels	`draft-ietf-mpls-rsvp-tunnel-applicability-02.txt`	October 2001
LSP Modification Using CR-LDP	`draft-ietf-mpls-crlsp-modify-03.txt`	September 2001
LSP Hierarchy with MPLS TE	`draft-ietf-mpls-lsp-hierarchy-02.txt`	August 2001
Link Management Protocol (LMP)	`draft-ietf-mpls-lmp-02.txt`	September 2001
Framework for MPLS-based Recovery	`draft-ietf-mpls-recovery-frmwrk-02.txt`	August 2001

Table 3–2 MPLS WG ID "Snapshot" (continued)

Title	Filename	Exp. Date
Multiprotocol Label Switching (MPLS) FEC-To-NHLFE (FTN) Management Information Base Using SMIv2	`draft-ietf-mpls-ftn-mib-01.txt`	September 2001
Fault Tolerance for LDP and CR-LDP	`draft-ietf-mpls-ldp-ft-01.txt`	August 2001
Generalized MPLS – Signaling Functional Description	`draft-ietf-mpls-generalized-signaling-03.txt`	October 2001
MPLS LDP Query Message Description	`draft-ietf-mpls-lsp-query-01.txt`	May 2001
Signaling Unnumbered Links in CR-LDP	`draft-ietf-mpls-crldp-unnum-01.txt`	August 2001
LDP Extensions for Optical User Network Interface (O-UNI) Signaling	`draft-ietf-mpls-ldp-optical-uni-00.txt`	April 2001
Signaling Unnumbered Links in RSVP-TE	`draft-ietf-mpls-rsvp-unnum-01.txt`	May 2001
Requirements for Support of Diff-Serv-aware MPLS Traffic Engineering	`draft-ietf-mpls-diff-te-reqts-00.txt`	May 2001

Table 3–2   MPLS WG ID "Snapshot" (continued)

Title	Filename	Exp. Date
Extensions to RSVP-TE and CR-LDP for Support of Diff-Serv-aware MPLS Traffic Engineering	`draft-ietf-mpls-diff-te-ext-01.txt`	August 2001
Generalized MPLS Signaling – CR-LDP Extensions	`draft-ietf-mpls-generalized-cr-ldp-02.txt`	October 2001
Generalized MPLS Signaling – RSVP-TE Extensions	`draft-ietf-mpls-generalized-rsvp-te-02.txt`	October 2001

1. As this book was being completed, this ID advanced on the standards track to RFC 3107, "Carrying Label Information in BGP-4."

For a full discussion of IDs and the IETF process relating to them, read RFC 2026, "The Internet Standards Process—Revision 3." (This document is also known as "Best Common Practice (BCP) 9.")

At this book was being written, there were over 30 IDs being worked on by the MPLS WG. These IDs could be divided into six general categories:

- SNMP Management Information Bases (MIBs)
- Label Distribution Protocol (LDP) signaling issues
- Constraint-based LDP (CR-LDP) signaling issues
- RSVP with TE extensions (RSVP-TE) signaling issues
- Generalized MPLS (GMPLS)
- Additional MPLS issues

The additional MPLS issues group contains drafts that deal with special topics and newly emerging areas of MPLS application.

MPLS WG SNMP MIB Internet Drafts

There are four current IDs defining experimental MIBs for MPLS-related objects. These include a general MIB for the overall LSR, an MIB for the LDP signaling protocol, an MIB for RSVP-TE signaling, and an MIB for managing the FEC-to-NHLFE (FTN) table and associated resources used for label switching and forwarding.

- "MPLS Label Switch Router Management Information Base Using SMIv2"
- "Definitions of Managed Objects for the Multiprotocol Label Switching, Label Distribution Protocol (LDP)"
- "MPLS Traffic Engineering Management Information Base Using SMIv2"
- "Multiprotocol Label Switching (MPLS) FEC-To-NHLFE (FTN) Management Information Base Using SMIv2 "

MPLS MIBs and SNMP-based MPLS management are covered in depth in Chapter 7, "The Management of MPLS."

MPLS WG LDP Internet Drafts

Four of the MPLS WG IDs deal with LDP issues:

- "LDP State Machine"—Additional LDP finite state machines (FSMs) are described in this draft. This draft augments the description of the LDP protocol and the main FSM found in the "LDP Specification" document. This document also includes the state machines for ATM-LSRs and the control blocks for setting up and using LSPs. The specification states that although this document is ATM-centric, the state machines can be adapted for other types of LSRs.
- "LDP Extensions for Optical User Network Interface (O-UNI) Signaling"—This document presents extensions to LDP to support the requirements for optical user network interface (O-UNI) signaling. These extensions include new type-length-values (TLVs) to support lightpath establishment at the O-UNI, and also the definition of two new LDP messages to allow for the exchanging of lightpath status information across the user network interface (UNI).

- "Fault Tolerance for LDP and CR-LDP"—This draft addresses fault tolerance for both the LDP and CR-LDP signaling protocols. This document proposes enhancements to these signaling protocols to make fault-tolerant implementations in LSRs easier.
- "MPLS LDP Query Message Description"—Three new LDP messages are defined in this specification. The encoding and procedures for `Query Message`, `Query-Reply Message`, and `Partial Query-Reply Message` are presented. An LER sends a `Query Message` when it wishes to retrieve information about an established LDP or CR-LDP-signaled LSP. The `Query-Reply Message` returns the queried data.

MPLS WG CR-LDP Internet Drafts

There are five IDs that specify CR-LDP and additional features and usage for this signaling protocol:

- "Constraint-Based LSP Setup using LDP"—CR-LDP signaling is defined in this document. CR-LDP is an extension of LDP signaling, which offers the capability of setting up constraint-based LSPs. This type of signaling is very useful for MPLS TE and MPLS-based VPN applications.
- "Applicability Statement for CR-LDP"—The applicability of CR-LDP is introduced in this draft. CR-LDP is an extension of LDP for TE, and its limitations and security considerations are discussed in the document.
- "LSP Modification Using CR-LDP"—This draft discusses how attributes, such as bandwidth, can be modified after constraint-based LSPs have been signaled and set up by CR-LDP. LSP modifications must be done without interrupting traffic flowing over the LSP. This document also discusses LSP rerouting and priority handling.
- "Improving Topology Data Base Accuracy With LSP Feedback Via CR-LDP"—This document deals with how network topology can be improved with a feedback mechanism that can be added to CR-LDP signaling. A topology database is the collection of all the links that can be used for calculating TE paths. This includes key network parameters such as link bandwidth.

- "Signaling Unnumbered Links in CR-LDP"—This draft defines the procedures and extensions needed for CR-LDP to support unnumbered links. Currently, this signaling protocol does not provide support for unnumbered links.

MPLS WG RSVP-TE Internet Drafts

The RSVP protocol has been extended to provide TE. Several documents have been submitted that specify these extensions and discuss associated features and usage of this protocol.

- "Extensions to RSVP for LSP Tunnels"—This draft is the main specification for RSVP-TE. It includes the definition of the key concept of a "tunnel." RSVP-TE extends RSVP with additional object definitions. A key application of RSVP-TE is for MPLS TE and the signaling of constraint-based paths.
- "Applicability Statement for Extensions to RSVP for LSP-Tunnels"—The applicability of RSVP-TE is introduced in this draft. Deployment guidelines and protocol limitations are discussed. This specification also includes a technical overview of RSVP-TE as it relates to LSP tunnels.
- "Signaling Unnumbered Links in RSVP-TE"—This draft defines the procedures and extensions needed for RSVP-TE to support unnumbered links. Currently, this signaling protocol does not provide support for unnumbered links.

MPLS WG GMPLS Internet Drafts

There is a set of drafts that deals with GMPLS. GMPLS extends MPLS by encompassing additional networking technologies and broadening the definition of what a label is. These additional technologies include TDM, wavelengths, and spatial switching.

- "Generalized MPLS – Signaling Functional Description"—This draft describes the MPLS extensions that are required by GMPLS for signaling.
- "Generalized MPLS Signaling—CR-LDP Extensions"—This document details the extensions that are required for the CR-LDP signaling protocol, which is required to support GMPLS.

- "Generalized MPLS Signaling—RSVP-TE Extensions"—This document details the extensions that are required for the RSVP-TE signaling protocol, which is required to support GMPLS.

MPLS WG Additional
MPLS Issues Internet Drafts

There is an additional set of IDs that deals with a number of ancillary MPLS issues:

- "Framework for MPLS Recovery"—This draft details a set of procedures for providing protection for traffic carried on different paths. This framework greatly adds to the reliability of the network. LSRs need to support fault detection, fault notification, and fault recovery mechanisms. Various MPLS signaling protocols also need to be extended to support the configuration of recovery.

- "MPLS Support of Differentiated Services"—This document proposes a solution for supporting Diff-Serv over MPLS networks. This solution provides a network administrator with the ability to select different behavior aggregates (BAs) for mapping onto LSPs for the purpose of matching various Diff-Serv parameters for a particular network. For example, a network administrator could decide whether different sets of BAs should be mapped onto the same LSP or onto separate LSPs.

- "Requirements for Support of Diff-Serv-aware MPLS Traffic Engineering"—This draft defines the requirements for supporting Diff-Serv for MPLS TE applications on a per-class-type basis.

- "Extensions to RSVP-TE and CR-LDP for Support of Diff-Serv-aware MPLS Traffic Engineering"—This document adds to the general MPLS TE Diff-Serv requirements document by defining the extensions required for two major TE signaling protocols.

- "ICMP Extensions for Multiprotocol Label Switching"—This draft proposes extensions to the ICMP to allow LSRs to add MPLS-specific information to ICMP messages.

- "Carrying Label Information in BGP-4"—This draft discusses the use of BGP-4 as an alternate method for distributing MPLS labels. The labels that would be used for a route known to BGP are piggy-backed on the BGP Update message that is used by the protocol to distribute route information.
- "LSP Hierarchy with MPLS-TE"—LSP hierarchy is the use of the MPLS label stack to perform various TE functions. This document introduces the concept of improving scalability by aggregating TE LSPs. The specification describes the aggregation as a four-part process:

1. The LSR creates a traffic-engineered LSP.
2. The LSR forms a forwarding adjacency from this LSP, advertising the LSP as a link to the IGP.
3. Other LSRs use the forwarding adjacencies for their own path computation.
4. LSPs originated by other LSRs are nested into the LSP by using a hierarchical label stack.

Signaling aspects are also introduced with the required procedures explained.

- "Link Management Protocol (LMP)"—The LMP is specified in this draft. LMP runs between adjacent nodes and is used for link provisioning and fault isolation. LMP is also used for control channel and node connectivity checks, and to isolate link, fiber, or channel failures within a network.

ADDITIONAL MPLS-RELATED INTERNET DRAFTS..

There are many other MPLS IDs, especially individual submissions. Following is a sample list of the many individual submissions dealing with MPLS from the IETF Internet Draft Web page (www.ietf.org/ID.html), dated April 25, 2001. The list includes the draft title, author(s), date of submission, and a brief description. In general, these IDs can become MPLS WG IDs, get subsumed as other WG IDs, or expire.

Extensions for MultiProtocol Label Switching

By Dan Tappan, Ronald Bonica, Der-Hwa Gan, 11/13/2000.

The current memo documents extensions to ICMP that permit Label Switching Routers to append MPLS header information to ICMP messages. These ICMP extensions support an MPLS aware traceroute application that network operators can use to trace paths through the MPLS user plane. Although these extensions are not being proposed as Internet Standards, they are documented here because they have been implemented by several vendors and deployed by several operators.

Using PIM to Distribute MPLS Labels for Multicast Routes

By Dino Farinacci, Tian-Bai Qian, Y Rekhter, E. Rosen, 11/29/2000.

This document specifies a method of distributing MPLS labels for multicast routes. The labels are distributed in the same PIM messages that are used to create the corresponding routes. The method is media-type independent, and therefore works for multi-access/multicast capable LANs, point-to-point links, and NBMA networks.

Transport of Layer 2 Frames Over MPLS

By L. Martini, 02/12/2001.

This document describes methods for transporting the Protocol Data Units (PDUs) of layer 2 protocols such as Frame Relay, ATM AAL5, Ethernet, and providing a SONET circuit emulation service across an MPLS network.

Link Bundling in MPLS Traffic Engineering

By Lou Berger, Y Rekhter, Kireeti Kompella, 03/02/2001.

In some cases a pair of Label Switching Routers (LSRs) may be connected by several (parallel) links. From the MPLS Traffic Engineering point of view for reasons of scalability it may be desirable to advertise all these links as a single link into OSPF and/or IS-IS. This document describes how to accomplish this. This document also defines corresponding signaling (RSVP-TE) support.

BGP/MPLS VPNs

By E Rosen, 03/01/2001.

This document describes a method by which a Service Provider may use an IP backbone to provide VPNs for its customers. MPLS is used for forwarding packets over the backbone, and BGP is used for distributing routes over the backbone. The primary goal of this method is to support the case in which a client obtains IP backbone services from a Service Provider or Service Providers with which it maintains contractual relationships. The client may be an enterprise, a group of enterprises which need an extranet, an Internet Service Provider, an application service provider, another VPN Service Provider which uses this same method to offer VPNs to clients of its own, etc. The method makes it very simple for the client to use the backbone services. It is also very scalable and flexible for the Service Provider, and allows the Service Provider to add value.

A Path Protection/Restoration Mechanism for MPLS Networks

By Srinivas Makam, Ken Owens, Vishal Sharma, Changcheng Huang, Ben Mack-Crane, 11/27/2000.

It is expected that MPLS-based recovery could become a viable option for obtaining faster restoration than layer 3 rerouting. To deliver reliable service, however, multi-protocol label switching (MPLS) requires a set of procedures to provide protection of the traffic carried on the label switched paths (LSPs). This imposes certain requirements on the path recovery process, and requires procedures for the configuration of working and protection paths, for the communication of fault information to appropriate switching elements, and for the activation of appropriate switchover actions. This document specifies a mechanism for path protection switching and restoration in MPLS networks.

End to end authentication for LDP

By Oliver Paridaens, Yves T'Joens, Peter De Schrijver, Jeremy De Clercq, 03/05/2001.

The Label Distribution Protocol (LDP), as currently defined, makes use of the TCP MD5 Signature option to protect (authentication and integrity) the LDP traffic between two adjacent LSRs. This document specifies extensions to LDP to enable end-to-end authentication between non-adjacent LSR's (i.e., not directly connected via a TCP connection) that are setting up an LSP. Two mechanisms are defined that also provide integrity protection of the information carried within LDP messages and protect against the malicious replay of LDP messages. Both proposed mechanisms require ordered control LDP and can also be applied to CR-LDP.

Link Management Protocol (LMP)

By Lou Berger, Hal Sandick, Y Rekhter, John Drake, B Rajagopalan, Kireeti Kompella, Debashis Basak, Jonathan Lang, Krishna Mitra, 11/30/2000.

Future networks will consist of photonic switches, optical crossconnects, and routers that may be configured with bundled links consisting of a number of user component links and an associated control channel. This draft specifies a link management protocol (LMP) that runs between neighboring nodes and will be used for both link provisioning and fault isolation. A unique feature of LMP is that it is able to isolate faults in both opaque and transparent networks, independent of the encoding scheme used for the component links. LMP will be used to maintain control channel connectivity, verify component link connectivity, and isolate link, fiber, or channel failures within the network.

Extensions to RSVP-TE for MPLS Path Protection

By Bora Akyol, 11/30/2000.

To deliver reliable service, multi-protocol label switching (MPLS) requires a set of procedures to enable protection of the traffic carried on label switched paths (LSPs). Thus existing signaling mechanisms must be extended appropriately to support such functionality. Recently, RSVP-TE has introduced extensions to RSVP to support the establishment of LSP tunnels. This draft extends RSVP-TE to support path protection in MPLS. Specifically, we provide signaling support for establishing working and protection LSPs and for propagating fault notification upon LSP failure.

MPLS Label Stack Encapsulation in IP

By Rick Wilder, Y. Katsube, P. Doolan, Tom Worster, Andrew Malis, 03/02/2001.

Several useful applications of MPLS tunnels based on LSPs with second level labels between non adjacent LSRs have been identified: IP-VPNs and VoIP over MPLS are just two examples. This tunnelling technique can easily be extended to non-MPLS core networks. This Internet-Draft explains the motivation for encapsulating MPLS messages in IP and provides the protocol specification of the encapsulation.

G.LSP Service Model framework in an Optical G-MPLS network

By Olivier Duroyon, Rudy Hoebeke, Hans De Neve, Dimitri Papadimitriou, 01/22/2001.

The objective of this draft is to propose an IP service model for a non-packet switch capable optical network where G.LSPs are dynamically triggered by the IP layer and subsequently advertised for IP routing. The business model assumes that several IP service domains, some of which represent different administrative entities, share the same optical backbone and focuses therefore primarily on an overlay model. G-MPLS signaling with UNI support is assumed as underlying control plane protocol.

OSPF as the PE/CE Protocol in BGP/MPLS VPNs

By E. Rosen, Peter Psenak, 02/28/2001.

[VPN] describes a method of providing a VPN service. That method allows a variety of different protocols to be used as the routing protocol between the Customer Edge (CE) router and the Provider Edge (PE) router. However, it does not fully specify the procedures which must be implemented within the Provider's network when OSPF is used as the PE/CE routing protocol. This document provides that specification.

SONET/SDH Circuit MEmulation Service Over MPLS (CEM)Encapsulation

By Andy Malis, 03/01/2001.

This document describes a method for encapsulating SONET/SDH Path signals for transport across an MPLS network.

Policy Framework MPLS Information Model for QoS and TE

By Ritu Chadha, 11/29/2000.

The purpose of this draft is to describe an information model for representing MPLS traffic engineering policies. RFC 2702,'Requirements for Traffic Engineering Over MPLS', is used as a basis for determining the types of information that need to be represented in such an information model. The latter document describes the functional capabilities required to implement policies that facilitate efficient and reliable network operations in an MPLS domain. The information model described in this draft attempts to capture the information required to enable the functional capabilities described in RFC 2702. This information model could be used by a management system to optimize network performance through the necessary network provisioning actions. An overview of policy-based management is given in this document, along with a description of the relationship of this work to other information models that are being defined in the IETF Policy Framework working group. This is followed by a detailed description of the information model, and a number of examples illustrating its use.

Traffic Engineering with Unnumbered Links

By Y. Rekhter, Kireeti Kompella, 09/28/2000.

Current signaling used by MPLS TE doesn't provide support for unnumbered links. This document defines procedures and extensions to the MPLS TE signaling that are needed in order to support unnumbered links.

A Framework for the LSP Setup Across IGP Areas for MPLS Traffic Engineering

By Sudheer Dharanikota, Senthil Venkatachalam, 11/06/2000.

In this draft, we propose architecture for the inter-area LSP setup based on criteria (combination of constraints). We derive the architectural requirements for the routing protocols, signaling protocols and the MIBs to support such an idea. We also demonstrate how such a mechanism will reduce the crankback during LSP setup. A possible outline of the modifications to the CSPF algorithm and examples are presented. In the companion document we elaborate on the extensions required for such architecture.

OSPF, IS-IS, RSVP, CR-LDP Extensions to Support inter-Area Traffic Engineering Using MPLS TE

By Sudheer Dharanikota, Senthil Venkatachalam, 11/07/2000.

In this draft, we propose the extensions required to the routing protocols, signaling protocols, and the MIB to support the idea of inter-area LSPs. A companion document provides the architectural requirements for such a concept. This document also provides the signaling extensions to support the crankback as defined in the architecture document.

Signaling Unnumbered Links in RSVP-TE

By Y. Rekhter, Kireeti Kompella, 10/06/2000.

Current signaling used by MPLS TE doesn't provide support for unnumbered links. This document defines procedures and extensions to RSVP-TE, one of the MPLS TE signaling protocols that are needed in order to support unnumbered links.

MPLS-based Layer 2 VPNs

By Kireeti Kompella, 11/17/2000.

Virtual Private Networks (VPNs) based on Frame Relay or ATM circuits have been around a long time. While these VPNs work well, the costs of maintaining separate networks for Internet traffic and VPNs and the administrative burden of provisioning these VPNs have led Service Providers to look for alternative solutions. In this document, we present a VPN solution where from the customer's point of view, the VPN is based on Layer 2 circuits, but the Service Provider maintains and manages a single MPLS-based network for IP, MPLS IP VPNs, and Layer 2 VPNs.

Use of CR-LDP or RSVP-TE to Extend
802.1Q Virtual LANs across MPLS Networks

By Tissa Senevirathne, Paul Billinghurst, 10/13/2000.

This document presents a discussion on possible methods for extending Layer 2 Virtual LANs across MPLS networks through the use of CR-LDP or RSVP. Special note is taken on extending 802.1Q Tagged VLANs across MPLS networks. A new Forward Equivalence class called VLAN Forwarding Equivalence class (VFEC) is defined. Creating traffic engineered LSP based on P bit of the 802.1Q Tag is also a key focus of this document.

Signaling Unnumbered Links in CR-LDP

By A. Kullberg, Y. Rekhter, Kireeti Kompella, 10/11/2000.

Current signaling used by MPLS TE doesn't provide support for unnumbered links. This document defines procedures and extensions to CR-LDP, one of the MPLS TE signaling protocols, that are needed in order to support unnumbered links.

BGP-MPLS VPN extension for IPv6 VPN
over an IPv4 infrastructure

By Tri Nguyen, Gerard Gastaud, Dirk Ooms, Jeremy De Clercq, 03/05/2001.

This document describes a method by which a Service Provider may use an MPLS enabled IPv4 backbone to provide VPNs for its IPv6 customers. This proposal makes use of the method to build network based VPNs described in the RFC2547-Bis Internet draft. In BGP/ MPLS VPN, MPLS is used for forwarding packets over the backbone, and BGP is used for distributing VPN routes over the service provider backbone. This document proposes to use one of the defined codings for the Router Distinguisher to support an IPv6 VPN address family. It defines a coding for the SAFI-field in the case of labeled VPN- IPv6 routes.

MPLS/BGP Virtual Private Network
Management Information Base
Using SMIv2

By Luyuan Fang, Thomas Nadeau, Stephen Brannon, Fabio Chiussi, Joseph Dube, 11/13/ 2000.

This memo defines an experimental portion of the Management Information Base (MIB) for use with network management protocols in the Internet community. In particular, in response to customer demands and strong input from vendors, it describes managed objects for modeling and managing Multi-Protocol Label Switching(MPLS)/Border Gateway Protocol (BGP) Virtual Private Networks(VPNs).

Some Comments on GMPLS
and Optical Technologies

By Vishal Sharma, Greg Bernstein, 11/13/2000.

GMPLS is being considered as an extension to the MPLS framework to include optical, non-packet switched technologies. This draft reviews the motivation for doing so from an end-user's perspective and points out some key requirements/impacts that this will have on the extensions to the routing and label distribution/signaling protocols.

Multi-area MPLS Traffic Engineering

By Y. Rekhter, Kireeti Kompella, 03/06/2001.

An ISIS/OSPF routing domain may consists of multiple areas. This document postulates a set of mechanisms, and then outlines how these mechanisms could be used to establish/maintain Traffic Engineering LSPs that span multiple areas.

Multicast in MPLS/BGP VPNs

By Eric Rosen, 11/16/2000.

RFC2547bis describes a method of providing a VPN service. It specifies the protocols and procedures which must be implemented in order for a Service Provider to provide a unicast VPN. This document extends that specification by describing the protocols and procedures which a Service Provider must implement in order to support multicast traffic in a VPN, assuming that PIM [PIMv2] is the multicast routing protocol used within the VPN, and the SP network can provide PIM as well.

OSPF Extensions in Support of Generalized MPLS

By Kireeti Kompella, 03/02/2001.

This document specifies extensions to the OSPF routing protocol in support of Generalized Multi-Protocol Label Switching (previously known as Multi-Protocol Lambda Switching).

Enhancements to GMPLS Signaling for Optical Technologies

By Ben Mack-Crane, 11/17/2000.

GMPLS has now been proposed as an extension to the MPLS framework to include non packet-switched optical technologies, such as time-division multiplexing (PDH/SDH/SONET) and wavelength division multiplexing (lambdas/fibers). This draft proposes an enhanced label request format for such optical technologies, which accounts for some special characteristics of these technologies that differentiate them from packet-switched technologies. When enumerating our encoding, we focus, for clarity, on optical TDM technologies, since the standards for these are well-defined, but it will be seen that the proposal has very general applicability.

Extensions to ISIS for support of Diff-Serv-aware MPLS Traffic Engineering

By Francois Le Faucheur, 11/20/2000.

A companion document defines the requirements for support of Diff-Serv-aware MPLS Traffic Engineering on a per-Class- Type basis, as discussed in the Traffic Engineering Working Group Framework document. This document proposes corresponding extensions to ISIS for support of Traffic Engineering on a per-Class-Type basis.

The Notion of overbooking and Its Application to IP/MPLS Traffic Engineering

By Cheng Chen, 11/20/2000.

This contribution aims at examining the notion of overbooking in detail and its application on traffic engineering and capacity planning. For the ease of explanation, MPLS network with Diff-Serv support is used to demonstrate the concept in the subsequent sections.

Multi-service over MPLS

By Don Fedyk, Bernie St-Denis, 11/20/2000.

This document describes a generalized approach to carrying Multi- service protocol data units (PDUs) over an MPLS Network. This proposal defines standard MPLS encapsulations that support permanent virtual circuit (PVC) and switch virtual circuit (SVC) networking. The goal of this draft is to provide a framework that allows an MPLS network to support a range of services from simple circuit emulation services, to complete network inter-working. There are two distinct aspects to these services: the data plane and the control plane. The data plane must be defined to support nailed-up and switched services. This architecture covers the data plane but not the complete procedures for the control plane. The control plane is only defined from a nailed up perspective. The control plane for dynamic services maybe supported by other signaling protocols such as PNNI. Non MPLS signaling is not covered by this draft.

Using ECN to Signal Congestion Within an MPLS Domain

By Robert Jaeger, Mark Shayman, 11/20/2000.

We propose the addition of Explicit Congestion Notification (ECN) together with congestion signaling back to the ingress in order to provide notification to the ingress label switching router (LSR) if congestion is experienced along a label switched path (LSP). This information could be used by the ingress LSR to mitigate congestion by employing dynamic traffic engineering techniques such as shifting flows to alternate paths.

A Core MPLS IP VPN Architecture

By Karthik Muthukrishnan, 11/21/2000.

This memo presents an approach for building core Virtual Private Network (VPN) services in a service provider's MPLS backbone.

Encapsulation Methods for Transport of Layer 2 Frames Over MPLS

By Luca Martini, 02/19/2001.

This document describes methods for encapsulating the Protocol Data Units (PDUs) of layer 2 protocols such as Frame Relay, ATM AAL5, Ethernet for transport across an MPLS network.

Link Management Protocol (LMP) for WDM Transmission Systems

By A. Fredette, 03/06/2001.

A suite of protocols is being developed in the IETF to allow networks consisting of photonic switches (PXCs), optical crossconnects (OXCs), routers, switches, DWDM transmission systems, and optical add-drop multiplexors (OADMs) to use an MPLS-based control plane to dynamically provision resources and to provide network survivability using protection and restoration techniques.

Generalized MPLS Control Plane Architecture for Automatic Switched Transport Network

By Yong Xue, 11/22/2000.

Many solutions have been proposed to enable automatically switched transport networks (ASTN). This document describes a control plane architecture that can be applied to different packet and circuit switching technologies (including fiber, waveband, wavelength, PDH, and SONET/SDH). The control plane technology is based on IP/MPLS control plane protocols. As such, this document is based on the concepts introduced in MPLambdas and GMPLS-Signaling documents from an architectural perspective. It also describes how this control plane architecture could facilitate control plane integration of networks across technical, administrative, and business domains. This memo includes generic procedures, key concepts, and technical considerations for the generalized MPLS control plane architecture. It is intended to accentuate understanding of the application domains, create architectural alignment, and serve as guide for protocol engineering.

Framework for MPLS-based Control of Optical SDH/SONET Networks

By E. Mannie, Vishal Sharma, Greg Bernstein, 11/22/2000.

The suite of protocols that define Multi-Protocol Label Switching (MPLS) is in the process of enhancement to generalize its applicability to the control of non-packet based switching, that is, optical switching. One area of prime consideration is to use this generalized MPLS in upgrading the control plane of optical transport networks. This paper illustrates this process by describing how MPLS is being extended to control SONET/SDH networks. SONET/SDH networks are exemplary examples of this process since they possess a rich multiplex structure, a variety of protection/restoration options, are well defined, and are widely deployed. The extensions to MPLS routing protocols to disseminate information needed in transport path computation and network operations are discussed along with the extensions to MPLS label distribution protocols needed for provisioning of transport circuits. New capabilities that an MPLS control plane would bring to SONET/SDH networks, such as new restoration methods and multi-layer circuit establishment, are also discussed.

Extensions to CRLDP for MPLS Path Protection

By Ken Owens, 11/27/2000.

To deliver reliable service, multi-protocol label switching (MPLS) requires a set of procedures to enable protection of the traffic carried on label switched paths (LSPs). Thus existing signaling mechanisms must be extended appropriately to support such functionality. Recently, CR-LDP has introduced extensions to LDP to support the establishment of LSP tunnels. This draft extends CR-LDP to support path protection in MPLS. Specifically, we provide signaling support for establishing working and backup LSPs.

Crankback Routing Extensions
for MPLS Signaling

By A. Iwata, G Ash, Adrian Farrel, Norihito Fujita, 11/27/2000.

This draft proposes crankback routing extensions for CR-LDP signaling and for RSVP-TE signaling. Recently, several routing protocol extensions for advertising resource information in addition to topology information have been proposed for use in distributed constraint-based routing. In such a distributed routing environment, however, the information used to compute a constraint-based path may be out of date. This means that LSP setup requests may be blocked by links or nodes without sufficient resources. This draft specifies crankback routing extensions for CR-LDP and RSVP-TE so that the label request can be retried on an alternate path that detours around the blocked link or node upon a setup failure. Furthermore, the crankback routing schemes can also be applied to LSP restoration by indicating the location of the failure link or node. This would significantly improve the successful recovery ratio for failed LSPs, especially in situations where a large number of setup requests are triggered at the same time.

Tracing Requirements for Generic Tunnels

By David Meyer, Ronald Bonica, Kireeti Kompella, 02/22/2001.

This document specifies requirements for a generic route tracing application. The application must provide all functionality that 'traceroute' (from RFC 2151) currently provides. It also must provide enhanced capabilities with regard to tracing through tunnels (e.g., IP-in-IP, MPLS).

MTU Signaling Extensions for LDP

By Kireeti Kompella, Benjamin Black, 01/02/2001.

Proper functioning of RFC 1191 path MTU detection requires that IP routers have knowledge of the MTU for each link to which they are connected. As currently specified in [LDP], LDP does not have the ability to signal the MTU for an LSP to ingress LSRs. This document specifies extensions to the LDP label distribution protocol in support of LSP MTU signaling.

Secure MPLS - Encryption and
Authentication of MPLS Payloads

By Oliver Paridaens, Tissa Senevirathne, 02/20/2001.

This document specifies a mechanism for securing the MPLS data plane, i.e., securing any data carried over MPLS. This work is split into two aspects: use of IKE to establish the required security association for secure MPLS and definition of the encapsulation formats required for the encryption and authentication of MPLS payloads. Extensions, under the form of a new Domain of Interpretation, are defined for the use of IKE to set up Security Associations for secure MPLS.

Extending the Number of LSP Fragments
Beyond the 256 Limit

By Amir Hermelin, 01/12/2001.

This document describes a mechanism to allow a system to originate more than 256 LSP fragments, a limit set by the original Intermediate System to Intermediate System (IS-IS) Routing protocol, as described in ISO 10589. This mechanism can be used in IP-only, OSI-only, and dual routers. The document describes behaviors that are backwards compatible with implementations that do not support this feature. These behaviors are specified in a way that allows previous implementations to correctly process the extended fragment information.

Link Management Protocol Management Information Base Using SMIv2

By Martin Dubuc, 02/27/2001.

This memo defines an experimental portion of the Management Information Base (MIB) for use with network management protocols in the Internet community. In particular, it describes managed objects for modeling the Link Management Protocol (LMP).

TTL Processing in MPLS Networks

By Bora Akyol, Puneet Agarwal, 02/22/2001.

This document describes TTL processing in hierarchical MPLS networks.

SONET/SDH Circuit Emulation Service Over MPLS (CEM) Management Information Base Using SMIv2

By Dave Danenberg, 02/22/2001.

This memo defines an experimental portion of the Management Information Base (MIB) for use with network management protocols in the Internet community. In particular, it describes managed objects for modeling an adaptation of SONET/SDH circuits over a Multiprotocol Label Switching (MPLS) Label Switch Router (LSR).

Expanded Explicit Route Object for RSVP-TE

By Bora Akyol, 02/23/2001.

This document expands the Explicit Route Object (ERO) defined in RSVP-TE document. The primary reason for the expansion of the ERO is to simplify the processing of abstract nodes and loose routes as well as to specify globally unique interface identifiers in case of unnumbered interfaces.

Intra-Domain GMPLS Control Plane Architecture for Automatically Switched Transport Network

By Yangguang Xu, 02/23/2001.

Many solutions have been proposed to enable Automatically Switched Transport Networks (ASTN). This document describes an IP/MPLS based intra-domain control plane architecture that can be applied to different circuit switching technologies (including OTN, PDH and SONET/SDH). This memo includes generic procedures, key concepts, and technical considerations for the common control plane architecture. It is intended to accentuate understanding of the application domains, create architectural alignment, and serve as guide for protocol engineering.

MPLS Multicast Traffic Engineering

By Dirk Ooms, 02/23/2001.

There are several reasons for operators to construct multicast trees by another means than multicast routing protocols. This document lists these reasons and describes 2 ways of building a multicast traffic-engineered tree: root-initiated tree and leaf-initiated tree. Finally it defines extensions to CR-LDP to support MPLS multicast traffic engineering.

Optical Inter Domain Routing Requirements

By B. Rajagopalan, Greg Bernstein, 02/23/2001.

GMPLS is being considered as an extension to the MPLS framework to include optical non-packet switched technologies. This draft discusses requirements for inter domain routing protocols such as BGP for use in the optical domain.

Mobile IPv6 support in MPLS

By Jun Choi, 02/23/2001.

This document discusses how to build the large-scale mobile IPv6 network along with the MPLS network. It proposes that CR-LDP/RSVP-TE can be applied to set up the QoS guaranteed Label switched path (LSP) tunnels between an LER of mobile node and an LER of correspondent node. It means that the IPv6-in-IPv6 tunnels can be replaced by one or multiple LSPs on the MPLS network. This follows design principles such as idle mobile node consideration and QoS guarantee, smooth handoff, no change of Mobile IPv6 etc.

Achieving Assured Service Levels through Source Routed MPLS

By M. Gibson, 02/23/2001.

This memo sets out an MPLS-based solution to the IP service delivery problems as set out in RFC 2990. The solution is based on source routing of IP flows using MPLS label stacks. The solution elements are introduced sequentially and a usage scenario is mapped out that aligns with the work in the ISSLL working group.

Modification and Reorganization to GMPLS Signaling Functional Specification

By Yangguang Xu, 02/26/2001.

This draft proposes re-organization and modification to current GMPLS signaling and specifies a set of objects that are common to different network interfaces. Changes from GMPLS Signaling document are: G-Label Request and G-Label objects are re-formatted; Upstream Label, Suggested Label and Label Set are merged into one Suggested Label Set; and, bi-directional LSP creation procedure is clarified and simplified.

OAM Functionality for MPLS Networks

By Neil Harrison, 02/26/2001.

This Internet draft provides requirements and mechanisms for OAM (Operation and Maintenance) for the user-plane in MPLS networks. A connectivity verification'CV' OAM packet is defined, which is transmitted periodically from LSP source to LSP sink. The CV flow could be used to detect defects related to misrouting of LSPs as well as link and nodal failure, and if required to trigger protection switching to the protection path.

Considerations about possible security extensions to BGP/MPLS VPN

By Jeremy De Clercq, 02/26/2001.

The aim of this text is to contribute to the design work of the Provider Provisioned VPN Working Group. This text contains the motivation and requirements for extending the BGP/MPLS VPN model with security measures. Further, the draft explores some possible extensions to meet the listed requirements.

GMPLS Signalling Extensions for G.709 Optical Transport Networks

By Michele Fontana, 02/26/2001.

Along with the current development of packet over lambda switching, there is considerable development in transport systems based on the ITU-T G.709 specification. For that purpose, the inter-working of G.709 capable devices on top lambda switched networks is relevant to new optical developments at the OIF and IETF.

TTL Processing expansion for 1-hop LSP

by Shigeki Matsushima, 02/26/2001.

Some MPLS-VPN service provider want to hide their network topology from their customers. The value of TTL field of IP packets is decreased the amount of hop counts on a LSP at an egress LSR. Therefore at this time, It is possible that the customer know the number of routers onto a LSP of MPLS-VPN service provider.

Diff-Serv-aware MPLS Traffic Engineering Network Management Information Base Using SMIv2

By Thomas Nadeau, 02/26/2001.

This memo defines an experimental portion of the Management Information Base (MIB) for use with network management protocols in the Internet community. In particular, in response to customer demands and strong input from vendors, it describes managed objects for modeling and managing Diff-Serv-aware MPLS Traffic Engineering.

Generalized Switch Management Protocol (gsmp)

By Ben Mack-Crane, Janathan Sadler, 02/26/2001.

Work has been progressing in the Multi-protocol Label Switching (MPLS) working group on the application of MPLS technology to non-packet switching networks. Specifically, development of the Generalized MPLS (GMPLS) signaling draft has allowed for Optical, SONET/SDH, and spatial switching to be controlled by IP protocols.

Analysis of the Security of the MPLS Architecture

By Michael Behringer, 02/26/2001.

This document analyses the security of the MPLS architecture, especially in comparison with other VPN technologies such as ATM and Frame Relay. The target audience is service providers and VPN users. The document consists of two main parts: First the requirements for security in VPN services are defined, second MPLS is examined with respect to these requirements. The analysis shows that MPLS networks can be equally secured as traditional layer-2 networks such as ATM and Frame Relay.

A Core MPLS IP VPN Link Broadcast And Virtual Router Discovery

By Chandrasekar Kathirvelu, 02/27/2001.

An IPVPN consists of many routers, some physically discrete and some virtual, housed in a Provider Edge router. The problem that presents itself is that these virtual routers need do find each other over a virtual topology and they need to send broadcast datagrams as mandated in routing protocols (such as the neighbor discovery datagram and routing updates in OSPF, the routing updates in RIPV2, etc.) and user data over this virtual topology. This memo presents an approach for solving these problems.

Generalized MPLS Recovery Mechanisms

By Y. Rekhter, John Drake, Jonathan Lang, 02/27/2001.

This draft discusses protection and restoration mechanisms for fault management within the GMPLS framework.

Applicability Statement for Traffic Engineering with MPLS

By Blaine Christian, 02/27/2001.

This memo describes the applicability of Multiprotocol Label Switching (MPLS) to traffic engineering in IP networks. Special considerations for deployment of MPLS for traffic engineering in operational contexts are discussed and the limitations of the MPLS approach to traffic engineering are highlighted. This document is intended for the Internet informational track.

Generalized Multi-Protocol Label Switching (GMPLS) Architecture

By Peter Ashwood-Smith, 02/27/2001.

Future data and transmission networks will consist of elements such as routers, switches, DWDM systems, Add-Drop Multiplexors (ADMs), photonic cross-connects (PXCs) or optical cross- connects (OXCs), etc that will use Generalized MPLS (GMPLS) to dynamically provision resources and to provide network survivability using protection and restoration techniques.

Optical Multicast - A Framework

By E. Mannie, Dirk Ooms, Dimitri Papadimitriou, Jim Jones, 02/28/2001.

This contribution defines the optical multicast concepts and the related applications in optical networks. The objective is to extend the multicast concept for transparent and all-optical networks and subsequently the definition of the signaling protocol extensions for optical multicast-capable networks.

Link Bundling Information Base Using SMIv2

By Sudheer Dharanikota, Martin Dubuc, Thomas Nadeau, 02/28/2001.

This memo defines an experimental portion of the Management Information Base (MIB) for use with network management protocols in the Internet community. In particular, it describes managed objects for modeling link bundling as described in bundling draft.

Hierarchical VPN over MPLS Transport

By Karthik Muthukrishnan, 02/28/2001.

This memo presents an approach for building hierarchical Virtual Private Network (VPN) services. This approach uses Multiprotocol Label Switching (MPLS). The central vision is for the service provider to provide a virtual router service to other SPs without participating in VPNs of those SPs.

Extensions to MPLS-based Layer 2 VPNs

By Himanshu Shah, Xavier Briard, Jim Tsillas, 03/22/2001.

The Provisioning of VPN based on Layer 2 circuits across MPLS-base network has been described in draft-kompella-mpls-l2vpn-02.txt. The draft describes how provider's edge routers distribute configured VPN information amongst themselves. This information is then processed to map layer 2 circuits of customer's edge devices to remote customer devices of the same VPN through MPLS cloud via adjoining provider's edge devices. The proposal requires a priori guestimating of customer's growth needs for the VPN and accordingly over provisioning of a contiguous set of (preferably per platform) MPLS labels.

Reducing over-provisioning for MPLS based L2VPN

By Himanshu Shah, 03/22/2001.

This document will describe how provider's edge router can reduce the over-provisioning of resources and in some cases do away with the range configuration so that new sites can be added to an existing VPN topologies without incurring configuration changes to other provider's edge routers in the VPN.

MPLS-RELATED WORK IN OTHER IETF WORKING GROUPS.............................

In early 2001, the IETF created a temporary area called sub-IP and moved the MPLS WG from the routing area to there. Sub-IP in this context refers to Layer 2 and 1 technologies that are below network layer 3 IP. The sub-IP effort deals specifically with the measurement and control of sub-IP technologies, with the aim of supporting their use in the Internet or private IP networks.

The current set of sub-IP working groups are:

- MPLS
- Common Control and Measurement Plane (CCAMP)
- General Switch Management Protocol (GSMP)
- IP over Optical (IPO)
- IP over Resilient Packet Rings (IPORPR)
- Provider-Provisioned Virtual Private Networks (PPVPNs)
- Internet Traffic Engineering (TEWG)

There are also several other IETF working groups involved in MPLS-related activities that are outside of the newly created sub-IP area. These include the RSVP WG, the SNMP Configuration WG, the Policy WG, and several others that deal with issues that may include MPLS.

OTHER MPLS STANDARDIZATION EFFORTS...

As the impact of MPLS spreads beyond the sole province of the IETF, there are several other standardization organizations that are becoming involved with topics related to MPLS. These other organizations include the International Telecommunications Union (ITU), the ATM Forum, and several industry forums that have been created to deal with MPLS and similar technologies.

The International
Telecommunications Union (ITU)

The ITU (formerly the CCITT) is the standards body for defining carrier-class protocols in the telecommunications realm.

There are three ITU study groups (SGs) that are currently involved in the MPLS area:

- SG 11: MPLS Signaling (proposed)
- SG 13: MPLS Network Architecture
- SG 15: MPLS and IP Equipment Requirements

The ITU Web site is accessible at: `http://www.itu.int/home/index.html`

The ATM Forum

The ATM Forum is an international, non-profit group that was formed for the purpose of accelerating the use of ATM products and services by creating interoperability specifications.

There are two ATM working groups that are part of the ATM Forum and are doing work that involves MPLS:

- Traffic Management WG
- ATM-IP Collaboration WG

For the latest information on these efforts, consult the ATM Forum Web site at: `www.atmforum.com` .

FORUMS FOR MPLS ....

There are several industry forums that deal with MPLS and MPLS-related issues. These include:

- The MPLS Forum
- Optical Internetworking Forum (OIF)
- Optical Domain Service Interconnect (ODSI) Forum
- Multiservice Switching Forum (MSF)

Many industry forums have direct charters, allowing them to meet, perform their work, and disband. It is always advised to refer to a particular forum's Web site to stay abreast of their latest developments, meeting dates and agendas, and other related matters. The Web sites also contain membership information.

The MPLS Forum

The MPLS Forum is an international forum comprising various organizations that deal with MPLS. It was formed in early 2000, and it allows the various interested parties to meet and discuss current and pending MPLS-related topics. A main goal of the MPLS Forum is to promote MPLS compatibility and interoperability. The MPLS Forum works closely with all of the major MPLS standardization groups and other industry forums. The MPLS Forum's mission statement from its home Web page is shown in Figure 3–2. The URL for the MPLS Forum is: www.mplsforum.org.

> The MPLS Forum is an international forum advancing the successful deployment of multi-vendor MPLS networks and their associated applications. The Forum will achieve this through interoperability initiatives, implementation agreements, and education programs.

Figure 3–2   The MPLS Forum mission statement.

Table 3–3 contains a list of the founding members:

Table 3–3   MPLS Forum Founding Members

Company	
Advanced Internet Lab, GMU	Marconi
Broadband Office	NetPlane
Data Connection, Ltd.	Nokia
Ennovate Networks	Telcordia Technologies
GlobeSpan	Tenor Networks
Integral Access	Valiant Networks
Inverness Systems	Vivace Networks
Lucent Technologies	Qwest

Table 3–4 is an additional list of principal members:

Table 3–4   MPLS Forum Principal Members

Company	
AccessLan Communications	Jasmine Networks
Agilent Technologies	Maple Networks
Alcatel	MAYAN Networks Corporation
Amber Networks	Native Networks
Atrica Incorporated	NTT Corporation
Bay Microsystems	Orchestream
BellSouth	Pluris
Caspian Networks	Redback Networks
Celox Networks	Riverstone Networks
Charlotte's Web Networks	Sequoia Networks
CoreEl Microsystems	Siemens AG
Crescent Networks	TeraBeam Networks
Entridia	Terawave Communications
E.T.R.I.	Turin Networks
Extreme Networks	US West
Fujitsu	UUNET Technologies
Gotham Networks	Vertex Networks
Huawei America, Incorporated	Williams Communications
Interspeed	

It is interesting to notice the type and variety of companies and organizations that join the various MPLS industry forums.

Optical Internetworking Forum (OIF)

The OIF deals with issues specifically relating to the O-UNI. It specifies a set of protocols to accomplish this. The use of MPLS with optical technologies is discussed more fully in Chapter 10, "Future MPLS Developments and Directions." The mission of the forum (from the home page) is shown in Figure 3–3:

> The mission of the Optical Internetworking Forum (OIF) is to foster the development and deployment of interoperable products and services for data switching and routing using optical networking technologies. The OIF will encourage co-operation among telecom industry participants including equipment manufacturers, telecom service providers and end users; promote global development of optical internetworking products; promote nationwide and worldwide compatibility and interoperability; encourage input to appropriate national and international standards bodies; and identify, select, and augment as appropriate and publish optical internetworking specifications drawn from appropriate national and international standards.

Figure 3–3   The OIF mission statement.

The OIF Web site is: `http://www.oiforum.com`.

Optical Domain Service Interconnect (ODSI) Forum

The ODSI Forum is another industry coalition aimed at developing a standard user interface for optical equipment and a set of protocols to perform related tasks. Figure 3–4 on the next page explains the goals of the ODSI Forum. Since interoperability testing was completed in December 2000, ODSI successfully completed its charter and is now in the mode of promoting the attributes of the ODSI specification to standards organizations.

The ODSI Web site is: `http://www.odsi-coalition.com`.

Multiservice Switching Forum (MSF)

The MSF is an international association of service providers and systems suppliers that is developing and promoting open-architecture, multiservice switching systems. It was founded in 1998 and contains technical working groups that meet to discuss various related standards in this area. Table 3–5 on the next page is a list of members:

The MSF Web site is: `http://www.msforum.org`.

The goal of the ODSI coalition is to rapidly accelerate the practical evolution and use of the optical network through the development and promotion of an `open interface` that effectively links the optical network with higher-layer service networks and elements. To keep pace with market demands, the ODSI coalition formed in early 2000 to collaborate on a practical technical framework that leverages existing protocols and interfaces.

The primary goals of the ODSI coalition have been to:

Develop a technical recommendation that will enable service layer devices (e.g., IP routers, ATM switches, SONET/SDH ADMs) to dial-up high-speed bandwidth and services from the optical domain

Validate solutions through 'proof-of-concept' interoperability testing

Hand-off proposals and results to official standards group

Figure 3–4   The ODSI goals statement.

Table 3–5   Multiservice Switching Forum Members

Company	
Alcatel	Network Equipment Technologies
ANDA Networks	Nokia
Armillaire Technologies, Inc.	Nortel Networks
Belgacom	NTT
British Telecommunications PLC	OKI
Calix Networks	Orange
Cisco Systems	Pelago Networks
Cplane	Qwest Communications
Data Connection Limited	Samsung Group
Efficient Networks, Inc.	Santera Systems, Inc.
Ericsson	SBC Communications Inc.
ETRI	Siemens
France Telecom	Swisscom

Table 3–5   Multiservice Switching Forum Members (continued)

Company	
Fujitsu Network Communications, Inc.	Tachion
General Bandwidth	Telcordia Technologies
Intel	Telecom Italia S.P.A.
KPN	Telica
LG InfoComm U.S.A.	Turin Networks
Lucent Technologies	UNH Interoperability Labs
Mahi Networks, Inc.	Verizon Communications
Marconi PLC	VocalData
Mercury Corporation	Voxpath Networks
Mitel	Westwave
NEC Corporation	

IMPORTANT MPLS URLS ....

More and more information about MPLS is becoming available on the Web, including the MPLS WG mailing list, the MPLS Resource Center Web site, the MPLS World News Web site, and several other Web sites set up by individuals for disseminating MPLS information.

The MPLS WG Mailing List

The MPLS WG has a mailing list that can be joined to obtain information on the latest MPLS developments within the IETF.

General discussion questions can be sent to: `mpls@uu.net`.

To subscribe, send mail to: `mpls-request@uu.net` When subscribing (or unsubscribing), place `subscribe` (or `unsubscribe`) in the message with your e-mail address.

There is also an archive for this mailing list available at: `http://cell.onecall.net/cell-relay/archives/mpls/mpls.index.html`.

The MPLS Resource Center

The MPLS Resource Center site maintains a listing of Frequently Asked Questions (FAQs) devoted to MPLS and other valuable MPLS-related information. The MPLS FAQs and other MPLS-related links are available at: `www.mplsrc.com`.

The MPLS World News

MPLS World News maintains a very informational Web site on MPLS at: `www.mplsworld.com`.

Noritoshi Demizu's Multilayer Routing Web Site

Noritoshi Demizu maintains an extensive Web site on MPLS and other related topics. It can be found at: `http://www.watersprings.org/links/mlr`.

3.8.5 International Engineering Consortium (IEC) Tutorials

The International Engineering Consortium (IEC) Tutorials contain a great deal of information about communications, including MPLS. The Trillium and NetPlane tutorials at `www.iec.org/tutorials` deal specifically with MPLS topics.

BOOKS ON MPLS ....

Currently, there are four published books and one announced that specifically deal with MPLS:

- Davie, Bruce S. and Yakov Rekhter. *MPLS: Technology and Applications*. San Diego: Academic Press, 2000.
- Pepelnjak, Ivan and Jim Guichard. *MPLS and VPN Architectures: A Practical Guide to Understanding, Designing, and Deploying MPLS and MPLS-enabled VPNs* (Cisco Networking Fundamentals). Indianapolis, IN: Cisco Press, 2001.
- Black, Ulyess. *MPLS and Label Switching Networks*. Upper Saddle River, NJ: Prentice Hall PTR, 2001.

- Gray, Eric. *MPLS: Implementing the Technology*. Boston: Addison-Wesley, 2001.
- Alwayn, Vivek. *Advanced MPLS Design and Implementation*. Indianapolis, IN: Cisco Press, 2001. (Note: This book was not yet published as this one was being written.)

There are many other related networking books that contain sections on MPLS. For a comprehensive listing of these books, see the bibliography.

SUMMARY ....

Chapter 3 introduced MPLS documentation and other important resources that can aid in understanding the many facets of MPLS. It listed the MPLS RFCs and IDs and summarized MPLS standardization. It included information on important Web sites, books dealing with MPLS, and other MPLS details.

REFERENCE FOR CHAPTER 3 ....

1. from `www.bartleby.com/100/249.77.html`.

MPLS Core Technologies and Protocols

4

Science is a way of thinking,
but it can only advance on a basis of technique. [1]

— *Magnus Pyle*

The design and implementation of the MPLS architecture is realized through a comprehensive set of core technologies and protocols. The MPLS technology relies on related Internet standard protocols to complement its control plane, label switching, and forwarding techniques. MPLS works closely with Internet routing protocols to help understand where LSPs can be set up in the network. Several MPLS WG proposals advocate the use of various protocols for label distribution and signaling. SNMP is recommended as the network management protocol for monitoring and controlling MPLS resources. MPLS also interoperates with a number of other important networking technologies, including ATM, FR, Ethernet, SONET, and PPP. It should be noted that a great deal of the original MPLS work centered on the use of MPLS with ATM. While the interworking of ATM and IP is still an important use of MPLS in overlay networks, there is tremendous momentum in the utilization of MPLS in pure IP networks.

The key MPLS technologies comprise three main groups:

- The MPLS control plane and data forwarding plane
- The complementary routing IGPs
- The MPLS label distribution and signaling protocols

The MPLS control plane and data forwarding plane are the main subjects of this chapter. IGPs are used in conjunction with MPLS to discover network topology and state. The network topology includes such important information as the adjacent routers and next hops, and the connecting links and various attributes of those links, such as bandwidth. The current set of IGPs used by service providers with MPLS today include IS-IS, OSPF, and BGP-4. There are ongoing efforts in the IETF to add TE extensions to these IGPs to collect additional information about routes for use by MPLS. The MPLS label distribution and signaling protocols that are also important for this framework are covered in Chapter 5, "MPLS Signaling and Label Distribution."

As with all emerging technologies, MPLS comes with a new set of terminology and acronyms that must be mastered for all of the concepts to be fully understood. MPLS is largely based on existing routing and switching building blocks, so many of the terms will sound familiar, but MPLS also introduces several new neologisms.

FEC, LSR, and LSP are three acronyms that are key to understanding MPLS, and one encounters them frequently when dealing with this technology. With the help of a few supporting terms such as "domain," "label," and "MPLS node," and a general familiarity of routing and switching terms, the groundwork for understanding the MPLS architecture is started. Table 4–1 on the next page contains the first three MPLS acronyms everyone should master when starting to comprehend MPLS core technologies. For any other unfamiliar terms encountered, the reader should refer to the glossary at the end of the book.

The MPLS protocol is the set of rules that govern how network layer protocols with MPLS headers can be forwarded through an internetwork of MPLS nodes. An MPLS node is a network device that is running the software and hardware that are required to implement the MPLS control and data forwarding planes. It must be able to operate at least one network layer routing protocol. An MPLS node must also be able to forward

Table 4–1   Three Key MPLS Acronyms

FEC	*Forwarding Equivalence Class*—A set of network layer packets that are forwarded over the same path and in the same manner. With MPLS, this set of packets can typically use the same label (although there may be cases when packets from an FEC use multiple labels).
LSR	*Label-Switching Router*—A network node—such as an IP router or ATM switch—that is instrumented with MPLS software and hardware. This includes awareness of MPLS control protocols, operation of one (or more) Layer 3 routing protocols, and proper MPLS label manipulation (forwarding and switching).
LSP	*Label-Switched Path*—A path beginning at an ingress LSR, traversing zero or more transit LSRs, and ending at an egress LSR. All packets that contain the same label value travel the same LSP.

packets by operating on their MPLS labels. The architecture notes that an MPLS node may also be optionally capable of forwarding non-MPLS, or "native" Layer 3 packets.

A collection of MPLS nodes is called an "MPLS domain." This domain is typically managed and controlled under one administration. Currently, all of the service provider MPLS networks exist as single domains. Inter-MPLS domain interoperability—for example, running MPLS tunnels between service providers—is a current area of intense development and interoperability testing. The MPLS domain concept is similar to the notion of an AS, as that term is used in conventional IP routing. The idea that a group of network devices running the same protocol (or a set of interoperable protocols) is controlled by a single administrative entity paves the way for the use of policies. A policy is a set of rules that enforces a particular action depending on the configured filters that have been set up. The template for a policy rule can be generalized as: if (this filter is true), then (perform this action). Policies will become an important part in realizing and controlling most MPLS applications.

Each MPLS node in an MPLS domain contains its control and data forwarding planes. To summarize the operation of the control plane and data forwarding plane within each MPLS node, Figure 4–1 on the next page displays how the main MPLS concepts of FEC, LSR, and LSP are related.

In addition to these three key concepts, MPLS core technologies and protocols deal with several additional related technology details, including packet looping handling, MPLS multicast, IGP TE extensions, and how the protocol works with various lower layer protocol encapsulations.

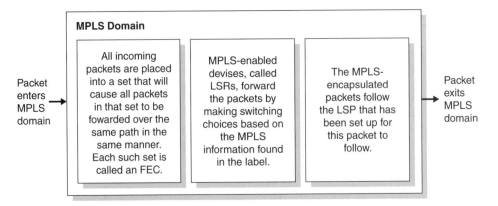

Figure 4–1   FEC, LSR, and LSP in the MPLS domain.

There are also a number of important MPLS design and implementation issues that need to be discussed. These include taking a look at the MPLS reference model as well as a sample context diagram (CD) and data flow diagrams (DFDs). There are also a number of Web sites that contain sample MPLS source code, which can be very useful when the reader needs to look at MPLS at the implementation level.

THE FORWARDING EQUIVALENCE CLASS (FEC) ....

In the most general sense, information flowing over a network comprises data units that support all of the requisite headers for each layer of communication involved in getting the information from its source to its destination. At Layer 3, the information flow comprises a set of network layer packets encapsulated with the network layer header. For the IP, each network layer packet contains the IP address of the destination computer for the packet in the header. The routing logic running in the router computes the shortest path for the packet by applying its algorithms to the specific network topology. The routing table is used to determine the next hop for any incoming packet based on a longest destination prefix match in the table and possibly other metrics. Conventional IP routing must analyze any incoming IP packet that comes into the network by doing a lookup in this table.

One can consider the set of all possible IPv4 destinations for the 32-bit addresses—a number slightly less than 2^{32} minus one (there are several reserved and invalid IP version 4 addresses)—as the "universe" of all possible IPv4 destinations (sometimes called the "omega," or Ω, in set notation). For any network device to accept and then forward an addressed packet along its way to its destination, the network device must be properly enabled by having its control plane and data forwarding plane set up correctly.

Within each MPLS node, the set of all possible destinations can be partitioned into independent subsets. Each of these subsets is called an FEC. All packets in the same FEC are forwarded down the same path in the same manner. After the MPLS node has classified the possible incoming packets into FECs, it must map each FEC into a next hop so that the forwarding operation works correctly.

An important point to make here is that, in MPLS, the network layer header only needs to be analyzed once: when the packet enters the MPLS domain. This is a major difference when compared to conventional IP routing, which requires the packet header to be analyzed at each hop.

The MPLS architecture cites five distinct advantages that MPLS has over conventional network layer forwarding. These advantages may increase bandwidth utilization in networks and allow for the deployment of many new applications.

1. There can be a class of switches in a network that can do MPLS forwarding (label lookup and replacement), but these switches are not capable of analyzing any Layer 3 headers in a timely manner.

2. MPLS FEC membership can be much richer than in IP. LSPs are not strictly based on SPF destination address resolution, but can be based on various addresses, ports, and other header information such as QoS parameters found in the network, transport, and application headers.

3. Where a packet enters the network can be used to affect the forwarding decision. This is not possible with conventional routing because the ingress router identity does not stay with the packet.

4. FEC determination can be made more complex without affecting any of the transit routers that merely swap labels along the LSP.

5. Through policy or TE, packet flows can be altered to construct explicit paths. An explicit route is represented by the labels that have been set up in the LSP. In conventional IP routing, the packet IP header needs to carry the route along with it as the source routing option.

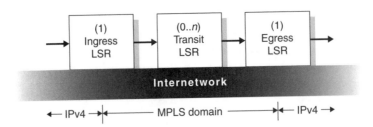

Figure 4–2   The MPLS domain model.

The point of entry to any MPLS domain is a special MPLS node called the "ingress LSR." The incoming network layer packet is classified to follow a set path through the MPLS cloud by being tagged with the appropriate label. These labels become indexes into tables that tell the intermediate MPLS nodes how and where to route this network layer packet with its MPLS header through the domain to its proper exit point. The exit point of every MPLS path is controlled by another special edge router called the "egress LSR." The egress LSR removes the MPLS header and sends the packet on its way, using the information that is present in the network layer header. For IPv4, IP routing is evoked using the network layer header information (SPF based on destination address).

A simple model of the MPLS domain comprises the ingress LSR, zero or more intermediate LSRs (called "transit LSRs"), and the egress LSR. All MPLS nodes are connected to some type of internetwork. Our introductory model of an MPLS domain, including the LSRs, is shown in Figure 4–2.

The ingress, transit, and egress LSRs must be capable of understanding and processing the appropriate network layer protocol in addition to MPLS. While IPv4 is used in the general discussion of MPLS protocols, the exact treatment for other networking technologies is discussed later in the chapter.

Figure 4–3 on the next page shows how an MPLS node acting as an ingress LSR chooses the next hop for any incoming packet by determining the FEC membership of the incoming packet. The FEC membership is a logical FEC mapping table that associates the FEC and label. The outgoing packet mapping process assigns the proper label and forwards the MPLS packet to the proper outgoing interface after its FEC membership has been established.

Before the actual MPLS forwarding can occur, each ingress LSR must create its own FEC mapping table by employing a partioning process. An example of an FEC mapping table is shown in Table 4–2. One of

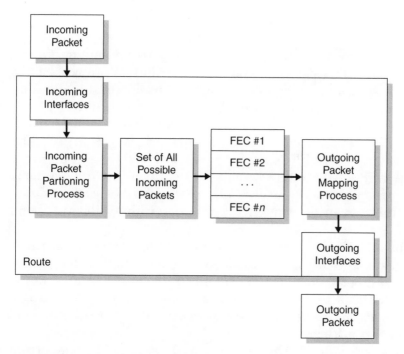

Figure 4–3   Choosing the next hop.

the great advantages of MPLS is that the set of rules for FEC membership is configurable and not tied to a single algorithm, such as the Dijkstra algorithm used by some interior routing protocols.

Table 4–2   FEC Mapping Table

FEC_1—A set of rules that determines that this particular group of network layer (Layer 3) packets will be forwarded in the same manner.	Uses LABEL_1*
. . .	. . .
FEC_n—A set of rules that determines that this particular group of network layer (Layer 3) packets will be forwarded in the same manner.	Uses LABEL_n*

*Packets belonging to an FEC may get mapped to multiple labels (for example, if stream merging is not being used).

MPLS uses a control-driven process to determine the FEC membership table. The knowledge of which FEC any incoming packet will be a member of is always determined before any MPLS data packets flow over the interfaces. The signaling and label distribution protocols and network management configuration for manual paths create the tables necessary to determine FEC membership. Anytime a packet arrives at an ingress LSR, there is a lookup to determine its FEC membership. This is in contrast to the data-driven scheme used by several pre-MPLS label swapping designs, where FECs are set up as traffic arrives at an ingress node and the LSP needs to be created. This is much more dynamic than the control-driven process, but it is not used in MPLS because data packets can be dropped in the time it takes to determine FEC membership and set up the LSP.

The MPLS label is used in the forwarding process after the path has been set up. The MPLS label is a short, fixed-length value that has local significance between two adjacent LSRs. The label represents the FEC with which this packet has been associated. **It is important to note that in MPLS, the label is never an encoding of the network layer destination address.**

Label swapping is the central paradigm in MPLS. Important issues associated with this include:

- The MPLS header
- Label operations
- Label spaces
- Label modes
- Other MPLS header processing issues

The MPLS Header

For data link layer switching technologies such as ATM and FR, the top-level MPLS label is inserted in the native label field for that particular protocol. For ATM, the VPI/VCI field is used for this MPLS label; for FR, the DLCI field is used.

In cases where MPLS is being used to forward Layer 3 IP packets and where the underlying Layer 2 technology does not support a native label field, an MPLS header must be inserted between the Layer 2 and Layer 3 headers. The process of inserting this MPLS header into the packet is a type of "encapsulation." An encapsulation protocol carries one (or more) higher level protocols transparently inside the data information

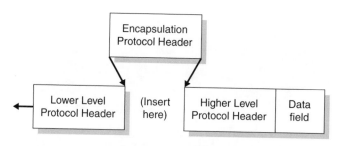

Figure 4–4   General protocol encapsulation.

payload of the encapsulated protocol's datagram. Essentially, a new header is introduced that makes the encapsulated header and data field the new data field. The general model for how encapsulation works is shown in Figure 4–4.

The MPLS header that is added to the Layer 3 header is often called the "shim" header to introduce the metaphor of how the MPLS (Layer 2.5) header is wedged into the packet at the proper place between the Layer 2 and Layer 3 headers.

One of the strengths of the MPLS architecture is its definition of a label stack. A label stack is a sequence of MPLS headers, or more formally, "label stack entries." The stack can contain one or more MPLS headers. This stacking allows for the creation of hierarchical LSPs that can be used for many new services. These services include network management, VPNs, TE, and others yet to be specified.

Another way of viewing MPLS is as a set of procedures for creating and processing labeled packets. The formula for a labeled packet is:

Network layer packet + MPLS label stack

Each MPLS header within the label stack is 32 bits (4 octets) in length and comprises four fields:

- The MPLS label
- The Experimental (EXP) Bits field
- The Stack (S) Bit field
- The Time To Live (TTL) field

Figure 4–5 on the next page shows the MPLS header.

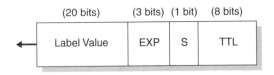

Figure 4–5 The MPLS header.

The ordering of the MPLS header within a network packet (e.g., IPv4) is shown in Figure 4–6. It is always placed between the Layer 2 and Layer 3 headers.

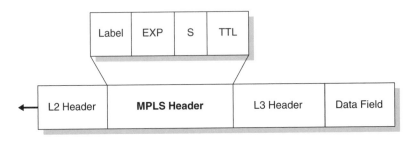

Figure 4–6 An MPLS "shim" header in IPv4.

The MPLS Label Field The MPLS Label field carries the value of the MPLS label that is used for all of the subsequent label operations: pushing, popping, and swapping. It is 20 bits in length.

A label only has local significance between the two communicating LSRs.

It was originally believed because the label length is "short" when compared to conventional network and link layer addresses (IPv4 is 32 bits, etc.), that this feature would increase the switching speed of MPLS packets through the network. Recent advances—particularly in hardware design—have mitigated this, as most routers and switches operate at wire speed. The labels are unstructured and stored in a label information base (LIB). The label values can range from 0 to 20**20-1, except for reserved values.

There are several reserved label values that are being specified by the MPLS WG (as defined in the MPLS label stack encoding RFC). These reserved labels are shown in Table 4–3 on the next page.

Table 4–3   Reserved MPLS Labels

Label Value	Label Meaning
0	**IPv4 Explicit NULL Label**—Indicates that the label stack must be popped. Subsequent forwarding of the packet will be based on the IPv4 network header. This label can only be used as the bottom-most label entry in a label stack.
1	**Router Alert Label**—This label is used in a similar manner to the "Router Alert Option" defined for IP packets. RFC 2113, "IP Router Alert Option," describes this option fully. This label value can be used anywhere in the label stack, except at the bottom. Furthermore, because the label cannot be the last label in the stack, this option is network layer-independent. When an LSR receives this label value, the packet is sent to the local software module that would process this information. The next innermost label determines the subsequent forwarding of the MPLS packet. Note that if the packet is forwarded further, this label must be pushed back on to the stack before forwarding.
2	**IPv6 Explicit NULL Label**—Indicates that the label stack must be popped. Subsequent forwarding of the packet will be based on the IPv6 network header. This label can only be used as the bottom-most label entry in a label stack.
3	**Implicit NULL Label**—This is a "virtual" label in the sense that this value can be distributed, but never appears in the MPLS header encapsulation. This label causes the LSR to pop the stack instead of the normal swap operation, where a new label value would be introduced. (This label value needs to be reserved because it is documented in the LDP specification.)
4—15	Reserved for future definition.

The Experimental Bits (EXP) Field   The Experimental Bits field contains three bits that are reserved for further study and experimentation. Work is being done to define a consistent standard for these bits to be used for differentiated services (Diff-Serv) and providing classes of service. Note that this field was originally called the Class of Service (CoS) field, and this is still seen in several documents.

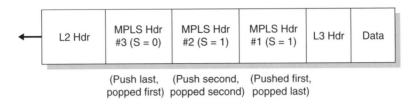

(Push last,   (Push second,   (Pushed first,
popped first) popped second) popped last)

Figure 4–7   A sample MPLS label stack.

The Stack (S) Bit Field   .The one-bit Stack Bit field is the mechanism used to support hierarchical MPLS label stacking. The last (that is, the innermost) label header has its S bit set to indicate that it is the last header in the stack. The S bit should be zero for all other MPLS header entries. The next field in the packet should always be the Layer 3 network header. Since MPLS always acts on the outermost –or "top"—level first, the MPLS stack is created as a last-in, first-out (LIFO) arrangement. An example three-level label stack is shown in Figure 4–7.

MPLS header #1 was the first MPLS header pushed on to the packet, then header #2, and finally, header #3. Label switching is always done on the top layer, and the labels are popped off as determined by the egress node for any LSP the packet is traveling in.

The Time To Live (TTL) Field   The TTL field in an MPLS header works in a similar fashion to the TTL field in an IP header; it is a mechanism to prevent looping. It indicates the number of hops a packet can traverse before the count reaches zero and TTL processing must be performed on it. If the packet is not destined for the local node when the count reaches zero, it can be silently discarded or trigger the generation of an ICMP message. The action the LSR takes is typically based on configuration. The MPLS Label Stack Entry TTL field is shown in Figure 4–8. The valid value range for this field is from 0 to 255.

Figure 4–8   The MPLS Label Stack Entry TTL field.

Label Operations

There are three basic operations performed on MPLS labels. These are shown in Table 4–4.

Table 4–4   MPLS Label Operations

Push	Places the MPLS label on the network layer packet. Always done at the ingress LSR. When more than one label is placed in a packet, the label stack entries are always organized as a LIFO stack.
Swap	Swaps labels. This is done at transit nodes. The incoming label is used as an index to find the new outgoing label that is swapped in the MPLS header.
Pop	Removes MPLS label. Done at the egress node.

Label "Spaces"

There are two basic notions of label spaces for MPLS: per-platform label space and per-interface label space. Each label space consists of the assignable labels from 0 to 1048574, with 0 through 15 having reserved and special semantics (see the section titled "The MPLS Label Field"). The decision on whether per-platform or per-interface space should be implemented on a particular LSR is a function of how the interfaces are used.

Per-Platform Label Space   Per-platform label space means that there is one set of labels for the entire LSR. All interfaces share this common label pool. This is shown in Figure 4–9 on the next page.

Per-Interface Label Space   MPLS can also support a label space per interface. Each interface utilizes its own private label pool and any labels on different interfaces must be distributed and assigned independently. This type of configuration is used particularly with ATM-LSRs, which require independent label spaces for each interface. Figure 4–10 shows an example of per-interface label space.

Label Modes

The MPLS architecture specifies that the label binding decision—that is, associating a specific label with a particular FEC—is always done by the

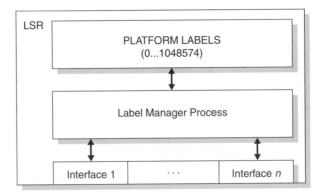

Figure 4–9   Per-platform label space.

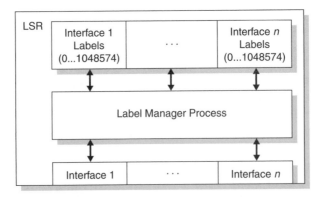

Figure 4–10   Per-interface label space.

downstream LSR. This is called "downstream assignment." The LSR then notifies its upstream peer of the binding decision by distributing the label in this downstream-to-upstream direction. This is shown in Figure 4–11 on the next page.

In the static configuration case, each respective LSR must have its labels properly configured. In the signaled case, the signaling protocol assigns the labels at each LSR it visits. Each upstream LSR must ensure that the label it receives is acceptable before it binds the label for traffic forwarding. This check includes making sure the label value is available

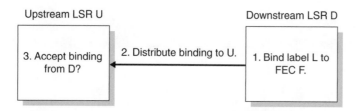

Figure 4–11   MPLS label assignment and distribution.

and that it is in bounds for the label range supported by the particular LSR.

There are several important label-related issues associated primarily with configuration, binding distribution, and the use of MPLS resources available at the LSR. These issues include:

- Label assignment modes
- Label distribution modes
- Label retention modes
- Label merging

Label Assignment Modes   When an FEC is created by mapping address prefixes that are distributed by an IGP and used for creating hop-by-hop LSPs#Author: Is there a more understandable way to say this?, there are two possible label assignment modes that can be used when the labels are distributed. These are:

- Independent LSP control
- Ordered LSP control

With independent LSP control, each LSR makes its own decision whether to bind a label to the discovered FEC and distribute the new binding upstream. This is similar to how conventional IP routing is done when new routes are discovered. Independent LSP control is shown in Figure 4–12 on the next page.

Ordered LSP control is more restricted than independent control in that label binding only occurs for a particular FEC if either the LSR has the role of egress node for that FEC or if the LSR has already

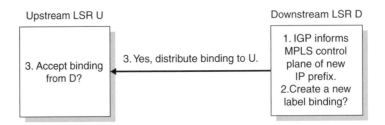

Figure 4–12   MPLS independent label assignment.

received a label binding for the FEC from its next hop for that FEC. This is shown in Figure 4–13.

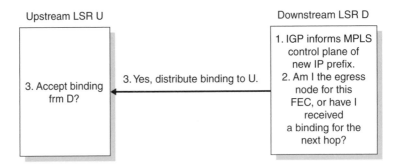

Figure 4–13   MPLS ordered label assignment.

Label Distribution Modes   There are also two possible label distribution methods that can be used with MPLS:

- Downstream-on-demand
- Unsolicited downstream

Downstream-on-demand label distribution is for hop-by-hop LSPs. It allows the LSR to explicitly request a label binding for a particular FEC from its downstream, next-hop neighbor.

Unsolicited downstream is the mode used when an LSR wishes to distribute bindings to its peers when they have not explicitly requested those label bindings. The labels are distributed in the downstream direction.

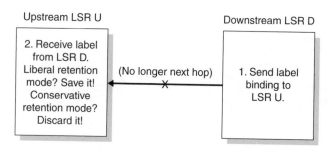

Figure 4–14   MPLS label retention modes.

The MPLS architecture allows either or both label distribution modes to be employed, depending on implementation details such as the interface characteristics and other available MPLS resources. However, for each set of label distribution adjacencies, the upstream LSR and downstream LSR must agree and use the same label distribution mode for hop-by-hop LSPs.

Label Retention Modes   Another characteristic of labels is their retention mode, that is, how long they "hang around" in the incoming label map and are still valid. As with other implementation decisions, label retention mode is a resources versus processing compromise.

An upstream LSR has a decision to make when it receives a label binding from a downstream LSR that is not currently the upstream LSR's next hop for the FEC. It can either "save" the label binding or it can discard it. Each of these two behaviors is implemented as a label retention mode. This is shown in Figure 4–14.

There are two primary label retention modes used with MPLS:

- Liberal label retention mode
- Conservative label retention mode

Liberal label retention mode is when the upstream LSR saves any label bindings it has received from non-next-hop downstream LSRs. Conservative label retention mode is when the label binding is discarded.

Liberal label retention mode has the advantage that if the downstream LSR becomes the next hop for the corresponding FEC, the LSP can be used very quickly. This allows for much quicker response to routing modifications. Of course, if the binding has been discarded, it must be reassigned before the LSP can be used. With the conservative retention mode, less resources are required, but reactions to next-hop changes occur much slower.

Label Merging   Label merging is the ability of an LSR to bind multiple incoming labels to a single FEC for the purpose of swapping labels for a new, single-output label, and then forwarding the packets to a single-output interface as the same LSP.

Note that certain classes of MPLS-enabled devices, such as ATM-LSRs using switched virtual circuit (SVC) or switched virtual path (SVP) encodings, cannot do label merging.

Other MPLS Header Processing Issues

There are several other additional MPLS header processing issues that are all related and deal with handling exception conditions with packets. These issues include:

- Maximum transmit unit (MTU) size
- Packet fragmentation
- ICMP error message generation

Maximum Transmit Unit (MTU) Size   The MTU size deter-mines the largest packet that can be sent without fragmentation occur-ring. This is an important configuration item because receiving devices need to know the upper limit of the largest packet they can accept. With MPLS, proper planning must be done because the MPLS design accom-modates label stacking, which allows the overall packet size to grow by 32 bits for each new entry.

Packet Fragmentation   Packet fragmentation is the process of partitioning a packet into smaller fragments to allow it to proceed through devices that have their MTU parameter set to less than the size of the packet that has been received and needs to be forwarded. For IP-based packets, there is a "do not fragment" (DF) bit in the header that can be used to determine the proper action. The algorithm for IPv4 is pre-sented in RFC 3032, "MPLS Label Stack Encoding," as follows:

If a labeled IPv4 datagram is "too big", and the DF bit is not set in its IP header, then the LSR MAY silently discard the datagram.

Note that discarding such datagrams is a sensible procedure only if the "Maximum Initially Labeled IP Datagram Size" is set to a non-zero value in every LSR in the network which is capable of adding a label stack to an unlabeled IP datagram.

If the LSR chooses not to discard a labeled IPv4 datagram which is too big, or if the DF bit is set in that datagram, then it MUST execute the following algorithm:

1. Strip off the label stack entries to obtain the IP datagram.
2. Let N be the number of bytes in the label stack (i.e, 4 times he number of label stack entries).
3. If the IP datagram does NOT have the "Don't Fragment" bit set in its IP header:
   a. convert it into fragments, each of which MUST be at least N bytes less than the Effective Maximum Frame Payload Size.
   b. Prepend each fragment with the same label header that would have been on the original datagram had fragmentation not been necessary.
   c. Forward the fragments
4. If the IP datagram has the "Don't Fragment" bit set in its IP header:
   a. the datagram MUST NOT be forwarded
   b. Create an ICMP Destination Unreachable Message:
      i. set its Code field [3] to "Fragmentation Required and DF Set",
      ii. set its Next-Hop MTU field [4] to the difference between the Effective Maximum Frame Payload Size and the value of N
   c. If possible, transmit the ICMP Destination Unreachable Message to the source of the of the discarded datagram.

Sending ICMP Error Messages   MPLS can be configured to send ICMP error messages for IPv4. For any LSR to be capable of sending ICMP packets, it must be able to create the ICMP packet and then be able to send this packet to the IP packet's source. To accomplish this, the LSR must be able to determine first that the network layer header indicates that this is an IP packet, and second that the LSR can properly route the ICMP packet back to the source by using the packet's source IP address.

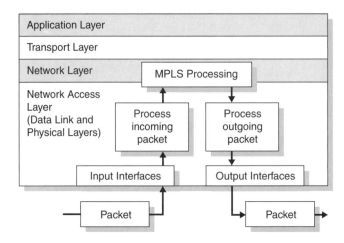

Figure 4–15   An LSR.

THE LABEL-SWITCHING ROUTER (LSR) ....

For all LSRs, there is a core set of functions involved in MPLS processing. This is shown in Figure 4–15 as a process takes in incoming packets from the input interface and processes them as outgoing packets to be placed on the proper output interface. The primary focus of the LSR is to forward MPLS packets by utilizing label switching operations. An LSR is capable of forwarding native IP packets, as well as running the IP routing protocols and MPLS control protocols.

LSPs exist within an MPLS domain. Within a domain, each MPLS-enabled router is capable of assuming one of three roles from the perspective of a particular LSP: the ingress, transit, or egress node. In Figure 4–16 on the next page, the roles of an MPLS-enabled router are shown. MPLS-enabled router D assumes the originating role of an ingress label edge router (LER) for LSP 1. For LSP 2, node D acts as a transit LSR and swaps labels. Finally, for LSP 3, node D takes on the role of an egress LSR and terminates the LSP. These three sample network LSPs are:

• Sample Network LSP 1: A--->B--->D
• Sample Network LSP 2: A--->D--->E
• Sample Network LSP 3: D--->E--->C

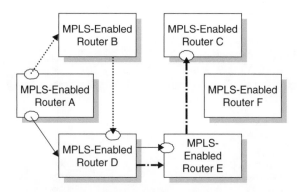

Figure 4–16   Example roles for MPLS-enabled routers.

Not to belabor the point, but people first becoming acquainted with MPLS often mistakenly assume that a particular router running MPLS has to act exclusively as an ingress, transit, or egress node. This is obviously not the case; the role of an MPLS-enabled router is always viewed from the perspective of its position within each particular LSP.

An LSR can be subclassed based on additional functionality it may perform. Three major types of LSRs are:

- Ingress LSR
- Transit LSR
- Egress LSR

Let's look at the major functional blocks of each type of LSR.

The Ingress LSR

The ingress router (a.k.a. the "head-end," or LER) is the "brains" of the LSP. This LSR is shown in Figure 4–17 on the next page. The ingress LSR handles the incoming packets as they enter the MPLS domain. The input IP packets have their headers analyzed, their FEC membership determined, and an initial label assigned. In terms of the LSP, the ingress LSR is the most upstream node in the path.

There are three major functional processing blocks for MPLS processing in the MPLS ingress LSR:

1. Analyze network layer header and assign FEC

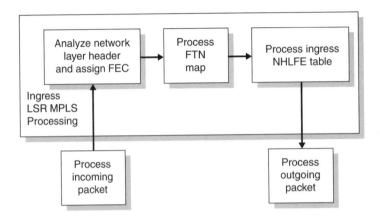

Figure 4–17   The ingress LSR processing model.

2. Process Forward Equivalency Class to Next Hop Label Forwarding Entry (FTN) map

3. Process ingress Next Hop Label Forwarding Entry (NHLFE) table

The NHLFE table is the data structure that is implemented in each LSR to forward an MPLS labeled packet. It contains several key data points that are associated with a set of MPLS packets. These include:

- The packet's next hop
- Label stack operation
- Data link encapsulation (optional)
- Encoding method for the label stack when transmitting the packet (optional)
- Other information needed for properly disposing of the packet, if necessary

The label stack operations are of four basic types:

- Push the label stack
- Swap the top label stack with a new label stack
- Pop the label stack
- Swap the top label stack with a new label, and then push one or more new labels on to the label stack

The MPLS architecture document also specifies additional behavior when an LSR's "next hop" has been set to the LSR itself. In this case, the label stack operation must be to pop the label stack. The LSR then must forward the resulting packet to itself. If there are no more label stack entries, the LSR then uses native forwarding based on the Layer 3 protocol.

The FTN[1] table is the key data structure resident in each LSR that acts in the ingress role for its set of LSPs. The purpose of the FTN is to accept an entering unlabeled packet and then determine which entry will be used to label and forward the packet as it enters the MPLS domain. The FTN maps each unlabeled incoming packet to an FEC for its association to the corresponding set of NHLFE table entries.

The Transit LSR

A transit router is like a player in a game of "hot potato." It gets an MPLS packet, the label is swapped, and the packet is sent to the next downstream LSR as quickly as possible. The next downstream LSR will either be the egress router or another transit router. The transit router's role is simple and straightforward. This is where any performance gains in the end-to-end routing of network layer packets are achieved through pure transit layer switching. The major process blocks of the transit LSR are shown in Figure 4–18.

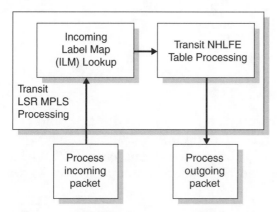

Figure 4–18   The transit LSR processing model.

---

1. The FTN acronym is interesting in the fact that it is actually an acronym of acronyms (a meta-acronym?). I suppose this trend parallels the IPv4 address depletion problem: we are running out of TLA (three-letter acronym) combinations. In this particular case, I suppose FECTNHLFE table would be a little unwieldy.

The Incoming Label Map (ILM) is the data structure resident in each transit and egress LSR. It uses the incoming label value as an index into the NHLFE table. The purpose of the ILM is to forward MPLS-labeled packets along its LSP. Note that there is one ILM if the LSR is using a per-platform label space and one per interface if the LSR is using a per-interface label space. Like the FTN, the architecture specification states that if the ILM maps a particular label to more than one NHLFE that contains more than one element, exactly one entry must be chosen before the packet can be swapped. This is an implementation detail and can possibly be used for equal cost, multipath load-balancing mechanisms.

Penultimate Hop Popping   An interesting subclass of the transit LSR is the penultimate-hop LSR. It is so named because this LSR is capable of a special case of MPLS processing called penultimate hop popping.

Because this is a **primer** ...

The word *penultimate* has been around since 1677 and means "next to the last."

The role of the penultimate LSR is shown in Figure 4–19.

Penultimate hop popping is a configurable option that allows for the removal (pop) of the MPLS label by the LSR—that is, the penultimate LSR—before arriving at the egress LSR.

The Egress LSR

The egress router does the cleanup for the LSP and can play an important role in certain label signaling and distribution protocols. The egress LSR does the final MPLS processing on each MPLS packet by removing the MPLS header and then sending the packet on its way using the de-

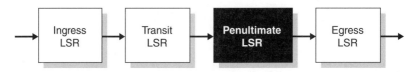

Figure 4–19   The penultimate transit LSR.

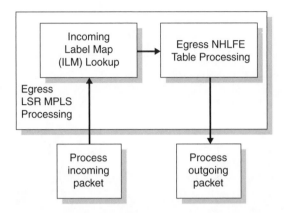

Figure 4–20   The egress LSR processing model.

encapsulated network layer header. In terms of the LSP, the egress LSR is the most downstream node in the path. The egress LSR is also a LER. The egress router's MPLS processing model is shown in Figure 4–20.

A Further Note on LSR Terminology

There are two idioms that frequently occur when MPLS terminology is used that may benefit from clarification. They deal with the relationship between MPLS nodes in a domain. Tongue-in-cheek, they are called the "river" metaphor and the "rabbit" metaphor.

The river metaphor compares an LSR's position in its LSP role to a position on a river. This relationship is shown in Figure 4–21.

LSR B is "downstream" from LSR A. Conversely, LSR A is "upstream" from LSR B. The notation "Rd" for LSR B and "Ru" for LSR A is often used when discussing this configuration. The data packet "river" is flowing in the direction of the arrows through LSR A and LSR B.

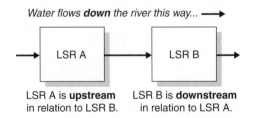

Figure 4–21   Upstream and downstream LSRs.

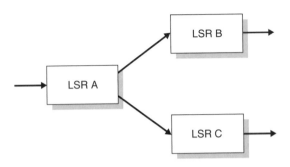

Figure 4–22   Next-hop LSRs.

Remember, the packets—like a river—flow down from source to destination.

The rabbit metaphor shown in Figure 4–22 shows LSRs B and C as next hops for LSR A. As next hops, these routers are responsible for advancing the packets they receive closer to their destination based on their forwarding tables.

Using MPLS, an LSP becomes a collection of next hops that starts at the ingress and is logically connected to the egress LSR.

THE LABEL-SWITCHED PATH (LSP) ....

An LSP is the route MPLS packets from a particular FEC use to travel across a set of LSRs that span an MPLS domain. It is a unidirectional path that always begins at the ingress LSR, traverses zero or more transit LSRs, and ends at the egress LSR. The portion of the LSP between any two LSRs is also called an "LSP hop" (or, less preferably, an "LSP segment").

An LSP is always unidirectional.

There are two main categories of LSPs:

• Static LSPs
• Signaled LSPs

A UML inheritance diagram that portrays the relationships among the various types of LSPs is shown in Figure 4–23 on the next page.

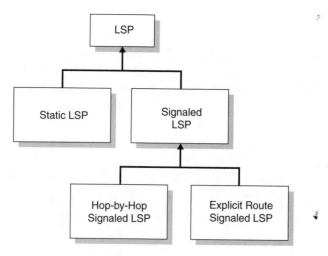

Figure 4–23 LSP hierarchy.

The Static LSP

A static LSP is an LSP that is manually configured at each LSR. No signaling is involved, and these types of LSPs are typically created by visiting each LSR and using network management to set the label, interface, and any pertinent path values.

The Signaled LSP

When a signaling protocol is used to set up an LSP, a signaled LSP is created. The hop-by-hop signaled LSP is also considered a best-effort path. Explicitly routed LSPs can offer specific service agreements.

The LDP is used for this type of LSP. Two specific examples of LDPs used for creating these types of LSPs are CR-LDP and RSVP-TE. More details concerning the protocols that are used for signaled LSPs are covered in Chapter 5, "MPLS Signaling and Label Distribution."

Additional LSP Attributes

There are additional LSP attributes beyond type. These include LSP preemption, protection, and rerouting. LSP preemption is arranging LSPs based on configurable priorities. This feature allows for preemption when a higher priority LSP needs to be set up, thus resulting in a lower priority LSP getting torn down. LSP protection allows for the creation of various types of backup LSPs. This feature is important for the MPLS path restoral application. Backup LSPs can be created in both "hot" and "cold" standby modes. Cold standby LSPs need to be activated when a failed LSP is detected and signaled; hot standby LSPs are preconfigured and automatically become active after any associated LSP fails. Rerouting is also a key part of the MPLS path restoral application. Rerouting is required when a failed LSR or link is detected. This is primarily accomplished via the various Hello and Keep Alive messages exchanged by the signaling protocols. A policy that activates path rerouting when a better LSP is discovered can also be implemented. This is often called "LSP optimization."

ADDITIONAL MPLS CORE TECHNOLOGY DETAILS ....

Additional MPLS core technology details include:

- MPLS packet looping
- MPLS multicast
- IGP TE extensions
- MPLS security considerations

MPLS Packet Looping

When a path is created that does not advance a packet toward its destination because a node in the path is erroneously revisited, a loop is created. Figure 4–24 depicts such a condition. Looping is an undesirable

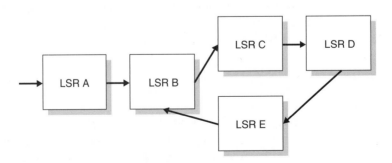

Figure 4–24   Example network with routing loop.

condition that can either be prevented or removed before loops use too much of a network's resources.

Loop Prevention Loop prevention is the use of logic to prevent loops from being configured. In Figure 4–24, the signaling software would recognize that the LSP trying to be set up contains a loop (A—B—C—D—E—B). The B node occurs twice in the LSP. The LSP creation would fail and the LSP setup would be appropriately modified.

Loop Mitigation Loop mitigation is a run-time check for loops. Variables within a packet or counters maintained at the routers detect loops and discard looping packets. Two popular metrics used for loop mitigation include counting the hops (using the TTL counter in the packet header) and the path vector value.

MPLS Multicast

While the current version of the MPLS architecture document states that MPLS multicast is "left for further study," there is a great deal of activity going on to investigate various architectural alternatives for this type of protocol.

IGP TE Extensions for MPLS

IGP TE extensions for MPLS have been added to provide additional link information. This additional information includes reserved bandwidth, allocated bandwidth, and link priorities (often called link affinity, or "colors"). This information is used in turn to update the LSR topology database to compute the constraint-based route calculation. This calculation often uses a modified Dikstra algorithm called constraint-based shortest path first (CSPF) to determine the optimal constraint-based LSP tunnels. The two primary IGPs being extended for MPLS are OSPF and IS-IS.

MPLS TE Extensions for OSPF The OSPF interior routing protocol has been extended for MPLS TE. The current reference is "Traffic Engineering Extensions to OSPF" (`draft-katz-yeung-ospf-traffic-04.txt`).

MPLS TE Extensions for IS-IS The IS-IS interior routing protocol has also been extended for MPLS TE. The latest work-in-progress

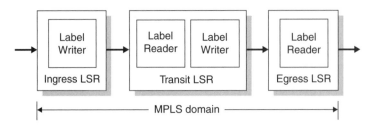

Figure 4–25   MPLS security considerations.

specification for these modifications is "IS-IS extensions for Traffic Engineering" (draft-ietf-isis-traffic-02.txt).

MPLS Security Considerations

Security is an important consideration for MPLS networks. Figure 4–25 shows the various roles that are present in the LSRs. A security policy is created on an MPLS domain basis to create and enforce security mechanisms such as authentication, authorization, and encryption.

MPLS ENCAPSULATION FORMATS ....

One of the great strengths of the MPLS design is that it can be encapsulated with a variety of Layer 2 protocols. These Layer 2 protocols include ATM, FR, PPP, and Ethernet.

ATM Encapsulation Format

The ATM encapsulation format is shown in Figure 4–26 on the next page.

FR Encapsulation Format

With FR, the current MPLS label gets carried in the DLCI field in the Q.922 FR header. This is shown in Figure 4–27 on the next page.

PPP Encapsulation Format

MPLS can be encapsulated in PPP. The MPLS Control Protocol (MPLSCP) is used for enabling and disabling label switching on the PPP link. MPLSCP employs the same packet exchange mechanism that is

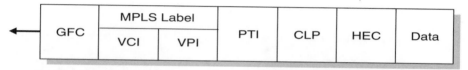

ATM Heater (5 bytes):
GFC: Generic Flow Control (4 bits)-For local sharing of congestion
    information.
VCI: Virtual Circuit Identifier (16 bits)-Identifies the virtual channel
    address.
VR: Virtual Path Identifier (8 bits)- Identifies the virtual path address
PTI: Payload Type Identifier (3 bits)-Distinguishes the difference
    between user data and maintenance traffic (e.g., management).
CLP: Cell Loss Priority (1 bit)- High or low priority for this cell
HEC: Header Error Control (8 bits)-Used by phyical layer to correct
    single errors or detect multiple errors in the cell header.

Figure 4–26   MPLS label into ATM frame.

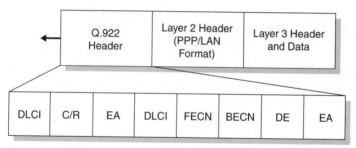

Note: DLCI size can be 10, 17, or 23 bits.

Figure 4–27   MPLS label into FR packet.

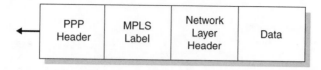

Figure 4–28   MPLS label into PPP packet.

used by the lower level Link Control Protocol (LCP) of the PPP protocol
suite. Exactly one MPLSCP packet is encapsulated in a PPP information
field. The PPP Protocol field is assigned a value of 8281 hexadecimal for
MPLS. This is shown in Figure 4–28.

Figure 4–29   MPLS label into Ethernet frame.

Ethernet Encapsulation Format

When MPLS packets are sent over Ethernet, exactly one labeled packet is carried in each frame. The label stack entries are placed between the data link layer header and the network layer header. Figure 4–29 shows MPLS Ethernet encapsulation. The Ethertype value in the Ethernet header is 8847 (hexadecimal) for unicast and 8848 (hexadecimal) for multicast. These Ethertype header values can be used with either the standard Ethernet format or with 802.3 LLC/SNAP encapsulation.

MPLS DESIGN AND IMPLEMENTATION ....

MPLS design and implementation can be modeled in several different ways. One method is to represent the MPLS core code as a context diagram (CD). This CD can be further refined as data flow diagrams (DFDs).

The MPLS Context Diagram (CD)

Figure 4-30 is an MPLS CD that shows the system as one central process.

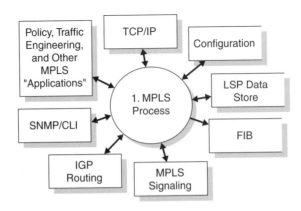

Figure 4–30   The MPLS CD.

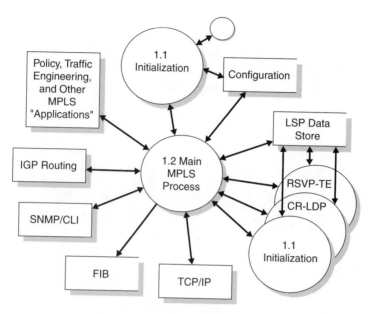

Figure 4–31   The MPLS top-level DFD model.

The MPLS Top-Level Data Flow Diagram (DFD)

The MPLS CD can be refined into a top-level DFD as shown in Figure 4–31.

This model can be iterated to many levels (second-level, third-level, etc.), owing to the complexity of MPLS and its associated processes and data stores.

An MPLS Reference Model

The MPLS reference model is shown in Figure 4–32 on the next page. It depicts the main process blocks that comprise an MPLS implementation.

MPLS SOURCE CODE
FOR IMPLEMENTATIONS ....

There are several commercial MPLS software stack vendors, including Data Connection, Future Software, Net Plane, Trillium, and Virata. Additionally, there are several MPLS source code implementations that are available for download via the Web. Three such implementations are:

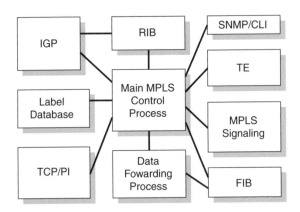

Figure 4–32   The MPLS reference model.

- The NIST MPLS switch
- The Source Forge MPLS for Linux Project
- CR-LDP source from Nortel

The NIST Switch

The NIST switch is an experimental set of MPLS software that runs on a common PC platform and allows the PC to act as an LSR. The software implements QoS and explicit routing through label switching. It also uses proposed extensions to RSVP to signal QoS requests and distribute labels.

The NIST switch runs over 10Mb and 100Mb Ethernet. It also supports ATM. The first supported operating systems for the PC platform included the UNIX variants FreeBSD and Linux.

Because it is being developed in a research environment, the code is freely available and designed to be easily altered. Each of its major modules such as the queuing algorithms, label databases, label distribution, routing algorithms, device support routines, and QoS policies are independently configurable modules that are readily modifiable and replaceable.

The NIST switch code is freely available as public domain source code. The code is based in part on other code that is covered by the BSD-style copyrights.

For more information and access to NIST switch source code and documentation, see the NIST switch Web site at: `http://www.antd.nist.gov/itg/nistswitch/`.

E-mail can be sent to: `nistswitch-dev@antd.nist.gov`

The Source Forge MPLS for Linux Project

MPLS for Linux is an open source effort to create a set of MPLS signaling protocols and an MPLS forwarding plane for the Linux operating system. The code is available at: `http://mpls-linux.sourceforge.net/`.

CR-LDP Source Code from Nortel

Nortel Networks has downloadable source code for the CR-LDP signaling protocol. The URL within the Nortel Web site is: `http://www.nortelnetworks.com/corporate/technology/mpls/source/index.html`.

SUMMARY ....

Architecture can only advance by deployment experience and improvements in technology. This chapter introduced the MPLS core technologies and major protocols. How MPLS uses the control plane and data forwarding plane to perform label switching is a key element of the framework.

Three main acronyms that apply to MPLS are: FEC, LSR, and LSP.

Because this is a **primer** ...

Below are the definitions for FEC, LSR, and LSP as found in the MPLS architecture document:
Forwarding Equivalence Class—A group of IP packets which are forwarded in the same manner (e.g., over the same path, with the same forwarding treatment).
Label-Switching Router—An MPLS node which is capable of forwarding native L3 packets.
Label-Switched Path—The path through one or more LSRs at one level of the hierarchy followed by packets in a particular FEC.

This chapter also dealt with other closely related areas, including looping, multicast, IGP TE extensions, and security extensions. The chapter also presented the MPLS encapsulation formats, design and implementation models, and references for source code implementations.

REFERENCE FOR CHAPTER 4 ....

1. Jonathan Green (ed.). *Morrow's International Dictionary of Contemporary Quotations*. New York: William Morrow & Company, Inc., 1982, p. 221.

MPLS
Signaling and
Label
Distribution

5

I took the one less traveled by,
and that has made all the difference. [1]

— *Robert Frost, "The Road Not Taken"*

With MPLS, labels are everything. Important activities surrounding labels include path signaling to set up the route MPLS packets will travel, as well as the label distribution that is required to assign the correct label to the correct MPLS-enabled router. After the paths have been signaled and labels distributed, the main MPLS function of label forwarding can begin. In addition to this functionality, there are ancillary tasks relating to labels, including label maintenance, retention times, ordering, and error handling, that must be performed.

Path signaling is the process whereby cooperating routers communicate acceptable paths based on parameters such as available resources, proper administrative permissions, and other policy decisions. Path signaling is dynamic, and each router along a path typically communicates with its neighbors to verify that communication will be possible. Signaling also allows for path establishment and teardown, priorities and preemption, optimization, failure recovery, and specification of QoS parameters.

A label distribution protocol is a set of rules and procedures that one LSR can use to inform another LSR—typically its upstream neighbor—about which label values will be used to forward MPLS traffic between them. The concatenation of next hops between LSRs becomes the path the MPLS packets will take. The path set up by these bilateral agreements about the label's meaning is called, of course, the label-switched path, or LSP. A label distribution protocol may use a specific control exchange, or the label values may be piggybacked on any number of standard routing protocols.

Label distribution protocols work with path signaling protocols to set up the control and label information that is required for MPLS data flows to operate correctly. This allows MPLS-enabled nodes to determine which labels are for use with which specific data flows.

According to the MPLS architecture, the decision to bind a particular label to a corresponding FEC is made by the LSR that is downstream from the perspective of the binding. It is the duty of this downstream LSR to inform its upstream LSR partner of the binding. To summarize, labels are downstream-assigned, and label bindings are distributed in the downstream-to-upstream direction. This is shown in Figure 5–1. (Note the differentiation between the control traffic and data packet flow traffic between the two nodes in the diagram.) It should also be reiterated that the MPLS architecture currently uses control-driven versus data-driven label assignment and binding. Label values and bindings are negotiated before any MPLS traffic ever flows on the data path for a particular label.

In addition to handling label distribution, the MPLS label protocols also handle creating explicit routes, dealing with TE parameters (bandwidth allocation, etc.), QoS issues, path restoral, and loop prevention.

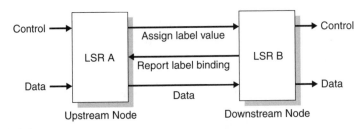

Figure 5–1 MPLS label assignment and binding

The MPLS architecture does not specifically preclude the distribution of labels via a single protocol or any other technique. This decision leaves the door open for standardizing multiple distribution protocols. Subsequently, several competing designs are being formulated within the MPLS WG. Each approach has its own benefits and drawbacks, and an LSR may choose to implement one or more of these protocols depending on the appropriate applicability.

The four current top contenders are:

- LDP[1]
- Constraint-based routing with LDP (CR-LDP)
- RSVP with TE extensions (RSVP-TE)
- Distributing labels with BGP-4

There are also additional proposals being formulated dealing with other routing protocols and label distribution techniques. The use of multicast protocols to distribute labels is being investigated.

Before discussing the signaling and distribution protocols themselves, there are two important concepts that are encountered when dealing with these protocols: the common message format and finite state machines (FSMs), which are generally used to control the flow of protocol messages.

The MPLS label signaling and distribution protocols communicate using messages. The most common format for these messages is the type-length-value (TLV) construct.

Because this is a primer ...

The type-length-value (TLV) construct is a method of encoding message parameters in an efficient and extensible manner. Each parameter is represented as a three-field tuple: the type field, the length field, and the value field. The type field is an implementation-specified value. The length contains the size of the value field in octets (exclusive of the length of the type and length fields). The value field holds the value. This construct is extensible because the value field can contain further nested TLVs, and there are generally reserved type fields that can be used for specific vendor purposes.

---

1. The acronym LDP is only used to refer specifically to the Label Distribution Protocol and is never used to refer to the general use of "label distribution protocol" (including LDP!).

The messages that contain the TLV constructs are used to advance the protocol state machines that are implemented by each protocol. Because more than one of these types of signaling and label distribution protocols can be implemented on an LSR, an FSM controls each instance of a protocol implementation. Often, FSMs are nested within the running state of the protocol FSM to control the state of each interface and session running the protocol.

Because this is a primer ...

A finite state machine (FSM) is a computational model that consists of states, events, and actions. There is a start state, intermediate states (such as "running"), and an end state, where the process completes. Each state can process a predefined set of events. When a valid event is received for the state (a "transition function"), a programmed action will occur. This action may cause the FSM to move to another state.
There are two common types of FSMs: a Mealy machine and a Moore machine, both named after their "inventors." The Mealy machine produces an output for each state event change, while the Moore machine produces an output while in each state.

THE LABEL DISTRIBUTION PROTOCOL (LDP)......................................

LDP is being designed from the ground up within the MPLS WG for the explicit purpose of specifying procedures for distributing MPLS labels. Because LDP works closely with IGP routing protocols, it is often called "MPLS hop-by-hop forwarding." LDP defines mechanisms for peer discovery, the basic label distribution protocol and its associated state machine, and LSP session initiation, maintenance, and termination. The standard also provides a mechanism for sending notifications and for loop detection for associated LSPs.

LDP Specifications

The primary reference for LDP is RFC 3036, "LDP Specification." Additionally, RFC 3037, "LDP Applicability," describes when LDP is relevant and appropriate in a particular MPLS context. RFC 3035, "MPLS Using LDP and ATM VC Switching," describes ways that ATM switches can be used as types of LSRs. These types of LSRs are called an ATM-LSRs.

In the MPLS WG, there are also five additional IDs that are being discussed and updated. They are listed in Table 5–1 by name, a brief description, and the current revision number as of this writing. For a more complete description of the LDP specification and its related documents, see Chapter 3, "MPLS Documentation and Resources."

Table 5–1   Current MPLS WG LDP IDs

Internet Draft Name	Description	Rev.
Definitions of Managed Objects for the Multiprotocol Label Switching, Label Distribution Protocol (LDP)	LDP MIB for SNMP	7
LDP State Machine	State machine for processing LDP messages	3
Fault Tolerance for LDP and CR-LDP	Enhancements to LDP for fault tolerance	1
MPLS LDP Query Message Description	Defines three new LDP messages for LSP queries	1
LDP Extensions for Optical User Network Interface (O-UNI) Signaling	Describes LDP extensions for O-UNI signaling	0

Introduction to LDP

LDP procedures allow LSRs that are running the LDP signaling protocol to create LSPs that have their end-points as either the next hop (i.e., the directly connected neighboring LSR, akin to conventional IP hop-by-hop forwarding), or as an egress LSR that is any number of transit LSRs away. The processes for discovering these two types of end-points are called basic discovery and extended discovery, respectively.

LDP recognizes a bidirectional association between two adjacent LSRs. These LSRs are called LDP peers, and they communicate over an LDP session that is created and run between them. An LSP can therefore be viewed as a series of LDP peers and their associated sessions. In Figure 5–2 on the next page, LSRs A and B are LDP peers communicating over LDP session 1, and LSRs B and C are LDP peers communicating over LDP session 2:

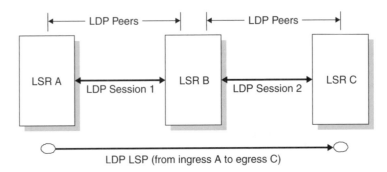

Figure 5-2 LDP peers and sessions.

LDP requires an FEC definition for each of its LSPs. Each FEC contains one or more parts called FEC elements. Each FEC element more specifically identifies which set of incoming packets will be mapped to an LSP at the ingress LSR. The LDP RFC notes that when an LSP is shared among multiple FEC elements, the LSP is terminated at or before the LSR where the FEC elements no longer share the same path.

The LDP specification currently defines two FEC elements:

- Address prefix—This element is an address prefix of any length from 0 to the full address size (inclusive).
- Host address—This element is a full host address.

The LDP specification defines the rules for mapping an incoming packet to its corresponding LSP. A complying implementation must apply these rules in order until the input packet can be mapped to its LSP. These rules are shown in Table 5–2 on the next page.

The LDP specification also points out several consequences of following this rule set path. First, an input packet can use an address prefix FEC element for the packet's egress router only if there is no other LSP that matches the packet's destination address. Second, if an input packet matches both a prefix address FEC element and a host address FEC element the tie is resolved by the packet using the host address FEC element's value. Finally, an input packet that does not match a specific host address FEC element may not use a corresponding LSP, even if the host address FEC element identifies the packet's egress router.

LDP is an application layer protocol that uses both UDP and TCP transport protocols to communicate with other LDP-enabled LSRs that can become its peer. Specifically, LDP on an LSR uses UDP for sending

Table 5–2   Rules for Determining LDP LSP Membership

Number	Rule
1	If there is exactly one LSP that has a **host address FEC element** that is identical to the input packet destination address, then the packet is mapped to that LSP.
2	If there is more than one LSP that contains a **host address FEC element** that is identical to the input packet destination address, then the packet is mapped to one of those LSPs. The procedure for selecting which LSP is an implementation consideration that is beyond the scope of the LDP specification.
3	If an input packet matches exactly one LSP, the packet is mapped to that LSP.
4	If a packet matches more than one LSP, the input packet is mapped to the LSP with the longest matching prefix. If there is no single LSP whose matching prefix is longest, the packet is mapped to one from the set of LSPs whose matching prefix is longer than the others. Again, this procedure for selecting one of these LSPs is an implementation consideration and not discussed in the LDP document.
5	If it is required that the input packet traverse a particular egress router, and there is an LSP that has an **address prefix FEC element** that is an address of that router, then the packet is mapped to that LSP. The procedure for obtaining this knowledge is also beyond the scope of the LDP RFC.

discovery messages to inform other LSRs of its potential candidacy as an LDP peer, and TCP for all other messages. The Session, Advertisement, and Notification messages require the reliable and orderly delivery transport that is provided by TCP for the LDP protocol to work properly.

The transport layer use by LDP is shown in Figure 5–3 on the next page. The well-known number for the UDP port for the LDP Hello messages is 646. The TCP port is also 646 for all other LDP messages.

The protocol associates an FEC with each LSP it creates for forwarding the packets that are destined for those LSPs in the forwarding plane. At the control plane, the LDP protocol implements its FSM.

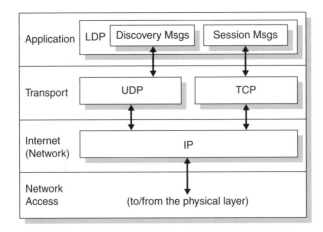

Figure 5–3   LDP as an application layer of the TCP/IP protocol suite.

LDP Messages

The LDP message unit comprises an LDP header and one or more LDP messages. Figure 5–4 on the next page shows the LDP message unit, which is also called the LDP PDU.

The LDP header is composed of three fields: version, length, and identifier. The version field contains the protocol number value. This field is 16 bits. The current value for this field is 1. The length field is a 16-bit value that contains the PDU length in octets. It is exclusive of the version and length fields. The maximum allowable length is 4096 bytes. Finally, the identifier field is used to identify the label space for the LSR that is sending the message. The field contains two sub-fields. The first four octets contain the router ID. The router ID is the IP address of this LSR. The final two octets contain an identifier for the LSR label space if the interface-wide label space, configuration is being used. If the LSR is using a platform-wide label space, this field will contain two zeroes. To summarize, the LDP header is ten octets.

The LDP message contains six fields. The "U" bit, the type, the length, the ID, a required parameters list, and an optional parameters list. The U bit is the unknown message bit that is used to determine if a notification for a received unknown message is sent to the sender (U bit =

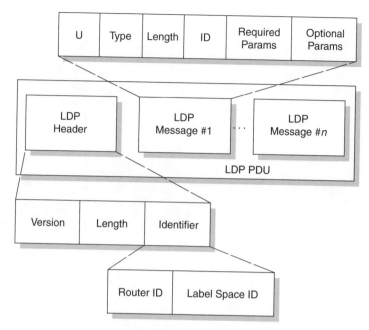

Figure 5–4 LDP PDU message format.

1) or not (U bit = 0). The message type identifies the various message types. This field is 15 bits long. The message length contains the octet length, starting with the message ID. This length field is 2 octets. The 32-bit message ID is used to uniquely tag Notification messages. The required parameters field is the variable set of mandatory message parameters for a particular message. Some messages do not require any parameters. If a message requires mandatory parameters, they must be in a specified order. Finally, the optional parameters field contains any additional optional parameters. If a message contains optional parameters, they may be present in any order.

LDP messages use the TLV encoding scheme within the required parameters and optional parameters fields. The current version of the protocol defines 21 LDP TLVs. They are shown in Table 5–3 on the next page.

The LDP specification defines 11 specific LDP messages that use these TLVs. The messages and their message types are presented in Table 5–4 on page 173.

Table 5–3 LDP TLV Tuples

TLV Name	Type Value
FEC	0x0100
Address List	0x0101
Hop Count	0x0103
Path Vector	0x0104
Generic Label	0x0200
ATM Label	0x0201
Frame Relay Label	0x0202
Status	0x0300
Extended Status	0x0301
Returned PDU	0x0302
Returned Message	0x0303
Common Hello Parameters	0x0400
IPv4 Transport Address	0x0401
Configuration Sequence Number	0x0402
IPv6 Transport Address	0x0403
Common Session Parameters	0x0500
ATM Session Parameters	0x0501
Frame Relay Session Parameters	0x0502
Label Request Message ID	0x0600
Vendor – Private	0x3E00 – 0x3EFF
Experimental	0x3F00 – 0x3FFF

Table 5–4   LDP Message Names and Types

Message Name	Message Type Value
Notification	0x0001
Hello	0x0001
Initialization	0x0200
Keep Alive	0x0201
Address	0x0300
Address Withdraw	0x0301
Label Mapping	0x0400
Label Request	0x0401
Label Withdraw	0x0402
Label Release	0x0403
Label Abort Request	0x0401

These 11 messages can be grouped into four basic types:

- Discovery messages—Discovery messages proclaim the availability of an LDP-enabled LSR for the MPLS domain. A Discovery message is also used to periodically remind other LSRs of a particular LSR's presence.
- Adjacency messages—Adjacency messages are required for establishing, maintaining, and terminating LDP sessions between any LDP peers.
- Label Advertisement messages—Label Advertisement messages are used to create, modify, and delete FEC-label mappings.
- Notification messages—Notification messages are used to send alert information and error messages. Specifically, there are two kinds of Notification messages: error notifications and advisory notifications.

LDP Discovery Messages   Discovery messages are used by an LSR to inform other LSRs in the domain that this particular LSR is available as a node for an LDP LSP. A Discovery message is a "Hello" poll

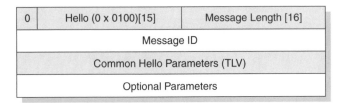

0	Hello (0 x 0100)[15]	Message Length [16]
Message ID		
Common Hello Parameters (TLV)		
Optional Parameters		

Figure 5–5   The Hello message format.

that is transmitted periodically using the UDP transport service to the "all routers on this subnet" group multicast address. When an LSR receives this message, it begins the LDP initialization procedure using the LDP Adjacency message set. After they are successfully initialized, the LSRs become peers and then begin exchanging Advertisement messages that deal with label specifics. The Discovery Type message is the LDP Hello Message, and its format is shown in Figure 5–5.

LDP Adjacency Messages   After an LSR is discovered, it initializes a TCP session with its newly found LDP peer by utilizing the LDP adjacency set of messages. There are four Adjacency messages defined for handling LDP sessions for peers: the Initialization message, the Keep Alive message, the Address message, and the Address Withdraw message.

The Initialization message is exchanged as the first message in the LDP session establishment procedure. The format of this message is shown in Figure 5–6.

The Keep Alive message is sent to help monitor the integrity of the LDP session transport connection. A Keep Alive timer is reset every time an LDP PDU is received during the TCP session, and each peer must ensure that the Keep Alive message is sent even if no other messages are

0	Initialization (0 x 0200)[15]	Message Length [16]
Message ID		
Common Session Parameters (TLV)		
Optional Parameters		

Figure 5–6   The Initialization message format.

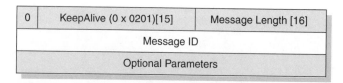

0	KeepAlive (0 x 0201)[15]	Message Length [16]
Message ID		
Optional Parameters		

Figure 5–7   The Keep Alive message format.

sent in order to assure the integrity of the connection. Figure 5–7 shows
the Keep Alive message format:

The Address message is sent by one peer to another to advertise its
interface addresses. The format of this message is shown in Figure 5–8.

0	Address (0 x 0300)[15]	Message Length [16]
Message ID		
Address List (TLV)		
Optional Parameters		

Figure 5–8   The Address message format.

The counterpart Address Withdraw message is used to inform a peer
to withdraw a previously advertised interface address. Its format is
shown in Figure 5–9.

0	Address Withdraw (0 x 0301)[15]	Message Length [16]
Message ID		
Address List (TLV)		
Optional Parameters		

Figure 5–9   The Address Withdraw message format.

LDP Label Advertisement Messages   Once an LDP session is
established between two peers, the label advertisement message set is
used to exchange specific information about managing the labels that will
be used in the LDP LSP.

0	Label Mapping (0 x 0400)[15]	Message Length [16]
Message ID		
FEC (TLV)		
Label (TLV)		
Optional Parameters		

Figure 5–10   The Label Mapping message format.

The Label Mapping message is sent to an LDP peer to advertise FEC-label bindings. The format of this message is shown in Figure 5–10.

The Label Request message is sent to an LDP peer to request a binding for an FEC. Figure 5–11 shows the format of this message.

0	Label Request (0 x 0401)[15]	Message Length [16]
Message ID		
FEC (TLV)		
Optional Parameters		

Figure 5–11   The Label Request message format.

The Label Abort Request message can be sent to abnormally terminate an outstanding Label Request message. The message format is shown in Figure 5–12.

0	Label Abort Req (0 x 0404)[15]	Message Length [16]
Message ID		
FEC (TLV)		
Label Request Message ID (TLV)		
Optional Parameters		

Figure 5–12   The Label Abort message format.

The Label Withdraw message signals to a peer that the peer should no longer use the specific FEC-label mappings the LSR had previously

0	Label Withdraw (0 x 0402)[15]	Message Length [16]
Message ID		
FEC (TLV)		
Label (TLV)*		
Optional Parameters		

*optional

Figure 5–13   The Label Withdraw message format.

advertised. This message should break the mapping between those FECs and their labels. The format of this message is shown in Figure 5–13.

When an LSR wishes to signal to an LDP peer that the LSR no longer needs a specific FEC-label mapping, the Label Release message is sent. Figure 5–14 shows the format of this message.

0	Label Release (0 x 0403)[15]	Message Length [16]
Message ID		
FEC (TLV)		
Label (TLV)*		
Optional Parameters		

*optional

Figure 5–14   The Label Release message format.

LDP Notification Messages   Notification messages are used to send alert information and error messages. LDP defines two types of notification messages:

- Error notifications—These notifications signal fatal errors. A fatal error causes the receiving peer to terminate its session and discard the corresponding label mappings.
- Advisory notifications—These notifications are used to pass status information about previous messages or general information about the session.

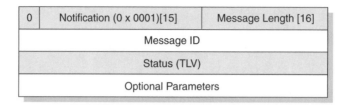

0	Notification (0 x 0001)[15]	Message Length [16]
Message ID	
Status (TLV)	
Optional Parameters	

Figure 5–15   The Notification message format.

The Notification message format is shown in Figure 5–15.

LDP Operational Issues

LDP supports four basic modes of label distribution:

- Downstream unsolicited independent control
- Downstream unsolicited ordered control
- Downstream-on-demand independent control
- Downstream-on-demand ordered control

LDP Scalability Issues

From RFC 3037, "LDP Applicability," the following LDP scalability issues are brought up for consideration when implementing LDP:

- LDP label distribution does not require a periodic refresh of its FEC-label bindings.
- Downstream-on-demand mode with conservative label retention can be used in situations where label resources may be scare, such as in ATM and FR environments.
- If resources are not an issue, LDP can be used in downstream unsolicited mode with liberal label retention mode. This configuration ensures that any changes in the next hops for an LSR would not require any label distribution because the labels would have already been distributed.
- LDP is limited in the total number of peering sessions by the number of allowable TCP connections.
- The use of path mitigation (the optional path vector loop detection mechanism) requires extra processing and resources at the LSR, and may impact scalability.

Security with LDP

LDP can optionally use the TCP Message Digest 5 (MD5) signature option. This prevents the insertion of spoofed TCP segments into LDP session connection streams. This use of the TCP MD5 signature option is similar to the way BGP uses this security feature. It is specified in RFC 2385, "Protection of BGP Sessions via the TCP MD5 Signature Option." The MD5 algorithm itself is presented in RFC 1321, "The MD5 Message-Digest Algorithm."

CONSTRAINT-BASED ROUTING WITH LDP (CR-LDP).......................................

CR-LDP is a variant of LDP that defines mechanisms for creating and maintaining explicitly routed LSPs. CR-LSP setup uses more information than can be derived from conventional IGPs. CR-LDP is used for MPLS applications such as TE and QoS, where extra knowledge about the routes is required. Also, CR-LDP is functionally equivalent to the RSVP-TE protocol.

CR-LDP Specifications

The main CR-LDP reference is still in discussion within the MPLS WG; therefore, the CR-LDP documents still exist as IDs at this writing. The main specification is "Constraint-based LSP Setup using LDP" (`draft-ietf-mpls-cr-ldp-05.txt`). There are also IDs being developed within the WG on CR-LDP for applicability, LSP modification, fault tolerance, signaling unnumbered links, support for Diff-Serv-aware TE, and GMPLS signaling.

Introduction to CR-LDP

CR-LDP is a set of extensions to LDP that facilitates the creation and use of constraint-based routing LSPs. Like LDP, CR-LDP uses similar messages for discovery, session establishment, label manipulation, and the sending of alert and error notifications.

RSVP TRAFFIC ENGINEERING EXTENSIONS (RSVP-TE)..........................

A major MPLS label signaling proposal involves the definition of extensions for the RSVP protocol to establish LSPs, distribute labels, and perform other label-related duties. The acronym for this effort is RSVP-TE. RSVP-TE builds on the RSVP protocol that was introduced in Chapter 2, "MPLS Background."

RSVP-TE Specifications

RSVP-TE is being developed under the auspices of the IETF MPLS WG. It is currently still in ID format. The current specification for this work is described in "RSVP-TE: Extensions to RSVP for LSP Tunnels," a work in progress by Daniel Awduche, Lou Berger, Der-Hwa Gan, Tony Li, Vijay Srinivasan, and George Swallow. (The current version is `draft-ietf-mpls-rsvp-lsp-tunnel-06.txt`.)

Introduction to RSVP-TE

The key concept of RSVP-TE is the notion of a "tunnel," or more specifically, an LSP tunnel. An LSP tunnel in this context specifically refers to the flow along an LSP from ingress to egress that is identified by its label. The label is always applied at the ingress LSR. An RSVP-TE LSP tunnel is shown in Figure 5–16.

A major application that uses LSP tunnels is TE. RSVP-TE is introduced here, and the general topic of MPLS TE is discussed fully in Chapter 6, "MPLS Operation and Uses."

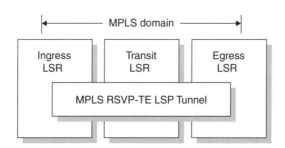

Figure 5–16   An RSVP-TE LSP tunnel.

RSVP-TE has six major features:

- The ability to establish LSP tunnels that may or may not require QoS differentiation.
- The ability to reroute an established LSP tunnel in a dynamic fashion.
- The ability to obtain the actual route that was traversed by an established LSP tunnel.
- The ability to identify and diagnose LSP tunnels as required.
- Under administrative control, the capability to preempt an established LSP tunnel.
- The ability to perform label allocation, distribution, and binding in the downstream-on-demand mode.

It should be noted that the current specification for RSVP-TE refers to unicast LSPs only; work on mulitcast LSPs is still under discussion.

Additional RSVP-TE Terminology

The RSVP-TE specification introduces additional MPLS-related terminology. These terms are presented in Table 5–5.

Table 5–5   Specific RSVP-TE Terminology

Abstract node: A set of nodes with an opaque internal topology that is grouped together as one for the signaling requirements of the ingress node. When the set only includes a single physical node, the additional term "simple abstract node" is used.

Explicitly routed LSP: An LSP that is not established via normal IP routing. The route is included as part of the signaling.

RSVP flow: A packet set with the same assigned label value set by the ingress node. Equivalent to an FEC.

Traffic engineered tunnel: A set of one or more LSP tunnels that carries a traffic trunk.

Traffic trunk: A set of flows grouped by their service class and placed on an LSP or set of LSPs.

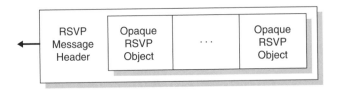

Figure 5–17   The RSVP generalized message format.

RSVP-TE uses several of the TE concepts and terms introduced in RFC 2702, "Requirements for Traffic Engineering over MPLS."

RSVP-TE Messages

RSVP is an extensible protocol. As defined in the RSVP functional specification (RFC 2205) and message processing rules (RFC 2209) specifications, additional objects can be defined that can be placed in RSVP for processing during RSVP message exchanges.

By adding these additional constructs to the protocol for MPLS, explicitly routed LSPs—tunnels—can be created. These tunnels are key to developing TE applications. The tunnels can be automatically routed away from various actual and potential network problems such as network failures, traffic congestion, priority traffic modifications, and other bottlenecks. In addition to these explicitly routed LSPs, RSVP-TE can also support LSP preemption and loop detection.

In the general case, an RSVP message contains a header and a set of objects that is used for each particular type of message. Figure 5–17 shows the generalized RSVP message format:

Within the RSVP message format, a further subdivision is possible. Certain RSVP objects are defined as a collection of one or more TLV triplets, or tuples, that can occur in the object.

For RSVP-TE, the main message exchange involves the ingress LSR sending the path message through the LSP tunnel to the egress. If the message has been processed correctly, the egress LSR sends a reservation message back to the ingress. The main RSVP-TE message flow is shown in Figure 5–18 on the next page.

To understand RSVP-TE, it is important to understand the Path and Reservation messages and the fields that comprise them.

The RSVP-TE Path Message   The first RSVP-TE message that is sent begins at the ingress LSR—also called the "sender" node in this con-

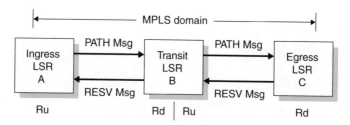

Figure 5–18   The top-level RSVP-TE message flow.

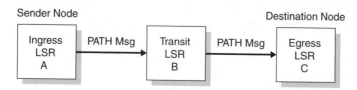

Figure 5–19   The RSVP Path message flow.

text—traverses the LSP tunnel, and then arrives at the egress LSR. The egress LSR is also called the "destination," or "receiver," node. The general flow of the Path message is shown in Figure 5–19.

The format of the Path message is shown in Figure 5–20. It should be noted that several of the fields are optional and need not be included in every Path message.

The purpose of the Path message is to establish the path for the LSP tunnel and derive key TE parameters.

The Path message contains five objects, three of which are optional:

- SESSION object
- LABEL_REQUEST object

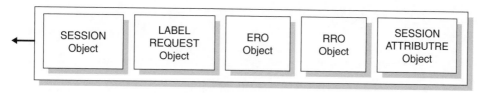

Figure 5–20   The RSVP Path message objects.

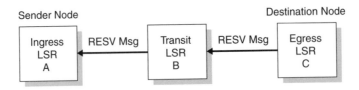

Figure 5–21   The RSVP Reservation (RESV) message flow.

- Explicit Route object (ERO; specifies the route as a sequence of abstract nodes)
- Record Route object (RRO)
- SESSION_ATTRIBUTE object

The RSVP-TE Reservation Message   The general flow of the Reservation message is shown in Figure 5–21.

The format of the Reservation message is shown in Figure 5–22. It should be noted that certain fields are optional and need not be included in every Reservation message.

The purpose of the RESV message is to verify that the LSP tunnel has been set up properly.

The RESV message contains four objects, one of which is optional:

- SESSION object
- LABEL object
- STYLE object (There are two types of RSVP-TE reservation styles: fixed filter (FF) and shared explicit (SE).)
- Record Route object (RRO)

RSVP-TE uses the downstream-on-demand label distribution technique.

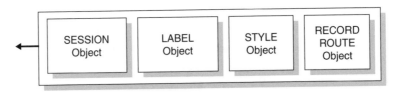

Figure 5–22   The RSVP Reservation (RESV) message objects.

RSVP-TE Reservation Styles

RSVP-TE defines two configurable reservation styles: fixed filter (FF) and shared explicit (SE). A reservation style is a set of options that is included in the RSVP-TE reservation request. In RSVP-TE, the reservation style is determined by the egress LSR.

Fixed Filter (FF) Style   The FF reservation style specifies the list of senders explicitly and makes a reservation for each one. Every sender has a dedicated reservation, and this is never shared with other senders. Each sender is uniquely identified by an IP address and LSP ID. The intent of the FF style is to create distinct reservations and maintain explicit sender selection.

Shared Explicit (SE) Style   The SE reservation style makes one reservation for a link that can be shared by a group of senders. Each sender can use a separate LSP. The intent of the SE style is to create a shared reservation with an explicit sender selection.

RSVP-TE Extensions

Several extensions have been defined for RSVP-TE to aid in its scalability (especially with regard to the soft-state nature of the protocol) and general deployment. These include Hello protocol extensions, refresh reduction, and new message extensions. Refresh reduction is described in RFC 2961, "RSVP Refresh Overhead Reduction Extensions."

DISTRIBUTING LABELS WITH BGP ....

Another design for distributing labels involves "piggybacking" the labels on conventional BGP Update messages.

Label Distribution with BGP Reference

This design is documented in the ID "Carrying Label Information in BGP-4" by Yakov Rekhter and Eric Rosen (see `www.ietf.org/internet-drafts/draft-ietf-mpls-bgp4-mpls-05.txt`).[2]

Introduction to Label Distribution with BGP

The Update messages that are used to distribute BGP routes would additionally carry the appropriate MPLS labels that are mapped to the same BGP route. Note that this design refers to BGP version 4 (BGP-4).

OTHER POSSIBLE MPLS LABEL DISTRIBUTION METHODS ....

MPLS signaling and label distribution protocols are continuing areas of discussion and exploration within the MPLS WG. Several other possible MPLS label distribution methods have been suggested. One involves the use of multicast to distribute labels.

COMPARING MPLS LABEL DISTRIBUTION METHODS ....

Since one or more label distribution techniques can be deployed, it is helpful to compare LDP with explicit route CR-LDP and RSVP-TE. LDP is used with conventional IGPs to create hop-by-hop LSPs. CR-LDP and RSVP-TE are used to create explicitly routed LSPs.

While functionally very similar between CR-LDP and RSVP-TE, the major distinction is that CR-LDP is a hard-state protocol, while RSVP-TE is a soft-state protocol. The two signaling protocols differ in message formats, how sessions are initiated and maintained, and many other implementation features. At this writing, the RSVP-TE protocol seems to be being deployed much more than CR-LDP.

---

2. As this book was being completed, this ID advanced on the standards track to RFC 3107, *"Carrying Label Information in BGP-4"*.

> **Because this is a primer ...**
>
> One distinguishing feature of communication protocols is whether they are "soft-state" or "hard-state." A soft-state protocol contains timers that periodically refresh the protocol information. Hard-state protocols do not use timers for this purpose and retain protocol information until it is explicitly removed.

SUMMARY...

Chapter 5 introduced and discussed MPLS signaling and label distribution. Because the architecture does not specify a particular methodology for accomplishing this, several methods were proposed, including LDP, CR-LDP, RSVP-TE, carrying labels with BGP, and others.

REFERENCE FOR CHAPTER 5...

1. from http://www.quoteland.com/qldb/author/127.

MPLS
Operation
and Uses

6

Distribution should undo excess,
And each man have enough. [1]

— *William Shakespeare*
King Lear, IV.I.72

The MPLS core technology and its associated label signaling and
distribution protocols are essential to the workings of MPLS. The
real reason for the dramatic rise in the interest in MPLS, however, is
because of its operation and uses: the applications. Applications are what
deliver revenue and what prompt people to become interested in the technology. The development of the "killer app" has long been held out as the
holy grail for further technology development and innovation.

Figure 6–1 on the next page shows a conceptual model of a fully realized MPLS-enabled network device, such as an LSR. Applications are
deployed within the device using MPLS as the enabling technology. The
three current Internet services—data, voice, and video—can be viewed as
vertical "slices" that are utilized by the various MPLS applications.
MPLS applications, in turn, are represented as horizontal layers that use

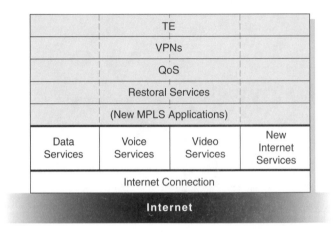

Figure 6–1   Internet services and MPLS applications.

the MPLS system software, hardware, and core technologies running on the device. MPLS uses the Internet to distribute and control the information flow that is necessary for the applications. Because of the tremendous amount of innovation in the Internet and MPLS areas, the model leaves room for new Internet services and new MPLS applications that are being conceived as you read these pages!

Internet services can be divided into three major groups: data, voice, and video. Each has its own resource requirements for operating reliably and effectively over the Internet. Packetized voice services generally require low delay and low delay variation. Voice applications can tolerate some data loss without perceptively degrading the performance. Packet data services can tolerate higher delay and higher delay variation than voice, and can also deal better with varying bandwidth. Most data applications can operate effectively with best-effort delivery, the current service quality found in most of the IP-based Internet today. Video, and its closely related service of multimedia (which is a more general service that delivers video, text, graphics, and animation in an integrated fashion), can accommodate a higher delay than voice, but requires no data loss to be effective. In general, multimedia-based applications can accept a greater delay variation, but they also have the no data loss requirement. Because these Internet services have such different requirements from the network, for MPLS applications to operate correctly, the services must be designed to efficiently use the network resources in the appropriate way.

MPLS applications are designed to provide schemes to more fully use network resources, including routes, links, and total bandwidth. There are also applications being defined for the creation of VPNs, and meeting the requirements for providing different levels of quality from various services. There is work being done to develop MPLS applications that can be used for path restoral and the diminution of network downtime and service outages. The flexibility of the MPLS architecture also provides the base for many other possible MPLS application developments.

There are four major MPLS applications currently being implemented and used in the Internet:

- TE
- VPN
- Internet QoS
- Path restoral services

Each of these topics could be the subject of its own book. Several new MPLS books deal mainly with VPN design and deployment, and there are others that concentrate on QoS and TE. One point that is not immediately clear is that these MPLS applications are closely related. MPLS applications are often used in combination by a service provider to realize improved network resource utilization and more reliable delivery of services. As the conceptual model shown is Figure 6–1 becomes deployed, these applications will play together to form a powerful information delivery solution (perhaps a "killer" technology?).

MPLS TE APPLICATION ....

TE is generally considered the first MPLS application that has been deployed. It was developed as an immediate need to offer alternative routing to the SPF algorithm used by conventional IP routing protocols. It is used to balance network overload by redistributing the traffic over alternatively chosen links and nodes. Because the IP routing protocols use similar techniques to create routes, a problem called "hyper-aggregation" can occur, where the traffic does not flow evenly when monitored at the network level. The objective of a network operations environment is to optimize how the network resources are used to provide the best possible performance and utilization.

What Is TE?

Looked at another way, TE is the process of matching traffic flows to available network resources. This is largely done by examining which resources are available and forcing the packet traffic to go through this specific directed path. The routing paths that are created are based on constraints. There are several constraints that are possible now in MPLS TE applications. These constraints range from bandwidth requirements and other network parameters to policies controlled by network management.

Because this is a **primer** ...

The terms traffic engineering routing (TE) and constraint-based routing (CBR) are two very similar—but slightly different—concepts. TE is often used in a restricted sense to refer to offline calculations of loose or strict explicit routes, while constraint-based routing is a more dynamic calculation of a traffic-engineered LSP (called a tunnel) at signaling time. Constraint-based routing is usually based on current routing attributes, including link colors, capacity, and utilization. Constraint-based routing is in "real-time," while TE routing is not.

An MPLS TE application must be able to compute the paths considering the known constraints. The constraints are stored in a data store in the LSR. This data store is often called the TE database. The TE database also contains data structures that store the topology of the network. This is also important information that is used by TE and constraint-based routing. This information must be propagated to the LSR peers so that there is common knowledge of the network and constraints present.

A final piece of the TE application is the ability to reserve the device and network resources that would be required to realize the constraints in the path. This reservation mechanism must also be dynamic, as the resource reservations need to be continually modified when the network is operational.

An MPLS TE application has additional mechanisms to operate, including extensions to the IGPs that are used in conjunction with the application (such as OSPF-TE and IS-IS-TE), the MPLS TE signaling protocols (RSVP-TE and CR-LDP), and perhaps, an algorithm used for

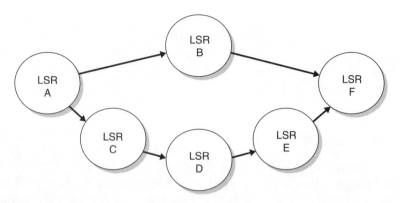

Figure 6–2   MPLS TE example.

path calculation. The current implementations are modifications to the Dijkstra algorithm called constrained shortest path first (CSPF). This algorithm uses constraints to create routes; it does not use the destination address's SPF method like conventional link-state IGPs.

Using TE in an MPLS Domain

Figure 6–2 shows how TE is used with MPLS. Conventional IP routing may calculate route A—B—F as the SPF route for a particular set of destination IP addresses bound for F. A TE routing CSPF calculation may use the TE databases in the nodes of this sample network and then create A—C—D—E—F as the traffic-engineered tunnel that would be appropriate for a given FEC whose traffic is destined for LSR F.

The benefits of an MPLS TE application include the capability to balance network traffic as a whole, plus the ability to route traffic around known congestion points in the network. Such an application acts as an aid to the path restoral application to provide viable alternative paths when various types of failure scenarios are encountered, and adds other niceties such as lowering operational costs, simplifying management, and optimizing the general efficiency of the network equipment and resources.

MPLS VPN APPLICATION ....

VPNs are currently being touted for their potential as a major revenue generating MPLS application for service providers. While the general concept of a VPN has been around almost as long as remote networking, its design and implementation with MPLS has uncovered several new and exciting twists. These issues include how VPN provisioning will be handled, who will do it, where the security will be implemented, how tariffs will be handled in an inter-service provider environment, and many others.

What Is a VPN?

First of all, what is a VPN? Or rather, what do "virtual," "private," and "network" mean when they are grouped together to form the VPN acronym? First, "virtual" means that the private communication resources of users at related sites get emulated over the shared public network infrastructure so that it appears that they are using a dedicated path. Next, "private" refers to the fact that the traffic is not commingled with non-VPN traffic. This usually involves a private address space and security mechanisms such as encryption and authentication. Finally "network" means more than one site is involved with the need for remote communications.

A VPN is a logical network that comprises two or more geographically separate physical networks that are connected in a secure way, often through a public internetwork such as the Internet. The general VPN model is shown in Figure 6–3. This figure shows two VPNs: one for network A and one for network B. The figure emphasizes the notion that a tunnel is created through the Internet to create a private and secure connection between the separate portions of each network. The term "site" is often used with VPNs to indicate a collection of users in one location. In Figure 6–3, sites 1 and 4 belong to one network, or enterprise. Network B comprises sites 2 and 3.

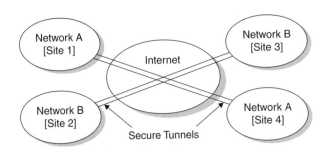

Figure 6–3   General VPN model.

There are three main types of VPNs: individual remote access, site-to-site, and extranet. Individual remote access offers the capability for a trusted user of a network to connect to the network from a remote off-network site. A site-to-site VPN connects separate portions of the same virtual network as shown in Figure 6–3. An extranet is another example of a VPN where one network allows another physical network to join for purposes of sharing information in a secure manner.

All of these VPNs share common features:

- Scalability
- Manageability
- Security
- Handling of private addresses

Scalability is a very desirable feature for VPNs because the VPNs often need to be expanded and enlarged as the business or enterprise implementing them expands. VPNs are often very dynamic when it comes to provisioning and configuration. VPNs must be manageable so that they can be configured, monitored, and controlled properly. Accounting management is also important for billing and other facets of customer care. Security is the feature that keeps the "P" in VPN. Security has become an increasingly key element in networking communications because of more frequent threats and attacks and the awareness of the importance of intellectual property and value of data as information. Because most VPNs now deal with IP, the ability of handling private addresses to assure the uniqueness of IP addresses is also essential.

In addition to the types of technologies that are used to implement them, VPNs are also categorized by the level of the OSI reference model in which they operate. There are two major classifications: Layer 2 VPNs and Layer 3 VPNs, although some have argued that MPLS VPNs are a new type—Layer 2.5 VPNs. It should also be noted that some vendors even tout Layer 4 VPNs. These operate on the Layer 4 header and are typically used for secure tunnels for a specific application. Common examples include e-mail and Web traffic. HTTP over the secure sockets layer (i.e., URLs prefixed with `https://`) is an example of a Layer 4 VPN.

Layer 2 VPN   A Layer 2 VPN uses link layer technologies and header analysis to create and deploy VPNs. This type of VPN typically understands how to encapsulate many different protocol types. Three of the most popular Layer 2 VPN protocols—Point-to-Point Tunneling Protocol (PPTP), Layer 2 Forwarding Protocol (L2F), and Layer 2 Tunneling Protocol (L2TP)[1]—offer similar functionality, but differ in the specifics of their implementation. All three protocols encapsulate PPP into an IP packet that gets sent between the remote access server or client and the terminating gateway device on the remote network through a secure tunnel.

Layer 2 VPNs were originally developed in the mid-1990s to connect remote users to a central site that contained an internal IP network. This is a successful and widespread technology that runs over FR or ATM.

Layer 3 VPN   A Layer 3 VPN operates on the network layer and uses the network header for implementing VPNs and routing. Whereas Layer 2 VPNs often encapsulate multiple protocols in IP, Layer 3 VPNs encapsulate IP packets with IP. Perhaps the major feature of Layer 3 VPNs is IP security (IPSec). IPSec is the IP encryption, authentication, and tunneling protocol standardized by the IETF.

MPLS VPN   Since the notion of a tunnel is an important aspect of MPLS, this technology seems a natural fit to create a VPN application. The "private" adjective in an MPLS VPN refers to the physical separation of traffic between the VPN LSP tunnels. It is very similar to the way virtual circuits are set up for ATM and FR VPN applications. Currently, there are two major directions in MPLS VPNs: BGP/MPLS VPNs and IP-based virtual router VPNs. Both approaches are based on the common VPN network model shown in Figure 6–4 on the next page.

The VPN customer site is connected to the service provider backbone by means of a connection between a customer edge (CE) router device and the provider edge (PE) routing device (which may contain virtual routers, or VRs). CE devices are preconfigured to connect to one (or more) PEs. In the VR model, multiple VRs can coexist on the same service provider PE device. CE devices can be attached to the PEs over any type of access data link (for example, ATM, FR, Ethernet, PPP, or IP tunneling mechanisms such as IPSec, L2TP, or GRE tunnels).

CE sites can be statically connected to the provider network via dedicated circuits or they can use dial-up links. Routing tables associated with each VR define the site-to-site reachability for each VPN. The inter-

---

1. L2TP is an Internet standard; it is documented in RFC 2661, *"Layer Two Tunneling Protocol "L2TP"."*

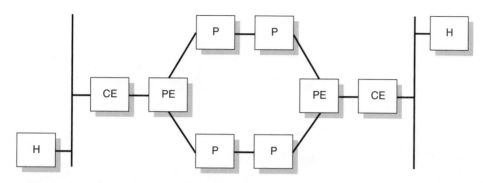

Figure 6–4   MPLS VPN reference model.

nal backbone provider routers (P) are not VPN-aware and do not keep a VPN state.

Both MPLS VPN approaches are similar in that they allow for service provider-created VPN service. A label stack is used to transport the MPLS VPN traffic from the customer site through the service provider core to the destination VPN customer site. In one approach, BGP is used to create special extended addresses for sending the packets through the MPLS core, and in the other, VRs keep separate MPLS path tables for each VPN. The actual implementation of these two approaches is markedly different, however, and which method will be deployed is a decision for the service provider based on vendor capabilities, interoperability, and other factors. There is a new IETF working group, Provider-Provisioned VPNs (PPVPNs)[2], that is developing a framework and related specifications to deal with these two and other types of VPNs.

MPLS/BGP VPNs   The MPLS/BGP VPN model involves the definition of extensions to the BGP exterior routing protocol for distributing routes over the backbone. These extensions are called BGP multiprotocol extensions (MG-BGP) and involve the creation of special extended addresses. These addresses are used to exchange reachability information among the PE routers. Only members of the same VPN exchange this reachability information. Each PE router in an MPLS/BGP VPN application maintains a separate routing table, called a VPN Routing and Forwarding table (VRF), for each VPN that it supports. Each VRF contains all of the routes for one customer. This effectively creates the virtual

---

2. See the PPVPN Web site at: `http://www.ietf.org/html.charters/`
`ppvpn-charter.html`

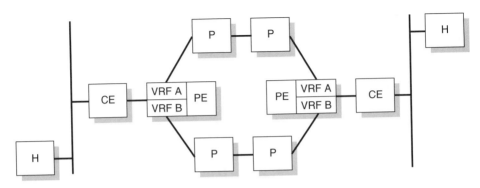

Figure 6–5 MPLS/BGP VPN example.

and private isolation that is required. This model allows for the use of overlapping private IP addressing by different enterprises. The MPLS/BGP VPN model is shown in Figure 6–5.

The main objective of this type of MPLS VPN implementation is to allow the service provider to provide the configuration and support of the VPN for the customer. A customer, in this case, can be an enterprise, a group of enterprises that need an extranet, another service provider, an application service provider, or even another VPN service provider that could use this MPLS application to offer VPNs to its own clients. This VPN model is a simple method for allowing customers to use network services in a scalable and flexible fashion. This model also allows the service provider to add value in areas such as management, security, and ease of use.

The MPLS/BGP VPN specification was first published as RFC 2547, *"BGP/MPLS VPNs."* It has subsequently been resubmitted to the WG, and is being refined again as an ID.[3]

MPLS IP-Based VR VPNs The other popular MPLS VPN model involves the use of VRs. A VR is a logical partitioning of a physical router into one or more logical (virtual) routers. Each VR maintains its own independent routing table for each VPN. Note that in this solution, BGP is not required for providing router reachability information. The VR VPN model is shown in Figure 6–6 on the next page.

The VR concept involves the portioning of a physical router into multiple VRs. Each VR utilizes the existing mechanisms and tools for configura-

---

3. The most current revision of the draft *"BGP/MPLS VPNs"* as of this writing is: `draft-rosen-rfc2547bis-03.txt`

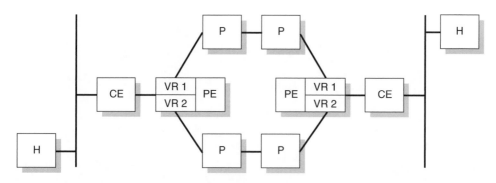

Figure 6–6   MPLS IP-based VPN example.

tion, provisioning, operation, accounting (e.g., billing), and maintenance. VRs can either share the physical routing resources or use separate instances. In this model, each VR has its own instance of routing to distribute VPN reachability information among the VR routers participating in the VPN application. The VPN application can use any routing protocol, and no specific VPN-related extensions are needed to the routing protocol for achieving the required VPN reachability. VPN configurations can be very flexible in how the VRs are connected in the backbone network with this VR model. The current draft states that this architecture can accommodate various backbone deployment scenarios: the VPN MPLS application service provider can own the backbone, or the VPN service provider can obtain the necessary backbone service from one or more other service providers.

The MPLS VPN model is still a work in progress and being defined as an ID.[4]

INTERNET QOS MPLS APPLICATION ....

An Internet QoS MPLS application introduces the notion that different types of service quality can be provided for the various types of traffic that are now traversing the Internet. This includes data, packetized voice, and video, which were discussed at the start of this chapter.

---

4. *"Network-based IP VPN Architecture using Virtual Routers"* (`draft-ietf-ppvpn-vpn-vr-00.txt`) is the current version of this proposal.

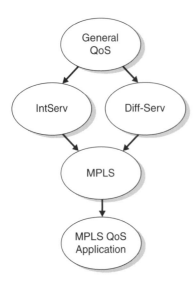

Figure 6–7   MPLS QoS application.

An MPLS QoS application is actually derived from applying general QoS techniques to the integrated services (IntServ) framework and Diff-Serv building block model of MPLS. This is shown in Figure 6–7.

General QoS

General QoS is the ability to guarantee at some quantifiable level that network nodes or applications can provide a satisfactory level of performance and reliability. QoS requires every element from the start of an application flow to its completion to be aware and respond to QoS requirements.

When QoS is applied to the Internet and the packet-based traffic that traverses it, QoS describes important parameters that are related to bandwidth, such as the assurance of low delay and minimal packet loss. The values of the requested parameters are a function of the nature of the Internet services used by a user application that requires a specific level of QoS.

Because this is a **primer** …

The terms quality of service and class of service are related, but slightly different concepts. QoS is the guarantee of providing a requested level of service. CoS is the category of service requested by each packet that is part of a particular application flow.

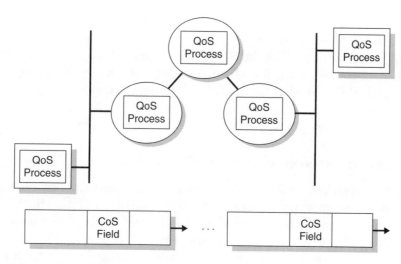

Figure 6–8   QoS versus CoS.

Figure 6–8 shows how QoS and CoS are related. They are very complementary technologies. They work together to provide a general quality of service to an application. Starting at the ingress of a route, the CoS field value is assigned. This CoS field is then analyzed by each QoS process running in the nodes along the way until the packet reaches its destination, hopefully within the specified QoS bounds that were established.

The IETF has created two efforts that directly relate to QoS and CoS: IntServ and Diff-Serv. IntServ and Diff-Serv can be used together with MPLS to realize an MPLS QoS application, although, as we will see, the Diff-Serv mechanism is what is used primarily with MPLS.

Integrated Services (IntServ)

The IntServ framework deals with resource reservations where network resources are apportioned to the needs of the application flows that will be using the device. The resources might also be controlled by IntServ policies created by network management. RSVP is the only currently implemented signaling protocol used for IntServ that communicates with the QoS processes running on the various nodes along the route.

The IntServ framework was defined to provide a source host to destination host (i.e., "end-to-end" connection) service connection definition for unicast and multicast application flows. IntServ uses RSVP to initiate a session between the end-points and to identify the service requirements of an application. This includes information such as the bandwidth, delay, and source of the data. The IntServ framework is not in widespread use because it does not scale for large networks (because of its "soft-state" nature; an FSM is needed for each IntServ session, creating a great deal of processing and signaling overhead). IntServ is specified in RFC 1633, "Integrated Services in the Internet Architecture: an Overview."

Differentiated Services (Diff-Serv)

Diff-Serv is often compared to a set of building blocks that can be used in various ways to prioritize packets in the QoS flow. With the Diff-Serv model, network traffic is classified by designated fields in the header and then examined at each node for the predefined treatment it should receive. The Diff-Serv effort was first focused on the TOS byte definition for the IP header, but has been expanded to a new definition called the Diff-Serv byte (DS) definition. The DS redefines the TOS byte syntax as well as its semantics.

Diff-Serv is defined in RFC 2475, "An Architecture for Differentiated Service."

The TOS Byte   The fundamental Diff-Serv concept is that each IP packet carries its CoS information within the packet header. A set of packets with the same TOS field value should receive the same treatment. The TOS field is shown in Figure 6–9 and was originally defined in RFC 791, "Internet Protocol Specification."

The TOS byte has two main fields: the precedence field and DTR field. The three bits of the precedence field are defined to mean:

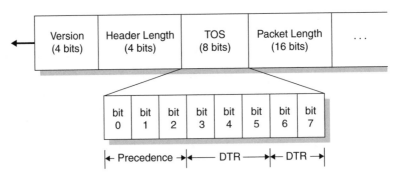

Figure 6–9   The IPv4 TOS field.

```
111 - Network Control
110 - Internetwork Control
101 - CRITIC/ECP
100 - Flash Override
011 - Flash
010 - Immediate
001 - Priority
000 - Routine
```

The DTR field contains a bit pattern that denotes delay, throughput, and reliability. The three parameters can be manipulated to create three basic choices that are a trade-off between low delay, high reliability, and high throughput:

```
Bit    3:  0 = Normal Delay,        1 = Low Delay
Bits   4:  0 = Normal Throughput,   1 = High Throughput
Bits   5:  0 = Normal Reliability,  1 = High Reliability
```

While the design of the TOS field was ahead of its time in concept, it did not receive much implementation in the field. This was mainly due to the fact that the exact way the precedence and DTR fields would be used within the network nodes was never fully agreed upon.

The DS Byte   The TOS field was later redefined as the Diff-Serv Byte field. The DS Byte field is shown in Figure 6–10. The DS Byte field uses the former TOS field location in the IPv4 header. The first six bits are used as an index value to a table implemented in the network node. This is called the Diff-Serv Codepoint (DSCP) field. The DSCP is unlike the TOS field because it is not a collection of bit fields. Thus, the six bits

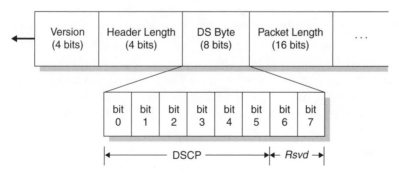

Figure 6–10   The IPv4 DS Byte field.

give 64 independent values. These values are called "codepoints." Bits 6 and 7 are reserved and are frequently referred to as the Currently Unused (CU) field.

The DSCP index maps to various data treatments that handle CoS. These data treatments are called per-hop behaviors (PHBs).

Per-Hop Behaviors   A PHB includes CoS handling mechanisms such as queue selection, scheduling issues, and congestion control. The currently defined PHBs include:

- Expedited forwarding (EF)
- Assured forwarding (AF)
- Default behavior (DE)

An EF PHB is required when loss, jitter, and delay must be low. With this PHB, the sum of all ingress rates in each node must not exceed the stated egress rate. This PHB generally prevents any queues in the node from increasing in size. This characteristic minimizes delay and delay variation.

An AF PHB defines a number of independent forwarding classes. Four are currently specified: AF1 through AF4. An AF PHB uses probability to determine service levels. Within each AF PHB, this is currently defined as three M subclasses that help determine the delivery probability. In times of congestion, the higher the M value, the greater the probability that a packet will be successfully delivered. This is a finer grained PHB in that each forwarding class can be independently configured for the node resources. This includes buffer space, queuing, and minimum egress capacity. The minimum egress capacity is realized by a scheduling algorithm. Three current scheduling algorithms that have been implemented are: weighted round-robin (WRR), class-based queuing (CBQ), and weighted fair queuing (WFQ).

A DE PHB is analogous to best-effort delivery, the current default behavior generally used in the Internet today. "Best–effort" means that the delivery will proceed after the other PHBs have been satisfied to deliver as many packets in as short a time as possible.

Because there are many codepoints still available, other PHB definitions are being debated. At this stage, they are still experimental.

A PHB is often divided into more friendly Diff-Serv service classes. The "Olympic medal" metaphor is commonly used to arrange these service classes into gold, silver, and bronze to correlate with the EF, AF, and DE PHBs, respectively.

The Diff-Serv building block toolkit contains another set of procedures in addition to DSCP and PHB. These procedures are called traffic conditioning procedures, and they further help to provide CoS and QoS handling.

Traffic Conditioning Procedures   While PHBs define the service quality, traffic conditioning procedures implement and enforce it. The full complement of traffic conditioning mechanisms is usually found in the edge LSRs of a network. The core routers need to implement just a subset of these. An edge LSR is shown in Figure 6–11. Also shown in the figure is an OSS that has three network management applications communicating to the LSR QoS objects via a management protocol.

In an edge LSR that contains a complete traffic conditioning implementation, there are five basic blocks: classify, meter, mark, shape, and drop.

The classify module is programmable and examines the IP header. This includes looking at the protocol field, source and destination IP addresses, and source and destination ports. The classify module maps the IP header fields to filters. A traffic profile is attached to a filter for a specific set of traffic.

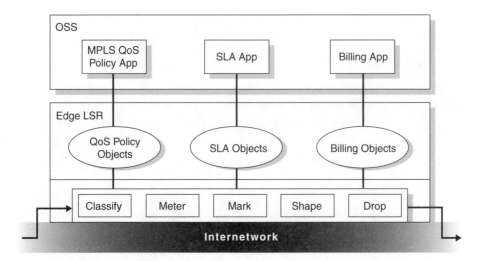

Figure 6–11   Traffic conditioning model.

The meter module maintains statistics on the traffic level parameters that can be used to help determine service level compliance. A customer SLA profile can include general parameters such as maximum data rate and average data rate, as well as more complex measurements such as maximum data burst at maximum rate. A notification process can be added to this module to alert the OSS that SLAs are being violated in the meter phase.

The mark process actively assigns the DSCP value in the IP header. The mark process uses information from the classify and meter modules to map a packet that is being processed with the correct PHB assignment.

Once a packet has been classified, metered, and marked, the shape process knows whether the packet is still within the configured traffic profile. If the traffic is within the profile, no action needs to be taken. If it exceeds the profile in some manner, the shaper "shapes" the traffic by buffering the packets to help regulate the traffic flow.

Finally, the drop mechanism is called when the shaped traffic exceeds the configured profile. This usually occurs when the shape buffers become full. The drop module discards the out-of-profile packets. Note that the shaping buffers are of different lengths, depending on the PHB, to properly provide the required QoS.

In addition to these five mechanisms, a basic router that supports QoS can also have additional queue management and scheduling. The control path also often contains admission control, policy control, and bandwidth brokers.

MPLS and QoS

MPLS uses a subset of QoS and applies several of the QoS mechanisms inside the MPLS domain. Figure 6–12 on the next page shows Internet QoS as an end-to-end proposition that is used to regulate application flows. Since MPLS operates in the transport network, which is within the IP-based QoS domain, its network nodes are part of a smaller subset, that is, the MPLS QoS domain.

IntServ and Diff-Serv can be used together with MPLS to realize an MPLS QoS application; although, as we will see, the Diff-Serv mechanism is what is primarily deployed.

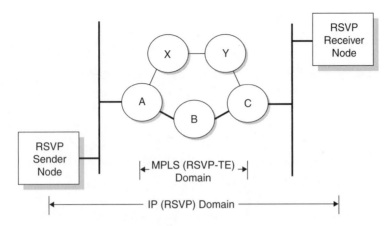

Figure 6–12   Internet QoS model for IP plus MPLS.

MPLS QoS Application

An MPLS QoS application is primarily derived from merging the Diff-Serv and MPLS concepts. The MPLS header originally contained a three-bit field that was called the CoS field. It was renamed the EXP, or Experimental field, to indicate that it may be used for additional purposes (found out through experimentation!).

The main working document for MPLS QoS applications is the ID work in progress titled "MPLS Support of Differentiated Services" (draft-ietf-mpls-diff-ext-09.txt). A new concept introduced with this work is the behavior aggregate (BA). A BA is the set of all IP packets that crosses a link and requires the same Diff-Serv behavior. This specification proposes a method for allowing the configuration of Diff-Serv BAs to be mapped onto LSPs for providing the best Diff-Serv objectives for the MPLS domain. A different set of BAs can be mapped onto the same LSP or onto separate LSPs. In this specification, the ingress LSR classifies and then marks the DSCP that corresponds to the BA. At the transit LSRs, the DSCP is used to select the configured PHB for traffic conditioning. Additionally, the specification promotes label space conservation and reduces the number of label setups and tear-downs required for signaling by only using multiple LSPs for a given FEC when required. The specification supports both the IPv4 and IPv6 formats for unicast traffic.

The two types of Diff-Serv LSPs defined in this draft are the EXP-Inferred-PSC LSP (E-LSP) and Label-Only-Inferred-PSC LSP (L-LSP).

EXP-Inferred-PSC LSPs (E-LSP)   An E-LSP can transport multiple ordered aggregates (OAs). The EXP field in the MPLS header is used by the LSR to assign the PHB to apply to the packet. An E-LSP can support up to eight BAs of a given FEC, irrespective of how many OAs these BAs span. The mapping from an EXP field to its PHB value for a given E-LSP can be either explicitly signaled at label setup time or it can be set up via preconfigured mappings.

Label-Only-Inferred-PSC LSPs (L-LSP)   The L-LSP can only transport one OA. The packet's scheduling treatment is inferred by the LSR exclusively from the MPLS label value, but the packet drop precedence can be additionally inferred from the EXP bits in the MPLS header. When the shim header is not used, as in ATM and FR, the drop precedence to be applied by the LSR to the labeled packet is conveyed inside the Layer 2 header encapsulation using link layer-specific drop precedence fields. For ATM, for example, the CLP field is used.

MPLS PATH
RESTORAL SERVICES APPLICATION ....

MPLS is offering many possible variations for path restoral applications. It is a simple concept with complex architectural and implementation considerations, and is currently a hotly-debated topic within the WG. Three primary path restoral scenarios are currently being considered for such an MPLS application:

- Local restoral
- End-to-end restoral
- Fast reroute

Three possible failure scenarios are shown in Figure 6–13 on the next page. The diagram shows that a failure can occur on a major LSP link, necessitating a switchover to an alternate LSP. This is called end-to-end restoral. Additionally, a link could fail so that a local switchover would cause the existing LSP to reroute around the failure (essentially

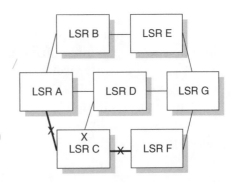

Figure 6–13 Failure points for an
MPLS path restoral application.

keeping the existing LSP intact), and the entire LSR could crash, bringing down all of the LSPs traveling through this router.

The principal behind fast reroute is to allow for the quick recovery of an LSP in the event of a node or link failure. Fast reroute provides a repair mechanism that is transparent to the user application, thus preventing problems such as application timeout, loss of data, or most other error conditions.

An MPLS path restoral application is very much a work in progress and many IDs have been written and discussed. Each draft covers areas that deal with failure and recovery scenarios.

One ID, "A Method for MPLS LSP Fast-Reroute Using RSVP Detours," (current version at this writing is `draft-gan-fast-reroute-00.txt`), was written by Der-Hwa Gan, Ping Pan, Arthi Ayyangar, and Kireeti Kompella. This document introduces a mechanism to establish backup RSVP-TE signaled tunnels. The application for this mechanism is particularly suited for large-scale networks. The proposal introduces two new RSVP-TE objects that allow RSVP-TE-enabled LSRs to create detours that can route around links and nodes as needed. This feature allows quick and automatic repair for an LSP, while successfully redirecting data to pre-computed and pre-established detour routes. A main tenet of this proposal is that packet loss is minimized.

Another path restoral ID is "A Method for Setting an Alternative Label Switched Paths to Handle Fast Reroute." The latest version, which was written by Dimitry Haskin and Ram Krishnan, is `draft-haskin-mpls-fast-reroute-05.txt`. This draft explains a method for setting up alternative LSPs to handle the fast rerouting of traffic when a primary LSP fails.

With all of the path restoral types, pre-established alternative paths can be used when packet loss due to an LSP failure is undesirable. Since predicting where a failure may occur within an LSP tunnel is difficult, path restoral applications involve complex computations and additional signaling to set up alternative paths to protect the entire tunnel. As an extreme case to fully protect the LSP tunnel, alternate LSPs should be set up at every transit node along the primary LSP.

The most commonly cited benchmark for path failure protection recovery is to emulate the 50-millisecond restoration provided in SONET self-healing rings.

OTHER MPLS APPLICATION DEVELOPMENTS..

There are doubtless many new MPLS applications being discussed and defined within the IETF. One possible application involves the use of hierarchical label stacking. Since the label stack mechanism offers flexibility in the number and uses of the MPLS label values, several proposals are emerging that deal with the number of labels and the values placed in them.

Another direction in MPLS application development is to provide support for inter-AS traffic. Mechanisms need to be put in place so that service providers can effectively pass MPLS traffic among themselves and resolve issues such as billing and SLA support. Work also continues in related areas such as multicast and security procedures. As the MPLS architecture evolves, new applications are sure to follow.

SUMMARY ....

This chapter discussed the practical application of MPLS operation and its uses. It introduced the main Internet services—data, voice, and video—and showed how these services could be used effectively by the current and emerging MPLS applications. The MPLS TE application deals with creating alternate routes through a network to more effectively use the entire physical network's capabilities. VPNs are MPLS applications that offer provider-based VPN service over the Internet using BGP protocol extensions or VRs. Internet QoS is used by an MPLS QoS application to implement and guarantee data delivery for the data, voice, and video services now being extensively used in the Internet. Path restoral services is a set of MPLS applications that offers mechanisms to recover from various link and router failures. The chapter concluded with a brief discussion of other possible MPLS application developments.

REFERENCE FOR CHAPTER 6..

1. from www.bartleby.com.

The Management of MPLS

7

A little knowledge that acts
is worth infinitely more than much knowledge that is idle. [1]

— *Kahlil Gibran,* **The Voice of the Master**

MPLS management is the monitoring and controlling of the applications, services, and all associated resources that exist inside an MPLS domain. SNMP is the most widely used standardized management framework used with MPLS. SNMP is recommended by the IETF as the preferred way of managing devices that are connected to the Internet.

NETWORK MANAGEMENT BASICS......................................

Network management is an essential component for deploying MPLS technology into a network. There are many vendors that offer different frameworks and platforms that can be used to manage LSRs, LSPs, and other key MPLS resources.

The functional requirements for comprehensive network management have been analyzed in great detail. The result of this analysis has been the subdivision of the network management functional areas into five major groupings. These groupings define "what" and are so commonly used in network management design and implementation today that they are often referred to by the collective acronym FCAPS. FCAPS stands for:

- Fault management
- Configuration management
- Accounting management
- Performance management
- Security management

When desirable features are defined for inclusion in network management systems, these features are usually mapped into one or more of the FCAPS functional areas. Network management applications are also categorized as one or more of these types. For example, a basic network manager would include a fault management application and a configuration management application. A full-featured manager would include applications covering the entire FCAPS suite.

Fault management detects, locates, and corrects problems in the network hardware and software. It determines and records that a fault has occurred, finds its location, and then attempts to mend the fault. An MPLS path restoral application, for example, could be informed that a fault occurred when the next hop on the active LSP was lost. It could then activate the standby LSP to keep the data forwarding path operational. Fault management maintains the state of the LSR and the links that comprise the LSPs using the device.

Configuration management knows and controls the state of the network domain. This includes knowing the devices and their interrelationships within the network. This management also specifically deals with the components that make up the LSR, including information on the system software and operating system, the types and status of the hardware boards, the states of the protocols, and all other related information.

Accounting management gauges the usage of network resources by various users and applications. It calculates usage with various algorithms that use the parameters of connection time, number of packets, packet addresses, etc. Internet billing uses accounting management to calculate tariffs, create SLAs, as well as maintain the MPLS QoS in the domain.

Performance management deals with the use of the network and often works closely with accounting management. Performance management deals specifically with how well the network is working. It allows network administrators to monitor key network variables such as throughput, response time, and general network availability. This type of management is helpful in pointing out where and how MPLS performance can improve.

Finally, security management is the regulation and administration of access to the network resources. It involves access validation and message security, which include authentication and encryption. The widespread deployment of the MPLS VPN application has made security management an important concern for the configuration and operation of these tunnels through the Internet.

NETWORK MANAGEMENT MODELS ....

Figure 7–1 (taken from [3]) shows the four models that comprise network management: the organization model, the information model, the functional model, and the communication model. In any effective network management framework, these four models must be present.

The organization model defines the basic components, what they do, and how they are related. In SNMP, for example, there are usually many

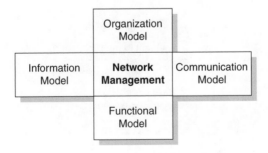

Figure 7–1 Network management models.

agents, each deployed in the device that is being managed, one or a few network management stations that run the applications that read and write to the agents, and a set of managed objects that represents the resources being monitored and controlled. The organization model defines a particular network management framework.

The information model describes the layout of the management information. For SNMP, the Structure of Management Information, or SMI, defines how the management information is structured. MIBs are used to describe specific objects. The functional model uses FCAPS to define the user requirements for what this network management implementation will do.

The protocols on how the management information is exchanged between the network management station and the agents are laid out in the communication model. The communication model can also be used to describe the interfaces between the layers that are providing and using management services. In SNMP, the protocol is also called SNMP (remember, the "P" in the acronym stands for "protocol").

As the importance of planes within the layer model has been shown with regard to the control plane and data forwarding plane in MPLS, it is appropriate to introduce the notion of the management plane and user plane. They are often called the "m-plane" and "u-plane," respectively. Both of these new planes are located in the application layer of the OSI model. The u-plane provides the interface to the m-plane so that key management information can be read and written. The m-plane implements the access to the management services. The four major MPLS planes are shown in Figure 7–2.

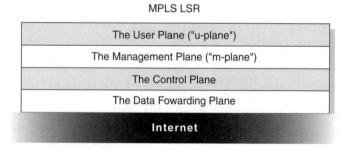

Figure 7–2   The "m-plane."

SNMP-BASED
MPLS NETWORK MANAGEMENT.....................................

The "S" in SNMP is often misunderstood by newcomers to mean simple, as in trivial or easy to understand. In actuality, the meaning of "simple," as it is used in SNMP, refers to the use of a basic model that employs agents that use as few resources as possible at the device under management. The complexity of the management task is, therefore, placed in the implementation of the network manager applications. This creates the basic SNMP model of simple agents being monitored and controlled by complex network management applications. There are many more details that go into the actual implementation of the technology. Appendix E, "A Detailed Introduction to SNMP," offers an overview of the main SNMP components and these details, and Appendix F, "RFC 2570: Introduction to SNMPv3," explains the latest version of the framework.

As has been stated, the IETF recommends that all devices connected to the Internet be SNMP-manageable. This, of course, includes MPLS LSRs. The SNMP framework specifies the major components that currently comprise SNMP. The framework can be divided into five key elements:

- The overall architecture
- A mechanism for describing and naming the managed objects and events called the SMI
- The management protocol for transferring the management information between a managed entity and a managing entity
- Protocol operations for accessing the management information
- Set of management "applications"

A key facet of SNMP is that managed objects are accessed through a virtual database called the MIB. MIB objects are defined by the rules specified in the SMI. Each resource that is to be managed in a device will implement the appropriate MIBs.

The MIB-II object ID (OID) hierarchy is shown in Figure 7–3 on the next page. It shows how the absolute numbering scheme that unambiguously defines every SNMP-manageable object is laid out.

There are four efforts underway in the MPLS WG for defining SNMP MIBs for MPLS management at this writing. (There is an additional MIB

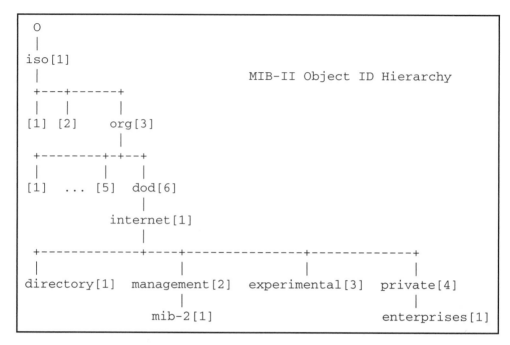

Figure 7–3 The MIB-II OID hierarchy.

that has just been introduced. It will contain the helper textual conventions that refine key object data type definitions.) One MIB defines the management objects necessary to manage the resources of the entire LSR from a top-level view. Another MIB defines the MIB objects for monitoring and controlling the LDP. An MIB has been defined for TE, and work is being done to define management objects for FTN table mapping. Each of these four efforts is currently described as a work in progress in the form of an ID:

- "MPLS Label Switch Router Management Information Base Using SMIv2" (LSR MIB)
- "Definitions of Managed Objects for the Multiprotocol Label Switching, Label Distribution Protocol (LDP)" (LDP MIB)
- "MPLS Traffic Engineering Management Information Base Using SMIv2" (TE MIB)
- "Multiprotocol Label Switching (MPLS) FEC-To-NHLFE (FTN) Management Information Base Using SMIv2" (FTN MIB)

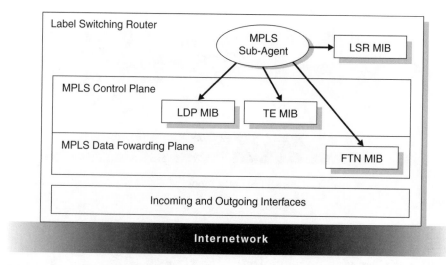

Figure 7–4   MPLS SNMP MIBs.

Figure 7–4 shows the relative location of the various MPLS MIB groups with respect to the model of an LSR. The LSR MIB contains objects that relate to the entire LSR. The LDP MIB manages the LDP signaling protocol, and the TE MIB controls the TE parameters and tunnels. Both sets of these objects represent resources in the control plane. The FTN MIB contains objects about key data structures found in the data forwarding plane, including key configuration and performance objects.

Beware: These five drafts are works in progress and in a state of flux. For the latest, definitive version of each MIB (whether it is in the draft format, or if it has progressed to RFC on the standards track), please consult the MPLS WG's home page.

Of course, in a fully SNMP-managed device, there are many additional MIBs to represent all of the objects that must be present in the network node for complete management, including standard MIBs, enterprise-specific MIBs, and any other MIBs that would be needed.

The LSR MIB

The LSR MIB defines the managed objects for monitoring and controlling an MPLS LSR. The current definition for the LSR MIB is the ID titled

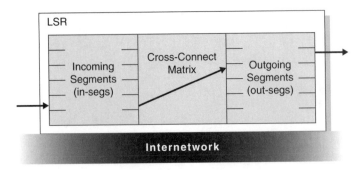

Figure 7–5 The transit LSR MIB model.

"MPLS Label Switch Router Management Information Base Using SMIv2" by Srinivasan, Viswanathan, and Nadeau.[1]

The LSR MIB allows for the configuration of both manual and dynamic LSPs for both point-to-multipoint and multipoint-to-point connections. It also allows interfaces to be enabled or disabled for running MPLS. Among other features, this MIB supports both per-platform and per-interface label spaces. The MIB also includes a full set of performance counters for monitoring in-segments, out-segments, and per-interface MPLS statistics.

A central concept of the LSR MIB model is the notion of a cross-connect. Figure 7–5 shows a point-to-point cross-connect that matches an incoming segment (in-segment) with an outgoing segment (out-segment) through the cross-connect matrix table. The LSR MIB supports the various combination of cross-connects: multipoint-to-point, point-to-point, and point-to-multipoint. In the multipoint-to-point connection, more than one in-segment is associated with an out-segment via the appropriate entries in the cross-connect table.

LSPs are configured using the LSR MIB by performing the following management steps:

1. Enable MPLS on the device interface.

2. Configure the appropriate in-segments and out-segments.

---

1. The current version for this MIB is available online at: `draft-ietf-mpls-lsr-mib-07.txt`

3. Set up the cross-connect table that matches the in-segments with the appropriate out-segments.

4. Specify any optional stack actions.

5. Specify any optional segment traffic parameters.

6. Monitor the meaningful LSR MIB statistics.

The LSR MIB comprises nine tables. The interface configuration table (`mplsInterfaceConfTable`) is used for enabling and disabling device interfaces to run MPLS. The `mplsInSegmentTable`, the `mplsOut-SegmentTable`, and the `mplsXCTable` are used to configure the in-segments, out-segments, and cross-connect matrix for each LSR, respectively. The `mplsLabelStackTable` can be used for configuring any optional label stack operations. The LSP-related traffic parameters can be optionally configured via the `mplsParamTable`. Finally, the LSR statistics can be queried in the `mplsInSegmentPerfTable`, `mplsOutSegment-PerfTable`, and `mplsInterfacePerfTable`.

All of the MPLS MIB modules can be tabularized into three important parts: textual conventions, the OID hierarchy that lists all MIB objects, and notifications. Table 7–1 on the next page contains the LSR MIB textual conventions that are currently defined. Eventually, all of the MPLS textual conventions found in the individual MIBs will be moved to the MPLS textual conventions MIB.

Table 7–2 contains the LSR MIB OID hierarchy.[2] This is the list of objects that comprise the LSR MIB.

---

2. The Access field acronyms are: NA = not accessible, RO = read-only, RC = read-create, AFN = accessible for notify, and RW = read-write. Certain objects, such as MODULE-IDENTITY and OBJECT IDENTIFIER, do not have access values and are noted with ***.

Table 7-1 LSR MIB Textual Conventions

Name	Syntax	Description
MplsLSPID	OCTET STRING (SIZE (0..31))	An identifier that is assigned to each LSP and is used to uniquely identify it. This is assigned at the head-end of the LSP and can be used by all LSRs to identify this LSP. This value is piggybacked by the signaling protocol when this LSP is signaled within the network. This identifier can then be used at each LSR to identify which labels are being swapped to other labels for this LSP. For IPv4 addresses, this results in a six-octet-long cookie.
MplsLabel	Unsigned32 (0..4294967295)	This value represents an MPLS label. Note that the contents of a label field are interpreted in an interface type-specific fashion. For example, the 20-bit-wide label carried in the MPLS shim header is contained in bits 0-19, and bits 20-31 must be zero. The frame relay label can be either 10 or 23 bits wide, depending on the size of the DLCI field, and bits 10-31 or 23-31 must be zero, respectively. For an ATM interface, bits 0-15 must be interpreted as the VCI, bits 16-23 as the VPI, and bits 24-31 must be zero. Note that the permissible label values are also a function of the interface type. For example, the value 3 has special semantics in the control plane for an MPLS shim header label and is not a valid label value in the data path.
MplsBitRate	Integer32(1..2147483647)	An estimate of bandwidth in units of 1,000 bits per second. If this object reports a value of 'n', then the rate of the object is somewhere in the range of 'n-500' to 'n+499'. For objects that do not vary in bit rate, or for those where no accurate estimation can be made, this object should contain the nominal bit rate.
MplsBurstSize	Integer32(1..2147483647)	The number of octets of MPLS data that the stream may send back-to-back without concern for policing.
MplsObjectOwner	INTEGER other(1), snmp(2), ldp(3), rsvp(4), crldp(5), policyAgent(6), unknown (7)	The entity that owns the object in question.

Table 7–2   The LSR MIB OID Hierarchy

Name	OID	ASN.1 Syntax	Access
mplsLsrMIB	1.3.6.1.3.96	MODULE-IDENTITY	***
mplsLsrObjects	1.3.6.1.3.96.1	OBJECT IDENTIFIER	***
mplsInterfaceConfTable	1.3.6.1.3.96.1.1	SEQUENCE OF MplsInterfaceConf Entry	NA
mplsInterfaceConfEntry	1.3.6.1.3.96.1.1.1	MplsInterfaceConf Entry	NA
mplsInterfaceConfIndex	1.3.6.1.3.96.1.1.1.1	InterfaceIndexOrZero	NA
mplsInterfaceLabelMinIn	1.3.6.1.3.96.1.1.1.2	MplsLabel	RO
mplsInterfaceLsbelMaxIn	1.3.6.1.3.96.1.1.1.3	MplsLabel	RO
mplsInterfaceLabelMinOut	1.3.6.1.3.96.1.1.1.4	MplsLabel	RO
mplsInterfaceLabelMaxOut	1.3.6.1.3.96.1.1.1.5	MplsLabel	RO
mplsInterfaceTotalBandwidth	1.3.6.1.3.96.1.1.1.6	MplsBitRate	RO
mplsInterfaceAvailableBandwidth	1.3.6.1.3.96.1.1.1.7	MplsBitRate	RO
mplsInterfaceLabelParticipationType	1.3.6.1.3.96.1.1.1.8	BITS	RO
mplsInterfaceConfStorageType	1.3.6.1.3.96.1.1.1.9	StorageType	RC
mplsInterfacePerfTable	1.3.6.1.3.96.1.2	SEQUENCE OF MplsInterfacePerf Entry	NA
mplsInterfacePerfEntry	1.3.6.1.3.96.1.2.1	MplsInterfacePerf Entry	NA
mplsInterfaceInLabelsUsed	1.3.6.1.3.96.1.2.1.1	Gauge32	RO
mplsInterfaceFailedLabelLookup	1.3.6.1.3.96.1.2.1.2	Counter32	RO
mplsInterfaceOutLabelsUsed	1.3.6.1.3.96.1.2.1.3	Gauge32	RO
mplsInterfaceOutFragments	1.3.6.1.3.96.1.2.1.4	Counter32	RO
mplsInSegmentTable	1.3.6.1.3.96.1.3	SEQUENCE OF MplsInSegmentEntry	NA
mplsInSegmentEntry	1.3.6.1.3.96.1.3.1	MplsInSegmentEntry	NA
mplsInSegmentIfIndex	1.3.6.1.3.96.1.3.1.1	InterfaceIndexOrZero	AFN
mplsInSegmentLabel	1.3.6.1.3.96.1.3.1.2	MplaLabel	AFN

Table 7–2 The LSR MIB OID Hierarchy (continued)

Name	OID	ASN.1 Syntax	Access
mplsInSegmentNPop	1.3.6.1.3.96.1.3.1.3	Integer32	RC
mplsInSegmentAddrFamily	1.3.6.1.3.96.1.3.1.4	AddressFamily Numbers	RC
mplsInSegmentXCIndex	1.3.6.1.3.96.1.3.1.5	Integer32	RO
mplsInSegmentOwner	1.3.6.1.3.96.1.3.1.6	MplsObjectOwner	RC
mplsInSegmentTrafficParamPtr	1.3.6.1.3.96.1.3.1.7	RowPointer	RC
mplsInSegmentRowStatus	1.3.6.1.3.96.1.3.1.8	RowStatus	RC
mplsInSegmentStorageType	1.3.6.1.3.96.1.3.1.9	StorageType	RC
mplsInSegmentPerfTable	1.3.6.1.3.96.1.4	SEQUENCE OF MplsInSegmentPerf Entry	NA
mplsInSegmentPerfEntry	1.3.6.1.3.96.1.4.1	MplsInSegmentPerf Entry	NA
mplsInSegmentOctets	1.3.6.1.3.96.1.4.1.1	Counter32	RO
mplsInSegmentPackets	1.3.6.1.3.96.1.4.1.2	Counter32	RO
mplsInSegmentErrors	1.3.6.1.3.96.1.4.1.3	Counter32	RO
mplsInSegmentDiscards	1.3.6.1.3.96.1.4.1.4	Counter32	RO
mplsInSegmentHCOctets	1.3.6.1.3.96.1.4.1.5	Counter64	RO
mplsInSegmentPerfDiscontinuityTime	1.3.6.1.3.96.1.4.1.6	TimeStamp	RO
mplsOutSegmentIndexNext	1.3.6.1.3.96.1.5	Integer32 (0..2147483647)	RO
mplsOutSegmentTable	1.3.6.1.3.96.1.6	SEQUENCE OF MplsOutSegmentEntry	NA
mplsOutSegmentEntry	1.3.6.1.3.96.1.6.1	MplsOutSegmentEntry	NA
mplsOutSegmentIndex	1.3.6.1.3.96.1.6.1.1	Integer32 (0..2147483647)	AFN
mplsOutSegmentIfIndex	1.3.6.1.3.96.1.6.1.2	InterfaceIndex	RC
mplsOutSegmentPushTopLabel	1.3.6.1.3.96.1.6.1.3	TruthValue	RC
mplsOutSegmentTopLabel	1.3.6.1.3.96.1.6.1.4	MplsLabel	RC
mplsOutSegmentNextHopIpAddrType	1.3.6.1.3.96.1.6.1.5	InetAddressType	RC

Table 7–2   The LSR MIB OID Hierarchy (continued)

Name	OID	ASN.1 Syntax	Access
mplsOutSegmentNextHopIpv4Addr	1.3.6.1.3.96.1.6.1.6	InetAddressIPv4	RC
mplsOutSegmentNextHopIpv6Addr	1.3.6.1.3.96.1.6.1.7	InetAddressIPv6	RC
mplsOutSegmentXCIndex	1.3.6.1.3.96.1.6.1.8	Integer32 (0..2147483647)	RO
mplsOutSegmentOwner	1.3.6.1.3.96.1.6.1.9	MplsObjectOwner	RC
mplsOutSegmentTrafficParamPtr	1.3.6.1.3.96.1.6.1.10	RowPointer	RC
mplsOutSegmentRowStatus	1.3.6.1.3.96.1.6.1.11	RowStatus	RC
mplsOutSegmentStorageType	1.3.6.1.3.96.1.6.1.12	StorageType	RC
mplsOutSegmentPerfTable	1.3.6.1.3.96.1.7	SEQUENCE OF MplsOutSegment PerfEntry	NA
mplsOutSegmentPerfEntry	1.3.6.1.3.96.1.7.1	MplsOutSegment PerfEntry	NA
mplsOutSegmentOctets	1.3.6.1.3.96.1.7.1.1	Counter32	RO
mplsOutSegmentPackets	1.3.6.1.3.96.1.7.1.2	Counter32	RO
mplsOutSegmentErrors	1.3.6.1.3.96.1.7.1.3	Counter32	RO
mplsOutSegmentDiscards	1.3.6.1.3.96.1.7.1.4	Counter32	RO
mplsOutSegmentHCOctets	1.3.6.1.3.96.1.7.1.5	Counter64	RO
mplsOutSegmentPerfDiscontinuityTime	1.3.6.1.3.96.1.7.1.6	TimeStamp	RO
mplsXCIndexNext	1.3.6.1.3.96.1.8	Integer32 (0..2147483647)	RO
mplsXCTable	1.3.6.1.3.96.1.9	SEQUENCE OF MplsXCEntry	NA
mplsXCEntry	1.3.6.1.3.96.1.9.1	MplsXCEntry	NA
mplsXCIndex	1.3.6.1.3.96.1.9.1.1	Integer32 (1..2147483647)	AFN
mplsXCLspId	1.3.6.1.3.96.1.9.1.2	MplsLSPID	RC
mplsXCLabelStackIndex	1.3.6.1.3.96.1.9.1.3	Integer32 (0..2147483647)	RC
mplsXCIsPersistent	1.3.6.1.3.96.1.9.1.4	TruthValue	RC
mplsXCOwner	1.3.6.1.3.96.1.9.1.5	MplsObjectOwner	RC

Table 7–2   The LSR MIB OID Hierarchy (continued)

Name	OID	ASN.1 Syntax	Access
mplsXCRowStatus	1.3.6.1.3.96.1.9.1.6	RowStatus	RC
mplsXCStorageType	1.3.6.1.3.96.1.9.1.7	StorageType	RC
mplsXCAdminStatus	1.3.6.1.3.96.1.9.1.8	INTEGER	RC
mplsXCOperStatus	1.3.6.1.3.96.1.9.1.9	INTEGER	RO
mplsMaxLabelStackDepth	1.3.6.1.3.96.1.10	Integer32 (1..2147483647)	RO
mplsLabelStackIndexNext	1.3.6.1.3.96.1.11	Integer32 (0..2147483647)	RO
mplsLabelStackTable	1.3.6.1.3.96.1.12	SEQUENCE OF MplsLabelStackEntry	NA
mplsLabelStackEntry	1.3.6.1.3.96.1.12.1	MplsLabelStackEntry	NA
mplsLabelStackIndex	1.3.6.1.3.96.1.12.1.1	Integer32 (1..2147483647)	NA
mplsLabelStackLabelIndex	1.3.6.1.3.96.1.12.1.2	Integer32 (1..2147483647)	NA
mplsLabelStackLabel	1.3.6.1.3.96.1.12.1.3	MplsLabel	RC
mplsLabelStackRowStatus	1.3.6.1.3.96.1.12.1.4	RowStatus	RC
mplsLabelStackStorageType	1.3.6.1.3.96.1.12.1.5	StorageType	RC
mplsTrafficParamIndexNext	1.3.6.1.3.96.1.13	Integer32 (0..2147483647)	RO
mplsTrafficParamTable	1.3.6.1.3.96.1.14	SEQUENCE OF MplsTrafficParam Entry	NA
mplsTrafficParamEntry	1.3.6.1.3.96.1.14.1	MplsTrafficParam Entry	NA
mplsTrafficParamIndex	1.3.6.1.3.96.1.14.1.1	Integer32 (1..2147483647)	NA
mplsTrafficParamMaxRate	1.3.6.1.3.96.1.14.1.2	MplsBitRate	RC
mplsTrafficParamMeanRate	1.3.6.1.3.96.1.14.1.3	MplsBitRate	RC
mplsTrafficParamMaxBurstSize	1.3.6.1.3.96.1.14.1.4	MplsBitRate	RC
mplsTrafficParamRowStatus	1.3.6.1.3.96.1.14.1.5	RowStatus	RC

Table 7–2 The LSR MIB OID Hierarchy (continued)

Name	OID	ASN.1 Syntax	Access
mplsTrafficParamStorageType	1.3.6.1.3.96.1.14.1.6	StorageType	RC
mplsXCTrapEnable	1.3.6.1.3.96.1.15	TruthValue	RW
mplsLsrNotifications	1.3.6.1.3.96.2	OBJECT IDENTIFIER	***
mplsLsrNotifyPrefix	1.3.6.1.3.96.2.0	OBJECT IDENTIFIER	***
mplsXCUp	1.3.6.1.3.96.2.0.1	NOTIFICATION-TYPE	***
mplsXCDown	1.3.6.1.3.96.2.0.2	NOTIFICATION-TYPE	***
mplsLsrConformance	1.3.6.1.3.96.3	OBJECT IDENTIFIER	***
mplsLsrGroups	1.3.6.1.3.96.3.1	OBJECT IDENTIFIER	***
mplsInterfaceGroup	1.3.6.1.3.96.3.1.1	OBJECT-GROUP	***
mplsInSegmentGroup	1.3.6.1.3.96.3.1.2	OBJECT-GROUP	***
mplsOutSegmentGroup	1.3.6.1.3.96.3.1.3	OBJECT-GROUP	***
mplsXCGroup	1.3.6.1.3.96.3.1.4	OBJECT-GROUP	***
mplsXCOptionalGroup	1.3.6.1.3.96.3.1.5	OBJECT-GROUP	***
mplsPerfGroup	1.3.6.1.3.96.3.1.6	OBJECT-GROUP	***
mplsHCInSegmentPerfGroup	1.3.6.1.3.96.3.1.7	OBJECT-GROUP	***
mplsHCOutSegmentPerfGroup	1.3.6.1.3.96.3.1.8	OBJECT-GROUP	***
mplsTrafficParamGroup	1.3.6.1.3.96.3.1.9	OBJECT-GROUP	***
mplsXCIsPersistentGroup	1.3.6.1.3.96.3.1.10	OBJECT-GROUP	***
mplsXCIsNotPersistentGroup	1.3.6.1.3.96.3.1.11	OBJECT-GROUP	***
mplsLabelStackGroup	1.3.6.1.3.96.3.1.12	OBJECT-GROUP	***
mplsSegmentDiscontinuityGroup	1.3.6.1.3.96.3.1.13	OBJECT-GROUP	***
mplsLsrNotificationGroup	1.3.6.1.3.96.3.1.14	OBJECT-GROUP	***
mplsLsrCompliances	1.3.6.1.3.96.3.2	OBJECT IDENTIFIER	***
mplsLsrModuleCompliance	1.3.6.1.3.96.3.2.1	MODULE-COMPLIANCE	***

Table 7–3 contains the LSR notifications currently defined.

Table 7–3 LSR MIB Notifications

Name	Description
MplsXCUp	This notification is generated when an `mplsXCOperStatus` object for one of the configured cross-connect entries is about to leave the `down` state and transition into some other state (but not into the `notPresent` state). This other state is indicated by the included value of `mplsXCOperStatus`.
MplsXCDown	This notification is generated when an `mplsXCOperStatus` object for one of the configured cross-connect entries is about to enter the `down` state and transition into some other state (but not into the `notPresent` state). This other state is indicated by the included value of `mplsXCOperStatus`.

The LSR MIB document contains a sample usage for setting up an LSP using this MIB. [2] The example is for a best-effort, unidirectional[3] LSP. The in-segment, cross-connect, and out-segment are shown in Figure 7–6. Incoming packets arrive at interface A, which has an `ifIndex` of 12. Outgoing packets will leave through interface B, which has an `ifIndex` of 13. It is assumed that the label stack has a depth of one.

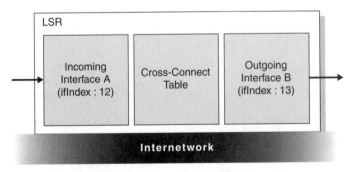

Figure 7–6 Example usage of the LSR MIB model.

---

3. The LSR MIB allows for the creation of bidirectional LSPs. At the ingress, for example, with a bi-directional tunnel, the in-segment would terminate at this point and the out-segment would originate here.

The first step is to set up the traffic parameters for both segments:

```
In mplsTrafficParamTable for the incoming direction:
{
    mplsTrafficParamIndex            = 5
    mplsTrafficParamMaxRate          = 100000,
    mplsTrafficParamMeanRate         = 100000,
    mplsTrafficParamMaxBurstSize     = 2000,
    mplsTrafficParamRowStatus        = createAndGo(4)
}
```

and:

```
In mplsTrafficParamTable for the outgoing direction:
{
    mplsTrafficParamIndex            = 6
    mplsTrafficParamMaxRate          = 100000,
    mplsTrafficParamMeanRate         = 100000,
    mplsTrafficParamMaxBurstSize     = 2000,
    mplsTrafficParamRowStatus        = createAndGo(4)
}
```

Next, the appropriate in-segment and out-segment entries with suitable traffic parameters are set up by pointing at the appropriate traffic parameter entries that were just created above:

```
In mplsInSegmentTable:
{
    mplsInSegmentIfIndex             = 12, -- incoming interface
    mplsInSegmentLabel               = 21, -- incoming label
    mplsInSegmentNPop                = 1,
    mplsInSegmentTrafficParamPtr     = mplsTrafficParamIndex.5,
    mplsInSegmentRowStatus           = createAndGo(4)
}
```

and:

```
In mplsOutSegmentTable:
{
    mplsOutSegmentIndex              = 1,
    mplsOutSegmentIfIndex            = 13, -- outgoing interface
    mplsOutSegmentPushTopLabel       = true(1),
    mplsOutSegmentTopLabel           = 22, -- outgoing label
    mplsOutSegmentTrafficParamPtr    = mplsTrafficParamIndex.6,
    mplsOutSegmentRowStatus          = createAndGo(4)
}
```

Finally, the cross-connect entry is created by associating the newly created in- and out-segments:

```
In mplsXCTable:
{
   mplsXCIndex              = 2,
   mplsXCLspId              = 'c021041502'H, -- 192.33.4.21.2
   mplsInSegmentIfIndex     = 12,
   mplsInSegmentLabel       = 21,
   mplsOutSegmentIndex      = 1,
   mplsXCIsPersistent       = false (1),
   mplsLabelStackIndex      = 0, -- only a single outgoing label
   mplsXCRowStatus          = createAndGo(4)
}
```

The MIB document notes that the `mplsInSegmentXCIndex` and `mplsOutSegmentXCIndex` objects will automatically be assigned the value 2 when these segments are referred to from the corresponding cross-connect entry.

The LDP MIB

The MIB objects for managing the LDP are defined in the ID titled "Definitions of Managed Objects for the Multiprotocol Label Switching, Label Distribution Protocol (LDP)" by Cucchiara, Sjostrand, and Luciani[4]. The LDP MIB contains the objects that can be accessed to configure LDP sessions on the specified LSR. In the MIB, each row represents an LDP session. There is also another table for discovered peers.

The current definition of the MIB is divided into six groups:

- The MPLS LDP general group
- The MPLS LDP generic group
- The MPLS LDP mapping group
- The MPLS LDP notifications group
- The MPLS LDP ATM group
- The MPLS LDP FR group

The general and notifications groups should always be supported. The generic group is for managing generic label implementations. The

---

4. The latest revision is available online as: `draft-ietf-mpls-ldp-mib-08.txt`

ATM and FR groups only need to be supported if the respective protocol is running on the LSR. The mapping group is used if the cross-connect tables from the LSR MIB are also implemented.

Table 7–4 contains the LDP MIB OID hierarchy.

Table 7–4   The LDP MIB OID Hierarchy

Name	OID	ASN.1 Syntax	Access
mplsMIB	1.3.6.1.2.1.10.n*	OBJECT IDENTIFIER	***
mplsLdpMIB	1.3.6.1.2.1.10.$n.x$**	MODULE-IDENTITY	***
mplsLdpObjects	1.3.6.1.2.1.10.$n.x$.1	OBJECT IDENTIFIER	***
mplsLdpLsrObjects	1.3.6.1.2.1.10.$n.x$.1.1	OBJECT IDENTIFIER	***
mplsLdpLsrId	1.3.6.1.2.1.10.$n.x$.1.1.1	MplsLsrIdentifier	RO
mplsLdpLsrLoopDetectionCapable	1.3.6.1.2.1.10.$n.x$.1.1.2	INTEGER	RO
mplsLdpEntityObjects	1.3.6.1.2.1.10.$n.x$.1.2	OBJECT IDENTIFIER	***
mplsLdpEntityIndexNext	1.3.6.1.2.1.10.$n.x$.1.2.1	Unsigned32 (0..4294967295)	RO
mplsLdpEntityTable	1.3.6.1.2.1.10.$n.x$.1.2.2	SEQUENCE OF MplsLdpEntity Entry	NA
mplsLdpEntityEntry	1.3.6.1.2.1.10.$n.x$.1.2.2.1	MplsLdpEntity Entry	NA
mplsLdpEntityLdpId	1.3.6.1.2.1.10.$n.x$.1.2.2.1.1	MplsLdpIndentifier	NA
mplsLdpEntityIndex	1.3.6.1.2.1.10.$n.x$.1.2.2.1.2	Unsigned32	NA
mplsLdpEntityProtocolVersion	1.3.6.1.2.1.10.$n.x$.1.2.2.1.3	Integer32	RC
mplsLdpEntityAdminStatus	1.3.6.1.2.1.10.$n.x$.1.2.2.1.4	INTEGER	RC
mplsLdpEntityOperStatus	1.3.6.1.2.1.10.$n.x$.1.2.2.1.5	INTEGER	RO
mplsLdpEntityTcpDscPort	1.3.6.1.2.1.10.$n.x$.1.2.2.1.6	Unsigned32	RC
mplsLdpEntityUdpDscPort	1.3.6.1.2.1.10.$n.x$.1.2.2.1.7	Unsigned32	RC
mplsLdpEntityMaxPduLength	1.3.6.1.2.1.10.$n.x$.1.2.2.1.8	Unsigned32	RC

Table 7–4   The LDP MIB OID Hierarchy (continued)

Name	OID	ASN.1 Syntax	Access
mplsLdpEntityKeepAliveHoldTimer	1.3.6.1.2.1.10.*n.x*.1.2.2.1.9	Integer32	RC
mplsLdpEntityHelloHoldTimer	1.3.6.1.2.1.10.*n.x*.1.2.2.1.10	Integer32	RC
mplsLdpEntityInitSesThreshold	1.3.6.1.2.1.10.*n.x*.1.2.2.1.11	Integer32	RC
mplsLdpEntityLabelDistMethod	1.3.6.1.2.1.10.*n.x*.1.2.2.1.12	INTEGER	RC
mplsLdpEntityLabelRetentionMode	1.3.6.1.2.1.10.*n.x*.1.2.2.1.13	INTEGER	RC
mplsLdpEntityPVLMisTrapEnable	1.3.6.1.2.1.10.*n.x*.1.2.2.1.14	INTEGER	RC
mplsLdpEntityPVL	1.3.6.1.2.1.10.*n.x*.1.2.2.1.15	Integer32	RC
mplsLdpEntityHopCountLimit	1.3.6.1.2.1.10.*n.x*.1.2.2.1.16	Integer32	RC
mplsLdpEntityTargPeer	1.3.6.1.2.1.10.*n.x*.1.2.2.1.17	TruthValue	RC
mplsLdpEntityTargPeerAddrType	1.3.6.1.2.1.10.*n.x*.1.2.2.1.18	AddressFamily Numbers	RC
mplsLdpEntityTargPeerAddr	1.3.6.1.2.1.10.*n.x*.1.2.2.1.19	MplsLdpGenAddr	RC
mplsLdpEntityOptionalParameters	1.3.6.1.2.1.10.*n.x*.1.2.2.1.20	MplsLabelTypes	RC
mplsLdpEntityDiscontinuityTime	1.3.6.1.2.1.10.*n.x*.1.2.2.1.21	TimeStamp	RO
mplsLdpEntitySorageType	1.3.6.1.2.1.10.*n.x*.1.2.2.1.22	StorageType	RC
mplsLdpEntityRowStatus	1.3.6.1.2.1.10.*n.x*.1.2.2.1.23	RowStatus	RC
mplsLdpEntityGenericObjects	1.3.6.1.2.1.10.*n.x*.1.2.3	OBJECT IDENTIFIER	***
mplsLdpEntityConfGenericLabel RangeTable	1.3.6.1.2.1.10.*n.x*.1.2.3.1	SEQUENCE OF MplsLdpEntityConf Generic LabelRangeEntry	NA
mplsLdpEntityConfGenericLabel RangeEntry	1.3.6.1.2.1.10.*n.x*.1.2.3.1.1	MplsLdpEntityConf GenericLabelRange Entry	NA
mplsLdpEntityConfGenLRMin	1.3.6.1.2.1.10.*n.x*.1.2.3.1.1.1	Unsigned32	NA
mplsLdpEntityConfGenLRMax	1.3.6.1.2.1.10.*n.x*.1.2.3.1.1.1	Unsigned32	NA
mplsLdpEntityConfGenIfIndxOr Zero	1.3.6.1.2.1.10.*n.x*.1.2.3.1.1.2	InterfaceIndexOr Zero	RC
mplsLdpEntityConfGenLRStorType	1.3.6.1.2.1.10.*n.x*.1.2.3.1.1.3	StorageType	RC
mplsLdpEntityConfGenLRRow Status	1.3.6.1.2.1.10.*n.x*.1.2.3.1.1.4	RowStatus	RC

Table 7–4 The LDP MIB OID Hierarchy (continued)

Name	OID	ASN.1 Syntax	Access
mplsLdpEntityAtmObjects	1.3.6.1.2.1.10.*n.x.*1.2.4	OBJECT IDENTIFIER	***
mplsLdpEntityAtmParmsTable	1.3.6.1.2.1.10.*n.x.*1.2.4.1	SEQUENCE OF MplsLdpEntityAtm ParamsEntry	NA
mplsLdpEntityAtmParmsEntry	1.3.6.1.2.1.10.*n.x.*1.2.4.1.1	MplsLdpEntityAtm ParamsEntry	NA
mplsLdpEntityAtmIfIndxOrZero	1.3.6.1.2.1.10.*n.x.*1.2.4.1.1.1	InterfaceIndexOr Zero	RC
mplsLdpEntityAtmMergeCap	1.3.6.1.2.1.10.*n.x.*1.2.4.1.1.2	INTEGER	RC
mplsLdpEntityAtmLRComponents	1.3.6.1.2.1.10.*n.x.*1.2.4.1.1.3	Unsigned32	RC
mplsLdpEntityAtmVcDirectionality	1.3.6.1.2.1.10.*n.x.*1.2.4.1.1.4	INTEGER	RC
mplsLdpEntityAtmLsrConnectivity	1.3.6.1.2.1.10.*n.x.*1.2.4.1.1.5	INTEGER	RC
mplsLdpEntityDefaultControlVpi	1.3.6.1.2.1.10.*n.x.*1.2.4.1.1.6	AtmVpIdentifier	RC
mplsLdpEntityDefaultControlVci	1.3.6.1.2.1.10.*n.x.*1.2.4.1.1.7	MplsAtm VcIdentifier	RC
mplsLdpEntityUnlabTrafVpi	1.3.6.1.2.1.10.*n.x.*1.2.4.1.1.8	AtmVpIdentifier	RC
mplsLdpEntityUnlabTrafVci	1.3.6.1.2.1.10.*n.x.*1.2.4.1.1.9	MplsAtm VcIdentifier	RC
mplsLdpEntityAtmStorType	1.3.6.1.2.1.10.*n.x.*1.2.4.1.1.10	StorageType	RC
mplsLdpEntityAtmRowStatus	1.3.6.1.2.1.10.*n.x.*1.2.4.1.1.11	RowStatus	RC
mplsLdpEntityConfAtmLabelRange Table	1.3.6.1.2.1.10.*n.x.*1.2.4.2	SEQUENCE OF MplsLdpEntityConf AtmLREntry	NA
mplsLdpEntityConfAtmLabelRange Entry	1.3.6.1.2.1.10.*n.x.*1.2.4.2.1	MplsLdpEntityConf AtmLREntry	NA
mplsLdpEntityConfAtmLRMinVpi	1.3.6.1.2.1.10.*n.x.*1.2.4.2.1.1	AtmVpIdentifier	NA
mplsLdpEntityConfAtmLRMinVci	1.3.6.1.2.1.10.*n.x.*1.2.4.2.1.2	MplsAtm VcIdentifier	NA
mplsLdpEntityConfAtmLRMaxVpi	1.3.6.1.2.1.10.*n.x.*1.2.4.2.1.3	AtmVpIdentifier	RC
mplsLdpEntityConfAtmLRMaxVci	1.3.6.1.2.1.10.*n.x.*1.2.4.2.1.4	MplsAtm VcIdentifier	RC
mplsLdpEntityConfAtmLRStorType	1.3.6.1.2.1.10.*n.x.*1.2.4.2.1.5	StorageType	RC

Table 7–4 The LDP MIB OID Hierarchy (continued)

Name	OID	ASN.1 Syntax	Access
mplsLdpEntityConfAtmLRRow Status	1.3.6.1.2.1.10.*n.x*.1.2.4.2.1.6	RowStatus	RC
mplsLdpEntityFrameRelayObjects	1.3.6.1.2.1.10.*n.x*.1.2.5	OBJECT IDENTIFIER	***
mplsLdpEntityFrameRelayParms Table	1.3.6.1.2.1.10.*n.x*.1.2.5.1	SEQUENCE OF MplsLdpEntityFr ParmsEntry	NA
mplsLdpEntityFrameRelayParms Entry	1.3.6.1.2.1.10.*n.x*.1.2.5.1.1	MplsLdpEntityFr ParamsEntry	NA
mplsLdpEntityFrIfIndxOrZero	1.3.6.1.2.1.10.*n.x*.1.2.5.1.1	InterfaceIndexOr Zero	RC
mplsLdpEntityFrMergeCap	1.3.6.1.2.1.10.*n.x*.1.2.5.1.2	INTEGER	RC
mplsLdpEntityFrLRComponents	1.3.6.1.2.1.10.*n.x*.1.2.5.1.3	Unisgned32	RC
mplsLdpEntityFrLen	1.3.6.1.2.1.10.*n.x*.1.2.5.1.4	INTEGER	RC
mplsLdpEntityFrVcDirectionality	1.3.6.1.2.1.10.*n.x*.1.2.5.1.5	INTEGER	RC
mplsLdpEntityFrParmsStorageType	1.3.6.1.2.1.10.*n.x*.1.2.5.1.6	StorageType	RC
mplsLdpEntityFrParmsRowStatus	1.3.6.1.2.1.10.*n.x*.1.2.5.1.7	RowStatus	RC
mplsLdpEntityConfFrLabelRange Table	1.3.6.1.2.1.10.*n.x*.1.2.5.2	SEQUENCE OF MplsLdpEntityConf FrLREntry	NA
mplsLdpEntityConfFrLabelRange Entry	1.3.6.1.2.1.10.*n.x*.1.2.5.2.1	MplsLdpEntityConf FrLREntry	NA
mplsLdpConfFrMinimumDlci	1.3.6.1.2.1.10.*n.x*.1.2.5.2.1.1	Integer32	NA
mplsLdpConfFrMaximumDlci	1.3.6.1.2.1.10.*n.x*.1.2.5.2.1.2	Integer32	RC
mplsLdpConfFrStorageType	1.3.6.1.2.1.10.*n.x*.1.2.5.2.1.3	StorageType	RC
mplsLdpConfFrRowStatus	1.3.6.1.2.1.10.*n.x*.1.2.5.2.1.4	RowStatus	RC
mplsLdpEntityStatsTable	1.3.6.1.2.1.10.*n.x*.1.2.6	SEQUENCE OF MplsLdpEntityStats Entry	NA
mplsLdpEntityStatsEntry	1.3.6.1.2.1.10.*n.x*.1.2.6.1	MplsLdpEntityStats Entry	NA
mplsLdpAttemptedSessions	1.3.6.1.2.1.10.*n.x*.1.2.6.1.1	Counter32	RO
mplsLdpSesRejectedNoHelloErrors	1.3.6.1.2.1.10.*n.x*.1.2.6.1.2	Counter32	RO
mplsLdpSesRejectedAdErrors	1.3.6.1.2.1.10.*n.x*.1.2.6.1.3	Counter32	RO

Table 7–4   The LDP MIB OID Hierarchy (continued)

Name	OID	ASN.1 Syntax	Access
mplsLdpSesRejectedMaxPduErrors	1.3.6.1.2.1.10.*n.x*.1.2.6.1.4	Counter32	RO
mplsLdpSesRejectedLRErrors	1.3.6.1.2.1.10.*n.x*.1.2.6.1.5	Counter32	RO
mplsLdpBadLdpIdentifierErrors	1.3.6.1.2.1.10.*n.x*.1.2.6.1.6	Counter32	RO
mplsLdpBadPduLengthErrors	1.3.6.1.2.1.10.*n.x*.1.2.6.1.7	Counter32	RO
mplsLdpBadMessageLengthErrors	1.3.6.1.2.1.10.*n.x*.1.2.6.1.8	Counter32	RO
mplsLdpBadTlvLengthErrors	1.3.6.1.2.1.10.*n.x*.1.2.6.1.9	Counter32	RO
mplsLdpMalformedTlvValueErrors	1.3.6.1.2.1.10.*n.x*.1.2.6.1.10	Counter32	RO
mplsLdpKeepALiveTimerExpErrors	1.3.6.1.2.1.10.*n.x*.1.2.6.1.11	Counter32	RO
mplsLdpShutdownNotifReceived	1.3.6.1.2.1.10.*n.x*.1.2.6.1.12	Counter32	RO
mplsLdpShutdownNotifSent	1.3.6.1.2.1.10.*n.x*.1.2.6.1.13	Counter32	RO
mplsLdpSessionObjects	1.3.6.1.2.1.10.*n.x*.1.3	OBJECT IDENTIFIER	***
mplsLdpPeerTable	1.3.6.1.2.1.10.*n.x*.1.3.1	SEQUENCE OF MplsLdpPeerEntry	NA
mplsLdpPeerEntry	1.3.6.1.2.1.10.*n.x*.1.3.1.1	MplsLdpPeerEntry	NA
mplsLdpPeerLdpId	1.3.6.1.2.1.10.*n.x*.1.3.1.1.1	MplsLdpIdentifier	NA
mplsLdpPeerLabelDistMethod	1.3.6.1.2.1.10.*n.x*.1.3.1.1.2	INTEGER	RO
mplsLdpPeerLoopDetectionForPV	1.3.6.1.2.1.10.*n.x*.1.3.1.1.3	INTEGER	RO
mplsLdpPeerPVL	1.3.6.1.2.1.10.*n.x*.1.3.1.1.4	Integer32	RO
mplsLdpHelloAdjacencyObjects	1.3.6.1.2.1.10.*n.x*.1.3.2	OBJECT IDENTIFIER	***
mplsLdpHelloAdjacencyTable	1.3.6.1.2.1.10.*n.x*.1.3.2.1	SEQUENCE OF MplsLdpHello AdjacencyEntry	NA
mplsLdpHelloAdjacencyEntry	1.3.6.1.2.1.10.*n.x*.1.3.2.1.1	MplsLdpHello AdjacencyEntry	NA
mplsLdpHelloAdjIndex	1.3.6.1.2.1.10.*n.x*.1.3.2.1.1.1	Unisgned32	NA
mplsLdpHelloAdjHoldTimeRem	1.3.6.1.2.1.10.*n.x*.1.3.2.1.1.2	TimeInterval	RO
mplsLdpHelloAdjType	1.3.6.1.2.1.10.*n.x*.1.3.2.1.1.3	INTEGER	RO
mplsLdpSesUpDownTrapEnable	1.3.6.1.2.1.10.*n.x*.1.3.3	INTEGER	RW

Table 7–4 The LDP MIB OID Hierarchy (continued)

Name	OID	ASN.1 Syntax	Access
mplsLdpSessionTable	1.3.6.1.2.1.10.*n.x.*1.3.4	SEQUENCE OF MplsLdpSession Entry	NA
mplsLdpSessionEntry	1.3.6.1.2.1.10.*n.x.*1.3.4.1	MplsLdpSession Entry	NA
mplsLdpSesState	1.3.6.1.2.1.10.*n.x.*1.3.4.1.1	INTEGER	RO
mplsLdpSesProtocolVersion	1.3.6.1.2.1.10.*n.x.*1.3.4.1.2	Integer32	RO
mplsLdpSesKeepAliveHoldTIme Rem	1.3.6.1.2.1.10.*n.x.*1.3.4.1.3	TimeInterval	RO
mplsLdpSesMaxPduLength	1.3.6.1.2.1.10.*n.x.*1.3.4.1.4	Unsigned32	RO
mplsLdpSesDiscontinuityTime	1.3.6.1.2.1.10.*n.x.*1.3.4.1.5	TimeStamp	RO
mplsLdpAtmSesTable	1.3.6.1.2.1.10.*n.x.*1.3.5	SEQUENCE OF MplsLdpAtmSes Entry	NA
mplsLdpAtmSesEntry	1.3.6.1.2.1.10.*n.x.*1.3.5.1	MplsLdpAtmSes Entry	NA
mplsLdpSesAtmLRLowerBoundVpi	1.3.6.1.2.1.10.*n.x.*1.3.5.1.1	AtmVpIdentifier	NA
mplsLdpSesAtmLRLowerBoundVci	1.3.6.1.2.1.10.*n.x.*1.3.5.1.2	MplsAtm VpIdentifier	NA
mplsLdpSesAtmLRUpperBoundVpi	1.3.6.1.2.1.10.*n.x.*1.3.5.1.3	AtmVpIdentifier	RO
mplsLdpSesAtmLRUpperBoundVci	1.3.6.1.2.1.10.*n.x.*1.3.5.1.4	MplsAtm VpIdentifier	RO
mplsLdpFrameRelaySesTable	1.3.6.1.2.1.10.*n.x.*1.3.6	SEQUENCE OF MplsLdpFrame RelaySesEntry	NA
mplsLdpFrameRelaySesEntry	1.3.6.1.2.1.10.*n.x.*1.3.6.1	MplsLdpFrame RelaySesEntry	NA
mplsLdpFrSesMinDlci	1.3.6.1.2.1.10.*n.x.*1.3.6.1.1	Integer32	NA
mplsLdpFrSesMaxDlci	1.3.6.1.2.1.10.*n.x.*1.3.6.1.2	Integer32	RO
mplsLdpFrSesLen	1.3.6.1.2.1.10.*n.x.*1.3.6.1.3	INTEGER	RO
mplsLdpSesStatsTable	1.3.6.1.2.1.10.*n.x.*1.3.7	SEQUENCE OF MplsLdpSesStats Entry	NA
mplsLdpSesStatsEntry	1.3.6.1.2.1.10.*n.x.*1.3.7.1	MplsLdpSesStats Entry	NA

Table 7–4   The LDP MIB OID Hierarchy (continued)

Name	OID	ASN.1 Syntax	Access
mplsLdpFrSesStatsUnkMesType Errors	1.3.6.1.2.1.10.*n*.*x*.1.3.7.1.1	Counter32	RO
mplsLdpFrSesStatsUnkTlvErrors	1.3.6.1.2.1.10.*n*.*x*.1.3.7.1.2	Counter32	RO
mplsFecObjects	1.3.6.1.2.1.10.*n*.*x*.1.3.8	OBJECT IDENTIFER	***
mplsFecIndexNext	1.3.6.1.2.1.10.*n*.*x*.1.3.8.1	Unsigned32 (0..4294967295)	RO
mplsFecTable	1.3.6.1.2.1.10.*n*.*x*.1.3.8.2	SEQUENCE OF MplsFecEntry	NA
mplsFecEntry	1.3.6.1.2.1.10.*n*.*x*.1.3.8.2.1	MplsFecEntry	NA
mplsFecIndex	1.3.6.1.2.1.10.*n*.*x*.1.3.8.2.1	Unsigned32	NA
mplsFecType	1.3.6.1.2.1.10.*n*.*x*.1.3.8.2.2	INTEGER	RC
mplsFecAddrLength	1.3.6.1.2.1.10.*n*.*x*.1.3.8.2.3	Integer32	RC
mplsFecAddrFamily	1.3.6.1.2.1.10.*n*.*x*.1.3.8.2.4	AddressFamilyNumbers	RC
mplsFecAddr	1.3.6.1.2.1.10.*n*.*x*.1.3.8.2.5	MplsLdpGenAddr	RC
mplsFecStorType	1.3.6.1.2.1.10.*n*.*x*.1.3.8.2.6	StorageType	RC
mplsFecRowStatus	1.3.6.1.2.1.10.*n*.*x*.1.3.8.2.7	RowStatus	RC
mplsLdpSesInLabelMapTable	1.3.6.1.2.1.10.*n*.*x*.1.3.9	SEQUENCE OF MplsSesInLabelMapEntry	NA
mplsLdpSesInLabelMapEntry	1.3.6.1.2.1.10.*n*.*x*.1.3.9.1	MplsSesInLableMapEntry	NA
mplsLdpSesInLabelIfIndex	1.3.6.1.2.1.10.*n*.*x*.1.3.9.1.1	InterfaceIndex	NA
mplsLdpSesInLabel	1.3.6.1.2.1.10.*n*.*x*.1.3.9.1.2	MplsLabel	NA
mplsLdpSesInLabelType	1.3.6.1.2.1.10.*n*.*x*.1.3.9.1.3	MplsLdpLabelTypes	RO
mplsLdpSesInLabelConnType	1.3.6.1.2.1.10.*n*.*x*.1.3.9.1.4	INTEGER	RO
mplsLdpSesOutLabelMapTable	1.3.6.1.2.1.10.*n*.*x*.1.3.10	SEQUENCE OF MplsLdpSesOutLabelMapEntry	NA
mplsLdpSesOutLabelMapEntry	1.3.6.1.2.1.10.*n*.*x*.1.3.10.1	MplsLdpSesOutLabelMapEntry	NA
mplsLdpSesOutLabelIfIndex	1.3.6.1.2.1.10.*n*.*x*.1.3.10.1.1	InterfaceIndex	NA

Table 7–4 The LDP MIB OID Hierarchy (continued)

Name	OID	ASN.1 Syntax	Access
mplsLdpSesOutLabel	1.3.6.1.2.1.10.*n.x*.1.3.10.1.2	MplsLabel	NA
mplsLdpSesOutLabelType	1.3.6.1.2.1.10.*n.x*.1.3.10.1.3	MplsLdpLabelTypes	RO
mplsLdpSesOutLabelConnType	1.3.6.1.2.1.10.*n.x*.1.3.10.1.4	INTEGER	RO
mplsLdpSesOutSegmentIndex	1.3.6.1.2.1.10.*n.x*.1.3.10.1.5	Integer32	RO
mplsLdpSesXCMapTable	1.3.6.1.2.1.10.*n.x*.1.3.11	SEQUENCE OF MplsLdpSesXCMap Entry	NA
mplsLdpSesXCMapEntry	1.3.6.1.2.1.10.*n.x*.1.3.11.1	MplsLdpSesXCMap Entry	NA
mplsLdpSesXCIndex	1.3.6.1.2.1.10.*n.x*1.3.11.1.1	Integer32 (1..2147483647)	RO
mplsXCsFecsTable	1.3.6.1.2.1.10.*n.x*.1.3.12	SEQUENCE OF MplsXCsFecsEntry	NA
mplsXCsFecsEntry	1.3.6.1.2.1.10.*n.x*.1.3.12.1	MplsXCsFecsEntry	NA
mplsXCsFecOperStatus	1.3.6.1.2.1.10.*n.x*.1.3.12.1.1	INTEGER	RO
mplsXCFecOperStatusLastChange	1.3.6.1.2.1.10.*n.x*.1.3.12.1.2	TimeStamp	RO
mplsLdpSesPeerAddrTable	1.3.6.1.2.1.10.*n.x*.1.3.13	SEQUENCE OF MplsLdpSesPeer AddrEntry	NA
mplsLdpSesPeerAddrEntry	1.3.6.1.2.1.10.*n.x*.1.3.13.1	MplsLspSesPeer AddrEntry	NA
mplsLdpSesPeerAddrIndex	1.3.6.1.2.1.10.*n.x*.1.3.13.1.1	Unsigned32 (1..4294967295)	NA
mplsLdpSesPeerNextHopAddrType	1.3.6.1.2.1.10.*n.x*.1.3.13.1.2	AddressFamily Names	RO
mplsLdpSesPeerNextHopAddr	1.3.6.1.2.1.10.*n.x*.1.3.13.1.3	MplsLdpGenAddr	RO
mplsLdpNotifications	1.3.6.1.2.1.10.*n.x*.2	OBJECT IDENTIFIER	***
mplsLdpNotificationPrefix	1.3.6.1.2.1.10.*n.x*.2.0	OBJECT IDENTIFIER	***
mplsLdpFailedInitSesThreshold Exceeded	1.3.6.1.2.1.10.*n.x*.2.1	NOTIFICATION-TYPE	***
mplsLdpPathVectorLimitMismatch	1.3.6.1.2.1.10.*n.x*.2.2	NOTIFICATION-TYPE	***

Table 7–4   The LDP MIB OID Hierarchy (continued)

Name	OID	ASN.1 Syntax	Access
mplsLdpSessionUp	1.3.6.1.2.1.10.*n.x*.2.3	NOTIFICATION-TYPE	***
mplsLdpSessionDown	1.3.6.1.2.1.10.*n.x*.2.4	NOTIFICATION-TYPE	***
mplsLdpConformance	1.3.6.1.2.1.10.*n.x*.3	OBJECT IDENTIFIER	***
mplsLdpGroups	1.3.6.1.2.1.10.*n.x*.3.1	OBJECT IDENTIFIER	***
mplsLdpGeneralGroup	1.3.6.1.2.1.10.*n.x*.3.1.1	OBJECT-GROUP	***
mplsLdpGenericGroup	1.3.6.1.2.1.10.*n.x*.3.1.2	OBJECT-GROUP	***
mplsLdpAtmGroup	1.3.6.1.2.1.10.*n.x*.3.1.3	OBJECT-GROUP	***
mplsLdpFrameRelayGroup	1.3.6.1.2.1.10.*n.x*.3.1.4	OBJECT-GROUP	***
mplsLdpMappingGroup	1.3.6.1.2.1.10.*n.x*.3.1.5	OBJECT-GROUP	***
mplsLdpNotificationsGroup	1.3.6.1.2.1.10.*n.x*.3.1.6	OBJECT-GROUP	***
mplsLdpCompliances	1.3.6.1.2.1.10.*n.x*.3.2	OBJECT IDENTIFIER	***
mplsLdpModuleCompliance	1.3.6.1.2.1.10.*n.x*.3.2.1	MODULE-COMPLIANCE	***

* To be assigned by IANA; the MPLS MIB will be a branch under the transmission branch under MIB-II.
** Also to be assigned by IANA; the LDP MIB will be a branch under the MPLS MIB branch.

Table 7–5 contains the four LDP MIB notifications as they are currently defined.

Table 7–5   LDP MIB Notifications

Name	Description
MplsLdpFailedInit SessionThreshold Exceeded	This notification is generated when the value of the `mplsLdpEntityFailedInitSessionTrapEnable` object is `enabled(1)` and the value of the `mplsLdpEntityFailedInitSessionThreshold` object has been exceeded.
MplsLdpPathVector LimitMismatch	This notification is generated when the value of the `mplsLdpEntityFailedInitSessionTrapEnable` object is `enabled(1)` and the `mplsLdpEntityPathVectorLimit` does NOT match the value of the `mplsLdpPeerPathVectorLimit` for a specific entity.
MplsLdpSessionUp	Generation of this trap occurs when the `mplsLdpSessionUpDownTrapEnable` object is `enabled(1)` and the value of `mplsLdpSessionState` changes from any state except `nonexistent(1)` to `operational(5)`.
MplsLdpSessionDown	Generation of this trap occurs when the `mplsLdpSessionUpDownTrapEnable` object is `enabled(1)` and the value of `mplsLdpSessionState` changes from `operational(5)` to any other state.

The TE MIB

The TE MIB defines the objects that are required to manage MPLS-based TE, including configuring MPLS tunnels and their associated parameters, as well as configuring the strict and loose hops that form the tunnels. The current definition for the TE MIB is the ID titled "MPLS Traffic Engineering Management Information Base Using SMIv2" by Srinivasan, Viswanathan, and Nadeau.[5]

---

5. The current version for this MIB is available online as: `draft-ietf-mpls-te-mib-06txt`

The configuration of a traffic-engineered tunnel requires four basic steps:

1. Set up the tunnel with the appropriate configuration parameters.
2. Set up the tunnel's in- and out-segments with their appropriate parameters.
3. Set up the cross-connect entries that associate the in- and out-segments belonging to the tunnel.
4. Specify any label stack actions.

There are seven tables in the TE MIB for setting up tunnels and their resources, specifying resource objects for CR-LDP signaled tunnels, and configuring strict and loose source-routed hops. The `mplsTunnelTable` can be used to create tunnels; the `mplsTunnelResourceTable` relates the resources required for the configured tunnels; the hops are configured via the `mplsTunnelHopTable`; and the `mplsTunnelARHopTable` contains the actual hops traversed by the tunnel, while the `mplsTunnelCHopTable` lists the hops computed by a constraint-based routing algorithm (specified in the `mplsTunnelHopTable`). The `mplsTunnelPerfTable` contains the tunnel performance counters, and the `mplsTunnelCRLDPResTable` contains information specifically about tunnels configured via CR-LDP signaling.

Table 7–6 contains the TE MIB textual conventions that are currently defined.

Table 7–6 TE MIB Textual Conventions

Name	Syntax	Description
MplsTunnelIndex	Integer32 (1..65535)	Index into mplsTunnelTable.
MplsTunnelInstanceIndex	Unsigned32 (0..65535)	Instance index into mplsTunnelTable.
MplsTunnelAffinity	Integer32	Include-any, include-all, or exclude-all constraint for link selection.
MplsLsrId	Integer32	A unique identifier for an MPLS LSR. This MAY represent an IPv4 address.

Table 7–6   TE MIB Textual Conventions (continued)

Name	Syntax	Description
MplsPathIndex	Integer32	A unique identifier used to identify a specific path used by a tunnel.
MplsPathIndexOrZero	Integer32	A unique identifier used to identify a specific path used by a tunnel. If this value is set to 0, it indicates that no path is in use.

Table 7–7 contains the TE MIB OID hierarchy.

Table 7–7   The TE MIB OID Hierarchy

Name	OID	ASN.1 Syntax	Access
mplsTeMIB	1.3.6.1.3.95	MODULE-IDENTITY	***
mplsTeScalars	1.3.6.1.3.95.1	OBJECT IDENTIFIER	***
mplsTunnelConfigured	1.3.6.1.3.95.1.1	Unsigned32	RO
mplsTunnelActive	1.3.6.1.3.95.1.2	Unsigned32	RO
mplsTunnelTEDistProto	1.3.6.1.3.95.1.3	BITS{other(0),ospf(1),isis(2)}	RO
mplsTunnelMaxHops	1.3.6.1.3.95.1.4	Unsigned32	RO
mplsTeObjects	1.3.6.1.3.95.2	OBJECT IDENTIFIER	***
mplsTunnelIndexNext	1.3.6.1.3.95.2.1	Integer32(0..65535)	RO
mplsTunnelTable	1.3.6.1.3.95.2.2	SEQUENCE OF MplsTunnelEntry	NA
mplsTunnelEntry	1.3.6.1.3.95.2.2.1	MplsTunnelEntry	NA
mplsTunnelIndex	1.3.6.1.3.95.2.2.1.1	MplsTunnelIndex	AFN
mplsTunnelInstance	1.3.6.1.3.95.2.2.1.2	MplsTunnelInstanceIndex	AFN
mplsTunnelIngressLSRId	1.3.6.1.3.95.2.2.1.3	MplsLsrId	AFN
mplsTunnelEgressLSRId	1.3.6.1.3.95.2.2.1.4	MplsLsrId	AFN
mplsTunnelName	1.3.6.1.3.95.2.2.1.5	DisplayString	RC

Table 7–7 The TE MIB OID Hierarchy (continued)

Name	OID	ASN.1 Syntax	Access
mplsTunnelDescr	1.3.6.1.3.95.2.2.1.6	DisplayString	RC
mplsTunnelIsIf	1.3.6.1.3.95.2.2.1.7	TruthValue	RC
mplsTunnelIfIndex	1.3.6.1.3.95.2.2.1.8	InterfaceIndexOrZero	RO
mplsTunnelXCPointer	1.3.6.1.3.95.2.2.1.9	RowPointer	RC
mplsTunnelSignallingProto	1.3.6.1.3.95.2.2.1.10	INTEGER	RC
mplsTunnelSetupPrio	1.3.6.1.3.95.2.2.1.11	INTEGER	RC
mplsTunnelHoldingPrio	1.3.6.1.3.95.2.2.1.12	INTEGER	RC
mplsTunnelSessonAttributes	1.3.6.1.3.95.2.2.1.13	BITS	RC
mplsTunnelOwner	1.3.6.1.3.95.2.2.1.14	INTEGER	RC
mplsTunnelLocalProtectInUse	1.3.6.1.3.95.2.2.1.15	TruthValue	RC
mplsTunnelResourcePointer	1.3.6.1.3.95.2.2.1.16	RowPointer	RC
mplsTunnelInstancePriority	1.3.6.1.3.95.2.2.1.17	Unsigned32	RC
mplsTunnelHopTableIndex	1.3.6.1.3.95.2.2.1.18	MplsPathIndexOrZero	RC
mplsTunnelARHopTableIndex	1.3.6.1.3.95.2.2.1.19	MplsPathIndexOrZero	RO
mplsTunnelCHopTableIndex	1.3.6.1.3.95.2.2.1.20	MplsPathIndexOrZero	RO
mplsTunnelPrimaryInstance	1.3.6.1.3.95.2.2.1.21	MplsTunnelInstanceIndex	RO
mplsTunnelPrimaryTimeUp	1.3.6.1.3.95.2.2.1.22	TimeTicks	RO
mplsTunnelPathChanges	1.3.6.1.3.95.2.2.1.23	Counter32	RO
mplsTunnelLastPathChange	1.3.6.1.3.95.2.2.1.24	TimeTicks	RO
mplsTunnelCreationTime	1.3.6.1.3.95.2.2.1.25	TimeStamp	RO
mplsTunnelStateTransitions	1.3.6.1.3.95.2.2.1.26	Counter32	RO
mplsTunnelIncludeAnyAffinity	1.3.6.1.3.95.2.2.1.27	MplsTunnelAffinity	RC
mplsTunnelIncludeAllAffinity	1.3.6.1.3.95.2.2.1.28	MplsTunnelAffinity	RC
mplsTunnelExcludeAllAffinity	1.3.6.1.3.95.2.2.1.29	MplsTunnelAffinity	RC
mplsTunnelPathInUse	1.3.6.1.3.95.2.2.1.30	MplsPathIndexOrZero	RC
mplsTunnelRole	1.3.6.1.3.95.2.2.1.31	INTEGER	RC
mplsTunnelTotalUpTime	1.3.6.1.3.95.2.2.1.32	TimeTicks	RC

Table 7–7   The TE MIB OID Hierarchy (continued)

Name	OID	ASN.1 Syntax	Access
mplsTunnelInstanceUpTime	1.3.6.1.3.95.2.2.1.33	TimeTicks	RC
mplsTunnelAdminStatus	1.3.6.1.3.95.2.2.1.34	INTEGER	RC
mplsTunnelOperStatus	1.3.6.1.3.95.2.2.1.35	INTEGER	RO
mplsTunnelRowStatus	1.3.6.1.3.95.2.2.1.36	RowStatus	RC
mplsTunnelStorageType	1.3.6.1.3.95.2.2.1.37	StorageType	RC
mplsTunnelHopListIndexNext	1.3.6.1.3.95.2.3	Unsigned32 (0..2147483647)	RO
mplsTunnelHopTable	1.3.6.1.3.95.2.4	SEQUENCE OF MplsTunnelHopEntry	NA
mplsTunnelHopEntry	1.3.6.1.3.95.2.4.1	MplsTunnelHopEntry	NA
mplsTunnelHopListIndex	1.3.6.1.3.95.2.4.1.1	MplsPathIndex	NA
mplsTunnelHopPathOptionIndex	1.3.6.1.3.95.2.4.1.2	MplsPathIndex	NA
mplsTunnelHopIndex	1.3.6.1.3.95.2.4.1.3	MplsPathIndex	NA
mplsTunnelHopAddrType	1.3.6.1.3.95.2.4.1.4	INTEGER	RC
mplsTunnelHopIpv4Addr	1.3.6.1.3.95.2.4.1.5	InetAddressIPv4	RC
mplsTunnelHopIpv4PrefixLen	1.3.6.1.3.95.2.4.1.6	Unsigned32	RC
mplsTunnelHopIpv6Addr	1.3.6.1.3.95.2.4.1.7	InetAddressIPv6	RC
mplsTunnelHopIpv6PrefixLen	1.3.6.1.3.95.2.4.1.8	Unsigned32	RC
mplsTunnelHopAsNumber	1.3.6.1.3.95.2.4.1.9	Unsigned32	RC
mplsTunnelHopLspId	1.3.6.1.3.95.2.4.1.10	MplsLSPID	RC
mplsTunnelHopType	1.3.6.1.3.95.2.4.1.11	INTEGER	RC
mplsTunnelHopIncludeExclude	1.3.6.1.3.95.2.4.1.12	INTEGER	RC
mplsTunnelHopPathOptionName	1.3.6.1.3.95.2.4.1.13	DispalyString	RC
mplsTunnelHopPathComp	1.3.6.1.3.95.2.4.1.14	INTEGER	RC
mplsTunnelHopRowStatus	1.3.6.1.3.95.2.4.1.15	RowStatus	RC
mplsTunnelHopStorageType	1.3.6.1.3.95.2.4.1.16	StorageType	RC
mplsTunnelResourceIndexNext	1.3.6.1.3.95.2.5	Unsigned32 (0..2147483647)	RO

Table 7–7   The TE MIB OID Hierarchy (continued)

Name	OID	ASN.1 Syntax	Access
mplsTunnelResourceTable	1.3.6.1.3.95.2.6	SEQUENCE OF MplsTunnelResource Entry	NA
mplsTunnelResourceEntry	1.3.6.1.3.95.2.6.1	MplsTunnelResource Entry	NA
mplsTunnelResourceIndex	1.3.6.1.3.95.2.6.1.1	Unsigned32	NA
mplsTunnelResourceMaxRate	1.3.6.1.3.95.2.6.1.2	MplsBitRate	RC
mplsTunnelResourceMeanRate	1.3.6.1.3.95.2.6.1.3	MplsBitRate	RC
mplsTunnelResourceMaxBurstSize	1.3.6.1.3.95.2.6.1.4	MplsBurstSize	RC
mplsTunnelResourceMeanBurstSize	1.3.6.1.3.95.2.6.1.5	MplsBurstSize	RC
mplsTunnelResourceExcessBurstSize	1.3.6.1.3.95.2.6.1.6	MplsBurstSize	RC
mplsTunnelResourceFrequency	1.3.6.1.3.95.2.6.1.7	INTEGER	RC
mplsTunnelResourceWeight	1.3.6.1.3.95.2.6.1.8	Unsigned32	RC
mplsTunnelResourceRowStatus	1.3.6.1.3.95.2.6.1.9	RowStatus	RC
mplsTunnelResourceStorageType	1.3.6.1.3.95.2.6.1.10	StorageType	RC
mplsTunnelARHopTable	1.3.6.1.3.95.2.7	SEQUENCE OF MplsTunnelARHopEntry	NA
mplsTunnelARHopEntry	1.3.6.1.3.95.2.7.1	MplsTunnelARHopEntry	NA
mplsTunnelARHopListIndex	1.3.6.1.3.95.2.7.1.1	MplsPathIndex	NA
mplsTunnelARHopIndex	1.3.6.1.3.95.2.7.1.2	MplsPathIndex	NA
mplsTunnelARHopAddrType	1.3.6.1.3.95.2.7.1.3	INTEGER	RO
mplsTunnelARHopIpv4Addr	1.3.6.1.3.95.2.7.1.4	InetAddressIPv4	RO
mplsTunnelARHopIpv4PrefixLen	1.3.6.1.3.95.2.7.1.5	Unsigned32	RO
mplsTunnelARHopIpv6Adr	1.3.6.1.3.95.2.7.1.6	InetAddressIPv6	RO
mplsTunnelARHopIpv6PrefixLen	1.3.6.1.3.95.2.7.1.7	Unsigned32	RO
mplsTunnelARHopAsNumber	1.3.6.1.3.95.2.7.1.8	Unsigned32	RO
mplsTunnelARHopLspId	1.3.6.1.3.95.2.7.1.9	MplsLSPID	RO
mplsTunnelCHopTable	1.3.6.1.3.95.2.8	SEQUENCE OF MplsTunnelCHopEntry	NA

Table 7–7 The TE MIB OID Hierarchy (continued)

Name	OID	ASN.1 Syntax	Access
mplsTunnelCHopEntry	1.3.6.1.3.95.2.8.1	MplsTunnelCHopEntry	NA
mplsTunnelCHopListIndex	1.3.6.1.3.95.2.8.1.1	MplsPathIndex	NA
mplsTunnelCHopIndex	1.3.6.1.3.95.2.8.1.2	MplsPathIndex	NA
mplsTunnelCHopAddrType	1.3.6.1.3.95.2.8.1.3	INTEGER	RO
mplsTunnelCHopIpv4Addr	1.3.6.1.3.95.2.8.1.4	InetAddressIPv4	RO
mplsTunnelCHopIpv4PrefixLen	1.3.6.1.3.95.2.8.1.5	Unsigned32	RO
mplsTunnelCHopIpv6Addr	1.3.6.1.3.95.2.8.1.6	InetAddressIPv6	RO
mplsTunnelCHopIpv6PrefixLen	1.3.6.1.3.95.2.8.1.7	Unsigned32	RO
mplsTunnelCHopAsNumber	1.3.6.1.3.95.2.8.1.8	Unsigned32	RO
mplsTunnelCHopType	1.3.6.1.3.95.2.8.1.9	INTEGER	RO
mplsTunnelPerfTable	1.3.6.1.3.95.2.9	SEQUENCE OF MplsTunnelPerfEntry	NA
mplsTunnelPerfEntry	1.3.6.1.3.95.2.9.1	MplsTunnelPerfEntry	NA
mplsTunnelPerfPackets	1.3.6.1.3.95.2.9.1.1	Counter32	RO
mplsTunnelPerfHCPackets	1.3.6.1.3.95.2.9.1.2	Counter64	RO
mplsTunnelPerfErrors	1.3.6.1.3.95.2.9.1.3	Counter32	RO
mplsTunnelPerfBytes	1.3.6.1.3.95.2.9.1.4	Counter32	RO
mplsTunnelPerfHCBytes	1.3.6.1.3.95.2.9.1.5	Counter64	RO
mplsTunnelCRLDPResTable	1.3.6.1.3.95.2.10	SEQUENCE OF MplsTunnelCRLDPResEntry	NA
mplsTunnelCRLDPResEntry	1.3.6.1.3.95.2.10.1	MplsTunnelCRLDPResEntry	NA
mplsTunnelCRLDPResMeanBurstSize	1.3.6.1.3.95.2.10.1.2	MplsBurstSize	RC
mplsTunnelCRLDPResExcessBurstSize	1.3.6.1.3.95.2.10.1.3	MplsBurstSize	RC
mplsTunnelCRLDPResFrequency	1.3.6.1.3.95.2.10.1.4	Integer32	RC
mplsTunnelCRLDPResWeight	1.3.6.1.3.95.2.10.1.5	Unisgned32	RC
mplsTunnelCRLDPResFlags	1.3.6.1.3.95.2.10.1.6	Unisgned32	RC
mplsTunnelCRLDPResRowStatus	1.3.6.1.3.95.2.10.1.7	RowStatus	RC

Table 7–7   The TE MIB OID Hierarchy (continued)

Name	OID	ASN.1 Syntax	Access
mplsTunnelCRLDPResStorageType	1.3.6.1.3.95.2.10.1.8	StorageType	RC
mplsTunnelTrapEnable	1.3.6.1.3.95.2.11	TruthValue	RW
mplsTeNotifications	1.3.6.1.3.95.3	OBJECT IDENTIFIER	***
mplsTeNotifyPrefix	1.3.6.1.3.95.3.0	OBJECT IDENTIFIER	***
MplsTunnelUp	1.3.6.1.3.95.3.0.1	NOTIFICATION-TYPE	***
MplsTunnelDown	1.3.6.1.3.95.3.0.2	NOTIFICATION-TYPE	***
mplsTunnelRerouted	1.3.6.1.3.95.3.0.3	NOTIFICATION-TYPE	***
mplsTunnelReoptimized	1.3.6.1.3.95.3.0.4	NOTIFICATION-TYPE	***
mplsTeConformance	1.3.6.1.3.95.4	OBJECT IDENTIFIER	***
MplsTeGroups	1.3.6.1.3.95.4.1	OBJECT IDENTIFIER	***
mplsTunnelGroup	1.3.6.1.3.95.4.1.1	OBJECT-GROUP	***
mplsTunnelManualGroup	1.3.6.1.3.95.4.1.2	OBJECT-GROUP	***
mplsTunnelSignaledGroup	1.3.6.1.3.95.4.1.3	OBJECT-GROUP	***
mplsTunnelScalarGroup	1.3.6.1.3.95.4.1.4	OBJECT-GROUP	***
mplsTunnelIsIntfcGroup	1.3.6.1.3.95.4.1.5	OBJECT-GROUP	***
mplsTunnelIsNotIntfcGroup	1.3.6.1.3.95.4.1.6	OBJECT-GROUP	***
mplsTunnelOptionalGroup	1.3.6.1.3.95.4.1.7	OBJECT-GROUP	***
mplsTunnelCRLDPResOptionalGroup	1.3.6.1.3.95.4.1.8	OBJECT-GROUP	***
mplsTeNotificationGroup	1.3.6.1.3.95.4.1.9	OBJECT-GROUP	***
mplsTeCompliances	1.3.6.1.3.95.4.2	OBJECT IDENTIFIER	***
mplsTeModuleCompliance	1.3.6.1.3.95.4.2.1	MODULE-COMPLIANCE	***

Table 7–8 on the next page contains the TE notifications as they are currently defined.

The TE MIB contains an example of a tunnel setup using a defined object. [4] The tunnel in the example is a best-effort, loosely-routed, unidirectional, traffic-engineered tunnel that spans two hops of a sample network. This MIB instance would be configured at the ingress, or "head-end," LSR.

Table 7–8 TE MIB Notifications

Name	Description
MplsTunnelUp	This notification is generated when an `mplsTunnelOperStatus` object for one of the configured tunnels is about to leave the down state and transition into some other state (but not into the `notPresent` state). This other state is indicated by the included value of `mplsTunnelOperStatus`.
MplsTunnelDown	This notification is generated when an `mplsTunnelOperStatus` object for one of the configured tunnels is about to enter the down state from some other state (but not from the `notPresent` state). This other state is indicated by the included value of `mplsTunnelOperStatus`.
MplsTunnelRerouted	This notification is generated when a tunnel is rerouted. If the actual path is used, then this object MAY contain the new path for this tunnel sometime after this trap is issued by the agent.
MplsTunnelReoptimized	This notification is generated when a tunnel is re-optimized. If the actual path is used, then this object MAY contain the new path for this tunnel sometime after this trap is issued by the agent.

```
In mplsTunnelTable:
{
  mplsTunnelIndex              = 1,
  mplsTunnelInstance           = 1,
  mplsTunnelIngressLSRId       = 123.123.125.1,
  mplsTunnelEgressLSRId        = 123.123.126.1,
  mplsTunnelName               = "My first tunnel",
  mplsTunnelDescr              = "Here to there",
  mplsTunnelIsIf               = true (1),
  mplsTunnelXCPointer          = mplsXCIndex.2.0.0.15,
  mplsTunnelSignallingProto    = none (1),
  mplsTunnelSetupPrio          = 0,
  mplsTunnelHoldingPrio        = 0,
  mplsTunnelSessionAttributes  = 0,
  mplsTunnelOwner              = snmp (1),
```

```
    mplsTunnelLocalProtectInUse   = false (0),
    mplsTunnelResourcePointer     = mplsTunnelResourceIndex.5,
    mplsTunnelInstancePriority    = 1,
    mplsTunnelHopTableIndex       = 1,
    mplsTunnelPrimaryInstance     = 0,
    mplsTunnelIncludeAnyAffinity  = 0,
    mplsTunnelIncludeAllAffinity  = 0,
    mplsTunnelExcludeAllAffinity  = 0,
    mplsTunnelPathInUse           = 1,
    mplsTunnelRole                = head(1),
    mplsTunnelRowStatus           = createAndGo (4)
}


In mplsTunnelResourceTable:
{
    mplsTunnelResourceIndex            = 5,
    mplsTunnelResourceMaxRate          = 0,
    mplsTunnelResourceMeanRate         = 0,
    mplsTunnelResourceMaxBurstSize     = 0,
    mplsTunnelResourceRowStatus        = createAndGo (4)
}
```

The next two instances of mplsTunnelHopEntry are used to specify the hops this tunnel needs to cross the network. The following entry represents the beginning of the network, that is, the first hop. Note that the MIB example uses a fictitious LSR identified by 123.123.125.1 as the ingress.

```
In mplsTunnelHopTable:
{
    mplsTunnelHopListIndex         = 1,
    mplsTunnelPathOptionIndex      = 1,
    mplsTunnelHopIndex             = 1,
    mplsTunnelHopAddrType          = 1,
    mplsTunnelHopIpv4Addr          = 123.123.125.1,
    mplsTunnelHopIpv4PrefixLen     = 9,
    mplsTunnelHopType              = loose (2),
    mplsTunnelHopRowStatus         = createAndGo (4)
}
```

The following entry represents the end of the sample two-node network. This is the egress, or last hop. The MIB uses the fictitious LSR identified by 123.123.126.1 as the egress LSR.

```
In mplsTunnelHopTable:
{
  mplsTunnelHopListIndex          = 1,
  mplsTunnelPathOptionIndex       = 1,
  mplsTunnelHopIndex              = 2,
  mplsTunnelHopAddrType           = 1,
  mplsTunnelHopIpv4Addr           = 123.123.126.1,
  mplsTunnelHopIpv4PrefixLen      = 9,
  mplsTunnelHopType               = loose (2),
  mplsTunnelHopRowStatus          = createAndGo (4)
}
```

The FEC-to-NHLFE (FTN) MIB

The FTN is the data structure present in any LSR acting in the ingress role for mapping each FEC set to its corresponding next-hop label forwarding entry (NHLFE) match. Remember, if there is more than one match, a mechanism based on a configured policy must choose the appropriate NHLFE partner. The FTN MIB is implemented in any LSR acting in the ingress role. It controls how the MPLS packets are selected for their labels and outgoing ports.

The FTN MIB manages the objects necessary to monitor and control this important data structure and any corresponding actions. The current definition for the FTN MIB is the ID titled "Multiprotocol Label Switching (MPLS) FEC-To-NHLFE (FTN) Management Information Base Using SMIv2" by Nadeau, Srinivasan, and Viswanathan.[6]

This work in progress currently defines the MIB as three tables:

- The FTN Mapping table (mplsFTNTable)
- The FTN Activation table (mplsFTNMapTable)
- The FTN Performance table (mplsFTNPerfTable)

The mplsFTNTable defines the set of rules against which incoming IP packets are matched and what actions should be taken on the matched packets. This table is where the FTN mappings can be specified. This table provides the standard five-tuple matching capability to all the IP addresses and ports to be defined. The mplsFTNMapTable defines how the rules are applied to specific interfaces. It maps the FTN table entries to

---

6. The current version for this MIB is available online as: draft-ietf-mpls-ftn-mib-01.txt

the interfaces present in the LSR. The `mplsFTNPerfTable` provides the performance counters for each active FTN entry based on interface. This table includes high capacity (i.e., 64-bit "buckets") when an interface causes the customary 32-bit counters to wrap too quickly.

Table 7–9 contains the FTN MIB textual conventions that are currently defined.

Table 7–9   FTN MIB Textual Conventions

Name	Syntax	Description
MplsPortAddr	INTEGER(0..65535)	A TCP or UDP port number. Along with an IP address, identifies a stream of IP traffic uniquely.
MplsFTNIndex	Integer32(1..2147483647)	Index for an FTN entry.
MplsFTNIndexOrZero	Integer32(0..2147483647)	Index for an FTN entry or zero.

Table 7–10 contains the listing for the FTN MIB OID hierarchy.

Table 7–10   The FTN MIB OID Hierarchy

Name	OID	ASN.1 Syntax	Access
mplsFTNMIB	1.3.6.1.3.*nnn**	MODULE-IDENTITY	***
mplsFTNNotifications	1.3.6.1.3.*nnn*.0	OBJECT IDENTIFIER	***
mplsFTNObjects	1.3.6.1.3.*nnn*.1	OBJECT IDENTIFIER	***
mplsFTNIndexNext	1.3.6.1.3.*nnn*.1.1	MplsFTNIndexOrZero	RO
mplsFTNTable	1.3.6.1.3.*nnn*.1.2	SEQUENCE OF MplsFTNEntry	NA
mplsFTNEntry	1.3.6.1.3.*nnn*.1.2.1	MPLSFTNEntry	NA
mplsFTNIndex	1.3.6.1.3.*nnn*.1.2.1.1	MplsFTNIndex	NA
mplsFTNRowStatus	1.3.6.1.3.*nnn*.1.2.1.2	RowStatus	RC
mplsFTNDescr	1.3.6.1.3.*nnn*.1.2.1.3	DisplayString	RC
mplsFTNApplied	1.3.6.1.3.*nnn*.1.2.1.4	TruthValue	RO

Table 7–10 The FTN MIB OID Hierarchy (continued)

Name	OID	ASN.1 Syntax	Access
mplsFTNMask	1.3.6.1.3.*nnn*.1.2.1.5	BITS	RC
mplsFTNAddrType	1.3.6.1.3.*nnn*.1.2.1.6	InetAddressType	RC
mplsFTNSourceIpv4AddrMin	1.3.6.1.3.*nnn*.1.2.1.7	InetAddressIPv4	RC
mplsFTNSourceIpv6AddrMin	1.3.6.1.3.*nnn*.1.2.1.8	InetAddressIPv6	RC
mplsFTNSourceIpv4AddrMax	1.3.6.1.3.*nnn*.1.2.1.9	InetAddressIPv4	RC
mplsFTNSourceIpv6AddrMax	1.3.6.1.3.*nnn*.1.2.1.10	InetAddressIPv6	RC
mplsFTNDestIpv4AddrMin	1.3.6.1.3.*nnn*.1.2.1.11	InetAddressIPv4	RC
mplsFTNDestIpv6AddrMin	1.3.6.1.3.*nnn*.1.2.1.12	InetAddressIPv6	RC
mplsFTNDestIpv4AddrMax	1.3.6.1.3.*nnn*.1.2.1.13	InetAddressIPv4	RC
mplsFTNDestIpv6AddrMax	1.3.6.1.3.*nnn*.1.2.1.14	InetAddressIPv6	RC
mplsFTNSourcePortMin	1.3.6.1.3.*nnn*.1.2.1.15	MplsPortAddr	RC
mplsFTNSourcePortMax	1.3.6.1.3.*nnn*.1.2.1.16	MplsPortAddr	RC
mplsFTNDestPortMin	1.3.6.1.3.*nnn*.1.2.1.17	MplsPortAddr	RC
mplsFTNDestPortMax	1.3.6.1.3.*nnn*.1.2.1.18	MplsPortAddr	RC
mplsFTNProtocol	1.3.6.1.3.*nnn*.1.2.1.19	INTEGER	RC
mplsFTNActionType	1.3.6.1.3.*nnn*.1.2.1.20	INTEGER	RC
mplsFTNActionPointer	1.3.6.1.3.*nnn*.1.2.1.21	RowPointer	RC
mplsFTNStorageType	1.3.6.1.3.*nnn*.1.2.1.22	StorageType	RC
mplsFTNMapTable	1.3.6.1.3.*nnn*.1.3	SEQUENCE OF MplsFTNMapEntry	NA
mplsFTNMapEntry	1.3.6.1.3.*nnn*.1.3.1	MPLSFTNMapEntry	NA
mplsFTNMapIfIndex	1.3.6.1.3.*nnn*.1.3.1.1	InterfaceIndexOrZero	RC
mplsFTNMapPrevIndex	1.3.6.1.3.*nnn*.1.3.1.2	MplsFTNIndexOrZero	RC
mplsFTNMapCurrIndex	1.3.6.1.3.*nnn*.1.3.1.3	MplsFTNIndex	RC
mplsFTNMapRowStatus	1.3.6.1.3.*nnn*.1.3.1.4	RowStatus	RC
mplsFTNMapStorageType	1.3.6.1.3.*nnn*.1.3.1.5	StorageType	RC
mplsFTNPerfTable	1.3.6.1.3.*nnn*.1.4	SEQUENCE OF MplsFTNPerfEntry	NA

Table 7–10 The FTN MIB OID Hierarchy (continued)

Name	OID	ASN.1 Syntax	Access
mplsFTNPerfEntry	1.3.6.1.3.*nnn*.1.4.1	MplsFTNPerfEntry	NA
mplsFTNMatchedPackets	1.3.6.1.3.*nnn*.1.4.1.1	Counter32	RO
mplsFTNMatchedOctets	1.3.6.1.3.*nnn*.1.4.1.2	Counter32	RO
mplsFTNMatchedHCPackets	1.3.6.1.3.*nnn*.1.4.1.3	Counter64	RO
mplsFTNMatchedHCOctets	1.3.6.1.3.*nnn*.1.4.1.4	Counter64	RO
mplsFTNConformance	1.3.6.1.3.*nnn*.2	OBJECT IDENTIFIER	***
mplsFTNGroups	1.3.6.1.3.*nnn*.2.1	OBJECT IDENTIFIER	***
mplsFTNRuleGroup	1.3.6.1.3.*nnn*.2.1.1	OBJECT-GROUP	***
mplsFTNMapGroup	1.3.6.1.3.*nnn*.2.1.2	OBJECT-GROUP	***
mplsFTNPerfGroup	1.3.6.1.3.*nnn*.2.1.3	OBJECT-GROUP	***
mplsFTNHCPerfGroup	1.3.6.1.3.*nnn*.2.1.4	OBJECT-GROUP	***
mplsFTNCompliances	1.3.6.1.3.*nnn*.2.2	OBJECT IDENTIFIER	***
mplsFTNModuleCompliance	1.3.6.1.3.*nnn*.2.2.1	MODULE-COMPLIANCE	***

There are currently no notifications defined for this MIB.

Additional MPLS MIB Efforts

The MPLS WG has completed a helper MIB that will be a central repository for the MPLS textual conventions. Textual conventions are a mechanism for limiting the scope of a data type definition to refine its meaning without having to create a new data type. This MIB is titled "Definition of Textual Conventions and OBJECT-IDENTITIES for Multi-Protocol Label Switching (MPLS) Management," and it was written by Thomas Nadeau, Joan Cucchiara, Cheenu Srinivasan, Arun Viswanathan, and Hans Sjostrand.[7] The current list of MPLS textual conventions is shown in Table 7–11.

The development of MIBs for MPLS is an ongoing effort as more and more MPLS resources are defined. There are several ongoing efforts that include the development of MIBs for many related MPLS topics. Most of

---

7. The current ID version for the TC MIB is: `draft-ietf-mpls-tc-mib-02.txt`

Table 7–11   MPLS Textual Conventions

Name	Syntax	Description
MplsAtmVcIdentifier	INTEGER32 (32..65535)	The VCI value for a VCL. The maximum VCI value cannot exceed the value allowable by atmInterfaceMaxVciBits, which is defined in the ATM MIB. The minimum value is 32; values 0 to 31 are reserved for other uses by the ITU and ATM Forum. 32 is typically the default value for the control VC.
MplsBitRate	Integer32 (1..2147483647)	An estimate of bandwidth in units of 1,000 bits per second. If this object reports a value of 'n', then the rate of the object is somewhere in the range of 'n-500' to 'n+499'. For objects that do not vary in bit rate, or for those where no accurate estimation can be made, this object should contain the nominal bit rate.
MplsBurstSize	Unsigned32 (1..4294967295)	An estimate of bandwidth in units of 1,000 bits per second. If this object reports a value of 'n', then the rate of the object is somewhere in the range of 'n-500' to 'n+499'. For objects that do not vary in bit rate, or for those where no accurate estimation can be made, this object should contain the nominal bit rate.
MplsExtendedTunnelId	Unsigned32	A unique identifier for an MPLS tunnel. This MAY represent an IPv4 address of the ingress or egress LSR for the tunnel. This value is derived from the extended tunnel ID in RSVP or the ingress router ID for CR-LDP.
MplsFTNIndex	Integer32 (1..2147483647)	Index for an FTN entry.
MplsFTNIndexOrZero	Integer32 (0..2147483647)	Index for an FTN entry or zero.

Table 7–11   MPLS Textual Conventions (continued)

Name	Syntax	Description
MplsInitialCreationSource	INTEGER	The entity that originally created the object in question. The values of this enumeration are defined as follows: other(1)—This is used when an entity has not been enumerated in this textual convention, but it is known by the agent. snmp(2)—The SNMP was used to configure this object initially. ldp(3)—The LDP was used to configure this object initially. rsvp(4)—The RSVP was used to configure this object initially. crldp(5)—The CR-LDP was used to configure this object initially. policyAgent(6)—A policy agent (perhaps in combination with one of the above protocols) was used to configure this object initially. unknown(7)—The agent cannot discern which component created the object.
MplsLSPID	OCTET STRING (SIZE (0..31))	An identifier that is assigned to each LSP and is used to uniquely identify it. This is assigned at the head-end of the LSP and can be used by all LSRs to identify this LSP. This value is piggybacked by the signaling protocol when this LSP is signaled within the network. This identifier can then be used at each LSR to identify which labels are being swapped to other labels for this LSP. For IPv4 addresses, this results in a six-octet-long cookie.
MplsLabel	Unsigned32 (0..4294967295)	This value represents an MPLS label as defined in RFC 3031, RFC 3032, RFC 3034, and RFC 3035.
MplsLdpGenAddr	OCTET STRING (SIZE (0..64))	The value of a network layer or data link layer address.
MplsLdpIdentifier	OCTET STRING (SIZE (6))	The LDP identifier is a six-octet quantity that is used to identify an LSR label space. The first four octets identify the LSR and must be a globally unique value, such as a 32-bit router ID assigned to the LSR. The last two octets identify a specific label space within the LSR.
MplsLdpLabelTypes	INTEGER	The Layer 2 label types that are defined for MPLS LDP/CRLDP are: generic(1), atm(2), and frameRelay(3).

Table 7–11   MPLS Textual Conventions (continued)

Name	Syntax	Description
MplsLsrIdentifier	OCTET STRING (SIZE (4))	The LSR identifier is the first four bytes of the LDP identifier.
MplaPathIndex	Unsigned32	A unique identifier used to specify apath used by a tunnel.
MplsPathIndexOrZero	Unsigned32	A unique identifier used to specify a path used by a tunnel. If this value is set to 0, it indicates that no path is in use.
MplsPortNumber	Integer32 (0..65535)	A TCP or UDP port number. Along with an IP address, identifies a stream of IP traffic uniquely.
MplsTunnelAffinity	Unsigned32	Include-any, include-all, or exclude-all constraint for link selection.
MplsTunnelIndex	Integer32 (1..65535)	Index into mplsTunnelTable.
MplsTunnelInstanceIndex	Unsigned32 (0..65535)	Instance index into mplsTunnelTable.

these efforts are early works in progress and are listed as individual submissions on the IETF Web site.

The ID "Diff-Serv-aware MPLS Traffic Engineering Network Management Information Base Using SMIv2" by Nadeau, Chiu, Townsend, Skalecki, and Tatham defines an MIB for managed objects for modeling and managing Diff-Serv-aware MPLS TE. An ID on link bundling managed objects, titled "Link Bundling Management Information Base Using SMIv2," was written by Dubuc, Dharanikota, Nadeau, and Lang. An LMP MIB ("Link Management Protocol Management Information Base Using SMIv2"), also by Dubuc, Dharanikota, Nadeau, and Lang, contains a description of the managed objects that will be necessary for monitoring and controlling the LMP to be used with GMPLS. An MIB that helps manage MPLS VPN applications titled "MPLS/BGP Virtual Private Network Management Information Base Using SMIv2" is being written by Nadeau, Fang, Brannon, Chiussi, Dube, and Tatham. This MIB will contain the objects necessary to manage MPLS/BGP VPNs.

CLI-BASED MPLS MANAGEMENT ....

Another important tool that is present in nearly every managed device is the command-line interface (CLI). The CLI is a terminal-based, proprietary interface that is often used for the low-level configuration and monitoring of the device. Most CLIs are text-based. Many CLIs use a common SNMP interface within the device to provide a consistent set of management values when the management information is read or written by either the CLI or SNMP agent.

POLICY-BASED MANAGEMENT ....

Policy-based management is a higher level abstraction that manages the network as a collection of similar resources. It allows management to move beyond its current charter of controlling each individual device and resource. Policy applications allow the network manager to provide and enforce a domain-wide, consistent configuration based on predetermined policies. Policy-based MPLS management will greatly facilitate the deployment and control of applications such as TE, QoS, VPNs, and path restoral.

The general model is shown in Figure 7–7. It points out how policy applications drive network management to create, deploy, and enforce domain-wide policies.

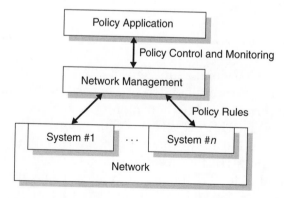

Figure 7–7   Policy-based network management model.

OTHER MPLS MANAGEMENT ISSUES ....

Two other important MPLS management issues include the development of management techniques and mechanisms for GMPLS and the new optical technologies. Also of interest is the rise of operation support systems (OSSs), which include SNMP network management and a host of new management technologies that are needed for the new requirements created by deploying MPLS.

The Link Monitoring Protocol (LMP)

The LMP is a management protocol that operates between two neighboring nodes that may be OXCs, PXCs, or any number of LSRs that possess optical interfaces. LMP is designed to maintain control channel connectivity, to assure that the physical channels carrying data are up and running, and also to handle the link details such as link statistics, failures, and so on.

Operation Support Systems (OSSs)

The OSS is the manager side of the management equation. The OSS provides the management infrastructure used in telecommunications and data communications deployments, which can incorporate SNMP and other management frameworks. The three most important facets of any OSS are customer care and billing, provisioning and order management, and network operations management.

SUMMARY ....

Chapter 7 dealt with a very important aspect of MPLS—its management. Since SNMP is the IETF-recommended framework for managing devices connected to the Internet, it plays an important role in the monitoring and control of MPLS. The MPLS WG has four main MIBs that are currently in the ID format, but may soon advance on the standards track as RFCs. These include an MIB that describes managed objects for the LSR, an MIB for LDP, an MIB for TE, and an MIB for the FTN mapping that is required at the ingress. The WG has also created an MIB that contains all of the MPLS textual conventions.

There are also several additional ongoing MIB development efforts. These areas include the management of MPLS/BGP VPNs, Diff-Serv, link bundling, and the LMP that will be used with GMPLS. Other MPLS management issues discussed include CLI, LMP, and OSS.

REFERENCES FOR CHAPTER 7..

1. Andrews, Robert. *The Columbia Dictionary of Quotations.* New York: Columbia University Press, 1993, p. 497.

2. Srinivasan, Chennu, Arun Viswanathan, and Thomas Nadeau. *MPLS Label Switch Router Management Information Base Using SMIv2* (work in progress). IETF MPLS Working Group Internet Draft, January 2001, pp. 8–10.

3. Subramanian, Mani. *Network Management: Principles and Practices.* Reading, MA: Addison-Wesley, 2000, p. 105.

4. Srinivasan, Chennu, Arun Viswanathan, and Thomas Nadeau. *MPLS Traffic Engineering Management Information Base Using SMIv2* (work in progress). IETF MPLS Working Group Internet Draft, March 2001, pp. 9–10.

Current MPLS Developments and Directions

8

> And thus do we of wisdom and of reach,
> With windlasses and with assays of bias,
> By indirections find directions out.[1] [1]
>
> — *William Shakespeare,*
> *Hamlet II*

There is little doubt that MPLS is stirring interest as a technology that will influence the Internet communications infrastructure. As work continues in standardizing the core MPLS technologies and associated label signaling and distribution protocols, related efforts are currently underway with MPLS groups and forums and in many associated technologies that may benefit from working with MPLS.

---

1. For all of us Shakespeare dilettantes, "windlasses" refers to roundabout methods, and the phrase "assays of bias" means oblique tests and trials.

CURRENT MPLS TECHNOLOGY DEVELOPMENTS ....

Current MPLS technology developments and protocol improvements include:

- "Everything" over MPLS
- Hierarchical stacking
- MPLS multicast
- Voice over MPLS (VoMPLS)
- Wireless MPLS

"Everything" over MPLS

An important, current MPLS development is the use of the technology to carry various types of Layer 2 transport traffic through specially configured LSP tunnels. There is interest in using MPLS as a universal data pipe, effectively creating an "everything" over MPLS network. MPLS is used in this scenario as an integrated access mechanism for many types of transport traffic within the entire network infrastructure. This technique can be used to create certain flavors of Layer 2 VPNs. The tunnels can also be used to carry virtual LAN (VLAN) Ethernet traffic across MPLS domains.

The prime Layer 2 technologies that are being investigated are ATM, FR, and Ethernet. Other lower-level transport technologies that are being looked at for this mechanism include PPP, Cisco's HDLC, and SONET/SDH and leased-line circuit emulation. The prime motivations for using MPLS in these scenarios is to leverage existing network equipment, provide circuit-based service emulation similar to the conventional circuit-switched networks in place, and be an any-to-any mesh network for these types of traffic.

The principal works in progress that define this current development are two IDs: "Transport of Layer 2 Frames Over MPLS" and "Encapsulation Methods for Transport of Layer 2 Frames Over MPLS.[2]"

---

2. As of this writing, the versions of these two IDs are: `draft-martini-l2circuit-trasn-mpls-06.txt` and `draft-martini-l2circuit-encap-mpls-02.txt`, respectively.

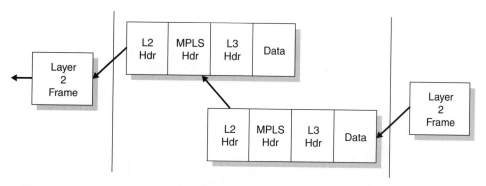

Figure 8–1   General encapsulation method.

In general, the Layer 2 frame is carried as data in the MPLS packet as shown in Figure 8–1. In most instances, the header of the Layer 2 frame can be removed at the ingress LSR and then recreated at the egress LSR by using extra encapsulation information that can either be signaled ahead of time or carried in a special control word as described in the specification.

ATM (AAL5) over MPLS   With the ATM Layer 2 technologies, MPLS supports the ATM switches found in the various connected edge networks. The VPI and VCI fields are translated by the ingress LSRs, which are at the edge of the MPLS network cloud. The LSRs maintain the VC label to the input and output ports as well as the VPI/VCI mapping. A sample network is shown in Figure 8–2 on the next page.

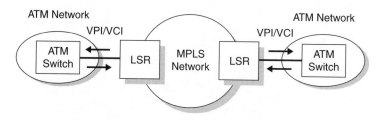

Figure 8–2   ATM and MPLS integrated access model.

FR over MPLS   For FR, MPLS supports the FR access devices (FRADs) that are typically found in the enterprise or customer FR network. As shown in Figure 8–3, on the next page, the ingress LSRs translate the DLCIs by maintaining the necessary tables for mapping the

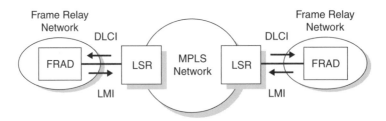

Figure 8–3   FR and MPLS integrated access model.

virtual circuit labels to the input and output interfaces and proper DLCI values. The data field of the MPLS packet in this configuration contains the entire FR PDU. The FECN and BECN bits are also carried, but this is transparent to MPLS. The ingress LSR maps the discard eligibility (DE) bit to a corresponding EXP value in the MPLS header. At the egress LSR, Q.933 and Q.922 errors and alarms can be generated.

Ethernet over MPLS   A sample Ethernet over MPLS network is shown in Figure 8–4. The ingress LSRs translate the Ethernet MAC addresses and maintain the MAC labels to input and output port mappings. The LSR can optionally maintain the VLAN mappings, also. For this type of encapsulation, the whole Layer 2 Ethernet frame (without the preamble and FCS) is carried in the MPLS packet data field. For VLANs, the VLAN tag is also transported. The ingress and egress LSRs may evaluate the priority field of the VLAN header for mapping into the EXP field of the MPLS header. The LSR may also optionally honor sequencing control.

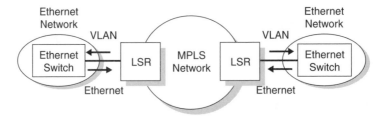

Figure 8–4   Ethernet and MPLS integrated access model.

Hierarchical Label Stacking

The ability to stack label entries to an arbitrary depth is one of the most powerful MPLS features. Various proposals have been forthcoming to create standardized hierarchies for transporting MPLS packets in an ordered and meaningful fashion. Currently, hierarchical label stacking is employed in BGP/MPLS VPNs, for example, to keep the core of the network ignorant of the specifics of the VPN application. There is discussion involving extending the semantics of inner labels for new possible application purposes, while the top labels are used to send the MPLS packet down to its LSPs.

MPLS Multicast

Multicast is the ability to send a single multicast packet to all intended recipients in the configured multicast group; that is, one packet is sent and many copies are received. This mechanism presents several unique challenges to technologies such as MPLS in the areas of TE and QoS. The way in which congestion is created and handled has different requirements for unicast IP and MPLS traffic.

One area where multicast is being investigated is with BGP/MPLS VPN applications. One current ID titled "Multicast in MPLS/BGP VPNs" by Rosen, Cai, Tappan, Wijnands, Rekhter, and Farinacci adds to the main BGP/MPLS VPN specification by describing the protocols and procedures that a service provider can implement to deploy multicast VPN traffic. The specification also indicates that the PIM multicast routing protocol must be used within the VPN.

MPLS multicast is currently a topic that is under investigation by the WG and several IDs should be forthcoming containing the various details necessary to support this within the Internet. As of this writing, neither CR-LPD nor RSVP-TE support multicast.

Voice over MPLS

The use of packetized voice technologies is growing in the Internet as data and voice networks slowly converge on a global scale. Investigation is being done in sending voice over MPLS as well as IP. Transmitting voice traffic over IP-based networks has many potential advantages. Service providers can deploy and support a single infrastructure for all important Internet services, including data, voice, and video. Voice traffic brings new constraints to a packet network, however. Voice-based applications require low delay and low-delay variation. They are tolerant to some small amount of voice packet data loss. These new requirements must be met by the network by providing an adequate QoS for voice traffic as it commingles with data and other traffic.

There are two current directions in marrying packetized voice and MPLS. One is Voice over IP over MPLS (VoIPoMPLS), which involves IP encapsulation of the voice packet. The other effort is VoMPLS, which places packetized voice samples directly over MPLS. IP encapsulation is not used in the latter technique. The current implementations of VoIPoMPLS use the Real-Time Protocol (RTP) as an application layer protocol over UDP for transport over IP over MPLS over a lower layer technology such as FR, ATM PPP, or Ethernet. There is a fair amount of packet header overhead (the RTP, UDP, and IP headers alone require 40 octets), and it requires a great deal of bandwidth to deliver the minimum quality for voice traffic.[3]

The MPLS technology has several features that make it an attractive candidate for working with voice to deliver new voice-over-packet services. But the technology must still deliver the required parameters for carrier class reliability and quality of voice. This includes the PCM encoding scheme (such as G.711 or G.726 encoding for speech), synchronization with the Stratum clock (G.811 standard), and channel echo cancellation.

At a recent IETF BOF meeting on VoMPLS, it was agreed to define a common framework and examine how related standards efforts could be brought into play. Key tenets of the VoMPLS framework include using LSPs as bearer channels for packetized voice traffic, introducing a new call control procedure for making calls, and identifying any other functional changes that might be done to MPLS to make it operate with voice. This would include compression schemes, suppression mechanisms, and others to be determined. The standard voice call control protocols (such as MEGACO, MGCP, and SIP) would need to operate with MPLS signaling protocols such as RSVP-TE and LDP.

In addition to VoMPLS, there is also work beginning on sending multimedia traffic over IP (MMoIP) networks that would use MPLS. This traffic has its own set of requirements and investigation is just beginning on a framework for this technology.

---

3. One benchmark for voice quality is the Mean Opinion Score (MOS). The MOS of a voice path must be greater than 4.0 for a carrier or service provider to tariff this service to a customer.

Wireless MPLS

The use of wireless technologies with MPLS is being investigated, primarily by several of the major wireless vendors as a way of introducing wireless traffic into the Internet in a controlled and standardized fashion. As with voice over MPLS technologies, wireless faces similar and additional hurdles for deployment, especially with regard to the latest "third-generation" (3G) wireless networks. Moving to the latest 3G networks will provide end-users the ability to send and receive high-capacity data from 9.6 Kbps to 2 Mbps for such data services as WWW access, while still providing a quality voice service.

Several framework proposals will be developed in the current environment. The MPLS applications of TE, QoS, and path restoral will play an important part in next-generation MPLS-based wireless networks.

MPLS PROTOCOL IMPROVEMENTS

While the main MPLS technology is being advanced, there are several protocol improvements and other advances that may improve the technology.

MPLS Header Compression

One current area of investigation is the use of MPLS header compression to increase the bandwidth efficiency of MPLS traffic. Two specifications have been created: one is titled "MPLS/IP Header Compression," and the other is "MPLS/IP Header Compression Over PPP." Both were written by Lou Berger and Jason Jeffords. They were originally presented at the July 2000 IETF meeting in Pittsburgh, Pennsylvania.

MPLS header compression schemes build on the standard IP header compression mechanisms presented in RFC 2507, "IP Header Compression," RFC 2508, "Compressing IP/UDP/RTP Headers for Low Speed Serial Links," and RFC 2509, "IP Header Compression Over PPP." These schemes would provide support for a variable number of MPLS label stack entries.

MPLS Security

Adding various security mechanisms to MPLS is also an important current development. While the basic security features that can be added to network technologies—such as access control, user and message authentication, message encryption, public key distribution techniques, and many others—are well-understood and have been deployed with IP for some time, there is renewed interest in using several of these features with MPLS.

The MPLS VPN application is garnering particular attention as the privacy of the data passed in the VPN tunnels must be ensured. Authentication digests and encryption of the message payload are being researched. Other areas of research include a security analysis of the overall MPLS architecture, end-to-end authentication of the LDP signaling messages, label stack authentication, and several others.

SUMMARY ....

Chapter 8 discussed current MPLS developments and protocol improvements. There are five current directions that are expanding the present scope and use of MPLS. These include the use of Layer 2 technologies over MPLS, hierarchical stacking, multicast, VoMPLS, and the use of MPLS in the wireless domain. Two areas that are being investigated for improving MPLS are header compression and the introduction of additional security mechanisms.

REFERENCES FOR CHAPTER 8 ....

1. Evans, Bergen. *Dictionary of Quotations.* New York: Delacorte Press, 1968, p. 756.

Current MPLS Implementations

9

The best way to have a good idea is to have lots of ideas. [1]

— *Linus Pauling*

W hether MPLS emerges as a new lynchpin in the Internet architecture or falters as a technology that could not find a place for one technical or political reason or another, many organizations are involved in implementing the technology. Current MPLS implementers can be broken down into several categories, including service providers, equipment vendors, software stack providers, test equipment manufacturers, testing organizations, universities, and several others.

The main purpose of this chapter is to give a very coarse-grained overview of several organizations involved in each category.[1] In no way is this chapter intended to be comprehensive, and due to the dynamic nature of new technologies in general, a complete list of any of the organizations in these categories would be a moving target.

---

1. An up-to-date list of MPLS vendors is kept at the MPLS Resource Center Web site: `www.mplsrc.com/vendor.shtml`

The Web is obviously an excellent place to retrieve more MPLS information from any of these organizations and to find more details. The listing of companies in the various MPLS forums is also a fine starting point to discover more data on MPLS products, which standards are being implemented, pricing, and so on; all of these companies are involved in MPLS implementation in one form or another. Also, as MPLS momentum grows, more and more organizations will become involved in all of these general categories.

SERVICE PROVIDERS UTILIZING MPLS..........................

The primary deliverer of MPLS technology and its applications is the service provider. A sampling of large national and global service providers that have announced MPLS deployments is shown in Table 9–1. This table is from early 2001, and will certainly be larger as this is being read. The reader is directed to each service provider's Web site to seek more specific MPLS information.

Service providers are interested in MPLS QoS, TE, and VPN applications as revenue producing opportunities. Many ISPs are designing and rolling out MPLS-based VPN services. Global One has an international service named Global Intranet VPN. Two ISPs in Japan include Japan-Telecom's Solteria VPN service and Super-VPN from NTT Communications. AT&T announced the addition of MPLS capabilities for QoS and VPNs to IP-enable their ATM network. This network will work with AT&T's IP-enabled FR service to create IP-based intranets and extranets without forcing customers to build separate IP networks or modify the IP applications they use. Both IP-enabled ATM and FR use MPLS. Each service provider in Table 9–1 provides one or more MPLS application.

Table 9–1   Service Providers Offering MPLS

Service Provider	Web Address
AT&T	www.att.com
British Telecom	www.bt.com
Cable & Wireless	www.cw.com
China Unicom	www.netchina.com.cn

Table 9–1   Service Providers Offering MPLS (continued)

Service Provider	Web Address
Concert	`www.concert.com`
CoreExpress	`www.coreexpress.com`
Digex	`www.digex.com`
Equant	`www.equant.com`
France Telecom	`www.francetelecom.fr`
Global One	`www.global-one.net`[1]
Global Crossing	`www.globalcrossing.com`
Infonet	`www.infonet.com`
Iteroute	`www.iteroute.com`
Japan Telecom	`www.japan-telecom.co.jp`
NTT	`www.ntt.co.jp`
Swisscom	`www.swisscom.com`
UUNET	`www.uunet.com`[2]
Worldcom	`www.worldcom.com`

1. Global One is now part of Equant.
2. UUNET is now part of Worldcom.

MPLS Equipment Vendors ....

MPLS equipment vendors manufacture MPLS gear for use throughout
the Internet: from core terabit routers and OXCs, to regional and metro
access routers, to smaller edge routers, ATM-LSRs, and FR MPLS
switches, to small MPLS traffic aggregation devices. The companies
range from established equipment vendors to many new startup ven-
tures. Each is creating standards-based MPLS implementations that will
play together in the next-generation Internet communication fabric.

Again, this is a high-level introduction to several of the major play-
ers. Please refer to their Web sites for more detailed information. Most of

these vendors have excellent white papers that deal with all aspects of MPLS. Also, consult the WWW for additional MPLS equipment vendors.

Alcatel

Alcatel is a leading vendor in the high-speed access and optical transport market, as well as being a major player in the areas of telecommunications and the Internet. Alcatel has several backbone and edge routing devices that support IP, ATM, and MPLS. One example of an Alcatel LSR is the 7670 Routing Switch Platform (RSP), which is designed for next-generation backbone networks. It integrates ATM, MPLS and IP routing on the same platform. The Alcatel Web site (www.alcatel.com) contains information on all of the Alcatel products that implement MPLS technology.

Avici

Avici produces a core terabit router platform called the terabit switch router (TSR). The TSR contains a software suite called Ipriori that includes MPLS. The Avici Web site is: www.avici.com.

Cisco Systems

Cisco Systems is a leading implementer of MPLS technology, starting with the tag switching technology that it developed in the 1990s. Cisco has a family of multiservice switches that use leading-edge MPLS technology with both IP and ATM networks. Cisco products implement a complete set of MPLS applications. The Cisco Internet Operating System (IOS) MPLS software integrates routing and switching to provide benefit to networks that are a pure IP architecture, as well as those with IP and ATM, or a mix of other Layer 2 technologies. The MPLS software is key for VPN and QoS applications. The Cisco Web site is: www.cisco.com.

Ennovate Networks

Ennovate Networks manufactures carrier-class, MPLS-enabled, IP multiservice switches. They also have an innovative IP VPN application. The Ennovate Networks Web site is: www.ennovatenetworks.com.

Ericsson

Ericsson provides a complete network-wide MPLS implementation with a family of ATM switches and IP routers. The Ericsson Web site is: www.ericsson.com.

Integral Access

Integral Access offers a set of devices, called the Pure Packet Node family, for MPLS-based access network solutions. The Pure Packet Node family enables service providers to guarantee QoS for packetized voice and to dynamically allocate bandwidth among voice, video, and data services. Their Web site is: www.integralaccess.com.

Juniper Networks

Juniper Networks has implemented a family of routers called the "M series" that performs at throughputs from 5 Gbps for an M5 to 160 Gbps for a terabit M160 core router. Juniper has also developed a custom operating system for its routers called JUNOS, which implements MPLS and the accompanying signaling protocols. The Juniper Web site is: www.juniper.net.

Lucent Technologies

Lucent Technologies is one of the oldest MPLS vendors with its IP Navigator product, which included one of the first commercial MPLS implementations. Lucent also markets the GX550 multiservice WAN switch and all of the accompanying MPLS applications. The Lucent Web site is: www.lucent.com.

Marconi

Marconi has developed a line of ATM-LSRs that includes MPLS applications. The ASX 4000 is an example of one such device. The Marconi Web site is: www.marconi.com.

Nortel

Through development and acquisition, Nortel has several families of MPLS devices, meeting customer requirements across a wide range of demands. These include the Passport series, the OPTera line, and the Shasta Broadband Service Node. The Nortel Web site is: www.nortel.com.

Riverstone

Riverstone Networks is a metropolitan area MPLS router vendor. River-stone has created a family of MPLS-enabled devices for implementing MPLS applications called the RS series. The Riverstone routers come in a variety of speeds and capabilities, including optical interfaces. The River-stone Web site is: www.riverstonenetworks.com.

Tenor Networks

Tenor Networks markets an MPLS core switch called the TN250G. It con-tains optical interfaces and supports the MPLS QoS application. Tenor has also developed TEMPo, an element management system that aids in the configuration, monitoring, and control of MPLS resources on Tenor LSRs. The Tenor Networks Web site is: www.tenornetworks.com.

MPLS SOFTWARE PROVIDERS..

MPLS protocol stack vendors often provide MPLS implementations as toolkits or collections of APIs that are added to a customer's device to cre-ate an MPLS-enabled device such as an LSR.

Data Connections Limited

 Data Connections Limited is an independent developer and supplier of MPLS, ATM, and other portable communications products. Data Connec-tion's DC-MPLS products provide a complete solution for all MPLS device vendors, including developers of core MPLS devices and IP-to-MPLS access devices. Their family of products includes label manage-ment software and LDP stacks. Their specific suite of MPLS products include DC-Label Manager, DC-RSVP-TE, and DC-CR-LDP. The Data Connections Limited Web site is: www.datcon.co.uk.

Future Software Limited

Future Software Limited is another MPLS stack vendor. Their product is called Future MPLS. Future MPLS software is their efficient and porta-ble implementation of the label switching capability mechanism required by IETF standards. This product supports RSVP-TE, LDP with CR-LSP, and MPLS forwarding functionality. The URL at Future Software Limited for MPLS information is: www.futsoft.com/mpls.htm.

NetPlane Systems

NetPlane Systems is a global supplier of portable networking protocol software and systems. Their software is specifically targeted for the control plane of a device. The company sells products that include implementations for MPLS, IP routing, ATM, Private Network—to—Network Interface (PNNI), FR, and simulated test tools. NetPlane's MPLS implementation is called the Label Traffic Control System (LTCS). The NetPlane Web site is: www.netplane.com.

Trillium

Trillium (an Intel company) provides a portable MPLS software product that integrates a label swapping forwarding paradigm with network layer routing, thus improving the price/performance of the network layer routing and scalability of the network layer and facilitating TE through an IP-based network. The Trillium Web site is: www.trillium.com.

Virata

Virata provides MPLS source code solutions in a package called Performance Optimized MPLS. This implementation includes interoperability-tested MPLS signaling support for LDP, CR-LDP, and RSVP-TE. Additionally, Virata delivers a complete TE solution by using their OSPF routing protocol (OSPF++) with integrated TE extensions. The Web address for Virata is: www.virata.com.

MPLS Testing Equipment Manufacturers ....

Several companies that develop and sell communication testing equipment have expanded the capabilities of their platforms to include MPLS testing. MPLS testing platforms come in both complete hardware and software solutions and software add-on modules to existing test equipment. Figure 9–1 on the next page shows a sample topology of several types of test devices deployed in a sample three-node MPLS network.

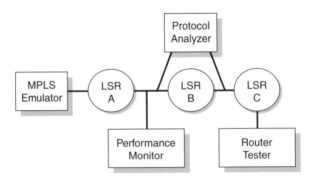

Figure 9–1 MPLS test equipment within a sample test network.

The following companies are a sample of several vendors that have delivered the MPLS test equipment used in various interoperability tests.

Agilent Technologies

Agilent Technologies produces testing equipment for MPLS and a variety of other network protocols. They offer two testing platforms—the QA Robot, which is a conformance test system, and the RouterTester, an MPLS and routing emulator—that can test MPLS features, as well as the LDP and RSVP-TE signaling protocols. The Agilent Web site is: www.agilent.com.

Ixia

Ixia has developed various types of traffic generators and performance analyzers that can be used to test MPLS. Ixia sells RSVP-TE emulation software that can be used to generate thousands of MPLS tunnels. The Ixia Web site is: www.ixiacom.com.

Radcom, Inc.

Radcom produces PrismLite, a protocol analyzer, and WireSpeed 622 PoS, which is a Packet over SONET (PoS) analyzer. Their Web site is: www.radcom-inc.com.

Spirent Communications

An MPLS-related device produced by Spirent is the ADTECH analyzer, generator, and emulator. The Spirent Web site is: www.spirentcom.com.

MPLS TESTING ORGANIZATIONS..................................

MPLS testing is a very important activity, especially in terms of interoperability. Several organizations have set up labs to test various vendor MPLS equipment for conformance, features, performance, and other important metrics.

Advanced Internet Lab (AIL) at George Mason University

The AIL is a testing facility located at George Mason University. Its mission is to provide a program of cutting-edge research, testing, and education in the critical areas of high-speed networking and Internet technology. MPLS interoperability is an initial testing objective for the lab. Major international networking vendors and ISPs help by sponsoring the testing effort. The AIL is supported by faculty and graduate research assistants from the School of Information Technology and Engineering (IT&E) and by the Office of the Vice President for Information Technology. In addition to MPLS work in interoperability testing, several other research programs in high-performance, large-bandwidth Internet core networks are also in progress. The AIL Web site is: www.ail.gmu.edu.

European Advanced Networking Test Center (EANTC) AG

The EANTC was founded in 1991 in Berlin, Germany. It offers global-based, vendor-neutral test facilities for testing many different communications protocols, including MPLS. In the last several years, the EANTC has held the MPLS Interoperability Group Test Event, where leading MPLS vendors can verify Alpha, Beta, or mature code interoperability against other current MPLS implementations of other vendors' products. The EANTC also offers related services, including consulting, support services, and seminars in ATM, MPLS, and other networking topics. The EANTC Web site is: www.eantc.com.

University of New Hampshire Interoperability Lab (IOL)

The IOL at the University of New Hampshire provides testing services for communication device vendors. In addition to research and development work, the IOL is used by over 100 vendors to verify the interoperability and conformance of their communications products. This IOL service is performed by independent, focused interest groups called "consortiums." Current IOL consortiums are operating to test the following: MPLS, Asymmetric Digital Subscriber Line (ADSL), ATM, bridge functions, DOCSIS, fast Ethernet (100 Base-T), fibre channel, Gigabit Ethernet, 10-Gigabit Ethernet, HDSL2, IPv6, iSCSI, routing, SHDSL, voice over broadband, VoIP, and wireless (IEEE 802.11). The IOL also provides educational and employment opportunities for qualified UNH undergraduate and graduate students. The IOL Web site is: `www.iol.unh.edu`.

OTHER ORGANIZATIONS INVOLVED WITH MPLS...

There are many other organizations involved in MPLS. Several universities have started programs that include MPLS design, implementation, and testing. A few national governments have also undertaken MPLS efforts to investigate the technology. Network management companies and OSS vendors have begun serious efforts to create management products. Other vendors have begun to create simulation and emulation devices that will aid in the design, configuration, and performance monitoring of MPLS networks. As MPLS matures, many new organizations will become involved in the effort in any number of ways.

SUMMARY ....

Chapter 9 introduced current MPLS implementations. The chapter included a sampling of the major organizations involved in various MPLS aspects, including service providers utilizing MPLS, equipment vendors, software protocol stack providers, testing equipment manufacturers, testing organizations, and others, such as universities. The intent of this chapter was to offer a sample of the many organizations that are involved in these activities. Web addresses were presented to point the reader toward more information in any of these particular areas.

REFERENCE FOR CHAPTER 9...

1. http://www.s-2000.com/quoteworld/ideas.html.

Future MPLS Developments and Directions

It's tough to make predictions,
especially about the future.[1]

— Yogi Berra

An invasion of armies can be resisted,
but not an idea whose time has come. [2]

— Victor Hugo

The MPLS architecture marries the simplicity of the label switching paradigm and its notion of a universal data forwarding plane with the open, standardized control plane protocols for signaling and label distribution. This union not only offers innovative approaches to complement the way conventional routing and switching are done today, it naturally lends itself to the use of the latest leading-edge technologies that are being used in next-generation networks. The MPLS architecture has shown itself to be adaptable for inclusion with future networking.

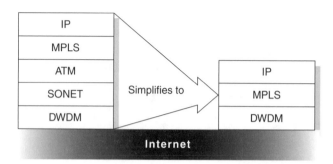

Figure 10–1   Internet layer simplification with optical and MPLS technologies.

The prime future networking technology is, in most people's estimation, optical networking. Work is advancing in many directions in this area. IP and MPLS look to be key components of the next–generation, optical-based Internet.

MPLS AND OPTICAL NETWORKING..................................

While the exact role of MPLS with optical networking is still being debated, IP will play a big role as the protocol for the optical control plane, as well as being used over the optical physical path as the data packet protocol. The distinction that is often made, "IP for optical" and "IP over optical," distinguishes the two different parts IP will play with optical technologies.

The main promise of optical networking is simplification. The way a layered model shows simplification is that fewer layers are required to perform the same functionality. Figure 10–1 shows a possible layer simplification model for migrating a current networking model used in the Internet to a simplified one that may be deployed in the future. Basically, the need for Layer 2 protocols such as ATM and the SONET layer are obviated by using IP and MPLS directly over the DWDM layer. The future DWDM layer will contain the optical switching logic.

IP for Optical

IP for optical is the use of the IP control plane protocols for managing the optical transport and photonic path control. Work done by the OIF and ODSI on the O-UNI is an example of an IP for optical technology.

IP over Optical

When IP is used to transport network layer packets over an optical network, the term "IP over optical" is often used. Two examples of this are IP over Packet over SONET (POS) links and IP over DWDM links.

Two new directions for MPLS within optical networking are MPLambdaS and GMPLS. They are very closely related and both deal with using MPLS with optical networking.

MPLAMBDAS...

The notion that the label swapping paradigm of MPLS could be extended to new optical technologies was first presented as a specification for the control of light paths, or optical trails. This technology was called MPLambdaS, that is, multiprotocol lambda (i.e., light wave) switching. The lambdas are the labels!

Each OXC device acts like an MPLS LSR with the MPLS control plane implemented for each OXC. A separate IP control channel is set up between neighboring OXCs. The light paths become the LSPs, and the selection of the lambdas and cross-connect ports is a process that is similar to the binding of labels. The MPLS explicit path signaling protocols—RSVP-TE and CR-LDP—are modified to establish the light paths. The IGPs—OSPF and IS-IS—are augmented with special extensions to accommodate optical details such as topology and resource discovery. The establishment of a light path LSP from an ingress OXC LSR to an egress OXC LSR requires that the cross-connect fabric in each transit OXC LSR be configured such that an input port is linked to the proper corresponding output port. Like conventional MPLS, MPLambdaS signaling allows the OXC to communicate the selected output port as the label value to the downstream OXC.

GENERALIZED MPLS (GMPLS) ....

GMPLS can be considered the application of MPLambdaS. GMPLS is an extension of the MPLS core technologies that utilizes the label swapping paradigm and control plane protocols with additional types of switching technologies. These technologies include time division switching (found in SONET ADMs, for example, where the time slots are labels), wavelength switching (found in OXCs where the frequencies are the labels), and spatial switching (found in networking devices that redirect traffic from an incoming port or fiber to a corresponding outgoing port or fiber). In the third case, the ports are equated to label values. Or, to "generalize" the different GMPLS switching applications, time division multiplexing (TDM), frequency division multiplexing (FDM), and space division multiplexing (SDM) are used. GMPLS extends MPLS by expanding the definition of a label. Labels are no longer additional fields in a network layer packet header, but can be optical lambdas, and so on.

There are four classes of paths that can be created with GMPLS signaling:

- Statistical multiplexed paths: conventional MPLS packets that use a shim header.
- TDM paths: each time slot is a label.
- FDM paths: each electromagnetic frequency (i.e., light wavelength) is a label.
- SDM paths: a position is a label (e.g., a fiber location in a bundle).

GMPLS defines several enhancements that are required for making MPLS work within optical networks. These include link bundling, unnumbered links, and the LMP. Link bundling is the aggregation of the link attributes of more than one parallel link into a single link bundle. The benefits of this include reducing the size of the link state database and improving several important scaling characteristics. Unnumbered links support links that are not configured with IP addresses. The use of alternative link identification simplifies many link management issues. The new proposed unnumbered link tag is the router ID/link number tuple. LMP is the additional management protocol needed for the specific optical requirements of monitoring and control between two optical neighbor nodes. LMP provides link connectivity verification, link property correlation, control channel management, and fault isolation.

MPLS AND OPTICAL FORUMS ....

MPLS forums were introduced in Chapter 3, "MPLS Documentation and Resources." Two of the MPLS forums deal directly with optical networking, particularly with user interface issues. These two forums are the OIF and the ODSI Forum.

Optical Internetworking Forum (OIF)

The main charter of the OIF is to specify the protocols and other specifications that are required to implement an open and standardized O-UNI for optical networks.

Table 10–1 lists the principal members of the OIF.

Table 10–1   OIF Principal Members

Accelerant Networks	Force 10 Networks	Optix Networks
Accelight Networks	Foundry Networks	Optobahn
Acorn Networks	France Telecom	OptronX
Actel	Free Electron Technology	PacketLight Networks
Acterna	Fujikura	Paracer
ADC	Fujitsu	Parama Networks
Aerie Networks	Furukawa	Paxonet Communications
Agilent Technologies	Furukawa Electric Technologies	PetaSwitch Solutions
Agility Communications	Galazar Networks	Phillips Semiconductors
Alcatel	Gazillion Bits	Photonami, Inc.
Algety Telecom	Gemfire	PhotonEx
Alidian Networks	General Dynamics	Photuris, Inc.
All Optical Networks, Inc.	Gennum Corporation	Phyworks
Allegro Networks	GigaTera	PicoLight
Alphion	Glimmerglass Networks	Pine Photonics Communications

Table 10–1   OIF Principal Members (continued)

Altera	Global Crossing North American Networks	Pluris
Alvesta Corporation	Gore & Associates	PMC Sierra
Amber Networks	Gtran	Polaris Networks, Inc.
AMCC	GWS Photonics	Power X Networks
America Online	Helic S.A.	Princeton Optical Systems
Ample Communications	Helix AG	Procket Networks
ANDO Corporation	Hi/fn	Qoptics
AON Networks	Hitachi	
Appian Communications	Honeywell	Quake Technologies
Applied Innovation	Huawei Technologies	Quantum Bridge
Applied Optoelectronics	Hyperchip	Qwest Communications
Aralight	IBM Corporation	Radiant Photonics
Astral Point Communications	Infineon Technologies	Raza Foundries
AT&T	Innovance Networks	Redback Networks
Atoga Systems	Inphi	RedClover Networks
Avici Systems	Integrated Device Technology	Redfern Broadband Networks
Axiowave Networks	Intel	RF Micro Devices
Axsun Technologies	Intelliden	RHK
Bandwidth9	Internet Machines	Riverstone Networks
Bay Microsystems	Internet Photonics	Sandia National Laboratories

Table 10–1   OIF Principal Members (continued)

BellSouth Telecommunications	Intune Technologies	Santur Corporation
Big Bear Networks	Iolon	Siemens
Bit Blitz Communications	Iris Labs	Sierra Monolithics
Bitmath	Japan Telecom	Silicon Access
Blaze Network Products	Jasmine Networks	Silicon Bridge
Blueleaf Networks	JDS Uniphase	Silicon Labs
Blue Sky Research	Jedai Broadband Networks	Silicon Packets
Bravida Corp	Jennic	SiOptic Networks, Inc.
BrightLink Networks	Juniper Networks	SITA Equant
Broadcom	KDDI R&D Laboratories	Solidum Systems Corporation
BT	KereniX	Solinet Systems
Cable & Wireless	Kestrel Solutions	Spirent Communications
Calient Networks	Kirana Networks	Sprint
Calix Networks	Kodeos Communications	StrataLight Communications
Caspian Networks	Korea Telecom	Sumitomo Electric Industries
Catamaran Communications	Lambda Crossing	Sycamore Networks
Celion Networks	Lara Networks, Inc.	Syntera Communications
Centerpoint Broadband Technologies	Laurel Networks	T-Networks, Inc.

Table 10-1 OIF Principal Members (continued)

Centillium Communications	LSI Logic	Tektronix
Chiaro Networks	Lucent Technologies	Telcordia Technologies
Chunghwa Telecom Labs	Lumentis	Tellabs
Cielo Communications	Luminous Networks	Tellium
Ciena Communications	LuxN	TelOptica
Cinta Corporation	LYNX – Photonic Networks	Tenor Networks
CIR	Mahi Networks	TeraBurst Networks
Cisco Systems	Maple Optical Systems	Terago Communications
CIVCOM	Marconi Communications	Texas Instruments
Computer & Communications Research Labs	Maxim Integrated Products	TILAB S.p.A.
Conexant	Memlink	Toshiba Corporation
CoreOptics	Metro-OptiX	Transparent Networks
Coriolis Networks	MindTree Consulting Pvt. Ltd	Trellis Photonics
Corning Incorporated	Mintera	TriCN Associates
Corona Optical Systems	Mitel Corporation	TriQuint Semiconductor
CPlane	Mitsubishi Electric Corporation	Tropic Networks
Crescent Networks	Movaz Networks, Inc.	TRW
CyOptics	Multilink Technology Corporation	Turin Networks

Table 10–1   OIF Principal Members (continued)

Cypress Semiconductor	National Security Agency, US. Dept of Defense	TyCom
Data Connection	National Semiconductor	US Conec
Deutsche Telekom	Nayna Networks	Valiant Networks
Ditech	NEC	Velio Communications
Dorsal Networks	Net Brahma Technologies	Verizon
Dowslake Microsystems	NetTest	Versatile Optical Networks, Inc.
E2O Communications	Network Associates	Village Networks
EBONE	Network Elements	VIPSwitch
ECI Telecom	Network Photonics	Virata Corporation
Edgeflow	New Focus	Vitesse Semiconductor
Efficient Channel Coding	NIST	Vivace Networks
El Paso Networks	Nokia	VSK Photonics
Elisa Communications	Nortel Networks	Wavium
Emcore Fiber Optics	NTT Coporation	West Bay Semiconductor
Emperative	NurLogic Design	White Rock Networks
Entridia	Ocular Networks	Williams Communication Group
Equipe Communications	OKI Electric Industry	WorldCom
Ericsson	Onex Communications	Xanoptix

Table 10-1   OIF Principal Members (continued)

ETRI	ONI Systems	Xelerated Packet Devices
Extreme Networks	OpNext	Xilinx
Ezchip	Opthos	XLight Photonics
Fast-Chip	Optical Switch	XStream Logic
FCI	Opticalwave Networks	Yotta Networks
Fiberhome Telecommunications	Optillion AB	Zepton Networks
Finisar Corporation	Optivera	ZettaCom

A list of auditing OIF members is shown in Table 10-2:

Table 10-2   OIF Auditing Members

ADVA AG Optical Networking	Japan Radio Co.	Sonera Carrier Networks Ltd.
Advantest America	KAIST	STMicroelectronics
Analog Devices	Marvell Technology	Telenor
API Networks	Matsushita Communication Industrial	Telia AB
Arcor AG	Multiplex	Tiburon Networks
BTT	Nakra Labs	UPC-CCABA
Cognigine Corporation	Norlight Telecommunications	Vectron International
Future Communications Software	NOVILIT	Vesta
GMD	Princeton Optronics	VTT Information Technology

Table 10–2   OIF Auditing Members (continued)

Hughes Software Systems	Roshnee Corporation	Wipro Technologies
Information & Communications University	Royal KPN	Zaiq Technologies
Intelligent Telecom	SBC	
ITSD, Ministry of Management Services	Sky Optix	

The OIF Web site is: http://www.oiforum.com.

Optical Domain Service Interconnect (ODSI) Forum

The ODSI Forum is another vendor-supported coalition aimed at developing a standard network user interface and supporting protocols for optical equipment. It was started in January 2000, and has developed a set of specifications. A MIB ("Definition of Managed Objects for ODSI Management") and an access control and accounting specification ("COPS Usage *with ODSI*") have been completed.[1] The ODSI Forum has also done interoperability testing on its protocols between various IP and optical devices. At this writing, the ODSI Forum has completed its initial stated objectives and continues to promote its specifications among various equipment vendor and testing organizations.

The list of ODSI companies and their Web site addresses is shown in Table 10–3 on the next page.

---

1. The completed documents as well as those in progress are available on the Web at: www.odsi-coalition.com/documents.asp

Table 10–3   ODSI Forum Members

Company	URL
Accelerated Networks, Inc	www.acceleratednetworks.com
ACT Networks, Inc.	www.actnetworks.com
ADC Telecommunications, Inc.	www.adc.com
ADVA AG Optical Networking	www.advaoptical.com
Advanced Switching Communications, Inc.	www.asc1.com
Alcatel	www.alcatel.com
Algety Telecom	www.algety.com
Alidian Networks, Inc.	www.alidian.com
Allegro Networks, Inc.	www.allegronetworks.com
Alloptic, Inc.	www.alloptic.com
Amber Networks	www.ambernetworks.com
ANDA Networks	www.andanetworks.com
Appian Communications, Inc.	www.appiancom.com
AppliedTheory Corporation	www.appliedtheory.com
Astral Point Communications, Inc	www.astralpoint.com
Atmosphere Networks, Inc.	www.atmospherenet.com
Atoga Systems, Inc.	www.atoga.com
Atrica, Inc.	www.atrica.com
Avici Systems, Inc.	www.avici.com
Broadband Access Systems, Inc.	www.basystems.com
Campio Communications, Inc.	www.campio.com
Caspian Networks	www.caspiannetworks.com
Catena Networks	www.catenanet.com
Carrier1	www.carrier1.com

Table 10–3   ODSI Forum Members (continued)

Company	URL
Celestica	www.celestica.com
CeLight, Inc.	--
Celox Networks	www.celoxnetworks.com
Charlotte's Web Networks Ltd.	www.cwnt.com
Chiaro Networks Ltd.	www.chiaro.com
Chiplogic, Inc.	www.chiplogic.com
Chromatis Networks	www.chromatis.com
Ciena Corporation	www.ciena.com
Cinta	www.cintacom.com
Convergent Networks	www.convergentnet.com
CoreExpress, Inc.	www.coreexpress.com
Coreon, Inc.	www.coreon.com
Coriolis Networks	www.coriolisnet.com
Corning Incorporated	www.corning.com
Corvia Networks, Inc.	www.corvia.com
Crescent Networks	www.crescentnets.com
CrossKeys Systems Corporation	www.crosskeys.com
Data Connection Ltd.	www.datcon.co.uk
Ditech Communications Corporation	www.ditechcom.com
Dynarc, Inc.	www.dynarc.com
ECI Telecom	www.ecitele.com
Edgeflow, Inc.	www.edgeflow.com
Electric Lightwave, Inc.	www.eli.net
Ellacoya Networks, Inc.	www.ellacoya.com

Table 10–3   ODSI Forum Members (continued)

Company	URL
Ennovate Networks, Inc.	www.ennovatenetworks.com
Enron Broadband Services	www.enron.net
EPIK Communications	www.epik.net
Equipe Communications	www.equipecom.com
Fitel Technologies, Inc.	www.fiteltech.com
GlobSpan (formerly Ficon Technology Inc.)	www.globespan.net
Gotham Networks, Inc.	www.gothamnetworks.com
Geyser Networks, Inc.	www.geysernetworks.com
Granite Systems	www.granite.com
Hyperchip	www.hyperchip.com
Iaxis	www.iaxis.com
ILOG, Inc.	www.ilog.com
Intermedia Communications, Inc.	www.intermedia.com
International Wire Communications, Inc.	www.iwcinc.net
ION Networks, Inc	www.ion-networks.com
Ionidea	www.ionidea.com
IPICOM, Inc.	www.ipicom.com
IPOptical, Inc.	www.ipoptical.com
IronBridge Networks, Inc.	www.ironbridgenetworks.com
Kestrel Solutions	www.kestrelsolutions.com
Lancast, Inc.	www.lancast.com
LayerOne, Inc.	www.layerone.com
Lightchip, Inc.	www.lightchip.com

Table 10–3   ODSI Forum Members (continued)

Company	URL
LTT Inc.	www.ltt.com
Lucent Technologies	www.lucent.com
Luminous Networks	www.luminousnetworks.com
Luxcore	www.luxcore.com
LuxN, Inc.	www.luxn.com
Maple Networks	www.maplenetworks.com
Metro-Optix	www.metro-optix.com
Native Networks	www.nativenetworks.com
NetPlane Systems, Inc. (formerly H&J)	www.netplane.com
Network Photonics, Inc.	www.networkphotonics.com
Ocular Networks	www.ocularnetworks.com
ONI Systems	www.onisystems.com
Optranet	www.optranet.com
OSS Corporation	www.osscorporation.com
Paragon Networks	www.paragon-networks.com
Pathnet	www.pathnet.com
PhotonEx	www.photonex.com
Photuris, Inc.	www.photuris.com
Pluris, Inc.	www.pluris.com
QDI	www.qdi-usa.com
Quantum Bridge Communications, Inc.	www.quantumbridge.com
Quarry Technologies	www.quarrytech.com
Redback Networks, Inc.	www.redback.com

Table 10–3 ODSI Forum Members (continued)

Company	URL
Redfern Broadband Networks	`networks.photonics.com.au`
Renka Corporation	`--`
Riverstone Networks	`www.riverstonenet.com`
Seabridge Ltd.	`www.seabridgenetworks.com`
Siara Systems, Inc.	`www.siara.com`
Siemens	`www.siemens.com`
Sirocco Systems, Inc.	`www.siroccosystems.com`
Sonus Networks	`www.sonusnet.com`
Sorrento Networks, Inc.	`www.sorrentonet.com`
Spirent Communications	`www.spirentcom.com`
Spring Tide Networks, Inc.	`www.springtidenet.com`
Storm Telecommunications Limited	`www.stormtel.com`
Sycamore Networks	`www.sycamorenet.com`
Syndesis Networks	`www.syndesis.com`
Tachion Networks, Inc.	`www.tachion.com`
Telica, Inc.	`www.telica.com`
Tellium, Inc.	`www.tellium.com`
Tenor Networks	`www.tenornetworks.com`
Terawave Communications	`www.terawave.com`
Tropic Networks, Inc.	`www.tropicnetworks.com`
Turin Networks	`www.turinnetworks.com`
Unisphere Solutions, Inc.	`www.unispheresolutions.com`
UUNET, an MCI WorldCom Co.	`www.uunet.com`
Valiant Networks, Inc.	`www.valiantnet.com`

Table 10–3   ODSI Forum Members (continued)

Company	URL
Village Networks	www.villagenetworks.com
VIPswitch	www.VIPswitch.com
Vivace Networks	www.vivacenetworks.com
Williams Communications	www.wilcom.com
Xros	www.xros.com

For more information, see the ODSI Web site: http://www.odsi-coalition.com.

ADDITIONAL MPLS DIRECTIONS ....

The use of MPLS with optical technologies is just one future MPLS direction. Deployment experience and experimentation will reveal many new areas where MPLS may lend itself as a helping technology. While the specifics are yet to be determined, there are several ongoing efforts in inter-AS communication, which will allow different service providers to share LSPs through their domains. The use of label stacking for creating hierarchies will become important in optical networking as well. Optimizations in how traffic will flow in the Internet (optimized multipath, equal-cost multipath, and a host of other designs that map MPLS packets over network links) are also future topics for MPLS development. How the architecture of MPLS and the architecture of the Internet will meld together is both a current and future development.

THE FUTURE OF MPLS...

MPLS is undeniably a rapidly emerging Internet technology. It offers tangible benefits that include lower cost for deployment, operation, and management, the offering of rolling out revenue by producing MPLS applications, multiprotocol operation with most of the popular layer 2 and layer 3 protocols, a simpler service delivery platform, and many new technical advantages. The separation of the control plane from the data forwarding plane is offering a flexibility that may make MPLS the control plane for the next generation of optical networks. It will move several current network technologies into the legacy category as MPLS provides more bandwidth that can be configured for services and applications much more quickly. MPLS is a complementary technology with IP, and the unstoppable growth of IP-based applications will make MPLS a suitable companion. As packetized voice and video travel on the same LSPs as data in a predictable and billable manner, MPLS will be one of the cornerstones of the next–generation, globally converged network.

While it is always difficult to predict the longer term future of MPLS, it does solve problems via its technology and applications that may bring the Internet architecture forward. It is not all a pretty picture, however, and there are concerns about security—particularly in the VPN area—and how several features will be complexly engineered (another ATM!). There is still a great deal of work and debate to be done as MPLS continues down its standardization path.

FINAL THOUGHTS ON MPLS..

Now that MPLS is gaining critical momentum through widespread deployment experience, the initial hype of better-than-ATM, faster-than-IP has given way to a critical evaluation of its role as an Internet technology. MPLS is not simply a way to make IP routers faster—we have new hardware solutions for that—but rather, its forwarding paradigm is simpler than conventional IP, and at the same time it enables more functionality by improving IP services and providing innovative IP applications that are only possible with MPLS.

MPLS will grow with future Internet services, including wireless on-demand video, long-distance and global IP telephony, Web-based unified messaging, and many others that will ignite the need for new and improved MPLS applications.

Edmund Burke once said, "You can never plan the future by the past." [3] With time, we will analyze whether MPLS successfully introduced change and whether the Internet has become a better place to send mission-critical information, e-mail, Web traffic, and all the other myriad types of data that may pass as MPLS-enabled packets.

SUMMARY..

Chapter 10 introduced the future of MPLS and the several technologies that are extending its architecture. Optical networking will most likely be the largest benefactor of extending MPLS technologies with GMPLS. Base IP will be used to control optical networks and will also be the encapsulating protocol of choice for sending data packets along optical fibers. Finally, industry forums will help standardize user interfaces.

REFERENCES FOR CHAPTER 10......................................

1. http://thinktank.virtualave.net/quotes.html.
2. http://www.s-2000.com/quoteworld/ideas.html.
3. http://www.quoteland.com.

An MPLS Chronology

A

Even if you are on the right track,
you'll get run over if you just sit there. [1]

— *Will Rogers*

W hile MPLS is a new technology, its underpinnings have been around for nearly a decade. First, IP traffic was overlaid on ATM networks, and then proposals began appearing in the middle of the last decade to marry IP signaling and routing protocols with the label swapping paradigm already in use in ATM and FR networks. Several vendors proposed label swapping techniques in products they introduced into the marketplace. The four major efforts were the cell switching router (CSR) from Toshiba, IP switching from Ipsilion, tag switching from Cisco, and IBM's aggregate route-based IP switching (ARIS). Several IETF standardization efforts were also begun to explore new architectures and routing techniques in the Internet. Finally, to pull the vendors' and various other attempts under the standardization umbrella, and after a great deal of interest at a BOF meeting, the IETF formed the MPLS WG in 1997.

The late 1990s showed intense interest in MPLS. Over 100 Internet drafts, plus implementation experience in TE, QoS, and VPNs, show that MPLS is gaining momentum. At the end of 1999, the first MPLS RFC appeared, MPLS progressed on the standards path as an architecture, and other major technology pieces became officially documented as RFCs. With the increased use of the Internet and native IP-based protocols such as MPLS, terabit routing, and optical technologies, there can be no doubt that MPLS is in full swing!

Following is a year-by-year timeline for MPLS gleaned from various sources. It is evident that MPLS is tied closely to the IETF and the MPLS WG, but there are several other important influences as well.

1992 ....

Presented as an informational RFC in May 1992, RFC 1322, "A Unified Approach to Inter-Domain Routing," by Estrin, Rekhter, and Hotz, is an influential proposal in advancing the architecture of the Internet.

1994 ....

In early 1994, Toshiba announces the CSR. This architecture is the first proposal for using the IP signaling protocols running in a CSR to control ATM switches. It is presented at the IETF IP over ATM WG meeting.

In June, R. Braden, D. Clark, and S. Shenker produce an informational RFC that describes the IntServ model: RFC 1633, "Integrated Services in the Internet Architecture: An Overview."

1995 ....

Work progresses by several vendors to produce frameworks that allow IP protocols to control ATM forwarding. Toshiba presents the CSR concept again at the spring IETF BOF meeting.

1996 ....

In early 1996, Ipsilon (acquired by Nokia) proposes IP switching. In May, an informational RFC, RFC 1953, "Ipsilon Flow Management Protocol Specification for IPv4 Version 1.0," is published. The companion informational RFC, RFC 1987, "Ipsilon's General Switch Management Protocol Specification Version 1.1," is published in August.

Cisco announces the tag switching framework.

IBM proposes ARIS.

The Nimrod Internet architecuture is presented as an informational RFC in August 1996. RFC 1992, "The Nimrod Routing Architecture," is written by Castineyra, Chiappa, and Steenstrup.

The first meeting to discuss MPLS in a BOF format occurs at the 37th IETF held in San Jose, California in December (9–13). The tag switching architecture is introduced, along with discussions on ARIS and CSR. The beginnings of label distribution schemes are also discussed, including multicast, the Tag Distribution Protocol (TDP), and the use of RSVP. Many of the central MPLS architectural cornerstones are put forth. These include network layer- and link layer-independence, the separation of the control plane and data forwarding plane, label distribution, and others that are part of the MPLS standards today.

1997 ....

In February, an informational RFC on the Toshiba CSR is released: RFC 2098, "Toshiba's Router Architecture Extensions for ATM: Overview." In the same month, an informational RFC is published that describes Cisco's tag switching architecture: RFC 2105, "Cisco Systems' Tag Switching Architecture Overview."

The charter for the MPLS WG is accepted by the IETF. The WG meets for the first time in April (7–11) at the 38th IETF in Memphis, Tennessee as a working group in the routing area. Four main topics discussed include: handling loops in MPLS, merging RSVP flows, ARIS support for LAN media switching, and ARIS features and how they can be used in MPLS. A major milestone of the WG is to produce the MPLS framework document. Work also begins on the MPLS architecture specification.

Also in April, RFC 2129, "Toshiba's Flow Attribute Notification Protocol (FANP) Specification," appears. It is an informational RFC that explains a protocol implemented in the CSR.

Initial interest in MPLS is particularly aimed at the TE application. Also, its potential for being a standards-based solution for providing VPNs is examined.

Cisco begins shipping MPLS products in the second half of the year.

The 39th IETF meeting takes place in Munich, Germany in August (11–15). The framework document and MPLS architecture are introduced and discussed. Other MPLS topics debated include MPLS encapsulation formats, ATM issues with virtual circuits, label distribution, QoS issues, scalability, and others.

The 40th IETF meeting is held at the end of the year (December 8–12) in Washington, D.C. The topics at this meeting include the proposal for a newly developed standardized label distribution protocol (LDP), using an existing standardized protocol such as RSVP for label distribution, loop prevention mechanisms, the label stack encoding specification, ATM issues, and several others.

1998 ....

Several companies begin offering MPLS-based VPN applications.

The 41st IETF occurs in March and April in Los Angeles, California (March 30–April 3). LDP is discussed in more detail as the specifics of the protocol become more defined. A discussion of carrying label information inside BGP-4 messages is also held. Other MPLS topics include VPNs, loop prevention, TE and management, architectural issues, and several other subjects that are now mainly of historical interest.

In August (23–28), the 42nd IETF is held in Chicago, Illinois. The current set of MPLS drafts is discussed. A slide presentation on RSVP-TE is also given.

The 43rd IETF meeting is held in the last month of the year (December 7–11) in Orlando, Florida. New discussions are held on the MPLS WG drafts. A draft for the MPLS TE MIB for the SNMP management of MPLS is also introduced.

Also in December, the Diff-Serv informational RFC is released. It is RFC 2475, "An Architecture for Differentiated Services." It is written by S. Blake, D. Black, M. Carlson, E. Davies, Z. Wang, and W. Weiss.

1999 ....

Several companies begin offering MPLS-based TE applications.

The 44th IETF meeting convenes in March (15–19) in Minneapolis, Minnesota. The current set of MPLS drafts are debated. This IETF meeting includes a QoS analysis for using TE over MPLS.

In July (11–16), the 45th IETF is held in Oslo, Norway. The bulk of the meeting involves the ongoing discussion of the MPLS drafts in progress. Specific presentations include: "A Method for Setting an Alternative Label Switched Paths to Handle Fast Reroute" and "MPLS Using RSVP and ATM VC Switching."

In September, the first MPLS RFC is published. RFC 2702, "Requirements for Traffic Engineering Over MPLS," is written by D. Awduche, J. Malcolm, J. Agogbua, M. O'Dell, and J. McManus. It is of informational status and presents TE and the concept of a "traffic trunk."

The 46th IETF is held in November (7–12) in Washington, D.C. In addition to the normal agenda-bashing and WG status updates, the current MPLS topics are presented and debated. Topics include: Diff-Serv over MPLS, QoS management, LDP and CR-LDP updates, MPLambdaS (which evolves into GMPLS), path rerouting, restoration, bypass labeling, OAM functionality, and several inoperability reports.

2000 ....

In March, the MPLS Forum is organized with 16 founding members. Also in March (26-31), the 47th IETF meeting occurs in Adelaide, Australia. This IETF continues discussion of the MPLS drafts.

In May, the first book on MPLS, *MPLS: Technology and Applications*, by Bruce Davie and Yakov Rekhter, is published.

The 48th IETF meets in July and August (July 31–August 4) in Pittsburgh, Pennsylvania. In addition to discussing the IDs, several presentations are given. These include: "MPLS/IP Header Compression," "MPLS/IP Header Compression over PPP," "Signaling Requirements at the Optical UNI," and "Policy Framework QoS Information Model for MPLS."

In December (10–15), the 49th IETF meeting is convened in San Diego, California. The current state of MPLS and the WG drafts are debated.

2001 ....

The MPLS WG becomes part of a new area within the IETF. The Sub-IP area is created to look at several related topics that deal with various lower layer technologies. Headed by area directors Scott Bradner and Bert Wijnen, this area includes seven new and established WGs:

- Multiprotocol Label Switching (MPLS)
- Common Control and Measurement Plane (CCAMP)
- General Switch Management Protocol (GSMP)
- IP over Optical (IPO)
- IP over Resilient Packet Rings (IPORPRs)
- Internet Traffic Engineering (TEWG)
- Provider-Provisioned Virtual Private Networks (PPVPNs)

Large-scale deployment of MPLS equipment and applications begins.

The core MPLS IDs are issued as standards track RFCs (proposed). The RFCs published in January include: RFC 3031, "Multiprotocol Label Switching Architecture"; RFC 3032, "MPLS Label Stack Encoding"; RFC 3033, "The Assignment of the Information Field and Protocol Identifier in the Q.2941 Generic Identifier and Q.2957 User-to-user Signaling for the Internet Protocol"; RFC 3034, "Use of Label Switching on Frame Relay Networks Specification"; RFC 3035, "MPLS using LDP and ATM VC Switching"; RFC 3036, "LDP Specification"; RFC 3037, "LDP Applicability"; and RFC 3038, "VCID Notification over ATM link for LDP." An experimental RFC, RFC 3063, "MPLS Loop Prevention Mechanism," is published in February.

The 50th IETF meeting is held in March (18–23) in Minneapolis, Minnesota. The advancement of many of the core MPLS IDs to RFCs is presented. Topics discussed include the emerging interest in optical technologies and GMPLS, security in MPLS, Operation and Maintenance (OAM), LDP, RSVP-TE, and many others.

Another standards track RFC, RFC 3107, "Carrying Label Information in BGP-4," is published.

The 51st IETF meeting is held in August (5–10) in London. In addition to the customary agenda-bashing and discussion of the WGs' status, the latest MPLS IDs are introduced and discussed. These include:

- "MPLS Signaling Extensions for Shared Fast Rerouting"
- "MPLS RSVP-TE Interoperability for Local Protection/Fast Reroute"
- "A Method for MPLS LSP Fast-Reroute Using RSVP Detours"
- "RSVP-TE Failure Recovery (Resynchronization after Failure)" Graceful Restart Mechanism for RSVP-TE"
- "MPLS Label Stack Authentication Methods and Algorithms"
- "MPLS Support of Differentiated Services using E-LSP"
- "Link Bundling Information Base Using SMIv2"

The meeting also includes the presentation of several MPLS TE IDs in the TEWG, such as "Alternative Technical Solution for MPLS DiffServ TE" and "MPLS Support of Differentiated Services Using E-LSP."

REFERENCE FOR APPENDIX A..

1. From www.quoteland.com.

MPLS-Related RFC Index

B

The following is a list of RFCs that pertain to MPLS-related topics, including routing, SNMP, the internet architecture, the TC/IP protocol suite, and other miscellanious related issues that may be of interest. They are presented in descending numerical order.

This list includes the RFC number, the title, the author(s) or editor(s), the date it was issued, and information on other RFCs that directly pertain to it. RFCs are now easily available over the Internet via anonymous FTP or in HTML format at several sites. A good starting point is to view a current RFC index (e.g., `ftp://ftp.isi.edu/in-notes/rfc-index.txt`).

Important specifications that are used for standardization are put on the standards track (see Table B–1 on the next page). A specification enters the standards track and can initially assume the status of proposed, experimental, or informational. Experimental and informational specifications either are not intended or do not fill the requirements to become full standards. Table B–1 lists the various standards levels.

A proposed standard must be stable, meet with good reception, and generally be considered to be of value. After at least six months (and two or more field implementations), a proposed standard may be considered for draft status. The minimum time requirement from being elevated to a full standard is then reduced to four months. Many solid implementations should be operating to prove the specification's worthiness. After a time, the specification may be replaced by a newer version; in that case, the former specification receives an historical status.

Table B–1   Specifications Standards Track

Standard Level	Description
Full Standard	The Internet Engineering Steering Group (IESG) has established this as an official standard protocol for the Internet. These protocols are assigned STD numbers (see RFC 1311). These are separated into two groups: (1) IP protocol and above, which are protocols that apply to the whole Internet; and (2) network-specific protocols, which are generally specifications for how to do IP on particular types of networks.
Draft Standard	The IESG is actively considering this protocol as a possible standard protocol. Substantial and widespread testing and comments are desired. Comments and test results should be submitted to the IESG. There is a possibility that changes will be made in a draft standard protocol before it becomes a standard protocol.
Proposed Standard	These are protocol proposals that may be considered by the IESG for standardization in the future. Implementation and testing by several groups is desirable. Revision of the protocol specification is likely.

Table B–1 Specifications Standards Track (continued)

Standard Level	Description
Experimental Standard	A system should not implement an experimental protocol unless it is participating in the experiment and has coordinated its use of the protocol with the developer of the protocol. Typically, experimental protocols are those that are developed as part of an ongoing research project not related to an operational service offering. While they may be proposed as service protocols at a later stage, and thus become proposed standard, draft standard, and then standard protocols, the designation of a protocol as experimental may sometimes be meant to suggest that the protocol, although perhaps mature, is not intended for operational use.
Informational Standard	Protocols developed by other standards organizations, or vendors, or that are for other reasons outside the purview of the IESG may be published as RFCs for the convenience of the Internet community as informational protocols.
Historic Standard	These are protocols that are unlikely to ever become standards in the Internet either because they have been superseded by later developments or they lack interest.

In addition to the standards status, an additional qualifier exists called the protocol status. This is explained in Table B–2.

Table B–2 Internet Standards Protocol Status

Protocol Status	Description
Required	The protocol **must** be implemented on a system.
Recommended	The protocol **should** be implemented on a system.
Elective	The protocol **may** be implemented on a system.
Limited use	The protocol **may** be implemented under special circumstances.
Not recommended	The protocol **should not** be implemented on a system.

Examples of protocol status for the TCP/IP suite include required for IP and TCP and recommended for SNMP. The three major standards that comprise SNMP version 1—the SMI, the MIB, and the protocol—are all full standards with recommended protocol status.

The following list contains the RFCs that are relevant to MPLS and MPLS-related standards and activities:

3107   "Carrying Label Information in BGP-4." Y. Rekhter and E. Rosen. May 2001 (Status: PROPOSED STANDARD).

3063   "MPLS Loop Prevention Mechanism." Y. Ohba, Y. Katsube, E. Rosen, and P. Doolan. February 2001 (Status: EXPERIMENTAL).

3037   "LDP Applicability." B. Thomas and E. Gray. January 2001 (Status: INFORMATIONAL).

3036   "LDP Specification." L. Andersson, P. Doolan, N. Feldman, A. Fredette, and B. Thomas. January 2001 (Status: PROPOSED STANDARD).

3035   "MPLS using LDP and ATM VC Switching." B. Davie, J. Lawrence, K. McCloghrie, E. Rosen, G. Swallow, Y. Rekhter, and P. Doolan. January 2001 (Status: PROPOSED STANDARD).

3034   "Use of Label Switching on Frame Relay Networks Specification." A. Conta, P. Doolan, and A. Malis. January 2001 (Status: PROPOSED STANDARD).

3033   "The Assignment of the Information Field and Protocol Identifier in the Q.2941 Generic Identifier and Q.2957 User-to-user Signaling for the Internet Protocol." M. Suzuki. January 2001 (Status: PROPOSED STANDARD).

3032   "MPLS Label Stack Encoding." E. Rosen, D. Tappan, G. Fedorkow, Y. Rekhter, D. Farinacci, T. Li, and A. Conta. January 2001 (Status: PROPOSED STANDARD).

3031   "Multiprotocol Label Switching Architecture." E. Rosen, A. Viswanathan, and R. Callon. January 2001 (Status: PROPOSED STANDARD).

2998   "A Framework for Integrated Services Operation over Diffserv Networks." Y. Bernet, P. Ford, R. Yavatkar, F. Baker, L. Zhang, M. Speer, R. Braden, B. Davie, J. Wroclawski, and E. Felstaine. November 2000 (Status: INFORMATIONAL).

2990   "Next Steps for the IP QoS Architecture." G. Huston. November 2000 (Status: INFORMATIONAL).

2983   "Differentiated Services and Tunnels." D. Black. October 2000 (Status: INFORMATIONAL).

2961   "RSVP Refresh Overhead Reduction Extensions." L. Berger, D. Gan, G. Swallow, P. Pan, F. Tommasi, and S. Molendini. April 2001 (Status: PROPOSED STANDARD).

2917   "A Core MPLS IP VPN Architecture." K. Muthukrishnan and A. Malis. September 2000 (Status: INFORMATIONAL).

2858   "Multiprotocol Extensions for BGP-4." T. Bates, Y. Rekhter, R. Chandra, and D. Katz. June 2000 ([Obsoletes RFC 2283] Status: PROPOSED STANDARD).

        "Requirements for Traffic Engineering Over MPLS." D. Awduche, J. Malcolm, J. Agogbua, M. O'Dell, and J. McManus. September 1999 (First MPLS RFC).

2684   "Multiprotocol Encapsulation over ATM Adaptation Layer 5." D. Grossman and J. Heinanen. September 1999 ([Obsoletes RFC 1483] Status: PROPOSED STANDARD).

2676   "QoS Routing Mechanisms and OSPF Extensions." G. Apostolopoulos, S. Kama, D. Williams, R. Guerin, A. Orda, and T. Przygienda. August 1999 (Status: EXPERIMENTAL).

2580   "Conformance Statements for SMIv2." K. McCloghrie, D. Perkins, and J. Schoenwaelder. April 1999 ([Obsoletes RFC 1904; also STD 0058] Status: STANDARD).

2579   "Textual Conventions for SMIv2." K. McCloghrie, D. Perkins, and J. Schoenwaelder. April 1999 ([Obsoletes RFC 1903; also STD 0058] Status: STANDARD).

2578   "Structure of Management Information Version 2 (SMIv2)." K. McCloghrie, D. Perkins, and J. Schoenwaelder. April 1999 ([Obsoletes RFC 1902; also STD 0058] Status: STANDARD).

2576   "Coexistence between Version 1, Version 2, and Version 3 of the Internet-standard Network Management Framework." R. Frye, D. Levi, S. Routhier, and B. Wijnen. March 2000 ([Obsoletes RFC 1908 and RFC 2089] Status: PROPOSED STANDARD).

2575   "View-based Access Control Model (VACM) for the Simple Network Management Protocol (SNMP)." B. Wijnen, R. Presuhn, and K. McCloghrie. April 1999 ([Obsoletes RFC 2275] Status: DRAFT STANDARD).

2574   "User-based Security Model (USM) for version 3 of the Simple Network Management Protocol (SNMPv3)." U. Blumenthal and B. Wijnen. April 1999 ([Obsoletes RFC 2274] Status: DRAFT STANDARD).

2573   "SNMP Applications." D. Levi, P. Meyer, and B. Stewart. April 1999 ([Obsoletes RFC 2273] Status: DRAFT STANDARD).

2572   "Message Processing and Dispatching for the Simple Network Management Protocol (SNMP)." J. Case, D. Harrington, R. Presuhn, and B. Wijnen. April 1999 ([Obsoletes RFC 2272] Status: DRAFT STANDARD).

2571   "An Architecture for Describing SNMP Management Frameworks." B. Wijnen, D. Harrington, and R. Presuhn. April 1999 ([Obsoletes RFC 2271] Status: DRAFT STANDARD).

2570   "Introduction to Version 3 of the Internet-standard Network Management Framework." J. Case, R. Mundy, D. Partain, and B. Stewart. April 1999 (Status: INFORMATIONAL).

2547   "BGP/MPLS VPNs." E. Rosen and Y. Rekhter. March 1999 (Status: INFORMATIONAL).

2475   "An Architecture for Differentiated Service." S. Blake, D. Black, M. Carlson, E. Davies, Z. Wang, and W. Weiss. December 1998 (Status: INFORMATIONAL).

2430   "A Provider Architecture for Differentiated Services and Traffic Engineering (PASTE)." T. Li and Y. Rekhter. October 1998 (Status: INFORMATIONAL).

2332   "NBMA Next Hop Resolution Protocol (NHRP)." J. Luciani, D. Katz, D. Piscitello, B. Cole, and N. Doraswamy. April 1998 (Status: PROPOSED STANDARD).

2283   "Multiprotocol Extensions for BGP-4." T. Bates, R. Chandra, D. Katz, and Y. Rekhter. February 1998 ([Obsoleted by RFC 2858] Status: PROPOSED STANDARD).

2210   "The Use of RSVP with IETF Integrated Services." J. Wroclawski. September 1997 (Status: PROPOSED STANDARD).

2209   "Resource ReSerVation Protocol (RSVP)—Version 1 Message Processing Rules." R. Braden and L. Zhang. September 1997 (Status: INFORMATIONAL).

2208   "Resource ReSerVation Protocol (RSVP)—Version 1 Applicability Statement Some Guidelines on Deployment." A. Mankin (ed.), F. Baker, B. Braden, S. Bradner, M. O`Dell, A. Romanow, A. Weinrib, and L. Zhang. September 1997 (Status: INFORMATIONAL).

2207   "RSVP Extensions for IPSEC Data Flows." L. Berger and T. O'Malley. September 1997 (Status: PROPOSED STANDARD).

2206   "RSVP Management Information Base using SMIv2." F. Baker, J. Krawczyk, and A. Sastry. September 1997 (Status: PROPOSED STANDARD).

2205 "Resource ReSerVation Protocol (RSVP)—Version 1 Functional Specification. R. Braden (ed.), L. Zhang, S. Berson, S. Herzog, and S. Jamin. September 1997 ([Updated by RFC 2750] Status: PROPOSED STANDARD).

2185 "Routing Aspects of IPv6 Transition." R. Callon and D. Haskin. September 1997 (Status: INFORMATIONAL).

2129 "Toshiba's Flow Attribute Notification Protocol (FANP) Specification." K. Nagami, Y. Katsube, Y. Shobatake, A. Mogi, S. Matsuzawa, T. Jinmei, and H. Esaki. April 1997 (Status: INFORMATIONAL).

2117 "Protocol Independent Multicast-Sparse Mode (PIM-SM): Protocol Specification." D. Estrin, D. Farinacci, A. Helmy, D. Thaler, S. Deering, M. Handley, V. Jacobson, C. Liu, P. Sharma, and L. Wei. June 1997 ([Obsoleted by RFC 2362] Status: EXPERIMENTAL).

2105 "Cisco Systems' Tag Switching Architecture Overview." Y. Rekhter, B. Davie, D. Katz, E. Rosen, and G. Swallow. February 1997 (Status: INFORMATIONAL).

2098 "Toshiba's Router Architecture Extensions for ATM: Overview." Y. Katsube, K. Nagami, and H. Esaki. February 1997 (Status: INFORMATIONAL).

1997 "BGP Communities Attribute." R. Chandra, P. Traina, and T. Li. August 1996 (Status: PROPOSED STANDARD).

1992 "The Nimrod Routing Architecture." I. Castineyra, N. Chiappa, and M. Steenstrup. August 1996 (Status: INFORMATIONAL).

1987 "Ipsilon's General Switch Management Protocol Specification Version 1.1." P. Newman, W. Edwards, R. Hinden, E. Hoffman, F. Ching Liaw, T. Lyon, and G. Minshall. August 1996 ([Updated by RFC 2297] Status: INFORMATIONAL).

"Internet Control Message Protocol (ICMPv6) for the Internet Protocol Version 6 (IPv6) Specification." A. Conta and S. Deering. December 1995 (Status: PROPOSED STANDARD).

1966 "BGP Route Reflection An alternative to full mesh IBGP." T. Bates and R. Chandrasekeran. June 1996 ([Updated by RFC 2796] Status: EXPERIMENTAL).

1954 "Transmission of Flow Labelled IPv4 on ATM Data Links Ipsilon Version 1.0." P. Newman, W. Edwards, R. Hinden, E. Hoffman, F. Ching Liaw, T. Lyon, and G. Minshall. May 1996 (Status: INFORMATIONAL).

1953 "Ipsilon Flow Management Protocol Specification for IPv4 Version 1.0." P. Newman, W. Edwards, R. Hinden, E. Hoffman, F. Ching Liaw, T. Lyon, and G. Minshall. May 1996 (Status: INFORMATIONAL).

1771   "A Border Gateway Protocol 4 (BGP-4)." Y. Rekhter and T. Li. March 1995 ([Obsoletes RFC 1654] Status: DRAFT STANDARD).

1633   "Integrated Services in the Internet Architecture: an Overview." R. Braden, D. Clark, and S. Shenker. June 1994 (Status: INFORMATIONAL).

1583   "OSPF Version 2." J. Moy. March 1994 ([Obsoletes RFC 1247; obsoleted by RFC 2178] Status: DRAFT STANDARD).

1577   "Classical IP and ARP over ATM." M. Laubach. January 1994 ([Obsoleted by RFC 2225] Status: PROPOSED STANDARD).

1953   "Ipsilon Flow Management Protocol Specification for IPv4 Version 1.0." P. Newman, W. Edwards, R. Hinden, E. Hoffman, F. Ching Liaw, T. Lyon, and G. Minshall. May 1996 (Status: INFORMATIONAL).

1483   "Using the OSI Directory to achieve User Friendly Naming (OSI-DS 24 (v1.2))." S. Hardcastle-Kille. July 1993 ([Obsoleted by RFC 1781] Status: EXPERIMENTAL).

1322   "A Unified Approach to Inter-Domain Routing." D. Estrin, Y. Rekhter, and S. Hotz. May 1992 (Status: INFORMATIONAL).

1321   "The MD5 Message-Digest Algorithm." R. Rivest. April 1992 (Status: INFORMATIONAL).

1215   "Convention for defining traps for use with the SNMP." M.T. Rose. March 1, 1991 (Status: INFORMATIONAL).

1213   "Management Information Base for Network Management of TCP/IP-based internets: MIB-II." K. McCloghrie and M.T. Rose. March 1, 1991 ([Obsoletes RFC 1158; updated by RFC 2011, RFC 2012, and RFC 2013; also STD 0017] Status: STANDARD).

1212   "Concise MIB definitions." M.T. Rose and K. McCloghrie. March 1, 1991. ([Also STD 0016] Status: STANDARD).

1158   "Management Information Base for network management of TCP/IP-based internets: MIB-II." M.T. Rose. May 1, 1990 ([Obsoleted by RFC 1213] Status: PROPOSED STANDARD).

1157   "Simple Network Management Protocol (SNMP)." J.D. Case, M. Fedor, M.L. Schoffstall, and C. Davin. May 1, 1990 ([Obsoletes RFC 1098; also STD 0015] Status: STANDARD).

1156   "Management Information Base for network management of TCP/IP-based internets." K. McCloghrie and M.T. Rose. May 1, 1990 ([Obsoletes RFC 1066] Status: HISTORIC).

1155 "Structure and identification of management information for TCP/IP-based internets." M.T. Rose and K. McCloghrie. May 1, 1990 ([Obsoletes RFC 1065; also STD 0016] Status: STANDARD).

0793 "Transmission Control Protocol." J. Postel. September 1, 1981 ([Also STD 0007] Status: STANDARD).

0791 "Internet Protocol." J. Postel. September 1, 1981 ([Obsoletes RFC 0760; also STD 0005] Status: STANDARD).

0768 "User Datagram Protocol." J. Postel. August 28, 1980 ([Also STD 0006] Status: STANDARD).

1 "Host Software." S. Crocker. April 17, 1969 (Status: UNKNOWN).

RFC 3031: Multiprotocol Label Switching

Network Working Group
Request for Comments: 3031
Category: Standards Track
E. Rosen
Cisco Systems, Inc.
A. Viswanathan

Force10 Networks, Inc.
R. Callon
Juniper Networks, Inc.
January 2001

Multiprotocol Label Switching Architecture

Status of this Memo

Copyright Notice

Abstract

   This document specifies the architecture for Multiprotocol Label
   Switching (MPLS).

Table of Contents

RFC 3031   MPLS Architecture   January 2001

RFC 3031   MPLS Architecture   January 2001

1. Specification

   The key words "MUST", "MUST NOT", "REQUIRED", "SHALL", "SHALL NOT",
   "SHOULD", "SHOULD NOT", "RECOMMENDED", "MAY", and "OPTIONAL" in this
   document are to be interpreted as described in RFC 2119.

2. Introduction to MPLS

   This document specifies the architecture for Multiprotocol Label
   Switching (MPLS).

   Note that the use of MPLS for multicast is left for further study.

Rosen, et al.   Standards Track   [Page 3]

RFC 3031   MPLS Architecture   January 2001

2.1. Overview

   As a packet of a connectionless network layer protocol travels from
   one router to the next, each router makes an independent forwarding
   decision for that packet. That is, each router analyzes the packet's
   header, and each router runs a network layer routing algorithm. Each
   router independently chooses a next hop for the packet, based on its
   analysis of the packet's header and the results of running the
   routing algorithm.

   Packet headers contain considerably more information than is needed
   simply to choose the next hop. Choosing the next hop can therefore
   be thought of as the composition of two functions. The first
   function partitions the entire set of possible packets into a set of
   "Forwarding Equivalence Classes (FECs)". The second maps each FEC to
   a next hop. Insofar as the forwarding decision is concerned,
   different packets which get mapped into the same FEC are
   indistinguishable. All packets which belong to a particular FEC and
   which travel from a particular node will follow the same path (or if
   certain kinds of multi-path routing are in use, they will all follow
   one of a set of paths associated with the FEC).

   In conventional IP forwarding, a particular router will typically
   consider two packets to be in the same FEC if there is some address
   prefix X in that router's routing tables such that X is the "longest
   match" for each packet's destination address. As the packet
   traverses the network, each hop in turn reexamines the packet and
   assigns it to a FEC.

   In MPLS, the assignment of a particular packet to a particular FEC is
   done just once, as the packet enters the network. The FEC to which
   the packet is assigned is encoded as a short fixed length value known
   as a "label". When a packet is forwarded to its next hop, the label
   is sent along with it; that is, the packets are "labeled" before they
   are forwarded.

   At subsequent hops, there is no further analysis of the packet's
   network layer header. Rather, the label is used as an index into a
   table which specifies the next hop, and a new label. The old label
   is replaced with the new label, and the packet is forwarded to its
   next hop.

   In the MPLS forwarding paradigm, once a packet is assigned to a FEC,
   no further header analysis is done by subsequent routers; all
   forwarding is driven by the labels. This has a number of advantages
   over conventional network layer forwarding.

- MPLS forwarding can be done by switches which are capable of
  doing label lookup and replacement, but are either not capable
  of analyzing the network layer headers, or are not capable of
  analyzing the network layer headers at adequate speed.

- Since a packet is assigned to a FEC when it enters the network,
  the ingress router may use, in determining the assignment, any
  information it has about the packet, even if that information
  cannot be gleaned from the network layer header. For example,
  packets arriving on different ports may be assigned to
  different FECs. Conventional forwarding, on the other hand,
  can only consider information which travels with the packet in
  the packet header.

- A packet that enters the network at a particular router can be
  labeled differently than the same packet entering the network
  at a different router, and as a result forwarding decisions
  that depend on the ingress router can be easily made. This
  cannot be done with conventional forwarding, since the identity
  of a packet's ingress router does not travel with the packet.

- The considerations that determine how a packet is assigned to a
  FEC can become ever more and more complicated, without any
  impact at all on the routers that merely forward labeled
  packets.

- Sometimes it is desirable to force a packet to follow a
  particular route which is explicitly chosen at or before the
  time the packet enters the network, rather than being chosen by
  the normal dynamic routing algorithm as the packet travels
  through the network. This may be done as a matter of policy,
  or to support traffic engineering. In conventional forwarding,
  this requires the packet to carry an encoding of its route
  along with it ("source routing"). In MPLS, a label can be used
  to represent the route, so that the identity of the explicit
  route need not be carried with the packet.

Some routers analyze a packet's network layer header not merely to
choose the packet's next hop, but also to determine a packet's
"precedence" or "class of service". They may then apply different
discard thresholds or scheduling disciplines to different packets.
MPLS allows (but does not require) the precedence or class of service
to be fully or partially inferred from the label. In this case, one
may say that the label represents the combination of a FEC and a
precedence or class of service.

RFC 3031   MPLS Architecture   January 2001

MPLS stands for "Multiprotocol" Label Switching, multiprotocol because its techniques are applicable to ANY network layer protocol. In this document, however, we focus on the use of IP as the network layer protocol.

A router which supports MPLS is known as a "Label Switching Router", or LSR.

2.2. Terminology

This section gives a general conceptual overview of the terms used in this document. Some of these terms are more precisely defined in later sections of the document.

DLCI	a label used in Frame Relay networks to identify frame relay circuits
forwarding equivalence class	a group of IP packets which are forwarded in the same manner (e.g., over the same path, with the same forwarding treatment)
frame merge	label merging, when it is applied to operation over frame based media, so that the potential problem of cell interleave is not an issue.
label	a short fixed length physically contiguous identifier which is used to identify a FEC, usually of local significance.
label merging	the replacement of multiple incoming labels for a particular FEC with a single outgoing label
label swap	the basic forwarding operation consisting of looking up an incoming label to determine the outgoing label, encapsulation, port, and other data handling information.
label swapping	a forwarding paradigm allowing streamlined forwarding of data by using labels to identify classes of data packets which are treated indistinguishably when forwarding.

RFC 3031   MPLS Architecture   January 2001

    label switched hop   the hop between two MPLS nodes, on which
                                    forwarding is done using labels.

    label switched path   The path through one or more LSRs at one
                                    level of the hierarchy followed by a
                                    packets in a particular FEC.

    label switching router   an MPLS node which is capable of
                                    forwarding native L3 packets

    layer 2   the protocol layer under layer 3 (which
                                    therefore offers the services used by
                                    layer 3). Forwarding, when done by the
                                    swapping of short fixed length labels,
                                    occurs at layer 2 regardless of whether
                                    the label being examined is an ATM
                                    VPI/VCI, a frame relay DLCI, or an MPLS
                                    label.

    layer 3   the protocol layer at which IP and its
                                    associated routing protocols operate
                                    link layer synonymous with layer 2

    loop detection   a method of dealing with loops in which
                                      loops are allowed to be set up, and data
                                    may be transmitted over the loop, but
                                    the loop is later detected

    loop prevention   a method of dealing with loops in which
                                    data is never transmitted over a loop

    label stack   an ordered set of labels

    merge point   a node at which label merging is done

    MPLS domain   a contiguous set of nodes which operate
                                    MPLS routing and forwarding and which
                                    are also in one Routing or
                                    Administrative Domain

    MPLS edge node   an MPLS node that connects an MPLS
                                    domain with a node which is outside of
                                    the domain, either because it does not
                                    run MPLS, and/or because it is in a
                                    different domain. Note that if an LSR
                                  has a neighboring host which is not
                                    running MPLS, that that LSR is an MPLS
                                    edge node.

MPLS egress node   an MPLS edge node in its role in
                          handling traffic as it leaves an MPLS
                          domain

MPLS ingress node   an MPLS edge node in its role in
                          handling traffic as it enters an MPLS
                          domain

MPLS label   a label which is carried in a packet
                          header, and which represents the
                          packet's FEC

MPLS node   a node which is running MPLS. An MPLS
                          node will be aware of MPLS control
                          protocols, will operate one or more L3
                          routing protocols, and will be capable
                          of forwarding packets based on labels.
                          An MPLS node may optionally be also
                          capable of forwarding native L3 packets.

MultiProtocol Label Switching an IETF working group and the
                          effort associated with the working
                          group

network layer   synonymous with layer 3

stack   synonymous with label stack

switched path   synonymous with label switched path

virtual circuit   a circuit used by a connection-oriented
                          layer 2 technology such as ATM or Frame
                          Relay, requiring the maintenance of
                          state information in layer 2 switches.

VC merge   label merging where the MPLS label is
                          carried in the ATM VCI field (or
                          combined VPI/VCI field), so as to allow
                          multiple VCs to merge into one single VC

VP merge   label merging where the MPLS label is
                          carried din the ATM VPI field, so as to
                          allow multiple VPs to be merged into one
                          single VP. In this case two cells would
                          have the same VCI value only if they
                          originated from the same node. This
                          allows cells from different sources to
                          be distinguished via the VCI.

RFC 3031   MPLS Architecture   January 2001

      VPI/VCI   a label used in ATM networks to identify
                                       circuits

2.3. Acronyms and Abbreviations

    ATM   Asynchronous Transfer Mode
    BGP   Border Gateway Protocol
    DLCI   Data Link Circuit Identifier
    FEC   Forwarding Equivalence Class
    FTN   FEC to NHLFE Map
    IGP   Interior Gateway Protocol
    ILM   Incoming Label Map
    IP   Internet Protocol
    LDP   Label Distribution Protocol
    L2   Layer 2 L3   Layer 3
    LSP   Label Switched Path
    LSR   Label Switching Router
    MPLS   MultiProtocol Label Switching
    NHLFE   Next Hop Label Forwarding Entry
    SVC   Switched Virtual Circuit
    SVP   Switched Virtual Path
    TTL   Time-To-Live
    VC   Virtual Circuit
    VCI   Virtual Circuit Identifier
    VP   Virtual Path
    VPI   Virtual Path Identifier

2.4. Acknowledgments

    The ideas and text in this document have been collected from a number
    of sources and comments received. We would like to thank Rick
    Boivie, Paul Doolan, Nancy Feldman, Yakov Rekhter, Vijay Srinivasan,
    and George Swallow for their inputs and ideas.

3. MPLS Basics

    In this section, we introduce some of the basic concepts of MPLS and
    describe the general approach to be used.

3.1. Labels

    A label is a short, fixed length, locally significant identifier
    which is used to identify a FEC. The label which is put on a
    particular packet represents the Forwarding Equivalence Class to
    which that packet is assigned.

Rosen, et al.   Standards Track   [Page 9]

RFC 3031   MPLS Architecture   January 2001

Most commonly, a packet is assigned to a FEC based (completely or
partially) on its network layer destination address. However, the
label is never an encoding of that address.

If Ru and Rd are LSRs, they may agree that when Ru transmits a packet
to Rd, Ru will label with packet with label value L if and only if
the packet is a member of a particular FEC F. That is, they can
agree to a "binding" between label L and FEC F for packets moving
from Ru to Rd. As a result of such an agreement, L becomes Ru's
"outgoing label" representing FEC F, and L becomes Rd's "incoming
label" representing FEC F.

Note that L does not necessarily represent FEC F for any packets
other than those which are being sent from Ru to Rd. L is an
arbitrary value whose binding to F is local to Ru and Rd.

When we speak above of packets "being sent" from Ru to Rd, we do not
imply either that the packet originated at Ru or that its destination
is Rd. Rather, we mean to include packets which are "transit
packets" at one or both of the LSRs.

Sometimes it may be difficult or even impossible for Rd to tell, of
an arriving packet carrying label L, that the label L was placed in
the packet by Ru, rather than by some other LSR. (This will
typically be the case when Ru and Rd are not direct neighbors.) In
such cases, Rd must make sure that the binding from label to FEC is
one-to-one. That is, Rd MUST NOT agree with Ru1 to bind L to FEC F1,
while also agreeing with some other LSR Ru2 to bind L to a different
FEC F2, UNLESS Rd can always tell, when it receives a packet with
incoming label L, whether the label was put on the packet by Ru1 or
whether it was put on by Ru2.

It is the responsibility of each LSR to ensure that it can uniquely
interpret its incoming labels.

3.2. Upstream and Downstream LSRs

Suppose Ru and Rd have agreed to bind label L to FEC F, for packets
sent from Ru to Rd. Then with respect to this binding, Ru is the
"upstream LSR", and Rd is the "downstream LSR".

To say that one node is upstream and one is downstream with respect
to a given binding means only that a particular label represents a
particular FEC in packets travelling from the upstream node to the
downstream node. This is NOT meant to imply that packets in that FEC
would actually be routed from the upstream node to the downstream
node.

Rosen, et al.   Standards Track   [Page 10]

3.3. Labeled Packet

   A "labeled packet" is a packet into which a label has been encoded.
   In some cases, the label resides in an encapsulation header which
   exists specifically for this purpose. In other cases, the label may
   reside in an existing data link or network layer header, as long as
   there is a field which is available for that purpose. The particular
   encoding technique to be used must be agreed to by both the entity
   which encodes the label and the entity which decodes the label.

3.4. Label Assignment and Distribution

   In the MPLS architecture, the decision to bind a particular label L
   to a particular FEC F is made by the LSR which is DOWNSTREAM with
   respect to that binding. The downstream LSR then informs the
   upstream LSR of the binding. Thus labels are "downstream-assigned",
   and label bindings are distributed in the "downstream to upstream"
   direction.

   If an LSR has been designed so that it can only look up labels that
   fall into a certain numeric range, then it merely needs to ensure
   that it only binds labels that are in that range.

3.5. Attributes of a Label Binding

   A particular binding of label L to FEC F, distributed by Rd to Ru,
   may have associated "attributes". If Ru, acting as a downstream LSR,
   also distributes a binding of a label to FEC F, then under certain
   conditions, it may be required to also distribute the corresponding
   attribute that it received from Rd.

3.6. Label Distribution Protocols

   A label distribution protocol is a set of procedures by which one LSR
   informs another of the label/FEC bindings it has made. Two LSRs
   which use a label distribution protocol to exchange label/FEC binding
   information are known as "label distribution peers" with respect to
   the binding information they exchange. If two LSRs are label
   distribution peers, we will speak of there being a "label
   distribution adjacency" between them.

   (N.B.: two LSRs may be label distribution peers with respect to some
   set of bindings, but not with respect to some other set of bindings.)

   The label distribution protocol also encompasses any negotiations in
   which two label distribution peers need to engage in order to learn
   of each other's MPLS capabilities.

THE ARCHITECTURE DOES NOT ASSUME THAT THERE IS ONLY A SINGLE LABEL
DISTRIBUTION PROTOCOL. In fact, a number of different label
distribution protocols are being standardized. Existing protocols
have been extended so that label distribution can be piggybacked on
them (see, e.g., [MPLS-BGP], [MPLS-RSVP-TUNNELS]). New protocols
have also been defined for the explicit purpose of distributing
labels (see, e.g., [MPLS-LDP], [MPLS-CR-LDP].

In this document, we try to use the acronym "LDP" to refer
specifically to the protocol defined in [MPLS-LDP]; when speaking of
label distribution protocols in general, we try to avoid the acronym.

3.7. Unsolicited Downstream vs. Downstream-on-Demand

The MPLS architecture allows an LSR to explicitly request, from its
next hop for a particular FEC, a label binding for that FEC. This is
known as "downstream-on-demand" label distribution.

The MPLS architecture also allows an LSR to distribute bindings to
LSRs that have not explicitly requested them. This is known as
"unsolicited downstream" label distribution.

It is expected that some MPLS implementations will provide only
downstream-on-demand label distribution, and some will provide only
unsolicited downstream label distribution, and some will provide
both. Which is provided may depend on the characteristics of the
interfaces which are supported by a particular implementation.
However, both of these label distribution techniques may be used in
the same network at the same time. On any given label distribution
adjacency, the upstream LSR and the downstream LSR must agree on
which technique is to be used.

3.8. Label Retention Mode

An LSR Ru may receive (or have received) a label binding for a
particular FEC from an LSR Rd, even though Rd is not Ru's next hop
(or is no longer Ru's next hop) for that FEC.

Ru then has the choice of whether to keep track of such bindings, or
whether to discard such bindings. If Ru keeps track of such
bindings, then it may immediately begin using the binding again if Rd
eventually becomes its next hop for the FEC in question. If Ru
discards such bindings, then if Rd later becomes the next hop, the
binding will have to be reacquired.

If an LSR supports "Liberal Label Retention Mode", it maintains the
bindings between a label and a FEC which are received from LSRs which
are not its next hop for that FEC. If an LSR supports "Conservative
Label Retention Mode", it discards such bindings.

Liberal label retention mode allows for quicker adaptation to routing
changes, but conservative label retention mode though requires an LSR
to maintain many fewer labels.

3.9. The Label Stack

So far, we have spoken as if a labeled packet carries only a single
label. As we shall see, it is useful to have a more general model in
which a labeled packet carries a number of labels, organized as a
last-in, first-out stack. We refer to this as a "label stack".

Although, as we shall see, MPLS supports a hierarchy, the processing
of a labeled packet is completely independent of the level of
hierarchy. The processing is always based on the top label, without
regard for the possibility that some number of other labels may have
been "above it" in the past, or that some number of other labels may
be below it at present.

An unlabeled packet can be thought of as a packet whose label stack
is empty (i.e., whose label stack has depth 0).

If a packet's label stack is of depth m, we refer to the label at the
bottom of the stack as the level 1 label, to the label above it (if
such exists) as the level 2 label, and to the label at the top of the
stack as the level m label.

The utility of the label stack will become clear when we introduce
the notion of LSP Tunnel and the MPLS Hierarchy (section 3.27).

3.10. The Next Hop Label Forwarding Entry (NHLFE)

The "Next Hop Label Forwarding Entry" (NHLFE) is used when forwarding
a labeled packet. It contains the following information:

1. the packet's next hop

2. the operation to perform on the packet's label stack; this is one
   of the following operations:

   a) replace the label at the top of the label stack with a
      specified new label

   b) pop the label stack

   c) replace the label at the top of the label stack with a
      specified new label, and then push one or more specified new
      labels onto the label stack.

It may also contain:

   d) the data link encapsulation to use when transmitting the packet

   e) the way to encode the label stack when transmitting the packet

   f) any other information needed in order to properly dispose of
      the packet.

Note that at a given LSR, the packet's "next hop" might be that LSR
itself. In this case, the LSR would need to pop the top level label,
and then "forward" the resulting packet to itself. It would then
make another forwarding decision, based on what remains after the
label stacked is popped. This may still be a labeled packet, or it
may be the native IP packet.

This implies that in some cases the LSR may need to operate on the IP
header in order to forward the packet.

If the packet's "next hop" is the current LSR, then the label stack
operation MUST be to "pop the stack".

3.11. Incoming Label Map (ILM)

The "Incoming Label Map" (ILM) maps each incoming label to a set of
NHLFEs. It is used when forwarding packets that arrive as labeled
packets.

If the ILM maps a particular label to a set of NHLFEs that contains
more than one element, exactly one element of the set must be chosen
before the packet is forwarded. The procedures for choosing an
element from the set are beyond the scope of this document. Having
the ILM map a label to a set containing more than one NHLFE may be
useful if, e.g., it is desired to do load balancing over multiple
equal-cost paths.

3.12. FEC-to-NHLFE Map (FTN)

The "FEC-to-NHLFE" (FTN) maps each FEC to a set of NHLFEs. It is
used when forwarding packets that arrive unlabeled, but which are to
be labeled before being forwarded.

RFC 3031   MPLS Architecture   January 2001

   If the FTN maps a particular label to a set of NHLFEs that contains
   more than one element, exactly one element of the set must be chosen
   before the packet is forwarded. The procedures for choosing an
   element from the set are beyond the scope of this document. Having
   the FTN map a label to a set containing more than one NHLFE may be
   useful if, e.g., it is desired to do load balancing over multiple
   equal-cost paths.

3.13. Label Swapping

   Label swapping is the use of the following procedures to forward a
   packet.

   In order to forward a labeled packet, a LSR examines the label at the
   top of the label stack. It uses the ILM to map this label to an
   NHLFE. Using the information in the NHLFE, it determines where to
   forward the packet, and performs an operation on the packet's label
   stack. It then encodes the new label stack into the packet, and
   forwards the result.

   In order to forward an unlabeled packet, a LSR analyzes the network
   layer header, to determine the packet's FEC. It then uses the FTN to
   map this to an NHLFE. Using the information in the NHLFE, it
   determines where to forward the packet, and performs an operation on
   the packet's label stack. (Popping the label stack would, of course,
   be illegal in this case.) It then encodes the new label stack into
   the packet, and forwards the result.

   IT IS IMPORTANT TO NOTE THAT WHEN LABEL SWAPPING IS IN USE, THE NEXT
   HOP IS ALWAYS TAKEN FROM THE NHLFE; THIS MAY IN SOME CASES BE
   DIFFERENT FROM WHAT THE NEXT HOP WOULD BE IF MPLS WERE NOT IN USE.

3.14. Scope and Uniqueness of Labels

   A given LSR Rd may bind label L1 to FEC F, and distribute that
   binding to label distribution peer Ru1. Rd may also bind label L2 to
   FEC F, and distribute that binding to label distribution peer Ru2.
   Whether or not L1 == L2 is not determined by the architecture; this
   is a local matter.

   A given LSR Rd may bind label L to FEC F1, and distribute that
   binding to label distribution peer Ru1. Rd may also bind label L to
   FEC F2, and distribute that binding to label distribution peer Ru2.
   IF (AND ONLY IF) RD CAN TELL, WHEN IT RECEIVES A PACKET WHOSE TOP
   LABEL IS L, WHETHER THE LABEL WAS PUT THERE BY RU1 OR BY RU2, THEN
   THE ARCHITECTURE DOES NOT REQUIRE THAT F1 == F2. In such cases, we
   may say that Rd is using a different "label space" for the labels it
   distributes to Ru1 than for the labels it distributes to Ru2.

In general, Rd can only tell whether it was Ru1 or Ru2 that put the particular label value L at the top of the label stack if the following conditions hold:

- Ru1 and Ru2 are the only label distribution peers to which Rd distributed a binding of label value L, and

- Ru1 and Ru2 are each directly connected to Rd via a point-to-point interface.

When these conditions hold, an LSR may use labels that have "per interface" scope, i.e., which are only unique per interface. We may say that the LSR is using a "per-interface label space". When these conditions do not hold, the labels must be unique over the LSR which has assigned them, and we may say that the LSR is using a "per-platform label space."

If a particular LSR Rd is attached to a particular LSR Ru over two point-to-point interfaces, then Rd may distribute to Ru a binding of label L to FEC F1, as well as a binding of label L to FEC F2, F1 != F2, if and only if each binding is valid only for packets which Ru sends to Rd over a particular one of the interfaces. In all other cases, Rd MUST NOT distribute to Ru bindings of the same label value to two different FECs.

This prohibition holds even if the bindings are regarded as being at different "levels of hierarchy". In MPLS, there is no notion of having a different label space for different levels of the hierarchy; when interpreting a label, the level of the label is irrelevant.

The question arises as to whether it is possible for an LSR to use multiple per-platform label spaces, or to use multiple per-interface label spaces for the same interface. This is not prohibited by the architecture. However, in such cases the LSR must have some means, not specified by the architecture, of determining, for a particular incoming label, which label space that label belongs to. For example, [MPLS-SHIM] specifies that a different label space is used for unicast packets than for multicast packets, and uses a data link layer codepoint to distinguish the two label spaces.

3.15. Label Switched Path (LSP), LSP Ingress, LSP Egress

A "Label Switched Path (LSP) of level m" for a particular packet P is a sequence of routers,

<R1, ..., Rn>

with the following properties:

1. R1, the "LSP Ingress", is an LSR which pushes a label onto P's label stack, resulting in a label stack of depth m;

2. For all i, 1<i<n, P has a label stack of depth m when received by LSR Ri;

3. At no time during P's transit from R1 to R[n-1] does its label stack ever have a depth of less than m;

4. For all i, 1<i<n: Ri transmits P to R[i+1] by means of MPLS, i.e., by using the label at the top of the label stack (the level m label) as an index into an ILM;

5. For all i, 1<i<n: if a system S receives and forwards P after P is transmitted by Ri but before P is received by R[i+1] (e.g., Ri and R[i+1] might be connected via a switched data link subnetwork, and S might be one of the data link switches), then S's forwarding decision is not based on the level m label, or on the network layer header. This may be because:

    a) the decision is not based on the label stack or the network layer header at all;

    b) the decision is based on a label stack on which additional labels have been pushed (i.e., on a level m+k label, where k>0).

In other words, we can speak of the level m LSP for Packet P as the sequence of routers:

1. which begins with an LSR (an "LSP Ingress") that pushes on a level m label,

2. all of whose intermediate LSRs make their forwarding decision by label Switching on a level m label,

3. which ends (at an "LSP Egress") when a forwarding decision is made by label Switching on a level m-k label, where k>0, or when a forwarding decision is made by "ordinary", non-MPLS forwarding procedures.

A consequence (or perhaps a presupposition) of this is that whenever an LSR pushes a label onto an already labeled packet, it needs to make sure that the new label corresponds to a FEC whose LSP Egress is the LSR that assigned the label which is now second in the stack.

We will call a sequence of LSRs the "LSP for a particular FEC F" if
it is an LSP of level m for a particular packet P when P's level m
label is a label corresponding to FEC F.

Consider the set of nodes which may be LSP ingress nodes for FEC F.
Then there is an LSP for FEC F which begins with each of those nodes.
If a number of those LSPs have the same LSP egress, then one can
consider the set of such LSPs to be a tree, whose root is the LSP
egress. (Since data travels along this tree towards the root, this
may be called a multipoint-to-point tree.) We can thus speak of the
"LSP tree" for a particular FEC F.

3.16. Penultimate Hop Popping

Note that according to the definitions of section 3.15, if <R1, ...,
Rn> is a level m LSP for packet P, P may be transmitted from R[n-1]
to Rn with a label stack of depth m-1. That is, the label stack may
be popped at the penultimate LSR of the LSP, rather than at the LSP
Egress.

From an architectural perspective, this is perfectly appropriate.
The purpose of the level m label is to get the packet to Rn. Once
R[n-1] has decided to send the packet to Rn, the label no longer has
any function, and need no longer be carried.

There is also a practical advantage to doing penultimate hop popping.
If one does not do this, then when the LSP egress receives a packet,
it first looks up the top label, and determines as a result of that
lookup that it is indeed the LSP egress. Then it must pop the stack,
and examine what remains of the packet. If there is another label on
the stack, the egress will look this up and forward the packet based
on this lookup. (In this case, the egress for the packet's level m
LSP is also an intermediate node for its level m-1 LSP.) If there is
no other label on the stack, then the packet is forwarded according
to its network layer destination address. Note that this would
require the egress to do TWO lookups, either two label lookups or a
label lookup followed by an address lookup.

If, on the other hand, penultimate hop popping is used, then when the
penultimate hop looks up the label, it determines:

   - that it is the penultimate hop, and

   - who the next hop is.

The penultimate node then pops the stack, and forwards the packet
based on the information gained by looking up the label that was
previously at the top of the stack. When the LSP egress receives the

RFC 3031   MPLS Architecture   January 2001

packet, the label which is now at the top of the stack will be the
label which it needs to look up in order to make its own forwarding
decision. Or, if the packet was only carrying a single label, the
LSP egress will simply see the network layer packet, which is just
what it needs to see in order to make its forwarding decision.

This technique allows the egress to do a single lookup, and also
requires only a single lookup by the penultimate node.

The creation of the forwarding "fastpath" in a label switching
product may be greatly aided if it is known that only a single lookup
is ever required:

  - the code may be simplified if it can assume that only a single
    lookup is ever needed

  - the code can be based on a "time budget" that assumes that only
    a single lookup is ever needed.

In fact, when penultimate hop popping is done, the LSP Egress need
not even be an LSR.

However, some hardware switching engines may not be able to pop the
label stack, so this cannot be universally required. There may also
be some situations in which penultimate hop popping is not desirable.
Therefore the penultimate node pops the label stack only if this is
specifically requested by the egress node, OR if the next node in the
LSP does not support MPLS. (If the next node in the LSP does support
MPLS, but does not make such a request, the penultimate node has no
way of knowing that it in fact is the penultimate node.)

An LSR which is capable of popping the label stack at all MUST do
penultimate hop popping when so requested by its downstream label
distribution peer.

Initial label distribution protocol negotiations MUST allow each LSR
to determine whether its neighboring LSRS are capable of popping the
label stack. A LSR MUST NOT request a label distribution peer to pop
the label stack unless it is capable of doing so.

It may be asked whether the egress node can always interpret the top
label of a received packet properly if penultimate hop popping is
used. As long as the uniqueness and scoping rules of section 3.14
are obeyed, it is always possible to interpret the top label of a
received packet unambiguously.

3.17. LSP Next Hop

   The LSP Next Hop for a particular labeled packet in a particular LSR
   is the LSR which is the next hop, as selected by the NHLFE entry used
   for forwarding that packet.

   The LSP Next Hop for a particular FEC is the next hop as selected by
   the NHLFE entry indexed by a label which corresponds to that FEC.

   Note that the LSP Next Hop may differ from the next hop which would
   be chosen by the network layer routing algorithm. We will use the
   term "L3 next hop" when we refer to the latter.

3.18. Invalid Incoming Labels

   What should an LSR do if it receives a labeled packet with a
   particular incoming label, but has no binding for that label? It is
   tempting to think that the labels can just be removed, and the packet
   forwarded as an unlabeled IP packet. However, in some cases, doing
   so could cause a loop. If the upstream LSR thinks the label is bound
   to an explicit route, and the downstream LSR doesn't think the label
   is bound to anything, and if the hop by hop routing of the unlabeled
   IP packet brings the packet back to the upstream LSR, then a loop is
   formed.

   It is also possible that the label was intended to represent a route
   which cannot be inferred from the IP header.

   Therefore, when a labeled packet is received with an invalid incoming
   label, it MUST be discarded, UNLESS it is determined by some means
   (not within the scope of the current document) that forwarding it
   unlabeled cannot cause any harm.

3.19. LSP Control: Ordered versus Independent

   Some FECs correspond to address prefixes which are distributed via a
   dynamic routing algorithm. The setup of the LSPs for these FECs can
   be done in one of two ways: Independent LSP Control or Ordered LSP
   Control.

   In Independent LSP Control, each LSR, upon noting that it recognizes
   a particular FEC, makes an independent decision to bind a label to
   that FEC and to distribute that binding to its label distribution
   peers. This corresponds to the way that conventional IP datagram
   routing works; each node makes an independent decision as to how to
   treat each packet, and relies on the routing algorithm to converge
   rapidly so as to ensure that each datagram is correctly delivered.

RFC 3031   MPLS Architecture   January 2001

In Ordered LSP Control, an LSR only binds a label to a particular FEC
if it is the egress LSR for that FEC, or if it has already received a
label binding for that FEC from its next hop for that FEC.

If one wants to ensure that traffic in a particular FEC follows a
path with some specified set of properties (e.g., that the traffic
does not traverse any node twice, that a specified amount of
resources are available to the traffic, that the traffic follows an
explicitly specified path, etc.) ordered control must be used. With
independent control, some LSRs may begin label switching a traffic in
the FEC before the LSP is completely set up, and thus some traffic in
the FEC may follow a path which does not have the specified set of
properties. Ordered control also needs to be used if the recognition
of the FEC is a consequence of the setting up of the corresponding
LSP.

Ordered LSP setup may be initiated either by the ingress or the
egress.

Ordered control and independent control are fully interoperable.
However, unless all LSRs in an LSP are using ordered control, the
overall effect on network behavior is largely that of independent
control, since one cannot be sure that an LSP is not used until it is
fully set up.

This architecture allows the choice between independent control and
ordered control to be a local matter. Since the two methods
interwork, a given LSR need support only one or the other. Generally
speaking, the choice of independent versus ordered control does not
appear to have any effect on the label distribution mechanisms which
need to be defined.

3.20. Aggregation

One way of partitioning traffic into FECs is to create a separate FEC
for each address prefix which appears in the routing table. However,
within a particular MPLS domain, this may result in a set of FECs
such that all traffic in all those FECs follows the same route. For
example, a set of distinct address prefixes might all have the same
egress node, and label swapping might be used only to get the the
traffic to the egress node. In this case, within the MPLS domain,
the union of those FECs is itself a FEC. This creates a choice:
should a distinct label be bound to each component FEC, or should a
single label be bound to the union, and that label applied to all
traffic in the union?

The procedure of binding a single label to a union of FECs which is
itself a FEC (within some domain), and of applying that label to all

Rosen, et al.   Standards Track   [Page 21]

traffic in the union, is known as "aggregation". The MPLS
architecture allows aggregation. Aggregation may reduce the number
of labels which are needed to handle a particular set of packets, and
may also reduce the amount of label distribution control traffic
needed.

Given a set of FECs which are "aggregatable" into a single FEC, it is
possible to (a) aggregate them into a single FEC, (b) aggregate them
into a set of FECs, or (c) not aggregate them at all. Thus we can
speak of the "granularity" of aggregation, with (a) being the
"coarsest granularity", and (c) being the "finest granularity".

When order control is used, each LSR should adopt, for a given set of
FECs, the granularity used by its next hop for those FECs.

When independent control is used, it is possible that there will be
two adjacent LSRs, Ru and Rd, which aggregate some set of FECs
differently.

If Ru has finer granularity than Rd, this does not cause a problem.
Ru distributes more labels for that set of FECs than Rd does. This
means that when Ru needs to forward labeled packets in those FECs to
Rd, it may need to map n labels into m labels, where n > m. As an
option, Ru may withdraw the set of n labels that it has distributed,
and then distribute a set of m labels, corresponding to Rd's level of
granularity. This is not necessary to ensure correct operation, but
it does result in a reduction of the number of labels distributed by
Ru, and Ru is not gaining any particular advantage by distributing
the larger number of labels. The decision whether to do this or not
is a local matter.

If Ru has coarser granularity than Rd (i.e., Rd has distributed n
labels for the set of FECs, while Ru has distributed m, where n > m),
it has two choices:

-   It may adopt Rd's finer level of granularity. This would
    require it to withdraw the m labels it has distributed, and
    distribute n labels. This is the preferred option.

-   It may simply map its m labels into a subset of Rd's n labels,
    if it can determine that this will produce the same routing.
    For example, suppose that Ru applies a single label to all
    traffic that needs to pass through a certain egress LSR,
    whereas Rd binds a number of different labels to such traffic,
    depending on the individual destination addresses of the
    packets. If Ru knows the address of the egress router, and if
    Rd has bound a label to the FEC which is identified by that
    address, then Ru can simply apply that label.

RFC 3031   MPLS Architecture   January 2001

In any event, every LSR needs to know (by configuration) what
granularity to use for labels that it assigns. Where ordered control
is used, this requires each node to know the granularity only for
FECs which leave the MPLS network at that node. For independent
control, best results may be obtained by ensuring that all LSRs are
consistently configured to know the granularity for each FEC.
However, in many cases this may be done by using a single level of
granularity which applies to all FECs (such as "one label per IP
prefix in the forwarding table", or "one label per egress node").

3.21. Route Selection

Route selection refers to the method used for selecting the LSP for a
particular FEC. The proposed MPLS protocol architecture supports two
options for Route Selection: (1) hop by hop routing, and (2) explicit
routing.

Hop by hop routing allows each node to independently choose the next
hop for each FEC. This is the usual mode today in existing IP
networks. A "hop by hop routed LSP" is an LSP whose route is
selected using hop by hop routing.

In an explicitly routed LSP, each LSR does not independently choose
the next hop; rather, a single LSR, generally the LSP ingress or the
LSP egress, specifies several (or all) of the LSRs in the LSP. If a
single LSR specifies the entire LSP, the LSP is "strictly" explicitly
routed. If a single LSR specifies only some of the LSP, the LSP is
"loosely" explicitly routed.

The sequence of LSRs followed by an explicitly routed LSP may be
chosen by configuration, or may be selected dynamically by a single
node (for example, the egress node may make use of the topological
information learned from a link state database in order to compute
the entire path for the tree ending at that egress node).

Explicit routing may be useful for a number of purposes, such as
policy routing or traffic engineering. In MPLS, the explicit route
needs to be specified at the time that labels are assigned, but the
explicit route does not have to be specified with each IP packet.
This makes MPLS explicit routing much more efficient than the
alternative of IP source routing.

The procedures for making use of explicit routes, either strict or
loose, are beyond the scope of this document.

3.22. Lack of Outgoing Label

When a labeled packet is traveling along an LSP, it may occasionally
happen that it reaches an LSR at which the ILM does not map the
packet's incoming label into an NHLFE, even though the incoming label
is itself valid. This can happen due to transient conditions, or due
to an error at the LSR which should be the packet's next hop.

It is tempting in such cases to strip off the label stack and attempt
to forward the packet further via conventional forwarding, based on
its network layer header. However, in general this is not a safe
procedure:

  - If the packet has been following an explicitly routed LSP, this
    could result in a loop.

  - The packet's network header may not contain enough information
    to enable this particular LSR to forward it correctly.

Unless it can be determined (through some means outside the scope of
this document) that neither of these situations obtains, the only
safe procedure is to discard the packet.

3.23. Time-to-Live (TTL)

In conventional IP forwarding, each packet carries a "Time To Live"
(TTL) value in its header. Whenever a packet passes through a
router, its TTL gets decremented by 1; if the TTL reaches 0 before
the packet has reached its destination, the packet gets discarded.

This provides some level of protection against forwarding loops that
may exist due to misconfigurations, or due to failure or slow
convergence of the routing algorithm. TTL is sometimes used for
other functions as well, such as multicast scoping, and supporting
the "traceroute" command. This implies that there are two TTL-
related issues that MPLS needs to deal with: (i) TTL as a way to
suppress loops; (ii) TTL as a way to accomplish other functions, such
as limiting the scope of a packet.

When a packet travels along an LSP, it SHOULD emerge with the same
TTL value that it would have had if it had traversed the same
sequence of routers without having been label switched. If the
packet travels along a hierarchy of LSPs, the total number of LSR-
hops traversed SHOULD be reflected in its TTL value when it emerges
from the hierarchy of LSPs.

RFC 3031   MPLS Architecture   January 2001

The way that TTL is handled may vary depending upon whether the MPLS
label values are carried in an MPLS-specific "shim" header [MPLS-
SHIM], or if the MPLS labels are carried in an L2 header, such as an
ATM header [MPLS-ATM] or a frame relay header [MPLS-FRMRLY].

If the label values are encoded in a "shim" that sits between the
data link and network layer headers, then this shim MUST have a TTL
field that SHOULD be initially loaded from the network layer header
TTL field, SHOULD be decremented at each LSR-hop, and SHOULD be
copied into the network layer header TTL field when the packet
emerges from its LSP.

If the label values are encoded in a data link layer header (e.g.,
the VPI/VCI field in ATM's AAL5 header), and the labeled packets are
forwarded by an L2 switch (e.g., an ATM switch), and the data link
layer (like ATM) does not itself have a TTL field, then it will not
be possible to decrement a packet's TTL at each LSR-hop. An LSP
segment which consists of a sequence of LSRs that cannot decrement a
packet's TTL will be called a "non-TTL LSP segment".

When a packet emerges from a non-TTL LSP segment, it SHOULD however
be given a TTL that reflects the number of LSR-hops it traversed. In
the unicast case, this can be achieved by propagating a meaningful
LSP length to ingress nodes, enabling the ingress to decrement the
TTL value before forwarding packets into a non-TTL LSP segment.

Sometimes it can be determined, upon ingress to a non-TTL LSP
segment, that a particular packet's TTL will expire before the packet
reaches the egress of that non-TTL LSP segment. In this case, the
LSR at the ingress to the non-TTL LSP segment must not label switch
the packet. This means that special procedures must be developed to
support traceroute functionality, for example, traceroute packets may
be forwarded using conventional hop by hop forwarding.

3.24. Loop Control

On a non-TTL LSP segment, by definition, TTL cannot be used to
protect against forwarding loops. The importance of loop control may
depend on the particular hardware being used to provide the LSR
functions along the non-TTL LSP segment.

Suppose, for instance, that ATM switching hardware is being used to
provide MPLS switching functions, with the label being carried in the
VPI/VCI field. Since ATM switching hardware cannot decrement TTL,
there is no protection against loops. If the ATM hardware is capable
of providing fair access to the buffer pool for incoming cells
carrying different VPI/VCI values, this looping may not have any
deleterious effect on other traffic. If the ATM hardware cannot

Rosen, et al.   Standards Track   [Page 25]

provide fair buffer access of this sort, however, then even transient
loops may cause severe degradation of the LSR's total performance.

Even if fair buffer access can be provided, it is still worthwhile to
have some means of detecting loops that last "longer than possible".
In addition, even where TTL and/or per-VC fair queuing provides a
means for surviving loops, it still may be desirable where practical
to avoid setting up LSPs which loop. All LSRs that may attach to
non-TTL LSP segments will therefore be required to support a common
technique for loop detection; however, use of the loop detection
technique is optional. The loop detection technique is specified in
[MPLS-ATM] and [MPLS-LDP].

3.25. Label Encodings

In order to transmit a label stack along with the packet whose label
stack it is, it is necessary to define a concrete encoding of the
label stack. The architecture supports several different encoding
techniques; the choice of encoding technique depends on the
particular kind of device being used to forward labeled packets.

3.25.1. MPLS-specific Hardware and/or Software

If one is using MPLS-specific hardware and/or software to forward
labeled packets, the most obvious way to encode the label stack is to
define a new protocol to be used as a "shim" between the data link
layer and network layer headers. This shim would really be just an
encapsulation of the network layer packet; it would be "protocol-
independent" such that it could be used to encapsulate any network
layer. Hence we will refer to it as the "generic MPLS
encapsulation".

The generic MPLS encapsulation would in turn be encapsulated in a
data link layer protocol.

The MPLS generic encapsulation is specified in [MPLS-SHIM].

3.25.2. ATM Switches as LSRs

It will be noted that MPLS forwarding procedures are similar to those
of legacy "label swapping" switches such as ATM switches. ATM
switches use the input port and the incoming VPI/VCI value as the
index into a "cross-connect" table, from which they obtain an output
port and an outgoing VPI/VCI value. Therefore if one or more labels
can be encoded directly into the fields which are accessed by these
legacy switches, then the legacy switches can, with suitable software
upgrades, be used as LSRs. We will refer to such devices as "ATM-
LSRs".

RFC 3031   MPLS Architecture   January 2001

    There are three obvious ways to encode labels in the ATM cell header
    (presuming the use of AAL5):

    1. SVC Encoding

        Use the VPI/VCI field to encode the label which is at the top
        of the label stack. This technique can be used in any network.
        With this encoding technique, each LSP is realized as an ATM
        SVC, and the label distribution protocol becomes the ATM
        "signaling" protocol. With this encoding technique, the ATM-
        LSRs cannot perform "push" or "pop" operations on the label
        stack.

    2. SVP Encoding

        Use the VPI field to encode the label which is at the top of
        the label stack, and the VCI field to encode the second label
        on the stack, if one is present. This technique some
        advantages over the previous one, in that it permits the use of
        ATM "VP-switching". That is, the LSPs are realized as ATM
        SVPs, with the label distribution protocol serving as the ATM
        signaling protocol.

        However, this technique cannot always be used. If the network
        includes an ATM Virtual Path through a non-MPLS ATM network,
        then the VPI field is not necessarily available for use by
        MPLS.

        When this encoding technique is used, the ATM-LSR at the egress
        of the VP effectively does a "pop" operation.

    3. SVP Multipoint Encoding

        Use the VPI field to encode the label which is at the top of
        the label stack, use part of the VCI field to encode the second
        label on the stack, if one is present, and use the remainder of
        the VCI field to identify the LSP ingress. If this technique
        is used, conventional ATM VP-switching capabilities can be used
        to provide multipoint-to-point VPs. Cells from different
        packets will then carry different VCI values. As we shall see
        in section 3.26, this enables us to do label merging, without
        running into any cell interleaving problems, on ATM switches
        which can provide multipoint-to-point VPs, but which do not
        have the VC merge capability.

        This technique depends on the existence of a capability for
        assigning 16-bit VCI values to each ATM switch such that no
        single VCI value is assigned to two different switches. (If an

Rosen, et al.   Standards Track   [Page 27]

adequate number of such values could be assigned to each
switch, it would be possible to also treat the VCI value as the
second label in the stack.)

If there are more labels on the stack than can be encoded in the ATM
header, the ATM encodings must be combined with the generic
encapsulation.

3.25.3. Interoperability among Encoding Techniques

If <R1, R2, R3> is a segment of a LSP, it is possible that R1 will
use one encoding of the label stack when transmitting packet P to R2,
but R2 will use a different encoding when transmitting a packet P to
R3. In general, the MPLS architecture supports LSPs with different
label stack encodings used on different hops. Therefore, when we
discuss the procedures for processing a labeled packet, we speak in
abstract terms of operating on the packet's label stack. When a
labeled packet is received, the LSR must decode it to determine the
current value of the label stack, then must operate on the label
stack to determine the new value of the stack, and then encode the
new value appropriately before transmitting the labeled packet to its
next hop.

Unfortunately, ATM switches have no capability for translating from
one encoding technique to another. The MPLS architecture therefore
requires that whenever it is possible for two ATM switches to be
successive LSRs along a level m LSP for some packet, that those two
ATM switches use the same encoding technique.

Naturally there will be MPLS networks which contain a combination of
ATM switches operating as LSRs, and other LSRs which operate using an
MPLS shim header. In such networks there may be some LSRs which have
ATM interfaces as well as "MPLS Shim" interfaces. This is one
example of an LSR with different label stack encodings on different
hops. Such an LSR may swap off an ATM encoded label stack on an
incoming interface and replace it with an MPLS shim header encoded
label stack on the outgoing interface.

3.26. Label Merging

Suppose that an LSR has bound multiple incoming labels to a
particular FEC. When forwarding packets in that FEC, one would like
to have a single outgoing label which is applied to all such packets.
The fact that two different packets in the FEC arrived with different
incoming labels is irrelevant; one would like to forward them with
the same outgoing label. The capability to do so is known as "label
merging".

Let us say that an LSR is capable of label merging if it can receive
two packets from different incoming interfaces, and/or with different
labels, and send both packets out the same outgoing interface with
the same label. Once the packets are transmitted, the information
that they arrived from different interfaces and/or with different
incoming labels is lost.

Let us say that an LSR is not capable of label merging if, for any
two packets which arrive from different interfaces, or with different
labels, the packets must either be transmitted out different
interfaces, or must have different labels. ATM-LSRs using the SVC or
SVP Encodings cannot perform label merging. This is discussed in
more detail in the next section.

If a particular LSR cannot perform label merging, then if two packets
in the same FEC arrive with different incoming labels, they must be
forwarded with different outgoing labels. With label merging, the
number of outgoing labels per FEC need only be 1; without label
merging, the number of outgoing labels per FEC could be as large as
the number of nodes in the network.

With label merging, the number of incoming labels per FEC that a
particular LSR needs is never be larger than the number of label
distribution adjacencies. Without label merging, the number of
incoming labels per FEC that a particular LSR needs is as large as
the number of upstream nodes which forward traffic in the FEC to the
LSR in question. In fact, it is difficult for an LSR to even
determine how many such incoming labels it must support for a
particular FEC.

The MPLS architecture accommodates both merging and non-merging LSRs,
but allows for the fact that there may be LSRs which do not support
label merging. This leads to the issue of ensuring correct
interoperation between merging LSRs and non-merging LSRs. The issue
is somewhat different in the case of datagram media versus the case
of ATM. The different media types will therefore be discussed
separately.

3.26.1. Non-merging LSRs

The MPLS forwarding procedures is very similar to the forwarding
procedures used by such technologies as ATM and Frame Relay. That
is, a unit of data arrives, a label (VPI/VCI or DLCI) is looked up in
a "cross-connect table", on the basis of that lookup an output port
is chosen, and the label value is rewritten. In fact, it is possible
to use such technologies for MPLS forwarding; a label distribution
protocol can be used as the "signalling protocol" for setting up the
cross-connect tables.

Unfortunately, these technologies do not necessarily support the
label merging capability. In ATM, if one attempts to perform label
merging, the result may be the interleaving of cells from various
packets. If cells from different packets get interleaved, it is
impossible to reassemble the packets. Some Frame Relay switches use
cell switching on their backplanes. These switches may also be
incapable of supporting label merging, for the same reason -- cells
of different packets may get interleaved, and there is then no way to
reassemble the packets.

We propose to support two solutions to this problem. First, MPLS
will contain procedures which allow the use of non-merging LSRs.
Second, MPLS will support procedures which allow certain ATM switches
to function as merging LSRs.

Since MPLS supports both merging and non-merging LSRs, MPLS also
contains procedures to ensure correct interoperation between them.

3.26.2. Labels for Merging and Non-Merging LSRs

An upstream LSR which supports label merging needs to be sent only
one label per FEC. An upstream neighbor which does not support label
merging needs to be sent multiple labels per FEC. However, there is
no way of knowing a priori how many labels it needs. This will
depend on how many LSRs are upstream of it with respect to the FEC in
question.

In the MPLS architecture, if a particular upstream neighbor does not
support label merging, it is not sent any labels for a particular FEC
unless it explicitly asks for a label for that FEC. The upstream
neighbor may make multiple such requests, and is given a new label
each time. When a downstream neighbor receives such a request from
upstream, and the downstream neighbor does not itself support label
merging, then it must in turn ask its downstream neighbor for another
label for the FEC in question.

It is possible that there may be some nodes which support label
merging, but can only merge a limited number of incoming labels into
a single outgoing label. Suppose for example that due to some
hardware limitation a node is capable of merging four incoming labels
into a single outgoing label. Suppose however, that this particular
node has six incoming labels arriving at it for a particular FEC. In
this case, this node may merge these into two outgoing labels.

Whether label merging is applicable to explicitly routed LSPs is for
further study.

RFC 3031   MPLS Architecture   January 2001

3.26.3. Merge over ATM

3.26.3.1. Methods of Eliminating Cell Interleave

   There are several methods that can be used to eliminate the cell
   interleaving problem in ATM, thereby allowing ATM switches to support
   stream merge:

      1. VP merge, using the SVP Multipoint Encoding

         When VP merge is used, multiple virtual paths are merged into a
         virtual path, but packets from different sources are
         distinguished by using different VCIs within the VP.

      2. VC merge

         When VC merge is used, switches are required to buffer cells
         from one packet until the entire packet is received (this may
         be determined by looking for the AAL5 end of frame indicator).

   VP merge has the advantage that it is compatible with a higher
   percentage of existing ATM switch implementations. This makes it
   more likely that VP merge can be used in existing networks. Unlike
   VC merge, VP merge does not incur any delays at the merge points and
   also does not impose any buffer requirements. However, it has the
   disadvantage that it requires coordination of the VCI space within
   each VP. There are a number of ways that this can be accomplished.
   Selection of one or more methods is for further study.

   This tradeoff between compatibility with existing equipment versus
   protocol complexity and scalability implies that it is desirable for
   the MPLS protocol to support both VP merge and VC merge. In order to
   do so each ATM switch participating in MPLS needs to know whether its
   immediate ATM neighbors perform VP merge, VC merge, or no merge.

3.26.3.2. Interoperation: VC Merge, VP Merge, and Non-Merge

   The interoperation of the various forms of merging over ATM is most
   easily described by first describing the interoperation of VC merge
   with non-merge.

   In the case where VC merge and non-merge nodes are interconnected the
   forwarding of cells is based in all cases on a VC (i.e., the
   concatenation of the VPI and VCI). For each node, if an upstream
   neighbor is doing VC merge then that upstream neighbor requires only
   a single VPI/VCI for a particular stream (this is analogous to the
   requirement for a single label in the case of operation over frame
   media). If the upstream neighbor is not doing merge, then the

Rosen, et al.   Standards Track   [Page 31]

RFC 3031   MPLS Architecture   January 2001

neighbor will require a single VPI/VCI per stream for itself, plus enough VPI/VCIs to pass to its upstream neighbors. The number required will be determined by allowing the upstream nodes to request additional VPI/VCIs from their downstream neighbors (this is again analogous to the method used with frame merge).

A similar method is possible to support nodes which perform VP merge. In this case the VP merge node, rather than requesting a single VPI/VCI or a number of VPI/VCIs from its downstream neighbor, instead may request a single VP (identified by a VPI) but several VCIs within the VP. Furthermore, suppose that a non-merge node is downstream from two different VP merge nodes. This node may need to request one VPI/VCI (for traffic originating from itself) plus two VPs (one for each upstream node), each associated with a specified set of VCIs (as requested from the upstream node).

In order to support all of VP merge, VC merge, and non-merge, it is therefore necessary to allow upstream nodes to request a combination of zero or more VC identifiers (consisting of a VPI/VCI), plus zero or more VPs (identified by VPIs) each containing a specified number of VCs (identified by a set of VCIs which are significant within a VP). VP merge nodes would therefore request one VP, with a contained VCI for traffic that it originates (if appropriate) plus a VCI for each VC requested from above (regardless of whether or not the VC is part of a containing VP). VC merge node would request only a single VPI/VCI (since they can merge all upstream traffic into a single VC). Non-merge nodes would pass on any requests that they get from above, plus request a VPI/VCI for traffic that they originate (if appropriate).

3.27. Tunnels and Hierarchy

Sometimes a router Ru takes explicit action to cause a particular packet to be delivered to another router Rd, even though Ru and Rd are not consecutive routers on the Hop-by-hop path for that packet, and Rd is not the packet's ultimate destination. For example, this may be done by encapsulating the packet inside a network layer packet whose destination address is the address of Rd itself. This creates a "tunnel" from Ru to Rd. We refer to any packet so handled as a "Tunneled Packet".

3.27.1. Hop-by-Hop Routed Tunnel

If a Tunneled Packet follows the Hop-by-hop path from Ru to Rd, we say that it is in an "Hop-by-Hop Routed Tunnel" whose "transmit endpoint" is Ru and whose "receive endpoint" is Rd.

RFC 3031   MPLS Architecture   January 2001

3.27.2. Explicitly Routed Tunnel

   If a Tunneled Packet travels from Ru to Rd over a path other than the
   Hop-by-hop path, we say that it is in an "Explicitly Routed Tunnel"
   whose "transmit endpoint" is Ru and whose "receive endpoint" is Rd.
   For example, we might send a packet through an Explicitly Routed
   Tunnel by encapsulating it in a packet which is source routed.

3.27.3. LSP Tunnels

   It is possible to implement a tunnel as a LSP, and use label
   switching rather than network layer encapsulation to cause the packet
   to travel through the tunnel. The tunnel would be a LSP <R1, ...,
   Rn>, where R1 is the transmit endpoint of the tunnel, and Rn is the
   receive endpoint of the tunnel. This is called a "LSP Tunnel".

   The set of packets which are to be sent though the LSP tunnel
   constitutes a FEC, and each LSR in the tunnel must assign a label to
   that FEC (i.e., must assign a label to the tunnel). The criteria for
   assigning a particular packet to an LSP tunnel is a local matter at
   the tunnel's transmit endpoint. To put a packet into an LSP tunnel,
   the transmit endpoint pushes a label for the tunnel onto the label
   stack and sends the labeled packet to the next hop in the tunnel.

   If it is not necessary for the tunnel's receive endpoint to be able
   to determine which packets it receives through the tunnel, as
   discussed earlier, the label stack may be popped at the penultimate
   LSR in the tunnel.

   A "Hop-by-Hop Routed LSP Tunnel" is a Tunnel that is implemented as
   an hop-by-hop routed LSP between the transmit endpoint and the
   receive endpoint.

   An "Explicitly Routed LSP Tunnel" is a LSP Tunnel that is also an
   Explicitly Routed LSP.

3.27.4. Hierarchy: LSP Tunnels within LSPs

   Consider a LSP <R1, R2, R3, R4>. Let us suppose that R1 receives
   unlabeled packet P, and pushes on its label stack the label to cause
   it to follow this path, and that this is in fact the Hop-by-hop path.
   However, let us further suppose that R2 and R3 are not directly
   connected, but are "neighbors" by virtue of being the endpoints of an
   LSP tunnel. So the actual sequence of LSRs traversed by P is <R1,
   R2, R21, R22, R23, R3, R4>.

Rosen, et al.   Standards Track   [Page 33]

When P travels from R1 to R2, it will have a label stack of depth 1.
R2, switching on the label, determines that P must enter the tunnel.
R2 first replaces the Incoming label with a label that is meaningful
to R3. Then it pushes on a new label. This level 2 label has a
value which is meaningful to R21. Switching is done on the level 2
label by R21, R22, R23. R23, which is the penultimate hop in the
R2-R3 tunnel, pops the label stack before forwarding the packet to
R3. When R3 sees packet P, P has only a level 1 label, having now
exited the tunnel. Since R3 is the penultimate hop in P's level 1
LSP, it pops the label stack, and R4 receives P unlabeled.

The label stack mechanism allows LSP tunneling to nest to any depth.

3.27.5. Label Distribution Peering and Hierarchy

Suppose that packet P travels along a Level 1 LSP <R1, R2, R3, R4>,
and when going from R2 to R3 travels along a Level 2 LSP <R2, R21,
R22, R3>. From the perspective of the Level 2 LSP, R2's label
distribution peer is R21. From the perspective of the Level 1 LSP,
R2's label distribution peers are R1 and R3. One can have label
distribution peers at each layer of hierarchy. We will see in
sections 4.6 and 4.7 some ways to make use of this hierarchy. Note
that in this example, R2 and R21 must be IGP neighbors, but R2 and R3
need not be.

When two LSRs are IGP neighbors, we will refer to them as "local
label distribution peers". When two LSRs may be label distribution
peers, but are not IGP neighbors, we will refer to them as "remote
label distribution peers". In the above example, R2 and R21 are
local label distribution peers, but R2 and R3 are remote label
distribution peers.

The MPLS architecture supports two ways to distribute labels at
different layers of the hierarchy: Explicit Peering and Implicit
Peering.

One performs label distribution with one's local label distribution
peer by sending label distribution protocol messages which are
addressed to the peer. One can perform label distribution with one's
remote label distribution peers in one of two ways:

    1. Explicit Peering

        In explicit peering, one distributes labels to a peer by
        sending label distribution protocol messages which are
        addressed to the peer, exactly as one would do for local label
        distribution peers. This technique is most useful when the
        number of remote label distribution peers is small, or the

RFC 3031   MPLS Architecture   January 2001

number of higher level label bindings is large, or the remote
label distribution peers are in distinct routing areas or
domains. Of course, one needs to know which labels to
distribute to which peers; this is addressed in section 4.1.2.

Examples of the use of explicit peering is found in sections
4.2.1 and 4.6.

2. Implicit Peering

In Implicit Peering, one does not send label distribution
protocol messages which are addressed to one's peer. Rather,
to distribute higher level labels to ones remote label
distribution peers, one encodes a higher level label as an
attribute of a lower level label, and then distributes the
lower level label, along with this attribute, to one's local
label distribution peers. The local label distribution peers
then propagate the information to their local label
distribution peers. This process continues till the
information reaches the remote peer.

This technique is most useful when the number of remote label
distribution peers is large. Implicit peering does not require
an n-square peering mesh to distribute labels to the remote
label distribution peers because the information is piggybacked
through the local label distribution peering. However,
implicit peering requires the intermediate nodes to store
information that they might not be directly interested in.

An example of the use of implicit peering is found in section
4.3.

3.28. Label Distribution Protocol Transport

A label distribution protocol is used between nodes in an MPLS
network to establish and maintain the label bindings. In order for
MPLS to operate correctly, label distribution information needs to be
transmitted reliably, and the label distribution protocol messages
pertaining to a particular FEC need to be transmitted in sequence.
Flow control is also desirable, as is the capability to carry
multiple label messages in a single datagram.

One way to meet these goals is to use TCP as the underlying
transport, as is done in [MPLS-LDP] and [MPLS-BGP].

3.29. Why More than one Label Distribution Protocol?

   This architecture does not establish hard and fast rules for choosing
   which label distribution protocol to use in which circumstances.
   However, it is possible to point out some of the considerations.

3.29.1. BGP and LDP

   In many scenarios, it is desirable to bind labels to FECs which can
   be identified with routes to address prefixes (see section 4.1). If
   there is a standard, widely deployed routing algorithm which
   distributes those routes, it can be argued that label distribution is
   best achieved by piggybacking the label distribution on the
   distribution of the routes themselves.

   For example, BGP distributes such routes, and if a BGP speaker needs
   to also distribute labels to its BGP peers, using BGP to do the label
   distribution (see [MPLS-BGP]) has a number of advantages. In
   particular, it permits BGP route reflectors to distribute labels,
   thus providing a significant scalability advantage over using LDP to
   distribute labels between BGP peers.

3.29.2. Labels for RSVP Flowspecs

   When RSVP is used to set up resource reservations for particular
   flows, it can be desirable to label the packets in those flows, so
   that the RSVP filterspec does not need to be applied at each hop. It
   can be argued that having RSVP distribute the labels as part of its
   path/reservation setup process is the most efficient method of
   distributing labels for this purpose.

3.29.3. Labels for Explicitly Routed LSPs

   In some applications of MPLS, particularly those related to traffic
   engineering, it is desirable to set up an explicitly routed path,
   from ingress to egress. It is also desirable to apply resource
   reservations along that path.

   One can imagine two approaches to this:

      - Start with an existing protocol that is used for setting up
         resource reservations, and extend it to support explicit
         routing and label distribution.

      - Start with an existing protocol that is used for label
         distribution, and extend it to support explicit routing and
         resource reservations.

The first approach has given rise to the protocol specified in [MPLS-RSVP-TUNNELS], the second to the approach specified in [MPLS-CR-LDP].

3.30. Multicast

This section is for further study

4. Some Applications of MPLS

4.1. MPLS and Hop by Hop Routed Traffic

A number of uses of MPLS require that packets with a certain label be forwarded along the same hop-by-hop routed path that would be used for forwarding a packet with a specified address in its network layer destination address field.

4.1.1. Labels for Address Prefixes

In general, router R determines the next hop for packet P by finding the address prefix X in its routing table which is the longest match for P's destination address. That is, the packets in a given FEC are just those packets which match a given address prefix in R's routing table. In this case, a FEC can be identified with an address prefix.

Note that a packet P may be assigned to FEC F, and FEC F may be identified with address prefix X, even if P's destination address does not match X.

4.1.2. Distributing Labels for Address Prefixes

4.1.2.1. Label Distribution Peers for an Address Prefix

LSRs R1 and R2 are considered to be label distribution peers for address prefix X if and only if one of the following conditions holds:

1. R1's route to X is a route which it learned about via a particular instance of a particular IGP, and R2 is a neighbor of R1 in that instance of that IGP

2. R1's route to X is a route which it learned about by some instance of routing algorithm A1, and that route is redistributed into an instance of routing algorithm A2, and R2 is a neighbor of R1 in that instance of A2

3. R1 is the receive endpoint of an LSP Tunnel that is within
   another LSP, and R2 is a transmit endpoint of that tunnel, and
   R1 and R2 are participants in a common instance of an IGP, and
   are in the same IGP area (if the IGP in question has areas),
   and R1's route to X was learned via that IGP instance, or is
   redistributed by R1 into that IGP instance

4. R1's route to X is a route which it learned about via BGP, and
   R2 is a BGP peer of R1

In general, these rules ensure that if the route to a particular
address prefix is distributed via an IGP, the label distribution
peers for that address prefix are the IGP neighbors. If the route to
a particular address prefix is distributed via BGP, the label
distribution peers for that address prefix are the BGP peers. In
other cases of LSP tunneling, the tunnel endpoints are label
distribution peers.

4.1.2.2. Distributing Labels

In order to use MPLS for the forwarding of packets according to the
hop-by-hop route corresponding to any address prefix, each LSR MUST:

1. bind one or more labels to each address prefix that appears in
   its routing table;

2. for each such address prefix X, use a label distribution
   protocol to distribute the binding of a label to X to each of
   its label distribution peers for X.

There is also one circumstance in which an LSR must distribute a
label binding for an address prefix, even if it is not the LSR which
bound that label to that address prefix:

3. If R1 uses BGP to distribute a route to X, naming some other
   LSR R2 as the BGP Next Hop to X, and if R1 knows that R2 has
   assigned label L to X, then R1 must distribute the binding
   between L and X to any BGP peer to which it distributes that
   route.

These rules ensure that labels corresponding to address prefixes
which correspond to BGP routes are distributed to IGP neighbors if
and only if the BGP routes are distributed into the IGP. Otherwise,
the labels bound to BGP routes are distributed only to the other BGP
speakers.

These rules are intended only to indicate which label bindings must
be distributed by a given LSR to which other LSRs.

RFC 3031   MPLS Architecture   January 2001

4.1.3. Using the Hop by Hop path as the LSP

If the hop-by-hop path that packet P needs to follow is <R1, ...,
Rn>, then <R1, ..., Rn> can be an LSP as long as:

1. there is a single address prefix X, such that, for all i,
   1<=i<n, X is the longest match in Ri's routing table for P's
   destination address;

2. for all i, 1<i<n, Ri has assigned a label to X and distributed
   that label to R[i-1].

Note that a packet's LSP can extend only until it encounters a router
whose forwarding tables have a longer best match address prefix for
the packet's destination address. At that point, the LSP must end
and the best match algorithm must be performed again.

Suppose, for example, that packet P, with destination address
10.2.153.178 needs to go from R1 to R2 to R3. Suppose also that R2
advertises address prefix 10.2/16 to R1, but R3 advertises
10.2.153/23, 10.2.154/23, and 10.2/16 to R2. That is, R2 is
advertising an "aggregated route" to R1. In this situation, packet P
can be label Switched until it reaches R2, but since R2 has performed
route aggregation, it must execute the best match algorithm to find
P's FEC.

4.1.4. LSP Egress and LSP Proxy Egress

An LSR R is considered to be an "LSP Egress" LSR for address prefix X
if and only if one of the following conditions holds:

1. R has an address Y, such that X is the address prefix in R's
   routing table which is the longest match for Y, or

2. R contains in its routing tables one or more address prefixes Y
   such that X is a proper initial substring of Y, but R's "LSP
   previous hops" for X do not contain any such address prefixes
   Y; that is, R is a "deaggregation point" for address prefix X.

An LSR R1 is considered to be an "LSP Proxy Egress" LSR for address
prefix X if and only if:

1. R1's next hop for X is R2, and R1 and R2 are not label
   distribution peers with respect to X (perhaps because R2 does
   not support MPLS), or

2. R1 has been configured to act as an LSP Proxy Egress for X

Rosen, et al.   Standards Track   [Page 39]

The definition of LSP allows for the LSP Egress to be a node which
does not support MPLS; in this case the penultimate node in the LSP
is the Proxy Egress.

4.1.5. The Implicit NULL Label

The Implicit NULL label is a label with special semantics which an
LSR can bind to an address prefix. If LSR Ru, by consulting its ILM,
sees that labeled packet P must be forwarded next to Rd, but that Rd
has distributed a binding of Implicit NULL to the corresponding
address prefix, then instead of replacing the value of the label on
top of the label stack, Ru pops the label stack, and then forwards
the resulting packet to Rd.

LSR Rd distributes a binding between Implicit NULL and an address
prefix X to LSR Ru if and only if:

    1. the rules of Section 4.1.2 indicate that Rd distributes to Ru a
       label binding for X, and

    2. Rd knows that Ru can support the Implicit NULL label (i.e.,
       that it can pop the label stack), and

    3. Rd is an LSP Egress (not proxy egress) for X.

This causes the penultimate LSR on a LSP to pop the label stack.
This is quite appropriate; if the LSP Egress is an MPLS Egress for X,
then if the penultimate LSR does not pop the label stack, the LSP
Egress will need to look up the label, pop the label stack, and then
look up the next label (or look up the L3 address, if no more labels
are present). By having the penultimate LSR pop the label stack, the
LSP Egress is saved the work of having to look up two labels in order
to make its forwarding decision.

However, if the penultimate LSR is an ATM switch, it may not have the
capability to pop the label stack. Hence a binding of Implicit NULL
may be distributed only to LSRs which can support that function.

If the penultimate LSR in an LSP for address prefix X is an LSP Proxy
Egress, it acts just as if the LSP Egress had distributed a binding
of Implicit NULL for X.

4.1.6. Option: Egress-Targeted Label Assignment

There are situations in which an LSP Ingress, Ri, knows that packets
of several different FECs must all follow the same LSP, terminating
at, say, LSP Egress Re. In this case, proper routing can be achieved

by using a single label for all such FECs; it is not necessary to
have a distinct label for each FEC. If (and only if) the following
conditions hold:

1. the address of LSR Re is itself in the routing table as a "host
   route", and

2. there is some way for Ri to determine that Re is the LSP egress
   for all packets in a particular set of FECs

Then Ri may bind a single label to all FECS in the set. This is
known as "Egress-Targeted Label Assignment."

How can LSR Ri determine that an LSR Re is the LSP Egress for all
packets in a particular FEC? There are a number of possible ways:

- If the network is running a link state routing algorithm, and
  all nodes in the area support MPLS, then the routing algorithm
  provides Ri with enough information to determine the routers
  through which packets in that FEC must leave the routing domain
  or area.

- If the network is running BGP, Ri may be able to determine that
  the packets in a particular FEC must leave the network via some
  particular router which is the "BGP Next Hop" for that FEC.

- It is possible to use the label distribution protocol to pass
  information about which address prefixes are "attached" to
  which egress LSRs. This method has the advantage of not
  depending on the presence of link state routing.

If egress-targeted label assignment is used, the number of labels
that need to be supported throughout the network may be greatly
reduced. This may be significant if one is using legacy switching
hardware to do MPLS, and the switching hardware can support only a
limited number of labels.

One possible approach would be to configure the network to use
egress-targeted label assignment by default, but to configure
particular LSRs to NOT use egress-targeted label assignment for one
or more of the address prefixes for which it is an LSP egress. We
impose the following rule:

- If a particular LSR is NOT an LSP Egress for some set of
  address prefixes, then it should assign labels to the address
  prefixes in the same way as is done by its LSP next hop for
  those address prefixes. That is, suppose Rd is Ru's LSP next

    hop for address prefixes X1 and X2. If Rd assigns the same
    label to X1 and X2, Ru should as well. If Rd assigns different
    labels to X1 and X2, then Ru should as well.

For example, suppose one wants to make egress-targeted label
assignment the default, but to assign distinct labels to those
address prefixes for which there are multiple possible LSP egresses
(i.e., for those address prefixes which are multi-homed.) One can
configure all LSRs to use egress-targeted label assignment, and then
configure a handful of LSRs to assign distinct labels to those
address prefixes which are multi-homed. For a particular multi-homed
address prefix X, one would only need to configure this in LSRs which
are either LSP Egresses or LSP Proxy Egresses for X.

It is important to note that if Ru and Rd are adjacent LSRs in an LSP
for X1 and X2, forwarding will still be done correctly if Ru assigns
distinct labels to X1 and X2 while Rd assigns just one label to the
both of them. This just means that R1 will map different incoming
labels to the same outgoing label, an ordinary occurrence.

Similarly, if Rd assigns distinct labels to X1 and X2, but Ru assigns
to them both the label corresponding to the address of their LSP
Egress or Proxy Egress, forwarding will still be done correctly. Ru
will just map the incoming label to the label which Rd has assigned
to the address of that LSP Egress.

4.2. MPLS and Explicitly Routed LSPs

There are a number of reasons why it may be desirable to use explicit
routing instead of hop by hop routing. For example, this allows
routes to be based on administrative policies, and allows the routes
that LSPs take to be carefully designed to allow traffic engineering
[MPLS-TRFENG].

4.2.1. Explicitly Routed LSP Tunnels

In some situations, the network administrators may desire to forward
certain classes of traffic along certain pre-specified paths, where
these paths differ from the Hop-by-hop path that the traffic would
ordinarily follow. This can be done in support of policy routing, or
in support of traffic engineering. The explicit route may be a
configured one, or it may be determined dynamically by some means,
e.g., by constraint-based routing.

MPLS allows this to be easily done by means of Explicitly Routed LSP
Tunnels. All that is needed is:

1. A means of selecting the packets that are to be sent into the
   Explicitly Routed LSP Tunnel;

2. A means of setting up the Explicitly Routed LSP Tunnel;

3. A means of ensuring that packets sent into the Tunnel will not
   loop from the receive endpoint back to the transmit endpoint.

If the transmit endpoint of the tunnel wishes to put a labeled packet
into the tunnel, it must first replace the label value at the top of
the stack with a label value that was distributed to it by the
tunnel's receive endpoint. Then it must push on the label which
corresponds to the tunnel itself, as distributed to it by the next
hop along the tunnel. To allow this, the tunnel endpoints should be
explicit label distribution peers. The label bindings they need to
exchange are of no interest to the LSRs along the tunnel.

4.3. Label Stacks and Implicit Peering

Suppose a particular LSR Re is an LSP proxy egress for 10 address
prefixes, and it reaches each address prefix through a distinct
interface.

One could assign a single label to all 10 address prefixes. Then Re
is an LSP egress for all 10 address prefixes. This ensures that
packets for all 10 address prefixes get delivered to Re. However, Re
would then have to look up the network layer address of each such
packet in order to choose the proper interface to send the packet on.

Alternatively, one could assign a distinct label to each interface.
Then Re is an LSP proxy egress for the 10 address prefixes. This
eliminates the need for Re to look up the network layer addresses in
order to forward the packets. However, it can result in the use of a
large number of labels.

An alternative would be to bind all 10 address prefixes to the same
level 1 label (which is also bound to the address of the LSR itself),
and then to bind each address prefix to a distinct level 2 label.
The level 2 label would be treated as an attribute of the level 1
label binding, which we call the "Stack Attribute". We impose the
following rules:

- When LSR Ru initially labels a hitherto unlabeled packet, if
  the longest match for the packet's destination address is X,
  and Ru's LSP next hop for X is Rd, and Rd has distributed to Ru
  a binding of label L1 to X, along with a stack attribute of L2,
  then

1. Ru must push L2 and then L1 onto the packet's label stack, and then forward the packet to Rd;

2. When Ru distributes label bindings for X to its label distribution peers, it must include L2 as the stack attribute.

3. Whenever the stack attribute changes (possibly as a result of a change in Ru's LSP next hop for X), Ru must distribute the new stack attribute.

Note that although the label value bound to X may be different at each hop along the LSP, the stack attribute value is passed unchanged, and is set by the LSP proxy egress.

Thus the LSP proxy egress for X becomes an "implicit peer" with each other LSR in the routing area or domain. In this case, explicit peering would be too unwieldy, because the number of peers would become too large.

4.4. MPLS and Multi-Path Routing

If an LSR supports multiple routes for a particular stream, then it may assign multiple labels to the stream, one for each route. Thus the reception of a second label binding from a particular neighbor for a particular address prefix should be taken as meaning that either label can be used to represent that address prefix.

If multiple label bindings for a particular address prefix are specified, they may have distinct attributes.

4.5. LSP Trees as Multipoint-to-Point Entities

Consider the case of packets P1 and P2, each of which has a destination address whose longest match, throughout a particular routing domain, is address prefix X. Suppose that the Hop-by-hop path for P1 is <R1, R2, R3>, and the Hop-by-hop path for P2 is <R4, R2, R3>. Let's suppose that R3 binds label L3 to X, and distributes this binding to R2. R2 binds label L2 to X, and distributes this binding to both R1 and R4. When R2 receives packet P1, its incoming label will be L2. R2 will overwrite L2 with L3, and send P1 to R3. When R2 receives packet P2, its incoming label will also be L2. R2 again overwrites L2 with L3, and send P2 on to R3.

Note then that when P1 and P2 are traveling from R2 to R3, they carry the same label, and as far as MPLS is concerned, they cannot be distinguished. Thus instead of talking about two distinct LSPs, <R1,

R2, R3> and <R4, R2, R3>, we might talk of a single "Multipoint-to-Point LSP Tree", which we might denote as <{R1, R4}, R2, R3>.

This creates a difficulty when we attempt to use conventional ATM switches as LSRs. Since conventional ATM switches do not support multipoint-to-point connections, there must be procedures to ensure that each LSP is realized as a point-to-point VC. However, if ATM switches which do support multipoint-to-point VCs are in use, then the LSPs can be most efficiently realized as multipoint-to-point VCs. Alternatively, if the SVP Multipoint Encoding (section 3.25.2) can be used, the LSPs can be realized as multipoint-to-point SVPs.

4.6. LSP Tunneling between BGP Border Routers

Consider the case of an Autonomous System, A, which carries transit traffic between other Autonomous Systems. Autonomous System A will have a number of BGP Border Routers, and a mesh of BGP connections among them, over which BGP routes are distributed. In many such cases, it is desirable to avoid distributing the BGP routes to routers which are not BGP Border Routers. If this can be avoided, the "route distribution load" on those routers is significantly reduced. However, there must be some means of ensuring that the transit traffic will be delivered from Border Router to Border Router by the interior routers.

This can easily be done by means of LSP Tunnels. Suppose that BGP routes are distributed only to BGP Border Routers, and not to the interior routers that lie along the Hop-by-hop path from Border Router to Border Router. LSP Tunnels can then be used as follows:

  1. Each BGP Border Router distributes, to every other BGP Border Router in the same Autonomous System, a label for each address prefix that it distributes to that router via BGP.

  2. The IGP for the Autonomous System maintains a host route for each BGP Border Router. Each interior router distributes its labels for these host routes to each of its IGP neighbors.

  3. Suppose that:

     a) BGP Border Router B1 receives an unlabeled packet P,

     b) address prefix X in B1's routing table is the longest match for the destination address of P,

     c) the route to X is a BGP route,

     d) the BGP Next Hop for X is B2,

     e) B2 has bound label L1 to X, and has distributed this binding
       to B1,

     f) the IGP next hop for the address of B2 is I1,

     g) the address of B2 is in B1's and I1's IGP routing tables as
       a host route, and

     h) I1 has bound label L2 to the address of B2, and distributed
       this binding to B1.

     Then before sending packet P to I1, B1 must create a label
     stack for P, then push on label L1, and then push on label L2.

4. Suppose that BGP Border Router B1 receives a labeled Packet P,
   where the label on the top of the label stack corresponds to an
   address prefix, X, to which the route is a BGP route, and that
   conditions 3b, 3c, 3d, and 3e all hold. Then before sending
   packet P to I1, B1 must replace the label at the top of the
   label stack with L1, and then push on label L2.

With these procedures, a given packet P follows a level 1 LSP all of
whose members are BGP Border Routers, and between each pair of BGP
Border Routers in the level 1 LSP, it follows a level 2 LSP.

These procedures effectively create a Hop-by-Hop Routed LSP Tunnel
between the BGP Border Routers.

Since the BGP border routers are exchanging label bindings for
address prefixes that are not even known to the IGP routing, the BGP
routers should become explicit label distribution peers with each
other.

It is sometimes possible to create Hop-by-Hop Routed LSP Tunnels
between two BGP Border Routers, even if they are not in the same
Autonomous System. Suppose, for example, that B1 and B2 are in AS 1.
Suppose that B3 is an EBGP neighbor of B2, and is in AS2. Finally,
suppose that B2 and B3 are on some network which is common to both
Autonomous Systems (a "Demilitarized Zone"). In this case, an LSP
tunnel can be set up directly between B1 and B3 as follows:

  - B3 distributes routes to B2 (using EBGP), optionally assigning
    labels to address prefixes;

  - B2 redistributes those routes to B1 (using IBGP), indicating
    that the BGP next hop for each such route is B3. If B3 has
    assigned labels to address prefixes, B2 passes these labels
    along, unchanged, to B1.

RFC 3031   MPLS Architecture   January 2001

    - The IGP of AS1 has a host route for B3.

4.7. Other Uses of Hop-by-Hop Routed LSP Tunnels

   The use of Hop-by-Hop Routed LSP Tunnels is not restricted to tunnels
   between BGP Next Hops. Any situation in which one might otherwise
   have used an encapsulation tunnel is one in which it is appropriate
   to use a Hop-by-Hop Routed LSP Tunnel. Instead of encapsulating the
   packet with a new header whose destination address is the address of
   the tunnel's receive endpoint, the label corresponding to the address
   prefix which is the longest match for the address of the tunnel's
   receive endpoint is pushed on the packet's label stack. The packet
   which is sent into the tunnel may or may not already be labeled.

   If the transmit endpoint of the tunnel wishes to put a labeled packet
   into the tunnel, it must first replace the label value at the top of
   the stack with a label value that was distributed to it by the
   tunnel's receive endpoint. Then it must push on the label which
   corresponds to the tunnel itself, as distributed to it by the next
   hop along the tunnel. To allow this, the tunnel endpoints should be
   explicit label distribution peers. The label bindings they need to
   exchange are of no interest to the LSRs along the tunnel.

4.8. MPLS and Multicast

   Multicast routing proceeds by constructing multicast trees. The tree
   along which a particular multicast packet must get forwarded depends
   in general on the packet's source address and its destination
   address. Whenever a particular LSR is a node in a particular
   multicast tree, it binds a label to that tree. It then distributes
   that binding to its parent on the multicast tree. (If the node in
   question is on a LAN, and has siblings on that LAN, it must also
   distribute the binding to its siblings. This allows the parent to
   use a single label value when multicasting to all children on the
   LAN.)

   When a multicast labeled packet arrives, the NHLFE corresponding to
   the label indicates the set of output interfaces for that packet, as
   well as the outgoing label. If the same label encoding technique is
   used on all the outgoing interfaces, the very same packet can be sent
   to all the children.

5. Label Distribution Procedures (Hop-by-Hop)

   In this section, we consider only label bindings that are used for
   traffic to be label switched along its hop-by-hop routed path. In
   these cases, the label in question will correspond to an address
   prefix in the routing table.

5.1. The Procedures for Advertising and Using labels

There are a number of different procedures that may be used to
distribute label bindings. Some are executed by the downstream LSR,
and some by the upstream LSR.

The downstream LSR must perform:

-   The Distribution Procedure, and

-   the Withdrawal Procedure.

The upstream LSR must perform:

-   The Request Procedure, and

-   the NotAvailable Procedure, and

-   the Release Procedure, and

-   the labelUse Procedure.

The MPLS architecture supports several variants of each procedure.

However, the MPLS architecture does not support all possible
combinations of all possible variants. The set of supported
combinations will be described in section 5.2, where the
interoperability between different combinations will also be
discussed.

5.1.1. Downstream LSR: Distribution Procedure

The Distribution Procedure is used by a downstream LSR to determine
when it should distribute a label binding for a particular address
prefix to its label distribution peers. The architecture supports
four different distribution procedures.

Irrespective of the particular procedure that is used, if a label
binding for a particular address prefix has been distributed by a
downstream LSR Rd to an upstream LSR Ru, and if at any time the
attributes (as defined above) of that binding change, then Rd must
inform Ru of the new attributes.

If an LSR is maintaining multiple routes to a particular address
prefix, it is a local matter as to whether that LSR binds multiple
labels to the address prefix (one per route), and hence distributes
multiple bindings.

5.1.1.1. PushUnconditional

   Let Rd be an LSR. Suppose that:

      1. X is an address prefix in Rd's routing table

      2. Ru is a label distribution peer of Rd with respect to X

   Whenever these conditions hold, Rd must bind a label to X and
   distribute that binding to Ru. It is the responsibility of Rd to
   keep track of the bindings which it has distributed to Ru, and to
   make sure that Ru always has these bindings.

   This procedure would be used by LSRs which are performing unsolicited
   downstream label assignment in the Independent LSP Control Mode.

5.1.1.2. PushConditional

   Let Rd be an LSR. Suppose that:

      1. X is an address prefix in Rd's routing table

      2. Ru is a label distribution peer of Rd with respect to X

      3. Rd is either an LSP Egress or an LSP Proxy Egress for X, or
         Rd's L3 next hop for X is Rn, where Rn is distinct from Ru, and
         Rn has bound a label to X and distributed that binding to Rd.

   Then as soon as these conditions all hold, Rd should bind a label to
   X and distribute that binding to Ru.

   Whereas PushUnconditional causes the distribution of label bindings
   for all address prefixes in the routing table, PushConditional causes
   the distribution of label bindings only for those address prefixes
   for which one has received label bindings from one's LSP next hop, or
   for which one does not have an MPLS-capable L3 next hop.

   This procedure would be used by LSRs which are performing unsolicited
   downstream label assignment in the Ordered LSP Control Mode.

5.1.1.3. PulledUnconditional

   Let Rd be an LSR. Suppose that:

      1. X is an address prefix in Rd's routing table

      2. Ru is a label distribution peer of Rd with respect to X

    3. Ru has explicitly requested that Rd bind a label to X and
       distribute the binding to Ru

Then Rd should bind a label to X and distribute that binding to Ru.
Note that if X is not in Rd's routing table, or if Rd is not a label
distribution peer of Ru with respect to X, then Rd must inform Ru
that it cannot provide a binding at this time.

If Rd has already distributed a binding for address prefix X to Ru,
and it receives a new request from Ru for a binding for address
prefix X, it will bind a second label, and distribute the new binding
to Ru. The first label binding remains in effect.

This procedure would be used by LSRs performing downstream-on-demand
label distribution using the Independent LSP Control Mode.

5.1.1.4. PulledConditional

Let Rd be an LSR. Suppose that:

    1. X is an address prefix in Rd's routing table

    2. Ru is a label distribution peer of Rd with respect to X

    3. Ru has explicitly requested that Rd bind a label to X and
       distribute the binding to Ru

    4. Rd is either an LSP Egress or an LSP Proxy Egress for X, or
       Rd's L3 next hop for X is Rn, where Rn is distinct from Ru, and
       Rn has bound a label to X and distributed that binding to Rd

Then as soon as these conditions all hold, Rd should bind a label to
X and distribute that binding to Ru. Note that if X is not in Rd's
routing table and a binding for X is not obtainable via Rd's next hop
for X, or if Rd is not a label distribution peer of Ru with respect
to X, then Rd must inform Ru that it cannot provide a binding at this
time.

However, if the only condition that fails to hold is that Rn has not
yet provided a label to Rd, then Rd must defer any response to Ru
until such time as it has receiving a binding from Rn.

If Rd has distributed a label binding for address prefix X to Ru, and
at some later time, any attribute of the label binding changes, then
Rd must redistribute the label binding to Ru, with the new attribute.
It must do this even though Ru does not issue a new Request.

RFC 3031   MPLS Architecture   January 2001

    This procedure would be used by LSRs that are performing downstream-
    on-demand label allocation in the Ordered LSP Control Mode.

    In section 5.2, we will discuss how to choose the particular
    procedure to be used at any given time, and how to ensure
    interoperability among LSRs that choose different procedures.

5.1.2. Upstream LSR: Request Procedure

    The Request Procedure is used by the upstream LSR for an address
    prefix to determine when to explicitly request that the downstream
    LSR bind a label to that prefix and distribute the binding.   There
    are three possible procedures that can be used.

5.1.2.1. RequestNever

    Never make a request. This is useful if the downstream LSR uses the
    PushConditional procedure or the PushUnconditional procedure, but is
    not useful if the downstream LSR uses the PulledUnconditional
    procedure or the the PulledConditional procedures.

    This procedure would be used by an LSR when unsolicited downstream
    label distribution and Liberal Label Retention Mode are being used.

5.1.2.2. RequestWhenNeeded

    Make a request whenever the L3 next hop to the address prefix
    changes, or when a new address prefix is learned, and one doesn't
    already have a label binding from that next hop for the given address
    prefix.

    This procedure would be used by an LSR whenever Conservative Label
    Retention Mode is being used.

5.1.2.3. RequestOnRequest

    Issue a request whenever a request is received, in addition to
    issuing a request when needed (as described in section 5.1.2.2). If
    Ru is not capable of being an LSP ingress, it may issue a request
    only when it receives a request from upstream.

    If Rd receives such a request from Ru, for an address prefix for
    which Rd has already distributed Ru a label, Rd shall assign a new
    (distinct) label, bind it to X, and distribute that binding.
    (Whether Rd can distribute this binding to Ru immediately or not
    depends on the Distribution Procedure being used.)

This procedure would be used by an LSR which is doing downstream-on-demand label distribution, but is not doing label merging, e.g., an ATM-LSR which is not capable of VC merge.

5.1.3. Upstream LSR: NotAvailable Procedure

If Ru and Rd are respectively upstream and downstream label distribution peers for address prefix X, and Rd is Ru's L3 next hop for X, and Ru requests a binding for X from Rd, but Rd replies that it cannot provide a binding at this time, because it has no next hop for X, then the NotAvailable procedure determines how Ru responds. There are two possible procedures governing Ru's behavior:

5.1.3.1. RequestRetry

Ru should issue the request again at a later time. That is, the requester is responsible for trying again later to obtain the needed binding. This procedure would be used when downstream-on-demand label distribution is used.

5.1.3.2. RequestNoRetry

Ru should never reissue the request, instead assuming that Rd will provide the binding automatically when it is available. This is useful if Rd uses the PushUnconditional procedure or the PushConditional procedure, i.e., if unsolicited downstream label distribution is used.

Note that if Rd replies that it cannot provide a binding to Ru, because of some error condition, rather than because Rd has no next hop, the behavior of Ru will be governed by the error recovery conditions of the label distribution protocol, rather than by the NotAvailable procedure.

5.1.4. Upstream LSR: Release Procedure

Suppose that Rd is an LSR which has bound a label to address prefix X, and has distributed that binding to LSR Ru. If Rd does not happen to be Ru's L3 next hop for address prefix X, or has ceased to be Ru's L3 next hop for address prefix X, then Ru will not be using the label. The Release Procedure determines how Ru acts in this case. There are two possible procedures governing Ru's behavior:

5.1.4.1. ReleaseOnChange

Ru should release the binding, and inform Rd that it has done so. This procedure would be used to implement Conservative Label Retention Mode.

5.1.4.2. NoReleaseOnChange

   Ru should maintain the binding, so that it can use it again
   immediately if Rd later becomes Ru's L3 next hop for X. This
   procedure would be used to implement Liberal Label Retention Mode.

5.1.5. Upstream LSR: labelUse Procedure

   Suppose Ru is an LSR which has received label binding L for address
   prefix X from LSR Rd, and Ru is upstream of Rd with respect to X, and
   in fact Rd is Ru's L3 next hop for X.

   Ru will make use of the binding if Rd is Ru's L3 next hop for X. If,
   at the time the binding is received by Ru, Rd is NOT Ru's L3 next hop
   for X, Ru does not make any use of the binding at that time. Ru may
   however start using the binding at some later time, if Rd becomes
   Ru's L3 next hop for X.

   The labelUse Procedure determines just how Ru makes use of Rd's
   binding.

   There are two procedures which Ru may use:

5.1.5.1. UseImmediate

   Ru may put the binding into use immediately. At any time when Ru has
   a binding for X from Rd, and Rd is Ru's L3 next hop for X, Rd will
   also be Ru's LSP next hop for X. This procedure is used when loop
   detection is not in use.

5.1.5.2. UseIfLoopNotDetected

   This procedure is the same as UseImmediate, unless Ru has detected a
   loop in the LSP. If a loop has been detected, Ru will discontinue
   the use of label L for forwarding packets to Rd.

   This procedure is used when loop detection is in use.

   This will continue until the next hop for X changes, or until the
   loop is no longer detected.

5.1.6. Downstream LSR: Withdraw Procedure

   In this case, there is only a single procedure.

   When LSR Rd decides to break the binding between label L and address
   prefix X, then this unbinding must be distributed to all LSRs to
   which the binding was distributed.

RFC 3031   MPLS Architecture   January 2001

It is required that the unbinding of L from X be distributed by Rd to
a LSR Ru before Rd distributes to Ru any new binding of L to any
other address prefix Y, where X != Y. If Ru were to learn of the new
binding of L to Y before it learned of the unbinding of L from X, and
if packets matching both X and Y were forwarded by Ru to Rd, then for
a period of time, Ru would label both packets matching X and packets
matching Y with label L.

The distribution and withdrawal of label bindings is done via a label
distribution protocol. All label distribution protocols require that
a label distribution adjacency be established between two label
distribution peers (except implicit peers). If LSR R1 has a label
distribution adjacency to LSR R2, and has received label bindings
from LSR R2 via that adjacency, then if adjacency is brought down by
either peer (whether as a result of failure or as a matter of normal
operation), all bindings received over that adjacency must be
considered to have been withdrawn.

As long as the relevant label distribution adjacency remains in
place, label bindings that are withdrawn must always be withdrawn
explicitly. If a second label is bound to an address prefix, the
result is not to implicitly withdraw the first label, but to bind
both labels; this is needed to support multi-path routing. If a
second address prefix is bound to a label, the result is not to
implicitly withdraw the binding of that label to the first address
prefix, but to use that label for both address prefixes.

5.2. MPLS Schemes: Supported Combinations of Procedures

Consider two LSRs, Ru and Rd, which are label distribution peers with
respect to some set of address prefixes, where Ru is the upstream
peer and Rd is the downstream peer.

The MPLS scheme which governs the interaction of Ru and Rd can be
described as a quintuple of procedures: <Distribution Procedure,
Request Procedure, NotAvailable Procedure, Release Procedure,
labelUse Procedure>. (Since there is only one Withdraw Procedure, it
need not be mentioned.) A "*" appearing in one of the positions is a
wild-card, meaning that any procedure in that category may be
present; an "N/A" appearing in a particular position indicates that
no procedure in that category is needed.

Only the MPLS schemes which are specified below are supported by the
MPLS Architecture. Other schemes may be added in the future, if a
need for them is shown.

5.2.1. Schemes for LSRs that Support Label Merging

If Ru and Rd are label distribution peers, and both support label
merging, one of the following schemes must be used:

1. <PushUnconditional, RequestNever, N/A, NoReleaseOnChange,
   UseImmediate>

   This is unsolicited downstream label distribution with
   independent control, liberal label retention mode, and no loop
   detection.

2. <PushUnconditional, RequestNever, N/A, NoReleaseOnChange,
   UseIfLoopNotDetected>

   This is unsolicited downstream label distribution with
   independent control, liberal label retention, and loop
   detection.

3. <PushConditional, RequestWhenNeeded, RequestNoRetry,
   ReleaseOnChange, *>

   This is unsolicited downstream label distribution with ordered
   control (from the egress) and conservative label retention
   mode. Loop detection is optional.

4. <PushConditional, RequestNever, N/A, NoReleaseOnChange, *>

   This is unsolicited downstream label distribution with ordered
   control (from the egress) and liberal label retention mode.
   Loop detection is optional.

5. <PulledConditional, RequestWhenNeeded, RequestRetry,
   ReleaseOnChange, *>

   This is downstream-on-demand label distribution with ordered
   control (initiated by the ingress), conservative label
   retention mode, and optional loop detection.

6. <PulledUnconditional, RequestWhenNeeded, N/A, ReleaseOnChange,
   UseImmediate>

   This is downstream-on-demand label distribution with
   independent control and conservative label retention mode,
   without loop detection.

7. <PulledUnconditional, RequestWhenNeeded, N/A, ReleaseOnChange, UseIfLoopNotDetected>

   This is downstream-on-demand label distribution with independent control and conservative label retention mode, with loop detection.

5.2.2. Schemes for LSRs that do not Support Label Merging

Suppose that R1, R2, R3, and R4 are ATM switches which do not support label merging, but are being used as LSRs. Suppose further that the L3 hop-by-hop path for address prefix X is <R1, R2, R3, R4>, and that packets destined for X can enter the network at any of these LSRs. Since there is no multipoint-to-point capability, the LSPs must be realized as point-to-point VCs, which means that there needs to be three such VCs for address prefix X: <R1, R2, R3, R4>, <R2, R3, R4>, and <R3, R4>.

Therefore, if R1 and R2 are MPLS peers, and either is an LSR which is implemented using conventional ATM switching hardware (i.e., no cell interleave suppression), or is otherwise incapable of performing label merging, the MPLS scheme in use between R1 and R2 must be one of the following:

1. <PulledConditional, RequestOnRequest, RequestRetry, ReleaseOnChange, *>

   This is downstream-on-demand label distribution with ordered control (initiated by the ingress), conservative label retention mode, and optional loop detection.

   The use of the RequestOnRequest procedure will cause R4 to distribute three labels for X to R3; R3 will distribute 2 labels for X to R2, and R2 will distribute one label for X to R1.

2. <PulledUnconditional, RequestOnRequest, N/A, ReleaseOnChange, UseImmediate>

   This is downstream-on-demand label distribution with independent control and conservative label retention mode, without loop detection.

3. <PulledUnconditional, RequestOnRequest, N/A, ReleaseOnChange,
   UseIfLoopNotDetected>

   This is downstream-on-demand label distribution with
   independent control and conservative label retention mode, with
   loop detection.

5.2.3. Interoperability Considerations

   It is easy to see that certain quintuples do NOT yield viable MPLS
   schemes. For example:

   - <PulledUnconditional, RequestNever, *, *, *>
     <PulledConditional, RequestNever, *, *, *>

     In these MPLS schemes, the downstream LSR Rd distributes label
     bindings to upstream LSR Ru only upon request from Ru, but Ru
     never makes any such requests. Obviously, these schemes are
     not viable, since they will not result in the proper
     distribution of label bindings.

     - <*, RequestNever, *, *, ReleaseOnChange>

     In these MPLS schemes, Rd releases bindings when it isn't using
     them, but it never asks for them again, even if it later has a
     need for them. These schemes thus do not ensure that label
     bindings get properly distributed.

   In this section, we specify rules to prevent a pair of label
   distribution peers from adopting procedures which lead to infeasible
   MPLS Schemes. These rules require either the exchange of information
   between label distribution peers during the initialization of the
   label distribution adjacency, or a priori knowledge of the
   information (obtained through a means outside the scope of this
   document).

   1. Each must state whether it supports label merging.

   2. If Rd does not support label merging, Rd must choose either the
      PulledUnconditional procedure or the PulledConditional
      procedure. If Rd chooses PulledConditional, Ru is forced to
      use the RequestRetry procedure.

      That is, if the downstream LSR does not support label merging,
      its preferences take priority when the MPLS scheme is chosen.

3. If Ru does not support label merging, but Rd does, Ru must
   choose either the RequestRetry or RequestNoRetry procedure.
   This forces Rd to use the PulledConditional or
   PulledUnConditional procedure respectively.

   That is, if only one of the LSRs doesn't support label merging,
   its preferences take priority when the MPLS scheme is chosen.

4. If both Ru and Rd both support label merging, then the choice
   between liberal and conservative label retention mode belongs
   to Ru. That is, Ru gets to choose either to use
   RequestWhenNeeded/ReleaseOnChange (conservative) , or to use
   RequestNever/NoReleaseOnChange (liberal). However, the choice
   of "push" vs. "pull" and "conditional" vs. "unconditional"
   belongs to Rd. If Ru chooses liberal label retention mode, Rd
   can choose either PushUnconditional or PushConditional. If Ru
   chooses conservative label retention mode, Rd can choose
   PushConditional, PulledConditional, or PulledUnconditional.

   These choices together determine the MPLS scheme in use.

6. Security Considerations

   Some routers may implement security procedures which depend on the
   network layer header being in a fixed place relative to the data link
   layer header. The MPLS generic encapsulation inserts a shim between
   the data link layer header and the network layer header. This may
   cause any such security procedures to fail.

   An MPLS label has its meaning by virtue of an agreement between the
   LSR that puts the label in the label stack (the "label writer"), and
   the LSR that interprets that label (the "label reader"). If labeled
   packets are accepted from untrusted sources, or if a particular
   incoming label is accepted from an LSR to which that label has not
   been distributed, then packets may be routed in an illegitimate
   manner.

7. Intellectual Property

   The IETF has been notified of intellectual property rights claimed in
   regard to some or all of the specification contained in this
   document. For more information consult the online list of claimed
   rights.

RFC 3031   MPLS Architecture   January 2001

8. Authors' Addresses

    Eric C. Rosen
    Cisco Systems, Inc.
    250 Apollo Drive
    Chelmsford, MA, 01824

    EMail: erosen@cisco.com

    Arun Viswanathan
    Force10 Networks, Inc.
    1440 McCarthy Blvd.
    Milpitas, CA 95035-7438

    EMail: arun@force10networks.com

    Ross Callon
    Juniper Networks, Inc.
    1194 North Mathilda Avenue
    Sunnyvale, CA 94089 USA

    EMail: rcallon@juniper.net

9. References

    [MPLS-ATM]   Davie, B., Lawrence, J., McCloghrie, K., Rekhter,
                            Y., Rosen, E., Swallow, G. and P. Doolan, "MPLS
                            using LDP and ATM VC Switching", RFC 3035,
                            January 2001.

    [MPLS-BGP]   "Carrying Label Information in BGP-4", Rekhter,
                            Rosen, Work in Progress.

    [MPLS-CR-LDP]   "Constraint-Based LSP Setup using LDP", Jamoussi,
                            Editor, Work in Progress.

    [MPLS-FRMRLY]   Conta, A., Doolan, P. and A. Malis, "Use of Label
                            Switching on Frame Relay Networks Specification",
                            RFC 3034, January 2001.

    [MPLS-LDP]   Andersson, L., Doolan, P., Feldman, N., Fredette,
                            A. and B. Thomas, "LDP Specification", RFC 3036,
                            January 2001.

[MPLS-RSVP-TUNNELS] "Extensions to RSVP for LSP Tunnels", Awduche,
                    Berger, Gan, Li, Swallow, Srinvasan, Work in
                    Progress.

[MPLS-SHIM]   Rosen, E., Rekhter, Y., Tappan, D., Fedorkow, G.,
                    Farinacci, D. and A. Conta, "MPLS Label Stack
                    Encoding", RFC 3032, January 2001.

[MPLS-TRFENG]   Awduche, D., Malcolm, J., Agogbua, J., O'Dell, M.
                    and J. McManus, "Requirements for Traffic
                    Engineering Over MPLS", RFC 2702, September 1999.

```
RFC 3031                    MPLS Architecture                January 2001


10. Full Copyright Statement

   Copyright (C) The Internet Society (2001).  All Rights Reserved.

   This document and translations of it may be copied and furnished to
   others, and derivative works that comment on or otherwise explain it
   or assist in its implementation may be prepared, copied, published
   and distributed, in whole or in part, without restriction of any
   kind, provided that the above copyright notice and this paragraph are
   included on all such copies and derivative works.  However, this
   document itself may not be modified in any way, such as by removing
   the copyright notice or references to the Internet Society or other
   Internet organizations, except as needed for the purpose of
   developing Internet standards in which case the procedures for
   copyrights defined in the Internet Standards process must be
   followed, or as required to translate it into languages other than
   English.

   The limited permissions granted above are perpetual and will not be
   revoked by the Internet Society or its successors or assigns.

   This document and the information contained herein is provided on an
   "AS IS" basis and THE INTERNET SOCIETY AND THE INTERNET ENGINEERING
   TASK FORCE DISCLAIMS ALL WARRANTIES, EXPRESS OR IMPLIED, INCLUDING
   BUT NOT LIMITED TO ANY WARRANTY THAT THE USE OF THE INFORMATION
   HEREIN WILL NOT INFRINGE ANY RIGHTS OR ANY IMPLIED WARRANTIES OF
   MERCHANTABILITY OR FITNESS FOR A PARTICULAR PURPOSE.


Acknowledgement

   Funding for the RFC Editor function is currently provided by the
   Internet Society.
```

RFC 3032: MPLS Label Stack Encoding

D

Network Working Group
Request for Comments: 3032
Category: Standards Track
E. Rosen
D. Tappan
G. Fedorkow
Cisco Systems, Inc.

                                                    Y. Rekhter
                                              Juniper Networks
                                                  D. Farinacci
                                                         T. Li
                                         Procket Networks, Inc.
                                                      A. Conta
                                         TranSwitch Corporation
                                                  January 2001

                        MPLS Label Stack Encoding

Status of this Memo

   This document specifies an Internet standards track protocol for the
   Internet community, and requests discussion and suggestions for
   improvements. Please refer to the current edition of the "Internet
   Official Protocol Standards" (STD 1) for the standardization state
   and status of this protocol. Distribution of this memo is unlimited.

Copyright Notice

Abstract

   "Multi-Protocol Label Switching (MPLS)" [1] requires a set of
   procedures for augmenting network layer packets with "label stacks",
   thereby turning them into "labeled packets". Routers which support
   MPLS are known as "Label Switching Routers", or "LSRs". In order to
   transmit a labeled packet on a particular data link, an LSR must
   support an encoding technique which, given a label stack and a
   network layer packet, produces a labeled packet. This document
   specifies the encoding to be used by an LSR in order to transmit
   labeled packets on Point-to-Point Protocol (PPP) data links, on LAN
   data links, and possibly on other data links as well. On some data
   links, the label at the top of the stack may be encoded in a
   different manner, but the techniques described here MUST be used to
   encode the remainder of the label stack. This document also
   specifies rules and procedures for processing the various fields of
   the label stack encoding.

RFC 3032   MPLS Label Stack Encoding   January 2001

Table of Contents

1. Introduction

   "Multi-Protocol Label Switching (MPLS)" [1] requires a set of
   procedures for augmenting network layer packets with "label stacks",
   thereby turning them into "labeled packets". Routers which support
   MPLS are known as "Label Switching Routers", or "LSRs". In order to
   transmit a labeled packet on a particular data link, an LSR must
   support an encoding technique which, given a label stack and a
   network layer packet, produces a labeled packet.

This document specifies the encoding to be used by an LSR in order to transmit labeled packets on PPP data links and on LAN data links. The specified encoding may also be useful for other data links as well.

This document also specifies rules and procedures for processing the various fields of the label stack encoding. Since MPLS is independent of any particular network layer protocol, the majority of such procedures are also protocol-independent. A few, however, do differ for different protocols. In this document, we specify the protocol-independent procedures, and we specify the protocol-dependent procedures for IPv4 and IPv6.

LSRs that are implemented on certain switching devices (such as ATM switches) may use different encoding techniques for encoding the top one or two entries of the label stack. When the label stack has additional entries, however, the encoding technique described in this document MUST be used for the additional label stack entries.

1.1. Specification of Requirements

The key words "MUST", "MUST NOT", "REQUIRED", "SHALL", "SHALL NOT", "SHOULD", "SHOULD NOT", "RECOMMENDED", "MAY", and "OPTIONAL" in this document are to be interpreted as described in RFC 2119 [2].

2. The Label Stack

2.1. Encoding the Label Stack

The label stack is represented as a sequence of "label stack entries". Each label stack entry is represented by 4 octets. This is shown in Figure 1.

```
 0                   1                   2                   3
 0 1 2 3 4 5 6 7 8 9 0 1 2 3 4 5 6 7 8 9 0 1 2 3 4 5 6 7 8 9 0 1
+-+-+-+-+-+-+-+-+-+-+-+-+-+-+-+-+-+-+-+-+-+-+-+-+-+-+-+-+-+-+-+-+ Label
|                Label                  | Exp |S|       TTL     | Stack
+-+-+-+-+-+-+-+-+-+-+-+-+-+-+-+-+-+-+-+-+-+-+-+-+-+-+-+-+-+-+-+-+ Entry

                 Label:  Label Value, 20 bits
                 Exp:    Experimental Use, 3 bits
                 S:      Bottom of Stack, 1 bit
                 TTL:    Time to Live, 8 bits

                           Figure 1
```

Rosen, et al.   Standards Track   [Page 3]

The label stack entries appear AFTER the data link layer headers, but BEFORE any network layer headers. The top of the label stack appears earliest in the packet, and the bottom appears latest. The network layer packet immediately follows the label stack entry which has the S bit set.

Each label stack entry is broken down into the following fields:

1. Bottom of Stack (S)

   This bit is set to one for the last entry in the label stack (i.e., for the bottom of the stack), and zero for all other label stack entries.

2. Time to Live (TTL)

   This eight-bit field is used to encode a time-to-live value. The processing of this field is described in section 2.4.

3. Experimental Use

   This three-bit field is reserved for experimental use.

4. Label Value

   This 20-bit field carries the actual value of the Label.

   When a labeled packet is received, the label value at the top of the stack is looked up. As a result of a successful lookup one learns:

   a) the next hop to which the packet is to be forwarded;

   b) the operation to be performed on the label stack before forwarding; this operation may be to replace the top label stack entry with another, or to pop an entry off the label stack, or to replace the top label stack entry and then to push one or more additional entries on the label stack.

   In addition to learning the next hop and the label stack operation, one may also learn the outgoing data link encapsulation, and possibly other information which is needed in order to properly forward the packet.

RFC 3032   MPLS Label Stack Encoding   January 2001

        There are several reserved label values:

            i. A value of 0 represents the "IPv4 Explicit NULL Label".
               This label value is only legal at the bottom of the label
               stack. It indicates that the label stack must be popped,
               and the forwarding of the packet must then be based on the
               IPv4 header.

           ii. A value of 1 represents the "Router Alert Label". This
               label value is legal anywhere in the label stack except at
               the bottom. When a received packet contains this label
               value at the top of the label stack, it is delivered to a
               local software module for processing. The actual
               forwarding of the packet is determined by the label
               beneath it in the stack. However, if the packet is
               forwarded further, the Router Alert Label should be pushed
               back onto the label stack before forwarding. The use of
               this label is analogous to the use of the "Router Alert
               Option" in IP packets [5]. Since this label cannot occur
               at the bottom of the stack, it is not associated with a
               particular network layer protocol.

          iii. A value of 2 represents the "IPv6 Explicit NULL Label".
               This label value is only legal at the bottom of the label
               stack. It indicates that the label stack must be popped,
               and the forwarding of the packet must then be based on the
               IPv6 header.

           iv. A value of 3 represents the "Implicit NULL Label". This
               is a label that an LSR may assign and distribute, but
               which never actually appears in the encapsulation. When
               an LSR would otherwise replace the label at the top of the
               stack with a new label, but the new label is "Implicit
               NULL", the LSR will pop the stack instead of doing the
               replacement. Although this value may never appear in the
               encapsulation, it needs to be specified in the Label
               Distribution Protocol, so a value is reserved.

            v. Values 4-15 are reserved.

2.2. Determining the Network Layer Protocol

   When the last label is popped from a packet's label stack (resulting
   in the stack being emptied), further processing of the packet is
   based on the packet's network layer header. The LSR which pops the
   last label off the stack must therefore be able to identify the
   packet's network layer protocol. However, the label stack does not
   contain any field which explicitly identifies the network layer

Rosen, et al.   Standards Track   [Page 5]

protocol. This means that the identity of the network layer protocol
must be inferable from the value of the label which is popped from
the bottom of the stack, possibly along with the contents of the
network layer header itself.

Therefore, when the first label is pushed onto a network layer
packet, either the label must be one which is used ONLY for packets
of a particular network layer, or the label must be one which is used
ONLY for a specified set of network layer protocols, where packets of
the specified network layers can be distinguished by inspection of
the network layer header. Furthermore, whenever that label is
replaced by another label value during a packet's transit, the new
value must also be one which meets the same criteria. If these
conditions are not met, the LSR which pops the last label off a
packet will not be able to identify the packet's network layer
protocol.

Adherence to these conditions does not necessarily enable
intermediate nodes to identify a packet's network layer protocol.
Under ordinary conditions, this is not necessary, but there are error
conditions under which it is desirable. For instance, if an
intermediate LSR determines that a labeled packet is undeliverable,
it may be desirable for that LSR to generate error messages which are
specific to the packet's network layer. The only means the
intermediate LSR has for identifying the network layer is inspection
of the top label and the network layer header. So if intermediate
nodes are to be able to generate protocol-specific error messages for
labeled packets, all labels in the stack must meet the criteria
specified above for labels which appear at the bottom of the stack.

If a packet cannot be forwarded for some reason (e.g., it exceeds the
data link MTU), and either its network layer protocol cannot be
identified, or there are no specified protocol-dependent rules for
handling the error condition, then the packet MUST be silently
discarded.

2.3. Generating ICMP Messages for Labeled IP Packets

Section 2.4 and section 3 discuss situations in which it is desirable
to generate ICMP messages for labeled IP packets. In order for a
particular LSR to be able to generate an ICMP packet and have that
packet sent to the source of the IP packet, two conditions must hold:

   1. it must be possible for that LSR to determine that a particular
      labeled packet is an IP packet;

   2. it must be possible for that LSR to route to the packet's IP
      source address.

Condition 1 is discussed in section 2.2. The following two
subsections discuss condition 2. However, there will be some cases
in which condition 2 does not hold at all, and in these cases it will
not be possible to generate the ICMP message.

2.3.1. Tunneling through a Transit Routing Domain

Suppose one is using MPLS to "tunnel" through a transit routing
domain, where the external routes are not leaked into the domain's
interior routers. For example, the interior routers may be running
OSPF, and may only know how to reach destinations within that OSPF
domain. The domain might contain several Autonomous System Border
Routers (ASBRs), which talk BGP to each other. However, in this
example the routes from BGP are not distributed into OSPF, and the
LSRs which are not ASBRs do not run BGP.

In this example, only an ASBR will know how to route to the source of
some arbitrary packet. If an interior router needs to send an ICMP
message to the source of an IP packet, it will not know how to route
the ICMP message.

One solution is to have one or more of the ASBRs inject "default"
into the IGP. (N.B.: this does NOT require that there be a "default"
carried by BGP.) This would then ensure that any unlabeled packet
which must leave the domain (such as an ICMP packet) gets sent to a
router which has full routing information. The routers with full
routing information will label the packets before sending them back
through the transit domain, so the use of default routing within the
transit domain does not cause any loops.

This solution only works for packets which have globally unique
addresses, and for networks in which all the ASBRs have complete
routing information. The next subsection describes a solution which
works when these conditions do not hold.

2.3.2. Tunneling Private Addresses through a Public Backbone

In some cases where MPLS is used to tunnel through a routing domain,
it may not be possible to route to the source address of a fragmented
packet at all. This would be the case, for example, if the IP
addresses carried in the packet were private (i.e., not globally
unique) addresses, and MPLS were being used to tunnel those packets
through a public backbone. Default routing to an ASBR will not work
in this environment.

In this environment, in order to send an ICMP message to the source
of a packet, one can copy the label stack from the original packet to
the ICMP message, and then label switch the ICMP message. This will

cause the message to proceed in the direction of the original
packet's destination, rather than its source. Unless the message is
label switched all the way to the destination host, it will end up,
unlabeled, in a router which does know how to route to the source of
original packet, at which point the message will be sent in the
proper direction.

This technique can be very useful if the ICMP message is a "Time
Exceeded" message or a "Destination Unreachable because fragmentation
needed and DF set" message.

When copying the label stack from the original packet to the ICMP
message, the label values must be copied exactly, but the TTL values
in the label stack should be set to the TTL value that is placed in
the IP header of the ICMP message. This TTL value should be long
enough to allow the circuitous route that the ICMP message will need
to follow.

Note that if a packet's TTL expiration is due to the presence of a
routing loop, then if this technique is used, the ICMP message may
loop as well. Since an ICMP message is never sent as a result of
receiving an ICMP message, and since many implementations throttle
the rate at which ICMP messages can be generated, this is not
expected to pose a problem.

2.4. Processing the Time to Live Field

2.4.1. Definitions

The "incoming TTL" of a labeled packet is defined to be the value of
the TTL field of the top label stack entry when the packet is
received.

The "outgoing TTL" of a labeled packet is defined to be the larger
of:

    a) one less than the incoming TTL,
    b) zero.

2.4.2. Protocol-independent rules

If the outgoing TTL of a labeled packet is 0, then the labeled packet
MUST NOT be further forwarded; nor may the label stack be stripped
off and the packet forwarded as an unlabeled packet. The packet's
lifetime in the network is considered to have expired.

Depending on the label value in the label stack entry, the packet MAY
be simply discarded, or it may be passed to the appropriate
"ordinary" network layer for error processing (e.g., for the
generation of an ICMP error message, see section 2.3).

When a labeled packet is forwarded, the TTL field of the label stack
entry at the top of the label stack MUST be set to the outgoing TTL
value.

Note that the outgoing TTL value is a function solely of the incoming
TTL value, and is independent of whether any labels are pushed or
popped before forwarding. There is no significance to the value of
the TTL field in any label stack entry which is not at the top of the
stack.

2.4.3. IP-dependent rules

We define the "IP TTL" field to be the value of the IPv4 TTL field,
or the value of the IPv6 Hop Limit field, whichever is applicable.

When an IP packet is first labeled, the TTL field of the label stack
entry MUST BE set to the value of the IP TTL field. (If the IP TTL
field needs to be decremented, as part of the IP processing, it is
assumed that this has already been done.)

When a label is popped, and the resulting label stack is empty, then
the value of the IP TTL field SHOULD BE replaced with the outgoing
TTL value, as defined above. In IPv4 this also requires modification
of the IP header checksum.

It is recognized that there may be situations where a network
administration prefers to decrement the IPv4 TTL by one as it
traverses an MPLS domain, instead of decrementing the IPv4 TTL by the
number of LSP hops within the domain.

2.4.4. Translating Between Different Encapsulations

Sometimes an LSR may receive a labeled packet over, e.g., a label
switching controlled ATM (LC-ATM) interface [9], and may need to send
it out over a PPP or LAN link. Then the incoming packet will not be
received using the encapsulation specified in this document, but the
outgoing packet will be sent using the encapsulation specified in
this document.

In this case, the value of the "incoming TTL" is determined by the
procedures used for carrying labeled packets on, e.g., LC-ATM
interfaces. TTL processing then proceeds as described above.

Sometimes an LSR may receive a labeled packet over a PPP or a LAN
link, and may need to send it out, say, an LC-ATM interface. Then
the incoming packet will be received using the encapsulation
specified in this document, but the outgoing packet will not be sent
using the encapsulation specified in this document. In this case,
the procedure for carrying the value of the "outgoing TTL" is
determined by the procedures used for carrying labeled packets on,
e.g., LC-ATM interfaces.

3. Fragmentation and Path MTU Discovery

Just as it is possible to receive an unlabeled IP datagram which is
too large to be transmitted on its output link, it is possible to
receive a labeled packet which is too large to be transmitted on its
output link.

It is also possible that a received packet (labeled or unlabeled)
which was originally small enough to be transmitted on that link
becomes too large by virtue of having one or more additional labels
pushed onto its label stack. In label switching, a packet may grow
in size if additional labels get pushed on. Thus if one receives a
labeled packet with a 1500-byte frame payload, and pushes on an
additional label, one needs to forward it as frame with a 1504-byte
payload.

This section specifies the rules for processing labeled packets which
are "too large". In particular, it provides rules which ensure that
hosts implementing Path MTU Discovery [4], and hosts using IPv6
[7,8], will be able to generate IP datagrams that do not need
fragmentation, even if those datagrams get labeled as they traverse
the network.

In general, IPv4 hosts which do not implement Path MTU Discovery [4]
send IP datagrams which contain no more than 576 bytes. Since the
MTUs in use on most data links today are 1500 bytes or more, the
probability that such datagrams will need to get fragmented, even if
they get labeled, is very small.

Some hosts that do not implement Path MTU Discovery [4] will generate
IP datagrams containing 1500 bytes, as long as the IP Source and
Destination addresses are on the same subnet. These datagrams will
not pass through routers, and hence will not get fragmented.

Unfortunately, some hosts will generate IP datagrams containing 1500
bytes, as long the IP Source and Destination addresses have the same
classful network number. This is the one case in which there is any
risk of fragmentation when such datagrams get labeled. (Even so,

fragmentation is not likely unless the packet must traverse an
ethernet of some sort between the time it first gets labeled and the
time it gets unlabeled.)

This document specifies procedures which allow one to configure the
network so that large datagrams from hosts which do not implement
Path MTU Discovery get fragmented just once, when they are first
labeled. These procedures make it possible (assuming suitable
configuration) to avoid any need to fragment packets which have
already been labeled.

3.1. Terminology

With respect to a particular data link, we can use the following
terms:

   - Frame Payload:

      The contents of a data link frame, excluding any data link
      layer headers or trailers (e.g., MAC headers, LLC headers,
      802.1Q headers, PPP header, frame check sequences, etc.).

      When a frame is carrying an unlabeled IP datagram, the Frame
      Payload is just the IP datagram itself. When a frame is
      carrying a labeled IP datagram, the Frame Payload consists of
      the label stack entries and the IP datagram.

   - Conventional Maximum Frame Payload Size:

      The maximum Frame Payload size allowed by data link standards.
      For example, the Conventional Maximum Frame Payload Size for
      ethernet is 1500 bytes.

   - True Maximum Frame Payload Size:

      The maximum size frame payload which can be sent and received
      properly by the interface hardware attached to the data link.

      On ethernet and 802.3 networks, it is believed that the True
      Maximum Frame Payload Size is 4-8 bytes larger than the
      Conventional Maximum Frame Payload Size (as long as neither an
      802.1Q header nor an 802.1p header is present, and as long as
      neither can be added by a switch or bridge while a packet is in
      transit to its next hop). For example, it is believed that
      most ethernet equipment could correctly send and receive
      packets carrying a payload of 1504 or perhaps even 1508 bytes,
      at least, as long as the ethernet header does not have an
      802.1Q or 802.1p field.

On PPP links, the True Maximum Frame Payload Size may be
virtually unbounded.

- Effective Maximum Frame Payload Size for Labeled Packets:

   This is either the Conventional Maximum Frame Payload Size or
   the True Maximum Frame Payload Size, depending on the
   capabilities of the equipment on the data link and the size of
   the data link header being used.

- Initially Labeled IP Datagram:

   Suppose that an unlabeled IP datagram is received at a
   particular LSR, and that the the LSR pushes on a label before
   forwarding the datagram. Such a datagram will be called an
   Initially Labeled IP Datagram at that LSR.

- Previously Labeled IP Datagram:

   An IP datagram which had already been labeled before it was
   received by a particular LSR.

3.2. Maximum Initially Labeled IP Datagram Size

   Every LSR which is capable of

      a) receiving an unlabeled IP datagram,
      b) adding a label stack to the datagram, and
      c) forwarding the resulting labeled packet,

   SHOULD support a configuration parameter known as the "Maximum
   Initially Labeled IP Datagram Size", which can be set to a non-
   negative value.

   If this configuration parameter is set to zero, it has no effect.

   If it is set to a positive value, it is used in the following way.
   If:

      a) an unlabeled IP datagram is received, and
      b) that datagram does not have the DF bit set in its IP header,
         and
      c) that datagram needs to be labeled before being forwarded, and
      d) the size of the datagram (before labeling) exceeds the value of
         the parameter,
   then
      a) the datagram must be broken into fragments, each of whose size
         is no greater than the value of the parameter, and

RFC 3032   MPLS Label Stack Encoding   January 2001

b) each fragment must be labeled and then forwarded.

For example, if this configuration parameter is set to a value of 1488, then any unlabeled IP datagram containing more than 1488 bytes will be fragmented before being labeled. Each fragment will be capable of being carried on a 1500-byte data link, without further fragmentation, even if as many as three labels are pushed onto its label stack.

In other words, setting this parameter to a non-zero value allows one to eliminate all fragmentation of Previously Labeled IP Datagrams, but it may cause some unnecessary fragmentation of Initially Labeled IP Datagrams.

Note that the setting of this parameter does not affect the processing of IP datagrams that have the DF bit set; hence the result of Path MTU discovery is unaffected by the setting of this parameter.

3.3. When are Labeled IP Datagrams Too Big?

A labeled IP datagram whose size exceeds the Conventional Maximum Frame Payload Size of the data link over which it is to be forwarded MAY be considered to be "too big".

A labeled IP datagram whose size exceeds the True Maximum Frame Payload Size of the data link over which it is to be forwarded MUST be considered to be "too big".

A labeled IP datagram which is not "too big" MUST be transmitted without fragmentation.

3.4. Processing Labeled IPv4 Datagrams which are Too Big

If a labeled IPv4 datagram is "too big", and the DF bit is not set in its IP header, then the LSR MAY silently discard the datagram.

Note that discarding such datagrams is a sensible procedure only if the "Maximum Initially Labeled IP Datagram Size" is set to a non-zero value in every LSR in the network which is capable of adding a label stack to an unlabeled IP datagram.

If the LSR chooses not to discard a labeled IPv4 datagram which is too big, or if the DF bit is set in that datagram, then it MUST execute the following algorithm:

   1. Strip off the label stack entries to obtain the IP datagram.

2. Let N be the number of bytes in the label stack (i.e, 4 times the number of label stack entries).

3. If the IP datagram does NOT have the "Don't Fragment" bit set in its IP header:

   a. convert it into fragments, each of which MUST be at least N bytes less than the Effective Maximum Frame Payload Size.

   b. Prepend each fragment with the same label header that would have been on the original datagram had fragmentation not been necessary.

   c. Forward the fragments

4. If the IP datagram has the "Don't Fragment" bit set in its IP header:

   a. the datagram MUST NOT be forwarded

   b. Create an ICMP Destination Unreachable Message:

      i. set its Code field [3] to "Fragmentation Required and DF Set",

      ii. set its Next-Hop MTU field [4] to the difference between the Effective Maximum Frame Payload Size and the value of N

   c. If possible, transmit the ICMP Destination Unreachable Message to the source of the of the discarded datagram.

3.5. Processing Labeled IPv6 Datagrams which are Too Big

   To process a labeled IPv6 datagram which is too big, an LSR MUST execute the following algorithm:

   1. Strip off the label stack entries to obtain the IP datagram.

   2. Let N be the number of bytes in the label stack (i.e., 4 times the number of label stack entries).

   3. If the IP datagram contains more than 1280 bytes (not counting the label stack entries), or if it does not contain a fragment header, then:

    a. Create an ICMP Packet Too Big Message, and set its Next-Hop MTU field to the difference between the Effective Maximum Frame Payload Size and the value of N

    b. If possible, transmit the ICMP Packet Too Big Message to the source of the datagram.

    c. discard the labeled IPv6 datagram.

4. If the IP datagram is not larger than 1280 octets, and it contains a fragment header, then

    a. Convert it into fragments, each of which MUST be at least N bytes less than the Effective Maximum Frame Payload Size.

    b. Prepend each fragment with the same label header that would have been on the original datagram had fragmentation not been necessary.

    c. Forward the fragments.

Reassembly of the fragments will be done at the destination host.

3.6. Implications with respect to Path MTU Discovery

The procedures described above for handling datagrams which have the DF bit set, but which are "too large", have an impact on the Path MTU Discovery procedures of RFC 1191 [4]. Hosts which implement these procedures will discover an MTU which is small enough to allow n labels to be pushed on the datagrams, without need for fragmentation, where n is the number of labels that actually get pushed on along the path currently in use.

In other words, datagrams from hosts that use Path MTU Discovery will never need to be fragmented due to the need to put on a label header, or to add new labels to an existing label header. (Also, datagrams from hosts that use Path MTU Discovery generally have the DF bit set, and so will never get fragmented anyway.)

Note that Path MTU Discovery will only work properly if, at the point where a labeled IP Datagram's fragmentation needs to occur, it is possible to cause an ICMP Destination Unreachable message to be routed to the packet's source address. See section 2.3.

If it is not possible to forward an ICMP message from within an MPLS
"tunnel" to a packet's source address, but the network configuration
makes it possible for the LSR at the transmitting end of the tunnel
to receive packets that must go through the tunnel, but are too large
to pass through the tunnel unfragmented, then:

-   The LSR at the transmitting end of the tunnel MUST be able to
    determine the MTU of the tunnel as a whole. It MAY do this by
    sending packets through the tunnel to the tunnel's receiving
    endpoint, and performing Path MTU Discovery with those packets.

-   Any time the transmitting endpoint of the tunnel needs to send
    a packet into the tunnel, and that packet has the DF bit set,
    and it exceeds the tunnel MTU, the transmitting endpoint of the
    tunnel MUST send the ICMP Destination Unreachable message to
    the source, with code "Fragmentation Required and DF Set", and
    the Next-Hop MTU Field set as described above.

4. Transporting Labeled Packets over PPP

The Point-to-Point Protocol (PPP) [6] provides a standard method for
transporting multi-protocol datagrams over point-to-point links. PPP
defines an extensible Link Control Protocol, and proposes a family of
Network Control Protocols for establishing and configuring different
network-layer protocols.

This section defines the Network Control Protocol for establishing
and configuring label Switching over PPP.

4.1. Introduction

PPP has three main components:

1. A method for encapsulating multi-protocol datagrams.

2. A Link Control Protocol (LCP) for establishing, configuring,
   and testing the data-link connection.

3. A family of Network Control Protocols for establishing and
   configuring different network-layer protocols.

In order to establish communications over a point-to-point link, each
end of the PPP link must first send LCP packets to configure and test
the data link. After the link has been established and optional
facilities have been negotiated as needed by the LCP, PPP must send
"MPLS Control Protocol" packets to enable the transmission of labeled
packets. Once the "MPLS Control Protocol" has reached the Opened
state, labeled packets can be sent over the link.

RFC 3032   MPLS Label Stack Encoding   January 2001

The link will remain configured for communications until explicit LCP
or MPLS Control Protocol packets close the link down, or until some
external event occurs (an inactivity timer expires or network
administrator intervention).

4.2. A PPP Network Control Protocol for MPLS

The MPLS Control Protocol (MPLSCP) is responsible for enabling and
disabling the use of label switching on a PPP link. It uses the same
packet exchange mechanism as the Link Control Protocol (LCP). MPLSCP
packets may not be exchanged until PPP has reached the Network-Layer
Protocol phase. MPLSCP packets received before this phase is reached
should be silently discarded.

The MPLS Control Protocol is exactly the same as the Link Control
Protocol [6] with the following exceptions:

   1. Frame Modifications

      The packet may utilize any modifications to the basic frame
      format which have been negotiated during the Link Establishment
      phase.

   2. Data Link Layer Protocol Field

      Exactly one MPLSCP packet is encapsulated in the PPP
      Information field, where the PPP Protocol field indicates type
      hex 8281 (MPLS).

   3. Code field

      Only Codes 1 through 7 (Configure-Request, Configure-Ack,
      Configure-Nak, Configure-Reject, Terminate-Request, Terminate-
      Ack and Code-Reject) are used. Other Codes should be treated
      as unrecognized and should result in Code-Rejects.

   4. Timeouts

      MPLSCP packets may not be exchanged until PPP has reached the
      Network-Layer Protocol phase. An implementation should be
      prepared to wait for Authentication and Link Quality
      Determination to finish before timing out waiting for a
      Configure-Ack or other response. It is suggested that an
      implementation give up only after user intervention or a
      configurable amount of time.

   5. Configuration Option Types

      None.

4.3. Sending Labeled Packets

   Before any labeled packets may be communicated, PPP must reach the
   Network-Layer Protocol phase, and the MPLS Control Protocol must
   reach the Opened state.

   Exactly one labeled packet is encapsulated in the PPP Information
   field, where the PPP Protocol field indicates either type hex 0281
   (MPLS Unicast) or type hex 0283 (MPLS Multicast). The maximum length
   of a labeled packet transmitted over a PPP link is the same as the
   maximum length of the Information field of a PPP encapsulated packet.

   The format of the Information field itself is as defined in section
   2.

   Note that two codepoints are defined for labeled packets; one for
   multicast and one for unicast. Once the MPLSCP has reached the
   Opened state, both label switched multicasts and label switched
   unicasts can be sent over the PPP link.

4.4. Label Switching Control Protocol Configuration Options

   There are no configuration options.

5. Transporting Labeled Packets over LAN Media

   Exactly one labeled packet is carried in each frame.

   The label stack entries immediately precede the network layer header,
   and follow any data link layer headers, including, e.g., any 802.1Q
   headers that may exist.

   The ethertype value 8847 hex is used to indicate that a frame is
   carrying an MPLS unicast packet.

   The ethertype value 8848 hex is used to indicate that a frame is
   carrying an MPLS multicast packet.

   These ethertype values can be used with either the ethernet
   encapsulation or the 802.3 LLC/SNAP encapsulation to carry labeled
   packets. The procedure for choosing which of these two
   encapsulations to use is beyond the scope of this document.

RFC 3032   MPLS Label Stack Encoding   January 2001

6. IANA Considerations

   Label values 0-15 inclusive have special meaning, as specified in
   this document, or as further assigned by IANA.

   In this document, label values 0-3 are specified in section 2.1.

   Label values 4-15 may be assigned by IANA, based on IETF Consensus.

7. Security Considerations

   The MPLS encapsulation that is specified herein does not raise any
   security issues that are not already present in either the MPLS
   architecture [1] or in the architecture of the network layer protocol
   contained within the encapsulation.

   There are two security considerations inherited from the MPLS
   architecture which may be pointed out here:

       - Some routers may implement security procedures which depend on
          the network layer header being in a fixed place relative to the
          data link layer header. These procedures will not work when
          the MPLS encapsulation is used, because that encapsulation is
          of a variable size.

       - An MPLS label has its meaning by virtue of an agreement between
          the LSR that puts the label in the label stack (the "label
          writer"), and the LSR that interprets that label (the "label
          reader"). However, the label stack does not provide any means
          of determining who the label writer was for any particular
          label. If labeled packets are accepted from untrusted sources,
          the result may be that packets are routed in an illegitimate
          manner.

8. Intellectual Property

   The IETF has been notified of intellectual property rights claimed in
   regard to some or all of the specification contained in this
   document. For more information consult the online list of claimed
   rights.

9. Authors' Addresses

Eric C. Rosen
Cisco Systems, Inc.
250 Apollo Drive
Chelmsford, MA, 01824

EMail: erosen@cisco.com

Dan Tappan
Cisco Systems, Inc.
250 Apollo Drive
Chelmsford, MA, 01824

EMail: tappan@cisco.com

Yakov Rekhter
Juniper Networks
1194 N. Mathilda Avenue
Sunnyvale, CA 94089

EMail: yakov@juniper.net

Guy Fedorkow
Cisco Systems, Inc.
250 Apollo Drive
Chelmsford, MA, 01824

EMail: fedorkow@cisco.com

Dino Farinacci
Procket Networks, Inc.
3910 Freedom Circle, Ste. 102A
Santa Clara, CA 95054

EMail: dino@procket.com

Tony Li
Procket Networks, Inc.
3910 Freedom Circle, Ste. 102A
Santa Clara, CA 95054

EMail: tli@procket.com

Alex Conta
TranSwitch Corporation
3 Enterprise Drive
Shelton, CT, 06484

EMail: aconta@txc.com

10. References

[1] Rosen, E., Viswanathan, A., and R. Callon, "Multiprotocol Label Switching Architecture", RFC 3031, January 2001.

[2] Bradner, S., "Key words for use in RFCs to Indicate Requirement Levels", BCP 14, RFC 2119, March 1997.

[3] Postel, J., "Internet Control Message Protocol", STD 5, RFC 792, September 1981.

[4] Mogul, J. and S. Deering, "Path MTU Discovery", RFC 1191, November 1990.

[5] Katz, D., "IP Router Alert Option", RFC 2113, February 1997.

[6] Simpson, W., Editor, "The Point-to-Point Protocol (PPP)", STD 51, RFC 1661, July 1994.

[7] Conta, A. and S. Deering, "Internet Control Message Protocol (ICMPv6) for the Internet Protocol Version 6 (IPv6) Specification", RFC 1885, December 1995.

[8] McCann, J., Deering, S. and J. Mogul, "Path MTU Discovery for IP version 6", RFC 1981, August 1996.

[9] Davie, B., Lawrence, J., McCloghrie, K., Rekhter, Y., Rosen, E. and G. Swallow, "MPLS Using LDP and ATM VC Switching", RFC 3035, January 2001.

11. Full Copyright Statement

   Copyright (C) The Internet Society (2001). All Rights Reserved.

Acknowledgement

   Funding for the RFC Editor function is currently provided by the
   Internet Society.

A Detailed Introduction to SNMP

The pure and simple truth is rarely pure and never simple. [1]

— *Oscar Wilde*

The Simple Network Management Protocol (SNMP) provides a standardized network management framework for enabling the control and monitoring of an internetwork and its devices. The requirements for managing such a diverse range of network devices and hosts include a simple—yet extensible—set of standards that must be as robust and unobtrusive as possible. Consequently, SNMP is vendor-independent and architected to be relatively easy to implement.

THE SIMPLE NETWORK MANAGEMENT PROTOCOL (SNMP)..............

SNMP was first developed in 1988 as a short-term solution for the network management framework to be used in managing devices connected to the Internet. The original plan was to supplant SNMP with the OSI network management standard, CMIP, after further standards development and implementation experience proved this feasible.[1]

The transition from SNMP to CMIP did not progress at the pace initially envisioned by the network management framework architects for a number of reasons. The CMIP implementations were slow to be realized, and at the same time, the first version of SNMP proliferated and gained a great deal of momentum and industry support. In fact, this transition never occurred. SNMP and CMIP are now two very different network management frameworks aimed at two different device groups. SNMP is the standard for internetwork TCP/IP-based networks (such as the Internet) and CMIP is a niche framework, primarily in use in large telecommunications networks and several other large organizations and universities.

SNMP's original charter of providing network management for Internet devices such as bridges, routers, and gateways has rapidly expanded to include nearly every possible networkable device. SNMP can also operate with non-TCP/IP network environments. Such a charter has allowed SNMP to be and evolve into a very popular and effective network management scheme. The recommendation from the Internet Architecture Board (IAB) that oversees standards development for the Internet states that any device that wishes to connect to the Internet and use the IP suite should have the capability to be managed by SNMP.

The first version of SNMP (called SNMPv1 for version 1) has enjoyed full Internet standard status for some time. Several subsequent attempts at a second version resulted in various dead-end proposals that now have either an experimental or historical status level. Version 3 of the framework (SNMPv3) is a fresh cut at evolving SNMP for the standards track by adding features that are required for the standard to move forward with today's internetwork environments. SNMPv3 is now being reviewed and test implementations are being fielded. It is up for draft status at this writing. The two main additions for SNMPv3 are security and remote administration features.

---

1. The details are described in RFC 1052, "IAB Recommendations for the Development of Internet Network Management Standards," from April 1988, and RFC 1109, "Report of the Second Ad Hoc Network Management Review Group," from August 1989.

Before we look closer at the specifics of the SNMP framework and the history of its three versions, it is important to understand the reference model. Understanding the SNMP manager/agent model is crucial before undertaking a Web-based management effort that includes the integration of SNMP functionality.

The SNMP Reference Model

The SNMP reference model, as diagrammed in Figure E–1, shows the general overall structure of the SNMP network management framework. This model includes the individual components of the system and the relationships among them.

The SNMP reference model comprises four major components:

- The internetwork
- The network protocols
- The network manager
- The managed network entity

The Internetwork As with all of our discussions on enterprise networking, for the SNMP reference model, an *internetwork* is the collection of one or more networks that uses a common protocol and is connected by gateways.[2] The TCP/IP protocols and IP global addressing scheme allow any two end-points on the internetwork to communicate

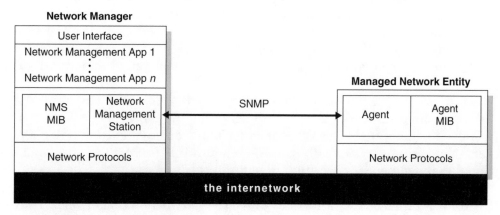

Figure E–1   The SNMP reference model.

---

2. "Gateway" was the original Internet term for router, that is, a device that implements Layers 1–3 of the OSI model.

with each other. Additionally, routing schemes provide for the proper delivery of messages in a timely and reliable way across the internetwork.

The Network Protocols   The network protocols are the rules that allow internetwork communication to be feasible. For internetwork communication using TCP/IP, various protocols operate at four of the well-defined layers of the TCP/IP model. A host, for example, will have implemented at least one, but probably many, protocols for each layer. The network protocols are collectively called the "protocol stack."

The Network Manager   The SNMP reference model shows the network manager as a network device that uses the network protocols and SNMP to communicate over the internetwork with the managed network entity. The network manager consists of four major components:

- The network management station (NMS)
- The NMS management information base (MIB) and database
- The set of network management applications
- The network management user interface

The NMS is the processing entity that monitors and controls the agents that it is responsible for and communicates with over the internetwork. It contains the SNMP engine that operates in the role as a manager entity. This relationship of the NMS and its agents is called a "community" in SNMP parlance. The NMS can read and write certain MIB objects in each agent to manage a network device. It can also store pertinent management information on each of the agents in its own database.

The MIB of the NMS contains a master list for the MIBs of all the agents in its community that it intends to manage. If an NMS is to control each agent's MIB variables, it must know or be able to discover the variable's presence. Typically, the NMS maintains its MIB and any additional management information in a database.

The network management applications are the programs that turn SNMP data into usable information for the network manager user. They are a vast array of programs that poll the agents, format get and set protocol requests, and handle the reception of trap messages. These network management applications are responsible for executing useful FCAPS network management functionality.

The applications use low-level SNMP data to make management information that is, in turn, utilized by the network administrator to make important enterprise business decisions. These decisions include replacing faulty or failed equipment, redistributing network resources, recognizing that more hardware and/or software need to be purchased and deployed, and so on. Other enterprise managements build on information from network management applications to enable these higher level applications to perform their decision-making and direct their information-gathering. These network management applications will be a key input to Web-based management frameworks, also.

The end-user's view of the network manager device is through the user interface at the network console. Most SNMP network managers offer a graphical user interface (GUI) to present performance statistics, accounting summaries, fault reports, configuration inventories, forms for creating queries, security breaches, topology maps, and so forth. Note that the specification of the user interface is not part of the SNMP standard and is considered an implementation detail. Presenting the network manager's SNMP console view through the Web browser is one of the first attempts at merging Web-based and SNMP-based management efforts.

The Managed Network Entity The SNMP reference model shows the managed network entity as the network device that contains the agent. It also uses the network protocols and SNMP to communicate over the internetwork with the network manager NMSs in its community. The managed network entity consists of two key components:

- The agent
- The agent MIB

The agent is the processing entity that receives requests from NMSs in its community, processes them if they are valid, and sends the appropriate response. Agents can also be configured to send trap messages to report asynchronous, predefined events. The agent implementation uses instrumentation routines that manipulate the local data structures to retrieve and write the various MIB objects under its control.

The MIB of the agent is its collection of managed objects. These are the "variables of interest" that have been defined in the standard way for describing how this managed network entity will be managed. The MIB groups that comprise a particular agent's MIB are dependent on the functionality of the device and which resources it manages. All agents include the MIB-II standard, that is, the lowest common denominator definition of SNMP management. MIB-II describes the basic TCP/IP and device objects that are necessary for a device to communicate and be managed by SNMP over the internetwork. These MIB-II objects include a system description, TCP and IP statistics, SNMP counter values, and so forth. The full description is in RFC 1213, "Management Information Base for network management of TCP/IP-based internets: MIB-II."

The SNMP Framework

The SNMP framework comprises three major components:

1. A data definition language, called the structure of management information (SMI).

2. Definitions of the management information, called the MIB.

3. The management protocol definition, also called SNMP (remember, the "P" in SNMP stands for "protocol").

The Structure of Management Information (SMI)   The   SMI lays the foundation for how management objects in the MIB are defined and encoded for transfer over the protocol. The SMI was first defined in August 1988, and later reached full standard status with RFC 1155. Enhancements to how the objects are defined through a more concise macro format definition and a formalization of the trap mechanism format were introduced in 1991 with RFC 1212 and RFC 1215, respectively. Note that RFC 1215 has informational status and is not, therefore, an official part of the SMI. Table E–1 shows an overview of the development of the SMI for SNMPv1.

Table E–1   SMI Summary

History	Date	RFC Number
SMI is first defined	August 1988	1065
SMI is modified	May 1990	1155
Concise MIB format is defined	March 1991	1212
Traps are defined	March 1991	1215

The SMI is the description of the common structures and generic types, along with the identification scheme, that are used in the implementation. The SMI is often likened to the schema definition used for defining databases. Just as a schema describes the format and layout of the objects in the database, the SMI describes the objects in the MIB. The key tenet of the SMI is that the formal definitions of the managed objects will be described using a language called Abstract Syntax Notation "dot" One (ASN.1).

The collection of managed objects, which are explicitly defined for each implementation as a particular MIB, are called *object types* in the formal SMI language.

Object types have three basic attributes that describe them. These attributes are:

- The object type *name*
- The object type *syntax*
- The object type *encoding*

Object Type Name   The object type name is a representation used as a means for uniquely identifying each object. It is also known as the *object identifier*. It is represented as a sequence of integers that traverse a global tree containing all the known objects in the SNMP management domain.

All of these known objects are defined in a hierarchy. The point of this hierarchy is to allocate the authority to assign names for objects to any interested and registered organization. Therefore, although any number of these groups may be assigning SNMP object names, this numbering scheme convention assures that all of the names created are unique and absolute because everyone knows the global scheme while being allocated and working in their own individual *branch*.

Every object that is to be managed is given a unique name. This object identifier name is properly placed in the global hierarchy where every object resides. Note the way the namespace is administered: Once a name is assigned, it cannot be reused by any other object. There is no object "conservation"—objects can be created (named), but never destroyed (removed).

This hierarchy is represented as a global "upside-down" tree that begins with an unnamed root node at the top and has nodes appended to it to represent the various objects that are named. Note that an object in these terms can be more than an SNMP-managed MIB object name. This global naming scheme also accommodates nodes for organizations, specifications, and other objects of interest that are named. The tree is very large and only when the tree is traversed to a specific subtree do you encounter the MIB variable names of SNMP.

The object identifier is represented as a string of decimal integers separated by periods. Each successive decimal group represents a deeper nesting level in the global naming hierarchy.

To be more specific, the root node has three child nodes appended to it that represent the organization in charge of administering that particular branch:

- The International Telegraph and Telephone Consultative Committee (CCITT) node
- (Note: The CCITT has now become the International Telecommunications Union-Telecommunications (ITU-T) branch.)
- The International Organization for Standardization (ISO) node
- A joint ISO-CCITT administration node

Each node is assigned a numerical value that usually begins with a zero and has subsequent peer-level objects assigned in incremental values. Figure E–2 shows the highest level of the naming tree.

The branch of interest for the SNMP world starts at the iso subtree. This subtree is, in turn, subdivided into four branches with nodes:

- standard node
- registration-authority node
- member-body node
- identified-organization node

```
o root-node
|
+--------------+---------------+
|              |               |
ccitt[0]     iso[1]     joint-iso-ccitt[2]
```

Figure E–2   Standard naming hierarchy.

Figure E–3 shows the sub-branch nodes for `iso`.

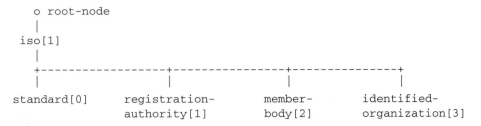

Figure E–3   iso naming branch.

The branch of interest for SNMP from the `iso` subtree continues down to the `identified-organization` branch. From there, Branch 6 (`dod`), belonging to the Department of Defense, has assigned its first node for use by the IAB (`internet`). For those keeping score, the object identifier for the IAB node can be represented as.

`1.3.6.1`, or `iso.identified-organization.dod.internet`, or `{ 1 3 6 1 }`

The `internet` node is further subdivided into four branches with their corresponding nodes:

- `directory` node
- `management` node
- `experimental` node
- `private` node

Figure E–4 on the next page displays the four `internet` branches administered by the IAB:

The `directory` branch is currently not used and is reserved for future OSI directory services to be implemented on the Internet.

The `management` branch contains objects that are defined in IAB documents, such as RFCs. Under this branch, the SNMP standard MIB is placed as Branch 1. Thus, all standard MIB objects, such as those found in MIB-II, begin with the same object identifier prefix: `1.3.6.1.2.1`. The Internet Assigned Numbers Authority (IANA) administers the `management` branch and all of its sub-branches.

Objects used on an experimental basis for testing and research can be placed in the `experimental` branch. The IANA also administers the numbering of the object identifiers in this branch (`1.3.6.1.3.1`).

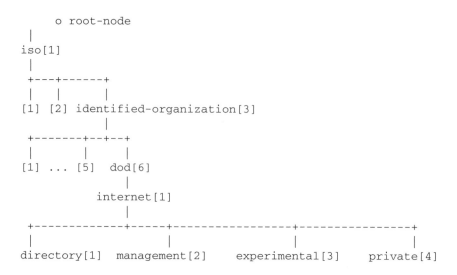

Figure E–4   IAB naming branch.

The `private` branch (`1.3.6.1.4.1`) is the repository for objects defined unilaterally, that is, named by one group or organization. The primary use of the `private` branch is for the addition of vendor MIB objects through the `enterprise` sub-branch. Each interested company can request a node number of the `enterprise` branch from the IANA, where the organization can append its own objects.[3] These objects are primarily the variables of interest that will be managed by SNMP for their specific products. Each company administers its object from this point in the naming tree.

Because all of these object identifiers are represented numerically, this organization lends itself naturally to lexicographic ordering. This is a very desirable feature in that it allows the NMS both to request all of the objects for any particular agent and to search a table without knowing its size beforehand.

---

3. The up-to-date list for enterprise numbers is available on the Web at: `ftp://ftp.isi.edu/in-notes/iana/assignments/enterprise-numbers`.

Object Type Syntax Syntax is the formal definition of an object type's structure using ASN.1. This syntax defines the abstract data structure corresponding to that particular object. Four standard attributes must be defined for each object to have properly declared objects for the MIB for SNMPv1. These four attributes are:

- Syntax type
- Access mode
- Status
- Name value

The syntax type is one of a set of predefined ASN.1 ObjectSyntax choices. Twelve choices are defined for version 1. These choices can be subdivided into three basic groups: simple, application-wide, and simply constructed. The simple category consists of INTEGER, OCTET STRING, OBJECT IDENTIFIER, and NULL. The application-wide group is composed of IpAddress, NetworkAddress, Counter, Gauge, TimeTicks, and Opaque. The simply constructed set contains list and table.

The access mode is a permission level that the agent examines per request for each object.

Four access values are defined: read-only, read/write, write-only, and not accessible. Read-only objects can be read but not written, read/write objects can be both read and written, write-only objects cannot be read but may be written, and not accessible objects cannot be read or written.

The status defines the managed node's responsibility for implementing this particular object. Three currently defined statuses are available: mandatory, optional, and obsolete. Mandatory objects must be implemented, optional objects may be implemented, and obsolete objects need no longer be implemented.

The name value is a short textual name, termed the *object descriptor,* that is equivalent to its corresponding object identifier.

Object Type Encoding Once the instances of the object types have been defined and declared, their values may be transmitted to and from the agent and NMS by applying the specified encoding rules of ASN.1 to the syntax for an object type. The transfer syntax notation used in SNMP is the basic encoding rules (BERs).

Abstract Syntax Notation One (ASN.1) ASN.1 is the high-level data type definition language used in SNMP to define managed objects. It is also used to describe the format of how SNMP messages can be sent between managers and agents. ASN.1 provides a standard way of representing data traveling across the internetwork. This standardization is an essential part of SNMP interoperability because the internal data within any one network device is represented in incompatible ways to different network computing device platforms. ASN.1 allows the management data to be represented in the same way for all SNMP managers and agents.

SNMP actually uses only a small subset of the full ASN.1 standard. The complete ISO ASN.1 definition is described in ISO Standard 8824, "Specification of Abstract Syntax Notation One (ASN.1)."

Basic Encoding Rules (BERs)   ISO Standard 8825, "Specification of Basic Encoding Rules for Abstract Syntax Notation One (ASN.1)," is the companion document to the ASN.1 specification. BER (often pronounced "brrrr") specifies how the syntax is encoded into octets and transferred over the internetwork. The BERs are an algorithm that takes the ASN.1 values and encodes the bits into the appropriate octet format for transmission over the internetwork. The BERs specify that the most significant bit is Bit 8 and the least significant bit is Bit 1. Bit 8 is the first bit presented to the network. This format is shown in Figure E–5.

Also noteworthy is the fact that integers that can be negative or positive are represented using two's complement notation. For non-negative integers, an unsigned representation can also be used to represent arbitrarily large positive numbers.

An important part of the BERs and ASN.1, as they are used in SNMP, is how the various data types are used as a component of a larger data item abstraction. This data item is a triplet composed of three variable-length parts: the tag, including the data type, the length, and the value. It is commonly referred to as the *TLV triplet*. The SNMP messages that pass back and forth between the NMS and agent are a complex nesting of ASN.1-encoded TLV data items. Figure E–6 on the next page shows the three parts that comprise the basic unit used in SNMP messages:

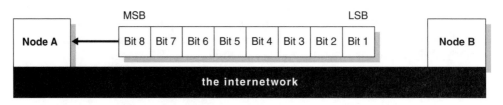

Figure E–5   How the BERs work.

Tag (or Type Identifier)	Length Identifier	Value (Contents)

Figure E–6   ASN.1 data item.

The Management Information Base (MIB)   The   MIB   defines
the collection of objects that can be accessed through the network management protocol. The first group of RFCs defining the MIB was referred
to as MIB-I ("MIB one"). Subsequent additions led to the current superset
of standard MIB objects. This new set, called MIB-II, is a full standard as
defined in RFC 1213. An overview of the MIB developments for version 1
appears in Table E–2.

Table E–2   Table E–2 MIB Summary

History	Date	RFC Number
MIB-I first defined	August 1988	1066
MIB-I modified	May 1990	1156
MIB-II introduced	May 1990	1158
MIB-II modified	March 1991	1213

Whereas the SMI provides the general framework for the definition
of managed objects, the MIB declares the particular instances for each
object and then binds a value to each one. The MIB is frequently referred
to as a *virtual database* of managed objects.

MIB-I was originally designed for a minimal SNMP implementation.
Most of the object definitions dealt with configuration or fault management, especially for routers and gateways. MIB-I contained 114 objects
divided into eight groups.

The subsequent MIB-II modification broadened SNMP's management scope by adding 57 new objects and two new groups. It is upwardly
compatible and basically reflects new requirements for the complexity of
managed nodes. This includes support for multiprotocol devices, objects
dealing with new media types, objects dealing with the SNMP itself, and
others. Refer to RFC 1213 for the exact list.

MIB Example: The System Description   The best way to see how
MIB objects are defined is by showing an example. The first group in

MIB-II, the system group, contains the top-level information about a managed device. This information includes the system description, its object ID, how long the agent has been running, a contact person, the system's name, its location, and what set level of services this agent offers.

Figure E–7 shows the first object in this group: the system description:

```
sysDescr OBJECT-TYPE
    SYNTAX  DisplayString (SIZE (0..255))
    ACCESS  read-only
    STATUS  mandatory
    DESCRIPTION
            "A textual description of the entity. This value
            should include the full name and version
            identification of the system's hardware type,
            software operating-system, and networking
            software. It is mandatory that this only contain
            printable ASCII characters."
    ::= { system 1 }
```

Figure E–7   The system description.

The ASN.1 OBJECT-TYPE macro, which defines the system description, is used to define all objects that would be defined for any MIB, whether they are standard objects in MIB-II or objects defined in an enterprise's own private MIB branch.

SNMP   SNMP is the definition of the application protocol for the network management service. It was first defined in August 1988, and later reached full standard status with RFC 1157. Table E–3 lists the major milestones in the protocol's development for version 1.

Table E–3   SNMP Protocol Summary

History	Date	RFC Number
SNMP first defined	August 1988	1067
SNMP modified	April 1989	1098
SNMP modified	May 1990	1157

The protocol is an asynchronous request and response protocol between an NMS and some agents. The protocol for version 1 supports five SNMP messages. Each message contains a header and a PDU, which contains the command and any associated data.

The NMS is capable of sending a message with any of three different PDUs. These three PDUs are the GetRequest-PDU, the GetNextRequest-PDU, and the SetRequest-PDU. The agent plays the opposite role and can send a message with two other PDUs: a response acknowledgment with the GetResponse-PDU to a properly processed request from an NMS and a message with a Trap-PDU. The trap message is an unsolicited event sent when an agent has discovered a predefined, extraordinary event that the manager wants to know about.

With SNMP, monitoring a network device's state is accomplished primarily by polling for appropriate values of meaningful agent MIB variables. The agent can send a limited number of traps to guide the NMS's focus and timing of that polling. The scheme favored for SNMP implementations is called *trap-directed polling*, where the trap sent by the agent causes the manager to poll for the objects associated with the condition indicated by the Trap-PDU.

The SNMP communicates its management information through the exchange of SNMP messages. Each message is completely and independently represented within a single datagram as presented to the UDP transport service. Each of these messages contains a version identifier, the SNMP community name, and the PDU.

The version identifier is a constant used for version control that the NMS and agents must know. Under SNMP, no version arbitration is available. If the NMS or agent receives an SNMP message containing an invalid or unsupported version number, the message is discarded. Under version 1, the version field always carries the value *0*; for SNMPv2, it must be *1*.

The SNMP community name is a string that identifies a particular group of NMSs and agents. Members of a community enforce authentication by using a crude password scheme. This simple use of a non-encrypted, plain text community name by communicating NMSs and their agents is called the *trivial authentication scheme*. For SNMPv1, it is the only SNMP security measure in place. The community name is represented as a string of octets. The community name "public" is often used as a default configuration setting.

SNMP Versions   While version 1 of the SNMP framework is a full Internet standard, subsequent efforts to create new standard versions have met with various fates. This has caused a great deal of confusion over the different versions and versions-of-versions of the protocol. This is further compounded by additional confusion over which version of the SMI is needed for each version of the protocol. Table E–4 shows the name, status, and description of each currently existing version of SNMP as of this writing.

Table E–4   SNMP Versions

Name	Status[1]	Description
SNMPv1	Full	The original version, defined by RFC 1157.
SNMPsec	Historic	The first attempt to add strong security to SNMPv1, defined by RFCs 1351, 1352, and 1353.
SNMPv2p	Historic	Party-based SNMP, which was another attempt to add strong security to SNMP, defined by RFCs 1441, 1445, 1446, 1448, and 1449.
SNMPv2c	Experimental	Community string-based SNMPv2, which was an attempt to combine the protocol operations of SNMPv2 with the security of SNMPv1, defined by RFCs 1901, 1905, and 1906.
SNMPv2u	Experimental	User-based SNMPv2, which provided security based on usernames and protocol operations of SNMPv2, defined by RFCs 1905, 1906, 1909, and 1910.
SNMPv2*	Experimental	An attempt to add the best features of SNMPv2p and SNMPv2u, defined by unpublished documents found at a Web site owned by SNMP Research (a leading SNMP vendor). (Usually pronounced "SNMP-V2-Star.")
SNMPv3	Proposed	Current effort to add strong security and remote administration to SNMP, defined in RFCs 2271–2275.

---

1. IETF standards-track documents can have a status of "proposed," "draft," "full," "experimental," or "historic." See Appendix B for a full description of these statuses.

Currently, only SNMPv1 has widespread usage, with implementations of SNMPv2c becoming more available. As SNMPv3 moves up through the standards process, it will begin to leave the lab and hopefully see more widespread vendor implementation and deployment.

HF?SNMP Version 1 (SNMPv1)   Even though it is celebrating its tenth birthday, version 1 still remains the predominant SNMP version in use. SNMPv1 is the first Internet standard network management framework, and as of this writing, the only version to reach full Internet standard. Its use is recommended for all devices connected to the Internet. Table E–5 shows the RFCs that make up the version 1 framework.

Table E–5   SNMPv1 RFCs

RFC	Title and Description
1155	"Structure and Identification of Management Information for TCP/IP-based Internets" Defines version 1 of the SMI (SMIv1); also referred to as STD 16.
1212	"Concise MIB Definitions" This specification defines the OBJECT-TYPE macro and other refinements to the SMI that improve the MIB definitions. This is also part of STD 16.
1157	"Simple Network Management Protocol (SNMP)" This is the definition of the version 1 protocol. It is STD 15.

RFC 1215, "Convention for Defining Traps for use with the SNMP," is also considered an important part of the version 1 framework, but it is not included in the formal standard set because it has informational status. The MIB-II definition found in RFC 1213 is defined using SMIv1.

HF?SNMP Version 2 (SNMPv2)   The second version of SNMP was an attempt to add new functionality. These hoped-for improvements included adding security and a supporting administrative framework, improving protocol operations, fixing any SNMPv1 deficiencies, designing manager-to-manager communications, and permitting remote SNMP-based configuration. The first major proposals put on the standards track appeared in April 1993 (RFCs 1441–1451). They were an ambitious attempt to address all of these areas. Implementation experience, however, revealed several problems.

The second major attempt at version 2 was released in January 1996 (RFCs 1902–1908). It was a much less comprehensive set of specifications than the first attempt at version 1. The new set of specifications did not include security and remote configuration. It did, however, include improved protocol operations with the addition of the GetBulk-PDU. It contained an improved SMI (SMI version 2, or SMIv2) and enhanced error handling and reporting. The main problem with this version of SNMP is that it lacked a standardized security and administration framework.

The current version that is being fielded is called SNMPv2c. The "c" suffix stands for "community." SNMPv2c still relies on the trivial community-based authentication scheme that was introduced with version 1 as described in RFC 1901, "Introduction to Community-based SNMPv2." This RFC only has experimental status.

The RFCs that make up the SNMPv2c framework and that are on the standards track are listed in Table E–6.

Table E–6   SNMPv2c RFCs

RFC	Title and Description
1902	"Structure of Management Information for Version 2 of the Simple Network Management Protocol (SNMPv2)" Describes the SMI.
1903	"Textual Conventions for Version 2 of the Simple Network Management Protocol (SNMPv2)" Adds to the SMI definition by including textual convention macro definitions.
1904	"Conformance Statements for Version 2 of the Simple Network Management Protocol (SNMPv2)" Defines conformance statements.
1905	"Protocol Operations for Version 2 of the Simple Network Management Protocol (SNMPv2)" Describes the new version 2 protocol.
1906	"Transport Mappings for Version 2 of the Simple Network Management Protocol (SNMPv2)" Details additional transports SNMPv2 can run on top of.
1907	"Management Information Base for Version 2 of the Simple Network Management Protocol (SNMPv2)" Lists the version II MIB.

Table E–6   SNMPv2c RFCs (continued)

RFC	Title and Description
1908	"Coexistence Between Version 1 and Version 2 of the Internet-standard Network Management Framework" Describes the details of the two versions working together.

There is widespread coexistence and support of both versions of the SMI. The main reason for this is the IETF policy that mandates that all new versions of MIB RFCs must specify their managed objects in the newer SMIv2 format.

SNMP Version 3 (SNMPv3)   For SNMP to move forward, security and administration features that were lacking in SNMPv2c had to be added. Work was begun in 1997 with the formation of the SNMPv3 WG to address these limitations. In December of that year, the Internet Engineering Standards Group (IESG) approved SNMPv3 IDs as a set of proposed standards, putting version 3 on the standards track.

This version builds on the experience gained with all the previous versions. It maintains the SNMP charter by remaining simple and extendible. It provides the modular architecture that allows the framework to evolve with the technology that it manages as well as with the advancements made in network management.

Most importantly, SNMPv3 provides security and remote administration services. Security services include authentication, privacy, and authorization.

The current RFCs that make up the SNMPv2c framework and that are on the standards track are listed in Table E–7.

Table E–7   SNMPv3 RFCs

RFC	Title and Description
2271	"An Architecture for Describing SNMP Management Frameworks" Describes the modular architecture and introduces the new terminology of "engines" and "applications."
2272	"Message Processing and Dispatching for the Simple Network Management Protocol (SNMP)" Details the message processing model.

Table E–7   SNMPv3 RFCs (continued)

RFC	Title and Description
2273	"SNMPv3 Applications" Lists the five types of applications defined for version 3 that describe how the protocol can be used: command generators, command responders, notification originators, notification receivers, and proxy forwarders.
2274	"User-based Security Model (USM) for version 3 of the Simple Network Management Protocol (SNMPv3)" Presents the security model.
2275	"View-based Access Control Model (VACM) for the Simple Network Management Protocol (SNMP)" Describes the method for how to control management information access.

Note that this definition of the SNMPv3 framework currently reuses the specifications defined for SNMPv2:

- RFC 1905: "Protocol Operations for Version 2 of the Simple Network Management Protocol (SNMPv2)"
- RFC 1906: "Transport Mappings for Version 2 of the Simple Network Management Protocol (SNMPv2)"

Because version 3 is the latest version, it must provide solutions to the problems introduced by creating multiple versions of a protocol. The problems that are being addressed by the SNMPv3 architects include migration paths among the versions, coexistence conflicts, and compliance levels within each version. As of this writing, work is progressing in several areas for advancing SNMPv3 to full Internet status. IDs[4] are currently circulating that provide an overall introduction to version 3, as well as solutions to the problems introduced by multiple versions.

What SNMP Provides   SNMP is perhaps the most successful management protocol ever deployed. By remaining a lightweight implementation with room to grow through its clearly defined extensions, SNMP has provided a solid solution for many types of network management problems. For the last 10 years, SNMP has shown itself capable of

---

4. IDs are available at: `ftp://ftp.ietf.org/internet-drafts/`

supporting a vast array of FCAPS management applications. It has proved scalable and it now manages enterprises with a large number of network devices of many different types.

While SNMP is the Internet standard for device management, it has been adapted to work over additional transports. SNMP has benefited from the ever-increasing popularity of the TCP/IP protocol suite, and riding on those coattails, the UDP transport has proved to be by far the most popular transport.

The manager/agent model has proved to be more scalable than first believed, and the feared limitations of the manager platform-centric model have been allayed by administering careful trap-directed polling policies. SNMP is the beginning of the manager-to-manager communications model to add another level to the management hierarchy. By creating management domains, network management problems can be discovered and corrected locally and the amount of management information that needs to be stored in a central place can be more closely regulated.

SNMP is also evolving, although not at the pace that was first envisioned. The first version of SNMP (SNMPv1) is very successful because it set up the original charter of balancing simplicity, flexibility, and extensibility. The second versions of SNMP struggled through the IETF standards process and implementation trials. The key additional requirements of security and remote configuration involved the introduction of complexity that made consensus difficult to achieve in 1993. SNMPv2c offers the same community authentication scheme used in version 1, and by January 1996, RFCs 1902–1908 offered few protocol and SMI enhancements. The SNMPv2c effort was very important, however, because it kept the SNMP evolution going. The problems of security and remote configuration *are* difficult, and the SNMPv3 effort will result in solutions, albeit five years later.

One of the greatest strengths that SNMP provides is a standardized approach that encourages the framework's flexibility and extensibility. The three major components defined in version 1—the SMI, MIB, and the protocol itself—are still the cornerstones for the version 3 framework. The fact that SNMP was developed within the Internet community has also helped to spread its popularity; SNMP documentation is "free." This fact has certainly engendered many commercial, reference manager, and agent implementations.

While 10 years of experience have shown that things could have been done differently, the SMI has shown itself to be a solid data definition language. And, although the ASN.1 syntax used for defining the MIBs can seem arcane and nonintuitive, hundreds of MIBs have been defined, allowing thousands of standard and enterprise-specific objects to be represented. By these means, SNMP has been extended to manage many new protocols and devices.

Another of SNMP's great strengths is the simplicity of the protocol. It is straightforward to implement and not resource-intensive for the agent. For version 1, the protocol contains only five request/response primitives:

- get-request
- set-request
- get-next-request
- get-response
- trap

The NMSs can retrieve the variables of interest to their applications by sending `get-request` and `get-next-request` messages. The former is a specific read operation, and the latter provides a tree traversal operator to determine which object instances are supported by an agent without the manager having to know ahead of time. The NMS can then modify an agent's variables by sending a `set-request` message. The agent can also send traps to the manager. For version 2, the `get-bulk` command was added to retrieve larger amounts of data (such as a table). Through these basic mechanisms, very complex and effective network management applications have been developed.

SNMP Shortcomings   Until the SNMPv3 effort is complete and implementations prove that the designs for security and remote configuration are stable, SNMP does not offer a complete solution for enterprise network management. Also, while SNMP is purposely not a full-fledged object-oriented design, the use of object-oriented technologies is growing rapidly, even with such low-level software as SNMP. The SNMP shortcomings are being addressed by advances in its own evolution.

REFERENCE FOR APPENDIX E

1. From www.quoteland.com.

RFC 2570:
Introduction to
SNMPv3

Network Working Group
Request for Comments: 2570
Category: Informational

J. Case
SNMP Research, Inc.
R. Mundy

TIS Labs at Network Associates, Inc.
D. Partain
Ericsson
B. Stewart
Cisco Systems
April 1999

Introduction to Version 3 of the
Internet-standard Network Management Framework

Status of this Memo

Copyright Notice

Abstract

   The purpose of this document is to provide an overview of the third
   version of the Internet-standard Management Framework, termed the
   SNMP version 3 Framework (SNMPv3). This Framework is derived from
   and builds upon both the original Internet-standard Management
   Framework (SNMPv1) and the second Internet-standard Management
   Framework (SNMPv2).

   The architecture is designed to be modular to allow the evolution of
   the Framework over time.

Table of Contents

1 Introduction

   This document is an introduction to the third version of the
   Internet-standard Management Framework, termed the SNMP version 3
   Management Framework (SNMPv3) and has multiple purposes.

   First, it describes the relationship between the SNMP version 3
   (SNMPv3) specifications and the specifications of the SNMP version 1
   (SNMPv1) Management Framework, the SNMP version 2 (SNMPv2) Management
   Framework, and the Community-based Administrative Framework for
   SNMPv2.

   Second, it provides a roadmap to the multiple documents which contain
   the relevant specifications.

   Third, this document provides a brief easy-to-read summary of the
   contents of each of the relevant specification documents.

   This document is intentionally tutorial in nature and, as such, may
   occasionally be "guilty" of oversimplification. In the event of a
   conflict or contradiction between this document and the more detailed
   documents for which this document is a roadmap, the specifications in

the more detailed documents shall prevail.

Further, the detailed documents attempt to maintain separation
between the various component modules in order to specify well-
defined interfaces between them. This roadmap document, however,
takes a different approach and attempts to provide an integrated view
of the various component modules in the interest of readability.

2 The Internet Standard Management Framework

The third version of the Internet Standard Management Framework (the
SNMPv3 Framework) is derived from and builds upon both the original
Internet-standard Management Framework (SNMPv1) and the second
Internet-standard Management Framework (SNMPv2).

All versions (SNMPv1, SNMPv2, and SNMPv3) of the Internet Standard
Management Framework share the same basic structure and components.
Furthermore, all versions of the specifications of the Internet
Standard Management Framework follow the same architecture.

2.1 Basic Structure and Components

An enterprise deploying the Internet Standard Management Framework
contains four basic components:

   * several (typically many) managed nodes, each with an SNMP entity
     which provides remote access to management instrumentation
     (traditionally called an agent);

   * at least one SNMP entity with management applications (typically
     called a manager),

   * a management protocol used to convey management information
     between the SNMP entities, and

   * management information.

The management protocol is used to convey management information
between SNMP entities such as managers and agents.

This basic structure is common to all versions of the Internet
Standard Management Framework; i.e., SNMPv1, SNMPv2, and SNMPv3.

2.2 Architecture of the Internet Standard Management Framework

The specifications of the Internet Standard Management Framework are
based on a modular architecture. This framework is more than just a
protocol for moving data. It consists of:

* a data definition language,

* definitions of management information (the Management
  Information Base, or MIB),

* a protocol definition, and

* security and administration.

Over time, as the Framework has evolved from SNMPv1, through SNMPv2,
to SNMPv3, the definitions of each of these architectural components
have become richer and more clearly defined, but the fundamental
architecture has remained consistent.

One prime motivator for this modularity was to enable the ongoing
evolution of the Framework as is documented in RFC 1052 [14]. When
originally envisioned, this capability was to be used to ease the
transition from SNMP-based management of internets to management
based on OSI protocols. To this end, the framework was architected
with a protocol-independent data definition language and Management
Information Base along with a MIB-independent protocol. This
separation was designed to allow the SNMP-based protocol to be
replaced without requiring the management information to be redefined
or reinstrumented. History has shown that the selection of this
architecture was the right decision for the wrong reason -- it turned
out that this architecture has eased the transition from SNMPv1 to
SNMPv2 and from SNMPv2 to SNMPv3 rather than easing the transition
away from management based on the Simple Network Management Protocol.

The SNMPv3 Framework builds and extends these architectural
principles by:

* building on these four basic architectural components, in some
  cases incorporating them from the SNMPv2 Framework by reference,
  and

* by using these same layering principles in the definition of new
  capabilities in the security and administration portion of the
  architecture.

Those who are familiar with the architecture of the SNMPv1 Management
Framework and the SNMPv2 Management Framework will find many familiar
concepts in the architecture of the SNMPv3 Management Framework.
However, in some cases, the terminology may be somewhat different.

3 The SNMPv1 Management Framework

   The original Internet-standard Network Management Framework (SNMPv1)
   is defined in the following documents:

     * STD 16, RFC 1155 [1] which defines the Structure of Management
       Information (SMI), the mechanisms used for describing and naming
       objects for the purpose of management.

     * STD 16, RFC 1212 [2] which defines a more concise description
       mechanism for describing and naming management information objects,
       but which is wholly consistent with the SMI.

     * STD 15, RFC 1157 [3] which defines the Simple Network Management
       Protocol (SNMP), the protocol used for network access to managed
       objects and event notification. Note this document also defines an
       initial set of event notifications.

   Additionally, two documents are generally considered to be companions
   to these three:

     * STD 17, RFC 1213 [13] which contains definitions for the base
       set of management information

     * RFC 1215 [25] defines a concise description mechanism for
       defining event notifications, which are called traps in the SNMPv1
       protocol. It also specifies the generic traps from RFC 1157 in the
       concise notation.

   These documents describe the four parts of the first version of the
   SNMP Framework.

3.1 The SNMPv1 Data Definition Language

   The first two and the last document describe the SNMPv1 data
   definition language. Note that due to the initial requirement that
   the SMI be protocol-independent, the first two SMI documents do not
   provide a means for defining event notifications (traps). Instead,
   the SNMP protocol document defines a few standardized event
   notifications (generic traps) and provides a means for additional
   event notifications to be defined. The last document specifies a
   straight-forward approach towards defining event notifications used
   with the SNMPv1 protocol. At the time that it was written, use of
   traps in the Internet-standard network management framework was
   controversial. As such, RFC 1215 was put forward with the status of
   "Informational", which was never updated because it was believed that
   the second version of the SNMP Framework would replace the first
   version. Note that the SNMPv1 data definition language is sometimes

referred to as SMIv1.

3.2 Management Information

The data definition language described in the first two documents was first used to define the now-historic MIB-I as specified in RFC 1066 [12], and was subsequently used to define MIB-II as specified in RFC 1213 [13].

Later, after the publication of MIB-II, a different approach to management information definition was taken from the earlier approach of having a single committee staffed by generalists work on a single document to define the Internet-standard MIB. Rather, many mini-MIB documents were produced in a parallel and distributed fashion by groups chartered to produce a specification for a focused portion of the Internet-standard MIB and staffed by personnel with expertise in those particular areas ranging from various aspects of network management, to system management, and application management.

3.3 Protocol Operations

The third document, STD 15, describes the SNMPv1 protocol operations performed by protocol data units (PDUs) on lists of variable bindings and describes the format of SNMPv1 messages. The operators defined by SNMPv1 are: get, get-next, get-response, set-request, and trap. Typical layering of SNMP on a connectionless transport service is also defined.

3.4 SNMPv1 Security and Administration

STD 15 also describes an approach to security and administration. Many of these concepts are carried forward and some, particularly security, are extended by the SNMPv3 Framework.

The SNMPv1 Framework describes the encapsulation of SNMPv1 PDUs in SNMP messages between SNMP entities and distinguishes between application entities and protocol entities. In SNMPv3, these are renamed applications and engines, respectively.

The SNMPv1 Framework also introduces the concept of an authentication service supporting one or more authentication schemes. In addition to authentication, SNMPv3 defines the additional security capability referred to as privacy. (Note: some literature from the security community would describe SNMPv3 security capabilities as providing data integrity, source authenticity, and confidentiality.) The modular nature of the SNMPv3 Framework permits both changes and additions to the security capabilities.

RFC 2570   Introduction to SNMPv3   April 1999

Finally, the SNMPv1 Framework introduces access control based on a
concept called an SNMP MIB view. The SNMPv3 Framework specifies a
fundamentally similar concept called view-based access control. With
this capability, SNMPv3 provides the means for controlling access to
information on managed devices.

However, while the SNMPv1 Framework anticipated the definition of
multiple authentication schemes, it did not define any such schemes
other than a trivial authentication scheme based on community
strings. This was a known fundamental weakness in the SNMPv1
Framework but it was thought at that time that the definition of
commercial grade security might be contentious in its design and
difficult to get approved because "security" means many different
things to different people. To that end, and because some users do
not require strong authentication, the SNMPv1 architected an
authentication service as a separate block to be defined "later" and
the SNMPv3 Framework provides an architecture for use within that
block as well as a definition for its subsystems.

4 The SNMPv2 Management Framework

The SNMPv2 Management Framework is fully described in [4-9] and
coexistence and transition issues relating to SNMPv1 and SNMPv2 are
discussed in [10].

SNMPv2 provides several advantages over SNMPv1, including:

  * expanded data types (e.g., 64 bit counter)

  * improved efficiency and performance (get-bulk operator)

  * confirmed event notification (inform operator)

  * richer error handling (errors and exceptions)

  * improved sets, especially row creation and deletion

  * fine tuning of the data definition language

However, the SNMPv2 Framework, as described in these documents, is
incomplete in that it does not meet the original design goals of the
SNMPv2 project. The unmet goals included provision of security and
administration delivering so-called "commercial grade" security with

  * authentication: origin identification, message integrity,
    and some aspects of replay protection;

  * privacy: confidentiality;

Case, et al.   Informational   [Page 7]

   * authorization and access control; and

   * suitable remote configuration and administration capabilities
     for these features.

The SNMPv3 Management Framework, as described in this document and
the companion documents, addresses these significant deficiencies.

5 The SNMPv3 Working Group

This document, and its companion documents, were produced by the
SNMPv3 Working Group of the Internet Engineering Task Force (IETF).
The SNMPv3 Working Group was chartered to prepare recommendations for
the next generation of SNMP. The goal of the Working Group was to
produce the necessary set of documents that provide a single standard
for the next generation of core SNMP functions. The single, most
critical need in the next generation is a definition of security and
administration that makes SNMP-based management transactions secure
in a way which is useful for users who wish to use SNMPv3 to manage
networks, the systems that make up those networks, and the
applications which reside on those systems, including manager-to-
agent, agent-to-manager, and manager-to-manager transactions.

In the several years prior to the chartering of the Working Group,
there were a number of activities aimed at incorporating security and
other improvements to SNMP. These efforts included:

   * "SNMP Security" circa 1991-1992 [RFC 1351 - RFC 1353],

   * "SMP" circa 1992-1993,

   * "The Party-based SNMPv2" circa 1993-1995 [RFC 1441 - RFC 1452].

Each of these efforts incorporated commercial grade, industrial
strength security including authentication, privacy, authorization,
view-based access control, and administration, including remote
configuration.

These efforts fed the development of the SNMPv2 Management Framework
as described in RFCs 1902 - 1908. However, the Framework described
in those RFCs had no standards-based security and administrative
framework of its own; rather, it was associated with multiple
security and administrative frameworks, including:

   * "The Community-based SNMPv2" (SNMPv2c) [RFC 1901],

   * "SNMPv2u" [RFCs 1909 - 1910] and

RFC 2570   Introduction to SNMPv3   April 1999

    * "SNMPv2*".

SNMPv2c had the endorsement of the IETF but no security and
administration whereas both SNMPv2u and SNMPv2* had security but
lacked the endorsement of the IETF.

The SNMPv3 Working Group was chartered to produce a single set of
specifications for the next generation of SNMP, based upon a
convergence of the concepts and technical elements of SNMPv2u and
SNMPv2*, as was suggested by an advisory team which was formed to
provide a single recommended approach for SNMP evolution.

In so doing, the Working Group charter defined the following
objectives:

  * accommodate the wide range of operational environments with
    differing management demands;

  * facilitate the need to transition from previous, multiple
    protocols to SNMPv3;

  * facilitate the ease of setup and maintenance activities.

In the initial work of the SNMPv3 Working Group, the group focused on
security and administration, including

  * authentication and privacy,

  * authorization and view-based access control, and

  * standards-based remote configuration of the above.

The SNMPv3 Working Group did not "reinvent the wheel," but reused the
SNMPv2 Draft Standard documents, i.e., RFCs 1902 through 1908 for
those portions of the design that were outside the focused scope.

Rather, the primary contributors to the SNMPv3 Working Group, and the
Working Group in general, devoted their considerable efforts to
addressing the missing link -- security and administration -- and in
the process made invaluable contributions to the state-of-the-art of
management.

They produced a design based on a modular architecture with
evolutionary capabilities with emphasis on layering. As a result,
SNMPv3 can be thought of as SNMPv2 with additional security and
administration capabilities.

Case, et al.   Informational   [Page 9]

In doing so, the Working Group achieved the goal of producing a
single specification which has not only the endorsement of the IETF
but also has security and administration.

6 SNMPv3 Framework Module Specifications

The specification of the SNMPv3 Management Framework is partitioned
in a modular fashion among several documents. It is the intention of
the SNMPv3 Working Group that, with proper care, any or all of the
individual documents can be revised, upgraded, or replaced as
requirements change, new understandings are obtained, and new
technologies become available.

Whenever feasible, the initial document set which defines the SNMPv3
Management Framework leverages prior investments defining and
implementing the SNMPv2 Management Framework by incorporating by
reference each of the specifications of the SNMPv2 Management
Framework.

The SNMPv3 Framework augments those specifications with
specifications for security and administration for SNMPv3.

The documents which specify the SNMPv3 Management Framework follow
the same architecture as those of the prior versions and can be
organized for expository purposes into four main categories as
follows:

  * the data definition language,

  * Management Information Base (MIB) modules,

  * protocol operations, and

  * security and administration.

The first three sets of documents are incorporated from SNMPv2. The
fourth set of documents are new to SNMPv3, but, as described
previously, build on significant prior related works.

6.1 Data Definition Language

The specifications of the data definition language includes STD 58,
RFC 2578, "Structure of Management Information Version 2 (SMIv2)"
[26], and related specifications. These documents are updates of
RFCs 1902 - 1904 [4-6] which have evolved independently from the
other parts of the framework and were republished as STD 58, RFCs
2578 - 2580 [26-28] when promoted from Draft Standard.

The Structure of Management Information (SMIv2) defines fundamental
data types, an object model, and the rules for writing and revising
MIB modules. Related specifications include STD 58, RFCs 2579, 2580.
The updated data definition language is sometimes referred to as
SMIv2.

STD 58, RFC 2579, "Textual Conventions for SMIv2" [27], defines an
initial set of shorthand abbreviations which are available for use
within all MIB modules for the convenience of human readers and
writers.

STD 58, RFC 2580, "Conformance Statements for SMIv2" [28], defines
the format for compliance statements which are used for describing
requirements for agent implementations and capability statements
which can be used to document the characteristics of particular
implementations.

6.2 MIB Modules

MIB modules usually contain object definitions, may contain
definitions of event notifications, and sometimes include compliance
statements specified in terms of appropriate object and event
notification groups. As such, MIB modules define the management
information maintained by the instrumentation in managed nodes, made
remotely accessible by management agents, conveyed by the management
protocol, and manipulated by management applications.

MIB modules are defined according the rules defined in the documents
which specify the data definition language, principally the SMI as
supplemented by the related specifications.

There is a large and growing number of standards-based MIB modules,
as defined in the periodically updated list of standard protocols
[STD 1, RFC 2400]. As of this writing, there are nearly 100
standards-based MIB modules with a total number of defined objects
approaching 10,000. In addition, there is an even larger and growing
number of enterprise-specific MIB modules defined unilaterally by
various vendors, research groups, consortia, and the like resulting
in an unknown and virtually uncountable number of defined objects.

In general, management information defined in any MIB module,
regardless of the version of the data definition language used, can
be used with any version of the protocol. For example, MIB modules
defined in terms of the SNMPv1 SMI (SMIv1) are compatible with the
SNMPv3 Management Framework and can be conveyed by the protocols
specified therein. Furthermore, MIB modules defined in terms of the
SNMPv2 SMI (SMIv2) are compatible with SNMPv1 protocol operations and
can be conveyed by it. However, there is one noteworthy exception:

the Counter64 datatype which can be defined in a MIB module defined
in SMIv2 format but which cannot be conveyed by an SNMPv1 protocol
engine.

6.3 Protocol Operations and Transport Mappings

The specifications for the protocol operations and transport mappings
of the SNMPv3 Framework are incorporated by reference to the two
SNMPv2 Framework documents.

The specification for protocol operations is found in RFC 1905,
"Protocol Operations for Version 2 of the Simple Network Management
Protocol (SNMPv2)" [7]. The SNMPv3 Framework is designed to allow
various portions of the architecture to evolve independently. For
example, it might be possible for a new specification of protocol
operations to be defined within the Framework to allow for additional
protocol operations.

The specification of transport mappings is found in RFC 1906,
"Transport Mappings for Version 2 of the Simple Network Management
Protocol (SNMPv2)" [8].

6.4 SNMPv3 Security and Administration

The SNMPv3 document series defined by the SNMPv3 Working Group
consists of seven documents at this time:

RFC 2570, "Introduction to Version 3 of the Internet-standard
Network Management Framework", which is this document.

RFC 2571, "An Architecture for Describing SNMP Management
Frameworks" [15], describes the overall architecture with special
emphasis on the architecture for security and administration.

RFC 2572, "Message Processing and Dispatching for the Simple
Network Management Protocol (SNMP)" [16], describes the possibly
multiple message processing models and the dispatcher portion that
can be a part of an SNMP protocol engine.

RFC 2573, "SNMP Applications" [17], describes the five types of
applications that can be associated with an SNMPv3 engine and
their elements of procedure.

RFC 2574, "The User-Based Security Model for Version 3 of the
Simple Network Management Protocol (SNMPv3)" [18], describes the
threats, mechanisms, protocols, and supporting data used to
provide SNMP message-level security.

RFC 2570   Introduction to SNMPv3   April 1999

   RFC 2575, "View-based Access Control Model for the Simple Network
   Management Protocol (SNMP)" [19], describes how view-based access
   control can be applied within command responder and notification
   originator applications.

   The Work in Progress, "Coexistence between Version 1, Version 2,
   and Version 3 of the Internet-standard Network Management
   Framework" [20], describes coexistence between the SNMPv3
   Management Framework, the SNMPv2 Management Framework, and the
   original SNMPv1 Management Framework.

7 Document Summaries

   The following sections provide brief summaries of each document with
   slightly more detail than is provided in the overviews above.

7.1 Structure of Management Information

   Management information is viewed as a collection of managed objects,
   residing in a virtual information store, termed the Management
   Information Base (MIB). Collections of related objects are defined
   in MIB modules. These modules are written in the SNMP MIB module
   language, which contains elements of OSI's Abstract Syntax Notation
   One (ASN.1) [11] language.   STD 58, RFCs 2578, 2579, 2580, together
   define the MIB module language, specify the base data types for
   objects, specify a core set of short-hand specifications for data
   types called textual conventions, and specify a few administrative
   assignments of object identifier (OID) values.

   The SMI is divided into three parts: module definitions, object
   definitions, and notification definitions.

   (1) Module definitions are used when describing information modules.
        An ASN.1 macro, MODULE-IDENTITY, is used to convey concisely the
        semantics of an information module.

   (2) Object definitions are used when describing managed objects. An
        ASN.1 macro, OBJECT-TYPE, is used to convey concisely the syntax
        and semantics of a managed object.

   (3) Notification definitions are used when describing unsolicited
        transmissions of management information. An ASN.1 macro,
        NOTIFICATION-TYPE, is used to convey concisely the syntax and
        semantics of a notification.

7.1.1 Base SMI Specification

STD 58, RFC 2578 specifies the base data types for the MIB module
language, which include: Integer32, enumerated integers, Unsigned32,
Gauge32, Counter32, Counter64, TimeTicks, INTEGER, OCTET STRING,
OBJECT IDENTIFIER, IpAddress, Opaque, and BITS. It also assigns
values to several object identifiers. STD 58, RFC 2578 further
defines the following constructs of the MIB module language:

* IMPORTS to allow the specification of items that are used
  in a MIB module, but defined in another MIB module.

* MODULE-IDENTITY to specify for a MIB module a description
  and administrative information such as contact and revision
  history.

* OBJECT-IDENTITY and OID value assignments to specify a
  an OID value.

* OBJECT-TYPE to specify the data type, status, and the semantics
  of managed objects.

* SEQUENCE type assignment to list the columnar objects in
  a table.

* NOTIFICATION-TYPE construct to specify an event notification.

7.1.2 Textual Conventions

When designing a MIB module, it is often useful to specify in a
short-hand way the semantics for a set of objects with similar
behavior. This is done by defining a new data type using a base data
type specified in the SMI. Each new type has a different name, and
specifies a base type with more restrictive semantics. These newly
defined types are termed textual conventions, and are used for the
convenience of humans reading a MIB module and potentially by
"intelligent" management applications. It is the purpose of STD 58,
RFC 2579, Textual Conventions for SMIv2 [27], to define the
construct, TEXTUAL-CONVENTION, of the MIB module language used to
define such new types and to specify an initial set of textual
conventions available to all MIB modules.

7.1.3 Conformance Statements

It may be useful to define the acceptable lower-bounds of
implementation, along with the actual level of implementation
achieved. It is the purpose of STD 58, RFC 2580, Conformance
Statements for SMIv2 [28], to define the constructs of the MIB module
language used for these purposes. There are two kinds of constructs:

(1) Compliance statements are used when describing requirements for
     agents with respect to object and event notification
     definitions. The MODULE-COMPLIANCE construct is used to convey
     concisely such requirements.

(2) Capability statements are used when describing capabilities of
     agents with respect to object and event notification
     definitions. The AGENT-CAPABILITIES construct is used to convey
     concisely such capabilities.

Finally, collections of related objects and collections of related
event notifications are grouped together to form a unit of
conformance. The OBJECT-GROUP construct is used to convey concisely
the objects in and the semantics of an object group. The
NOTIFICATION-GROUP construct is used to convey concisely the event
notifications in and the semantics of an event notification group.

7.2 Protocol Operations

The management protocol provides for the exchange of messages which
convey management information between the agents and the management
stations. The form of these messages is a message "wrapper" which
encapsulates a Protocol Data Unit (PDU).

It is the purpose of RFC 1905, Protocol Operations for SNMPv2 [7], to
define the operations of the protocol with respect to the sending and
receiving of the PDUs.

7.3 Transport Mappings

SNMP Messages may be used over a variety of protocol suites. It is
the purpose of RFC 1906, Transport Mappings for SNMPv2 [8], to define
how SNMP messages maps onto an initial set of transport domains.
Other mappings may be defined in the future.

Although several mappings are defined, the mapping onto UDP is the
preferred mapping. As such, to provide for the greatest level of
interoperability, systems which choose to deploy other mappings
should also provide for proxy service to the UDP mapping.

7.4 Protocol Instrumentation

   It is the purpose of RFC 1907, the Management Information Base for
   SNMPv2 document [9] to define managed objects which describe the
   behavior of an SNMPv2 entity.

7.5 Architecture / Security and Administration

   It is the purpose of RFC 2571, "An Architecture for Describing SNMP
   Management Frameworks" [15], to define an architecture for specifying
   SNMP Management Frameworks. While addressing general architectural
   issues, it focuses on aspects related to security and administration.
   It defines a number of terms used throughout the SNMPv3 Management
   Framework and, in so doing, clarifies and extends the naming of

   * engines and applications,

   * entities (service providers such as the engines in agents
     and managers),

   * identities (service users), and

   * management information, including support for multiple
     logical contexts.

   The document contains a small MIB module which is implemented by all
   authoritative SNMPv3 protocol engines.

7.6 Message Processing and Dispatch (MPD)

   RFC 2572, "Message Processing and Dispatching for the Simple Network
   Management Protocol (SNMP)" [16], describes the Message Processing
   and Dispatching for SNMP messages within the SNMP architecture. It
   defines the procedures for dispatching potentially multiple versions
   of SNMP messages to the proper SNMP Message Processing Models, and
   for dispatching PDUs to SNMP applications. This document also
   describes one Message Processing Model - the SNMPv3 Message
   Processing Model.

   It is expected that an SNMPv3 protocol engine MUST support at least
   one Message Processing Model. An SNMPv3 protocol engine MAY support
   more than one, for example in a multi-lingual system which provides
   simultaneous support of SNMPv3 and SNMPv1 and/or SNMPv2c.

RFC 2570   Introduction to SNMPv3   April 1999

7.7 SNMP Applications

It is the purpose of RFC 2573, "SNMP Applications" to describe the
five types of applications which can be associated with an SNMP
engine. They are: Command Generators, Command Responders,
Notification Originators, Notification Receivers, and Proxy
Forwarders.

The document also defines MIB modules for specifying targets of
management operations (including notifications), for notification
filtering, and for proxy forwarding.

7.8 User-based Security Model (USM)

RFC 2574, the "User-based Security Model (USM) for version 3 of the
Simple Network Management Protocol (SNMPv3)" describes the User-based
Security Model for SNMPv3. It defines the Elements of Procedure for
providing SNMP message-level security.

The document describes the two primary and two secondary threats
which are defended against by the User-based Security Model. They
are: modification of information, masquerade, message stream
modification, and disclosure.

The USM utilizes MD5 [21] and the Secure Hash Algorithm [22] as keyed
hashing algorithms [23] for digest computation to provide data
integrity

  * to directly protect against data modification attacks,

  * to indirectly provide data origin authentication, and

  * to defend against masquerade attacks.

The USM uses loosely synchronized monotonically increasing time
indicators to defend against certain message stream modification
attacks. Automatic clock synchronization mechanisms based on the
protocol are specified without dependence on third-party time sources
and concomitant security considerations.

The USM uses the Data Encryption Standard (DES) [24] in the cipher
block chaining mode (CBC) if disclosure protection is desired.
Support for DES in the USM is optional, primarily because export and
usage restrictions in many countries make it difficult to export and
use products which include cryptographic technology.

Case, et al.   Informational   [Page 17]

RFC 2570   Introduction to SNMPv3   April 1999

   The document also includes a MIB suitable for remotely monitoring and
   managing the configuration parameters for the USM, including key
   distribution and key management.

   An entity may provide simultaneous support for multiple security
   models as well as multiple authentication and privacy protocols. All
   of the protocols used by the USM are based on pre-placed keys, i.e.,
   private key mechanisms. The SNMPv3 architecture permits the use of
   asymmetric mechanisms and protocols (commonly called "public key
   cryptography") but as of this writing, no such SNMPv3 security models
   utilizing public key cryptography have been published.

7.9 View-based Access Control (VACM)

   The purpose of RFC 2575, the "View-based Access Control Model (VACM)
   for the Simple Network Management Protocol (SNMP)" is to describe the
   View-based Access Control Model for use in the SNMP architecture.
   The VACM can simultaneously be associated in a single engine
   implementation with multiple Message Processing Models and multiple
   Security Models.

   It is architecturally possible to have multiple, different, Access
   Control Models active and present simultaneously in a single engine
   implementation, but this is expected to be *_very_* rare in practice
   and *_far_* less common than simultaneous support for multiple
   Message Processing Models and/or multiple Security Models.

7.10 SNMPv3 Coexistence and Transition

   The purpose of "Coexistence between Version 1, Version 2, and Version
   3 of the Internet-standard Network Management Framework" is to
   describe coexistence between the SNMPv3 Management Framework, the
   SNMPv2 Management Framework, and the original SNMPv1 Management
   Framework. In particular, this document describes four aspects of
   coexistence:

   * Conversion of MIB documents from SMIv1 to SMIv2 format

   * Mapping of notification parameters

   * Approaches to coexistence between entities which support
      the various versions of SNMP in a multi-lingual network, in
      particular the processing of protocol operations in
      multi-lingual implementations, as well as behavior of
      proxy implementations

RFC 2570   Introduction to SNMPv3   April 1999

    * The SNMPv1 Message Processing Model and Community-Based
       Security Model, which provides mechanisms for adapting
       SNMPv1 and SNMPv2c into the View-Based Access Control Model
       (VACM) [19]

8 Security Considerations

   As this document is primarily a roadmap document, it introduces no
   new security considerations. The reader is referred to the relevant
   sections of each of the referenced documents for information about
   security considerations.

9 Editors' Addresses

   Jeffrey Case
   SNMP Research, Inc.
   3001 Kimberlin Heights Road
   Knoxville, TN 37920-9716
   USA
   Phone: +1 423 573 1434
   EMail: case@snmp.com

   Russ Mundy
   TIS Labs at Network Associates
   3060 Washington Rd
   Glenwood, MD 21738
   USA
   Phone: +1 301 854 6889
   EMail: mundy@tislabs.com

   David Partain
   Ericsson Radio Systems
   Research and Innovation
   P.O. Box 1248
   SE-581 12 Linkoping
   Sweden
   Phone: +46 13 28 41 44
   EMail: David.Partain@ericsson.com

   Bob Stewart
   Cisco Systems, Inc.
   170 West Tasman Drive
   San Jose, CA 95134-1706
   U.S.A.
   Phone: +1 603 654 6923
   EMail: bstewart@cisco.com

10 References

[1] Rose, M. and K. McCloghrie, "Structure and Identification of
     Management Information for TCP/IP-based internets", STD 16, RFC
     1155, May 1990.

[2] Rose, M. and K. McCloghrie, "Concise MIB Definitions", STD 16,
     RFC 1212, March 1991.

[3] Case, J., Fedor, M., Schoffstall, M. and J. Davin, "Simple
     Network Management Protocol", STD 15, RFC 1157, May 1990.

[4] SNMPv2 Working Group, Case, J., McCloghrie, K., Rose, M., and S.
     Waldbusser, "Structure of Management Information for Version 2
     of the Simple Network Management Protocol (SNMPv2)", RFC 1902,
     January 1996.

[5] SNMPv2 Working Group, Case, J., McCloghrie, K., Rose, M., and S.
     Waldbusser, "Textual Conventions for Version 2 of the Simple
     Network Management Protocol (SNMPv2)", RFC 1903, January 1996.

[6] SNMPv2 Working Group, Case, J., McCloghrie, K., Rose, M., and S.
     Waldbusser, "Conformance Statements for Version 2 of the Simple
     Network Management Protocol (SNMPv2)", RFC 1904, January 1996.

[7] SNMPv2 Working Group, Case, J., McCloghrie, K., Rose, M. and S.
     Waldbusser, "Protocol Operations for Version 2 of the Simple
     Network Management Protocol (SNMPv2)", RFC 1905, January 1996.

[8] SNMPv2 Working Group, Case, J., McCloghrie, K., Rose, M. and S.
     Waldbusser, "Transport Mappings for Version 2 of the Simple
     Network Management Protocol (SNMPv2)", RFC 1906, January 1996.

[9] SNMPv2 Working Group, Case, J., McCloghrie, K., Rose, M. and S.
     Waldbusser, "Management Information Base for Version 2 of the
     Simple Network Management Protocol (SNMPv2)", RFC 1907, January
     1996.

[10] SNMPv2 Working Group, Case, J., McCloghrie, K., Rose, M. and S.
     Waldbusser, "Coexistence between Version 1 and Version 2 of the
     Internet-standard Network Management Framework", RFC 1908,
     January 1996.

[11] Information processing systems - Open Systems Interconnection -
     Specification of Abstract Syntax Notation One (ASN.1),
     International Organization for Standardization. International
     Standard 8824, (December, 1987).

RFC 2570   Introduction to SNMPv3   April 1999

    [12] McCloghrie, K. and M. Rose, "Management Information Base for
         Network Management of TCP/IP-based Internets", RFC 1066, August
         1988.

    [13] McCloghrie, K. and M. Rose, "Management Information Base for
         Network Management of TCP/IP-based internets: MIB-II, STD 17,
         RFC 1213, March 1991.

    [14] Cerf, V., "IAB Recommendations for the Development of Internet
         Network Management Standards", RFC 1052, April 1988.

    [15] Harrington, D., Presuhn, R. and B. Wijnen, "An Architecture for
         Describing SNMP Management Frameworks", RFC 2571, April 1999.

    [16] Case, J., Harrington, D., Presuhn, R. and B. Wijnen, "Message
         Processing and Dispatching for the Simple Network Management
         Protocol (SNMP)", RFC 2572, April 1999.

    [17] Levi, D., Meyer, P. and B. Stewart, "SNMP Applications", RFC
         2573, April 1999.

    [18] Blumenthal, U. and B. Wijnen, "The User-Based Security Model for
         Version 3 of the Simple Network Management Protocol (SNMPv3)",
         RFC 2574, April 1999.

    [19] Wijnen, B., Presuhn, R. and K. McCloghrie, "View-based Access
         Control Model for the Simple Network Management Protocol
         (SNMP)", RFC 2575, April 1999.

    [20] Frye, R., Levi, D., Routhier, S., and B. Wijnen, "Coexistence
         between Version 1, Version 2, and Version 3 of the Internet-
         standard Network Management Framework", Work in Progress.

    [21] Rivest, R., "Message Digest Algorithm MD5", RFC 1321, April
         1992.

    [22] Secure Hash Algorithm. NIST FIPS 180-1, (April, 1995)
         http://csrc.nist.gov/fips/fip180-1.txt (ASCII)
         http://csrc.nist.gov/fips/fip180-1.ps (Postscript)

    [23] Krawczyk, H., Bellare, M. and R. Canetti, "HMAC: Keyed-Hashing
         for Message Authentication", RFC 2104, February 1997.

    [24] Data Encryption Standard, National Institute of Standards and
         Technology. Federal Information Processing Standard (FIPS)
         Publication 46-1. Supersedes FIPS Publication 46, (January,
         1977; reaffirmed January, 1988).

[25] Rose, M., "A Convention for Defining Traps for use with the SNMP", RFC 1215, March 1991.

[26] McCloghrie, K., Perkins, D., Schoenwaelder, J., Case, J., Rose, M. and S. Waldbusser, "Structure of Management Information Version 2 (SMIv2)", STD 58, RFC 2578, April 1999.

[27] McCloghrie, K., Perkins, D., Schoenwaelder, J., Case, J., Rose, M. and S. Waldbusser, "Textual Conventions for SMIv2", STD 58, RFC 2579, April 1999.

[28] McCloghrie, K., Perkins, D., Schoenwaelder, J., Case, J., Rose, M. and S. Waldbusser, "Conformance Statements for SMIv2", STD 58, RFC 2580, April 1999.

RFC 2570   Introduction to SNMPv3   April 1999

11 Full Copyright Statement

   Copyright (C) The Internet Society (1998). All Rights Reserved.

   This document and translations of it may be copied and furnished to
   others, and derivative works that comment on or otherwise explain it
   or assist in its implementation may be prepared, copied, published
   and distributed, in whole or in part, without restriction of any
   kind, provided that the above copyright notice and this paragraph are
   included on all such copies and derivative works. However, this
   document itself may not be modified in any way, such as by removing
   the copyright notice or references to the Internet Society or other
   Internet organizations, except as needed for the purpose of
   developing Internet standards in which case the procedures for
   copyrights defined in the Internet Standards process must be
   followed, or as required to translate it into languages other than
   English.

   The limited permissions granted above are perpetual and will not be
   revoked by the Internet Society or its successors or assigns.

   This document and the information contained herein is provided on an
   "AS IS" basis and THE INTERNET SOCIETY AND THE INTERNET ENGINEERING
   TASK FORCE DISCLAIMS ALL WARRANTIES, EXPRESS OR IMPLIED, INCLUDING
   BUT NOT LIMITED TO ANY WARRANTY THAT THE USE OF THE INFORMATION
   HEREIN WILL NOT INFRINGE ANY RIGHTS OR ANY IMPLIED WARRANTIES OF
   MERCHANTABILITY OR FITNESS FOR A PARTICULAR PURPOSE."

Acknowledgement

   Funding for the RFC Editor function is currently provided by
   the Internet Society.

Glossary
with Acronyms

MPLS terminology is derived from conventional routing, tag and IP switching, ATM and FR technologies, and several newly minted acronyms and terms.

A

Abstract Syntax Notation One (ASN.1):   OSI version of an abstract syntax notational language. Abstract syntax notation is used because it is implementation-dependent and can be used in a variety of internetwork environments to allow for interoperability. ASN.1 is defined in ISO documents 8824.2 and 8825.2.

Accounting Management (AM):   One of the five functional areas of network management. AM deals with network usage and utilization, billing, and other cost determinations.

Active route: A route selected from the possible set of routes stored in the RIB, which is used to reach a destination. Active routes are stored in the FIB.

Address: Unique identification of a network device that allows for unambiguous communications. Typically, a packet or frame contains both a source and destination address to facilitate communications.

Address Resolution Protocol (ARP):   Internet protocol that correlates a device's four-octet IP address to its corresponding six-octet Ethernet address. ARP is defined in RFC 826.

Agent: A processing entity on a managed network device that has the proper routines to access the management variables it controls. It generally responds to requests from an NMS. Agents can be considered management servers.

Aggregation: A procedure whereby a single label is bound to a union of FECs (and which is itself a FEC), and then this new label is applied to all of the packets that belong to the union. Aggregation reduces the number of labels needed for storage at an MPLS node as well as the label distribution overhead for a common traffic flow.

American National Standards Institute (ANSI):   Major standards definition group in the U.S. It represents the U.S. at the international ISO meetings that charter worldwide standards.

Application layer: The top layer of the OSI model that allows users to make use of network services.

Application Management (AM):   The monitoring, control, and configuration of applications running on the hosts connected on a network. It is a category of enterprise management.

Application-Specific Integrated Circuit (ASIC):   A special-purpose semiconductor circuit that is designed to meet a specific processing requirement. This is opposed to general-purpose chips such as microprocessors.

AS: *see* autonomous system.

ASIC: *see* application-specific integrated circuit.

ASN: *see* autonomous system number

Asynchronous Transfer Mode (ATM):   A set of network technologies developed within the ATM Forum that use fixed-size cells in a connection-based configuration to provide QoS and TE features. Within MPLS, ATM is considered a Layer 2 technology.

ATM: *see* asynchronous transfer mode.

Autonomous System (AS):   A set of related routers that are usually under one administrative and management control.

Autonomous System Number (ASN): A unique value that identifies an AS. The ASN range is from 1 to 65,535, although several values are reserved.

B

Basic Encoding Rules (BERs): OSI rules for defining the encoding of the data units and network transfer syntax. BERs are specified in ISO 8825.

BGP: *see* border gateway protocol.

Border Gateway Protocol (BGP): The prevalent external gateway protocol used in the Internet today. BGP is based on distance vector (DV) algorithms and uses TCP as its transport protocol. The primary purpose of BGP is to let different ASs exchange routing information for the purpose of forwarding network packets among them. This is called interdomain routing. The current version of BGP in use is 4.

C

CBR: *see* constraint-based routing.

Cell Switch Router (CSR): A router introduced by Toshiba in 1994 that uses an IP control plane with an ATM data forwarding plane.

Class of Service (CoS): A classification of data packets based on specific bits in the header that QoS systems can use to provide differentiated classes of service to all the packets that match that classification.

CLI: *see* command-line interface.

Client: A program or entity requesting services from a server.

Command-Line Interface (CLI): A text-based, proprietary management interface that is often used by craftsmen for low-level device configuration and monitoring.

Common Management Information Protocol (CMIP): An ISO-defined network management protocol used between OSI managers and agents. CMIP is defined in ISO Standard 9595.

Common Management Information Service (CMIS): An ISO-defined network management service that is offered by the CMIP management protocol.

Common Object Request Broker Architecture (CORBA):   An architecture that allows objects to communicate with other objects regardless of where they are located, what operating system they are executing, or even what programming language they are written in. CORBA was developed by the Object Management Group (OMG) consortium.

Constraint-Based Routing (CBR):   A type of routing that uses network parameters, or constraints, to determine the best route a set of packets should take.

Constraint-Based Routing with LDP (CR-LDP):   A label distribution protocol that is an extension to the LDP for the specific purpose of setting up traffic-engineered LSPs.

Configuration Management (CM):   One of the five functional areas of network management. CM deals with internetwork device setup and status.

Connection-oriented service: A service where a circuit is set up, used, and then taken down between two communicating parties. This type of service has three phases: connection establishment, data transfer, and communication release.

Connectionless service: A service where each packet is independent and contains full source and destination addressing so that a circuit does not need to be established between the two communicating parties.

Convergence: The point when information about any change in the network is propagated to all of the routers in the network for any routing protocols that require this information (such as BGP).

CoS: *see* class of service.

CR-LDP: *see* constraint-based routing with LDP.

CSR: *see* cell switch router.

D

Database: An organized collection of data that can be quickly accessed to create information for applications.

Data Encryption Standard (DES):   A   standardized   encryption scheme. DES was developed by the U.S. National Bureau of Standards and is part of SNMPv3 security.

Datagram: An independent packet containing both source and destination addresses. Typically used with connectionless service.

Data Link Connection Identifier (DLCI):   In FR, this is the label used to identify a circuit.

Data link layer: Layer 2 of the OSI seven-layer reference model that deals with the establishment and release of data link connections and the transmission of data units called frames on those connections.

Differentiated Services (Diff-Serv):   An IETF standard that is a set of building blocks that can be used to deliver QoS to networks. Diff-Serv usually comprises two components: per-hop behaviors (PHBs) and traffic conditioning.

Diff-Serv: *see* differentiated services.

DLCI: *see* data link connection identifier.

Domain: In MPLS, a set of contiguous nodes that is MPLS-enabled and is under a singular administrative control. In conventional routing, a domain is synonymous with an AS.

Domain Naming Service (DNS):   A hierarchical system for naming host computers on the Internet by grouping the subject hosts into categories. Typically, the names have meaningful extensions, such as .com for hosts in commercial businesses, .edu for computers in an educational setting, and so forth. DNS is defined in RFCs 1034 and 1035.

Dotted decimal notation: Also called "dotted quad" notation, this is the common notation for specifying IP addresses in the *n.n.n.n* format, where *n* represents one byte represented in decimal.

E

Egress node: An MPLS node that handles MPLS traffic as it leaves the MPLS domain. The egress node strips the label from the packet.

EGP: *see* exterior gateway protocol.

Electronic mail (e-mail):   A system where users and applications can exchange mail messages over an internetwork.

Encryption: An algorithm where message data is modified so that only the proper recipients can recover the true message.

Enterprise: A collection of hardware and software components that works together to allow a business to operate its systematic and purposeful activities in a cost-effective and efficient manner.

ER: *see* explicit route.

Ethernet: A LAN protocol that uses a carrier sense multiple access collision detection (CSMA/CD) policy for transmissions. It is a 10-Mbps standard that was originally developed by DEC, Intel, and Xerox. It is very similar to the IEEE 802.3 standard.

Explicit Route (ER): A route specifically set up to follow a predetermined path. This may or may not be the same route set up by a hop-by-hop routing protocol.

Exterior Gateway Protocol (EGP): A general class of routing protocols for routing network packets between ASs. EGPs are also called interdomain routing protocols. The most widely used EGP today is BGP-4.

Extranet: An external extension of an intranet that allows remote users secure access.

F

Fault, Configuration, Accounting, Performance, and Security (FCAPS) management: Five major functional areas addressed in network management.

Fault Management (FM): One of the five functional areas of network management. FM deals with network faults and their correction.

FEC: *see* forwarding equivalence class.

FIB: *see* forwarding information base.

Fiber Distributed Data Interface (FDDI): A protocol for transmitting data over fiber optic cable. FDDI is an ANSI standard that specifies a rate up to 100 Mbps.

Forwarding Equivalence Class (FEC): A set of network layer packets that is forwarded over the same path and in the same manner. With MPLS, this set of packets can typically use the same label (although there may be cases when packets from an FEC use multiple labels).

Forwarding Information Base (FIB): The set of active routes in a router that is used to forward packets.

Frame: A data link level unit of transmission. It contains a header, data, and trailer information.

Frame Relay (FR): A packet switching WAN protocol with speeds from 56 Kbps to 1.54 Mbps (T1) that provides greater throughput by having error detection and correction done by the higher level protocols.

G

Gateway: A protocol-independent, media-independent internetworking device that translates and routes various protocols. A gateway operates at Layer 7 of the OSI model (application layer).

Get: The SNMP "read" operation for a requested instance.

GetNext: The SNMP "read-next" operation, where the lexicographically next variable instance is returned, if available.

H

Host: A computer that is an end-station in a network. All the traffic arriving at a host is intended for host applications. Examples of hosts include personal computers (PCs), workstations, Web servers, and file servers. Hosts are also often called "end-nodes."

Host-to-host layer: The third layer of the TCP/IP network protocol that ensures reliable data transfer between TCP/IP hosts. It is similar to the transport layer of the OSI reference model.

I

ICMP: *see* Internet control message protocol.

IETF: *see* Internet engineering task force.

IGP: *see* interior gateway protocol.

Information Technology (IT): The general subject of managing information resources within an enterprise. IT must deal with the technological aspects of computers, networking, and data storage.

Ingress node: An MPLS node that handles MPLS traffic as it enters the MPLS domain. The ingress node applies the label to the packet.

Instance: The specific declaration of an object as realized by each agent implementation.

Institute of Electrical and Electronics Engineers (IEEE): The organization that helps define network standards. The IEEE ("eye-triple e") is active in creating and supporting many common communications specifications used today.

Integrated Services (IntServ): An IETF standard for providing QoS by reserving resources end-to-end for any particular application flow. The RSVP signaling protocol is used to signal for resources within the network.

Integrated Services Digital Network (ISDN): An   international standard proposed by the CCITT. ISDN specifies the transmission of voice, data, and video over telephone lines.

Interface: The clearly defined boundary between two functional layers.

Intermediate System-Intermediate System (IS-IS): An IGP originally developed by ISO that is now used in the Internet for IP routing.

Interior Gateway Protocol (IGP): A general class of routing protocols for routing network packets between nodes within an AS. IGPs are also called intra-domain routing protocols. Two of the most widely used IGPs today are OSPF and IS-IS.

International Organization for Standardization (ISO): The international standards body that specifies standards for many network protocols. ISO is noted for the seven-layer OSI reference model.

International Telecommunications Union-Telecommunications Sector (ITU-T): The international organization that makes technical recommendations on telephony and data communication systems. The ITU-T meets every four years. ITU-T was formerly known as the CCITT.

Internet: The large and ever-expanding set of interconnected computers that use the IP suite. The Internet links many university, government, research, and commercial sites. In a general sense, the Internet is a network of networks; the Internet is the largest internetwork in the world.

Internet Architecture Board (IAB): The group that oversees the general direction of Internet groups, protocols, and other matters.

Internet Control Message Protocol (ICMP): A part of the IP that sends special error and status messages. ICMP messages are used by PING. This protocol is specified in RFC 792.

Internet Engineering Task Force (IETF):   A technical group within the Internet Architecture Board that develops various Internet standards.

Internet layer: The second layer of the TCP/IP protocol suite that provides services for allowing data to traverse hosts that can reside on multiple networks.

Internet Protocol (IP):   Unreliable, connectionless, Internet layer protocol that uses IP addresses to send and receive messages. RFC 791 specifies this protocol.

Internetwork: A network of networks. These networks are usually connected by network devices such as routers.

IntServ: *see* integrated services.

Intranet: An internal network that uses Internet-based technologies and is connected to the Internet in a secure and controlled fashion.

IP: *see* Internet protocol.

IP address: A four-octet address specifying the network and host IDs. Both source and destination IP addresses exist.

IP suite: A set of protocols that implements the four layers of the TCP/IP protocols used for internetworking.

IP switching: A framework developed by Ipsilon (now part of Nokia) in 1996 that uses the IP control plane to manage ATM switches.

IS-IS: *see* intermediate system-intermediate system.

J

Java: A programming language.

L

Label: The short, fixed-length identifier used to identify an FEC. MPLS labels are locally significant.

Label distribution peers: Two adjacent LSRs that use an LDP to exchange label binding information. A label distribution adjacency is said to exist between them.

Label Distribution Protocol (LDP):   A protocol that uses hop-by-hop routing to create LSPs.

Label Edge Router (LER):   An ingress or egress LSR.

Label Information Base (LIB):   A database of information that contains label bindings and possibly additional information that may be needed by MPLS.

Label merge: The replacement of multiple incoming labels with a new, single, outgoing label. All of the incoming packets belong to the same FEC. The node where a merge is done is called the merge point.

Label stack: An ordered set of labels that is added to a network layer packet to create an MPLS labeled packet. The last ("bottom") label in the stack will always have its "S" bit set.

Label swap: The basic MPLS forwarding operation that involves a table lookup based on the incoming label as an index to determine the packet's next hop, new label, and any other additional information (encapsulation, port, etc.).

Label swapping: The general name for the entire MPLS paradigm of setting up a forwarding path and then swapping labels on packets as they traverse the domain from start (ingress) to finish (egress).

Label-Switched Path (LSP):   An MPLS route created to forward traffic from the ingress LSR to the egress LSR.

Label Switching Router (LSR):   An MPLS-enabled router or switch that forwards packets using label switching.

LAN: *see* local area network.

LDP: *see* label distribution protocol.

LER: *see* label edge router.

LIB: *see* label information base.

Lightweight Directory Access Protocol (LDAP):   A set of protocols for accessing internetwork directories in a standard way (e.g., e-mail addresses, public keys, special interest databases, etc.).

Local Area Network (LAN):   A collection of nodes and links that is geographically close and all connected on a single network, using a protocol such as Ethernet or token ring.

Loop detection: An algorithm that determines that the present path contains a looping condition. Note that data may be in the process of being transmitted on the path when the looping condition is detected.

Loop prevention: An algorithm for preventing a looping condition from occurring on a path so that data will never be sent over it.

LSP: *see* label-switched path.

LSP tunnel: An LSP that has been created with TE LDPs such as RSVP-TE and CR-LDP.

LSR: *see* label switching router.

M

MAC: *see* media access control.

Managed Object (MO): A general term for the variable of interest in a managed system.

Management Information Base (MIB): MIBs are virtual data bases that specify how SNMP management information should be defined.

Manager: A processing entity that requests and processes managed object values from corresponding agents. Managers are management clients.

Media Access Control (MAC): The Layer 2 addressing used by Ethernet.

Merge point: The specific LSR where the label merging operation is done.

Message Digest 5 (MD5): An authentication algorithm that is one of a series of authentication algorithms developed by Ron Rivest. MD5 was developed in 1991 and has proved to be very secure against various brute-force and other attacks.

MPLS: *see* multiprotocol label switching; incidentally, also the abbreviation for Minneapolis, Minnesota.

Multiprotocol Label Switching (MPLS): The set of open, standards-based Internet technologies that combine Layer 3 routing with Layer 2 switching to forward packets by utilizing short, fixed-length labels.

N

Network access layer: The lowest layer of the TCP/IP protocol suite that handles the connection between the host and the network.

Network layer: Layer 3 of the OSI seven-layer model that handles routing and circuits within a network.

Network Management (NM):   The monitoring, control, and configuration of devices connected on a network. It is a category of enterprise management.

Network Management Station (NMS):   A processing entity that makes requests of the agents it manages.

Node: The general term for a network device such as a bridge, router, switch (all intermediate nodes), or host (end-node).

O

Open Shortest Path First (OSPF):   An IGP routing protocol.

OSI Reference Model (OSI-RM):   The seven-layer model developed by ISO that is the fundamental architecture used in explaining the interactions of protocols and networks. Each layer builds on the services provided by the layer beneath it.

OSPF: *see* open shortest path first.

P

Packet: A unit of data that travels through a network.

Performance Management (PM):   One of the five functional areas of network management. PM deals with the efficiency and utilization of how the network is operating and how it is accessed.

Personal Computer (PC):   A host computer. Usually, there is a one-to-one correspondence of PC to user.

Physical layer: Layer 1 of the OSI seven-layer reference model that deals with the connection of the device to the media for transmitting the bitstream.

Packet Internet Groper (PING):   An Internet application that uses ICMP echo messages to test for basic connectivity between two IP-addressed nodes.

PNNI: *see* private network-network interface.

Poll: A periodic request for status.

Port: A communication connection point that may be realized in various ways in hardware or software.

PPP: *see* point-to-point protocol.

Point-to-Point Protocol (PPP): A family of IETF protocols for transporting many different Layer 3 protocol packets over a common link.

Presentation layer: The sixth layer of the OSI reference model that deals with data formats.

Private Network-Network Interface (PNNI): An ATM routing protocol that allows heterogeneous ATM switches to interoperate.

Process layer: The highest level of the TCP/IP protocol suite that provides the protocols needed to support applications such as e-mail and file transfer.

Protocol: A formal set of rules that defines standards between communicating parties.

Protocol Data Unit (PDU): A group of bytes in a known format that is delivered to and from peer applications. The SNMP PDU carries requests and responses between NMSs and agents.

Q

QoS: *see* quality of service.

Quality of Service (QoS): The guaranteed level of network service to a customer or application.

R

Repeater: A media-dependent network device that regenerates physical signals to extend the range of the media. A repeater operates at Layer 1 of the OSI model (physical layer).

Request for Comments (RFC): A document that contains information about the IP suite. RFCs contain a variety of information about other topics dealing with the Internet as well.

Resource Reservation Protocol (RSVP): An IETF protocol that is used to set up reservations for flows for IntServ within the Internet.

Resource Reservation Protocol with Traffic Engineering

Extensions (RSVP-TE):   A TE Label Distribution Protocol used for creating LSP tunnels.

Reverse Address Resolution Protocol (RARP):   Permits a host to discover its IP address. RARP is primarily used for diskless workstations.

RIB: *see* routing information base.

RIP: *see* routing information protocol.

Route: A path through the internetwork used to send and receive messages between two communicating hosts.

Router: A protocol-dependent, media-independent internetworking device that routes packets based on their destination address. A router operates at Layer 3 of the OSI model (network layer). Routers are also often called "intermediate nodes."

Routing Information Base (RIB):   A collection of all routes—active and inactive—present in a router. The active routes are always downloaded into the FIB.

Routing Information Protocol (RIP):   An IGP protocol.

RSVP: *see* resource reservation protocol.

RSVP-TE: *see* resource reservation protocol with traffic engineering extensions.

S

Secure SNMP: The name given to the first proposals for enhancements to SNMP version 1 (SNMPv1) to provide security features. Secure SNMP is defined in RFCs 1351–1353.

Security Management (SM):   One of the five functional areas of network management. SM deals with access permissions, protection, and user authentication.

Server: An application that handles requests from clients and then carries out any requested actions.

Service Level Agreement (SLA):   A QoS agreement for delivering services of a certain quality at a specific price.

Service management: The definition, monitoring, and reporting of services that an enterprise contracts from external sources or utilizes internally. Also expressed in an SLA.

Session layer: The fifth layer of the OSI reference model that deals with the reliable data exchange between users and the network.

Set: An SNMP "write" operation on a requested instance.

Simple Gateway Monitoring Protocol (SGMP): The network management framework that evolved into SNMP. SGMP is defined in RFC 1028.

Simple Management Protocol (SMP): A proposal in July 1992 to improve SNMPv1. SMP was used as the basis for SNMPv2.

Simple Network Management Protocol (SNMP): The network management framework defined by the Internet community utilizing the TCP/IP protocol suite. SNMP is defined by RFCs 1155, 1157, and 1213. The first version is also known as SNMPv1.

Simple Network Management Protocol version 2 (SNMPv2): A later enhancement to the SNMP framework. The SNMPv2 draft version is described in RFCs 1902–1908.

Simple Network Management Protocol version 3 (SNMPv3): The latest enhancement to the SNMP framework. SNMPv3 is described in RFCs 2271–2275.

Socket: A data structure that is used in a common interface for communicating with UDP, TCP, and IP.

SONET: *see* synchronous optical network.

Structure of Management Information (SMI): Rules for defining objects within a network management framework.

Subnetting: An extension of the IP addressing scheme where the network ID bytes can be further grouped into sub-networks.

Synchronous Optical Network (SONET): The ANSI-standard, high-speed, synchronous, physical layer network technology that is designed to be carried over optical media. SONET provides up to 2.5 Gbps.

Systems management: The monitoring, control, and configuration of the components within the devices connected on a network. This is a category of enterprise management and works closely with network management.

T

T1:   Digital transmission lines with speeds up to 1.54 Mbps. The framing specification for T1 is called DS1.

T3:   Digital transmission lines with speeds up to 44 Mbps. The framing specification for T3 is called DS3.

TCP: *see* transmission control protocol.

TE: *see* traffic engineering.

Telecommunications Management Network (TMN):   The telecommunications framework defined by the ITU-T for managing and controlling network elements and resources.

Telnet: An Internet protocol that defines remote terminal connection service.

Traffic Engineering (TE):   The process of mapping logical traffic flows and their requirements onto an existing physical network topology.

Transit node: An MPLS node that handles MPLS traffic within the MPLS domain. The transit node swaps the label found on the packet.

Transmission Control Protocol (TCP):   An Internet transport protocol that uses connection-oriented, end-to-end, reliable transmission. It is specified in RFC 793.

Transport layer: The fourth layer of the OSI model that provides end-to-end data integrity.

Trap: An SNMP alert that can be sent asynchronously by an agent to predetermined NMSs when a predefined condition has been detected.

U

UDP: *see* user datagram protocol.

UNIX: A popular multitasking, multi-user operating system developed by AT&T used on many internetworking devices.

User Datagram Protocol (UDP):   An Internet transport protocol that is connectionless, unreliable, and uses datagrams. It is defined in RFC 768.

V

VC: *see* virtual channel.

VCI: *see* virtual channel identifier.

VC merge: The label merging procedure for ATM, where the MPLS label is carried in the ATM VCI field (or combined VPI/VCI field) so as to allow multiple VCs to merge into one single VC. When the VPI field is used, the procedure is called "VP merge."

View: The set of managed objects in an agent's MIB that is available to the NMSs in its community.

Virtual Channel (VC):   In ATM, a communication channel that provides for the transport of ATM cells within an ATM network as a single stream of cells, in order, from user to user.

Virtual Channel Identifier(VCI):   An ATM header field that denotes a virtual channel.

Virtual Path (VP):   In ATM, a collection of related virtual channels.

Virtual Packet Identifier (VPI):   An ATM header field that denotes a virtual path.

Virtual Private Network (VPN):   A network that connects two or more physically separate networks into one logical network by using tunnels over a public communications fabric, such as the Internet. A VPN application ensures that the data sent on the VPN tunnel is "private" and kept logically separate from other general traffic.

Voice over IP (VoIP):   The specification for sending voice packets over RTP/UDP/IP through the Internet.

Voice over MPLS (VoMPLS):   The specification for sending voice packets directly over MPLS through the Internet.

VoIP: *see* voice over IP.

VoMPLS: *see* voice over MPLS.

VP: *see* virtual path.

VPI: *see* virtual packet identifier.

VPN: *see* virtual private network.

W

Wide Area Network (WAN):   A network that traverses long distances and often uses common carrier transmission services.

World Wide Web (WWW):   A client/server system running on the Internet that supports the storage, distribution, and display of various types of information. The information is usually formatted in HTML and addressed by its URL name. The WWW also supports links to other documents.

Workstation: A host computer or high-end PC.

Bibliography and Web Sites

I suggest that the only books that influence us
are those for which we are ready, and which have gone a little further
down the path than we have gone ourselves. [1]

— *E. M. Forster*

This bibliography contains a list of important MPLS Web sites and a listing of books and periodicals that pertain to MPLS and related topics. This list is certainly not comprehensive, but it contains a listing of MPLS resources that are very informative, well-written, and a good place to start in learning about MPLS. A periodic search of the Web will aid in keeping the reader up-to-date on the latest MPLS developments. The reader should also poll MPLS vendor sites, and one should certainly subscribe to the MPLS WG's mailing list to get the latest goings-on with the MPLS architecture and all of the related specifications and drafts.

WEB SITES

Check the Web sites of all the leading MPLS vendors for the latest MPLS information. Most vendors have extensive collections of whitepapers,

471

data sheets, and links to other sources of MPLS and related information. Important URLs for MPLS information include the following:

- **www.mplsrc.com:** The Web site of the MPLS Resource Center. This is an excellent site to start learning about MPLS. Read the FAQs if you are just starting.
- **www.mplsforum.org:** MPLS Forum Web site. Contains a great deal of information on what is going on in the Forum and in MPLS-related issues.
- **www.mplsworld.com:** The MPLS World News Web site.
- **www.watersprings.org:** Web site maintained by Noritoshi Demizu.
- **www.awduche.com:** Web site of Daniel Awduche, a leading MPLS contributor.
- **ail.gmu.edu/resources.htm:** The URL address for the Advanced Internet Lab.
- **www.lightreading.com:** The Web site for one of the leading online periodicals that contains frequent articles on MPLS vendors and issues. Hint: Use the search capability to see recent articles dealing with MPLS.

BOOKS ON MPLS

Davie, Bruce S. and Yakov Rekhter. *MPLS: Technology and Applications.* San Diego: Academic Press, 2000.

Pepelnjak, Ivan and Jim Guichard. *MPLS and VPN Architectures: A Practical Guide to Understanding, Designing, and Deploying MPLS and MPLS-enabled VPNs (Cisco Networking Fundamentals).* Indianapolis, IN: Cisco Press, 2001.

Black, Ulyess. *MPLS and Label Switching Networks.* Upper Saddle River, NJ: Prentice Hall PTR, 2001.

Gray, Eric. *MPLS: Implementing the Technology.* Boston: Addison-Wesley, 2001.

Alwayn, Vivek. *Advanced MPLS Design and Implementation.* Indianapolis, IN: Cisco Press, 2001.

BOOKS ON IP SWITCHING ....

Davie, Bruce S., Paul Doolan, and Yakov Rekhter. *Switching in IP Networks: IP Switching, Tag Switching, and Related Technologies.* Los Altos, CA: Morgan Kaufman Publishers, 1998.

Metz, Christopher Y. *IP Switching: Protocols and Architecture.* New York: McGraw-Hill, 1999.

BOOKS ON QUALITY OF SERVICE ....

Ferguson, Paul and Geoff Huston. *Quality of Service: Delivering QoS on the Internet and in Corporate Networks.* New York: Wiley Computer Publishing, 1998.

Wang, Zheng. *Internet QOS: Architectures and Mechanisms for Quality of Service.* San Diego: Academic Press (A Harcourt Science and Technology Company), 2001.

BOOKS ON ASSOCIATED TOPICS ....

Black, Darryl P. *Building Switched Networks: Multilayer Switching, QoS, IP Multicast, Network Policy, and Service Level Agreements.* Reading, MA: Addison-Wesley, 1999.

Subramaniam, Mani. *Network Management: Principles and Practice.* Reading, MA: Addison-Wesley, 2000.

Terplan, Kornel. *OSS Essentials.* New York: Wiley Computer Publishing, 2001.

BOOKS ON SNMP ....

Feit, Sidnie. *SNMP: A Guide to Network Management.* New York: McGraw-Hill. 1994.

Harnedy, Sean. *Total SNMP: Exploring the Simple Network Management Protocol.* Upper Saddle River, NJ: Prentice Hall PTR. 1997.

Perkins, David, and Evan McGinnis. *Understanding SNMP MIBs.* Upper Saddle River, NJ: Prentice Hall, 1997.

Rose, Marshall T. *The Simple Book: An Introduction to Networking Management rev. 2nd ed.* Upper Saddle River, NJ: Prentice Hall, 1996.

Rose, Marshall T., and Keith Z. McCloghrie. *How to Manage Your Network Using SNMP: The Network Management Practicum.* Upper Saddle River, NJ: Prentice Hall, 1995.

Stallings, William. *SNMP, SNMPv2, and RMON: Practical Network Management 2nd ed.* Reading, MA: Addison-Wesley, 1996.

MPLS Magazine Articles ....

Li, Tony. "MPLS and the Evolving Internet Architecture," *IEEE Communications Magazine*, December 1999, pp. 38–41.

Swallow, George. "MPLS Advantages for Traffic Engineering," *IEEE Communications Magazine*, December 1999, pp. 54–57.

Reference for Bibliography and Web Sites.......................................

1. from www.annabelle.net/topics/books.html.

Index